MERCURY READER

a custom publication

Cape Fear Community College

Pearson Custom Publishing

New York   Boston   San Francisco
London   Toronto   Sydney   Tokyo   Singapore   Madrid
Mexico City   Munich   Paris   Cape Town   Hong Kong   Montreal

Senior Vice President, Editorial and Marketing: Patrick F. Boles
Senior Sponsoring Editor: Natalie Danner
Development Editors: Mary Kate Paris and Katherine R. Gehan
Editorial Assistant: Jill Johnson
Operations Manager: Eric M. Kenney
Database Product Manager: Jennifer Berry
Rights Manager: Katie Huha
Art Director: Renée Sartell
Cover Designers: Renée Sartell and Sharon Treacy

Cover image courtesy of Conrad Pope.

Printed in the United States of America.

Please visit our websites at *www.pearsoncustom.com* and *www.mercuryreader.com*.

Attention bookstores: For permission to return any unsold stock, contact us at *pe-uscustomreturns@pearson.com*.

**Pearson
Custom Publishing**
is a division of

www.pearsonhighered.com

ISBN 10: 0-558-17850-2
ISBN 13: 978-0-558-17850-5

Contents

Individuals and Identity

Education and Language

Rights and Responsibilities

Activists and Leaders

Politics and Government

Poetry and Fiction

Poetry

Fiction

Appendix I: Ways of Writing

Appendix II: Rhetorical Modes

Appendix III: Links to Sample Essays

Hello!

We are delighted to welcome you to **English 111: Expository Writing** and your first semester of college credit English. By definition, expository writing thoroughly explains a subject. Expository writing is not strictly narration or description, process or exemplification, but it incorporates aspects of many rhetorical modes as it makes a complete, logical statement. We have designed an individualized text just for you to demonstrate and clarify this process.

The Mercury Reader: Ideas That Matter presents writing by ground-breaking authors representing a variety of time periods, experiences, backgrounds, and points of view. Some of these writers will be familiar to you, so you will have the opportunity to study their styles and messages through ever-deepening critical-thinking abilities. Other authors will be new to you and, as such, offer you opportunities to explore your own expanding understanding through their rhetoric.

The Mercury Reader supplies you with both fiction and nonfiction readings, with poetry as well as prose. The *Reader* also includes ample support materials regarding effective ways to explore and analyze a text, generate writing topics, and more. Visit the appendices in the back of the book for this valuable information.

And now, we hope you will turn to the table of contents of *The Mercury Reader* with the same satisfying anticipation that you use to approach your English composition course—with curiosity about your own voice as well as those of time-tested writers who wait to share their journeys with readers like you.

Welcome to Cape Fear Community College's ENG 111 course! Welcome to a renewed, expanded understanding of yourself, your beliefs, values, and writing abilities through active, engaged reading. We are very glad that you're here.

—The CFCC English Department

Individuals and Identity

Why I Want a Wife

Judy Brady

Judy Brady (1937–), born in San Francisco, studied painting and received a B.F.A. in 1962 in art from the University of Iowa. Then she married and raised a family in a traditional housewife role. She later commented that her male professors had talked her out of pursuing a career in education. In the late 1960s, she became active in the women's movement and began writing articles on feminism and other social issues. In 1990, she was the editor of Women and Cancer, *an anthology by women. The essay "Why I Want a Wife" appeared in the first issue of* Ms. *magazine in 1972.*

1   I belong to that classification of people known as wives. I am A Wife. And, not altogether incidentally, I am a mother.

Not too long ago a male friend of mine appeared on the scene fresh from a recent divorce. He had one child, who is, of course, with his ex-wife. He is looking for another wife. As I thought about him while I was ironing one evening, it suddenly occurred to me that I, too, would like to have a wife. Why do I want a wife?

I would like to go back to school so that I can become economically independent, support myself, and, if need be, support those dependent upon me. I want a wife who will work and send me to school. And while I am going to school I want a wife to take care of my children. I want a wife to keep track of the children's doctor and dentist appointments. And to keep track of mine, too. I want a wife to make sure my children eat properly and are kept clean. I want a wife who will wash the children's clothes and keep them mended. I want a wife who is a good nurturant attendant to my children, who arranges for their schooling, makes sure that they have an adequate social life with their peers, takes them to the park, the zoo, etc. I want a wife who takes care of the children when they are sick, a wife who arranges to be around when the children need special care, because, of course, I cannot miss classes at school. My wife must arrange to lose time at work and not lose the job. It may mean a small cut in my wife's income from time to time, but I guess I can tolerate that. Needless to say, my wife will arrange and pay for the care of the children while my wife is working.

I want a wife who will take care of *my* physical needs. I want a wife who will keep my house clean, a wife who will pick up after me. I want a wife who will keep my clothes clean, ironed, mended, replaced when need be, and who will see to it that my personal things are kept in their proper place so that I can find what I need the minute I need it. I want a wife who cooks the meals, a wife who is a *good* cook. I want a wife who will plan the menus, do the necessary grocery shopping, prepare the meals, serve them pleasantly, and then do the cleaning up while I do my studying. I want a wife who will care for me when I am sick and sympathize with my pain and loss of time from school. I want a wife to go along when our family takes a vacation so that someone can continue to care for me and my children when I need a rest and change of scene.

5   I want a wife who will not bother me with rambling complaints about a wife's duties. But I want a wife who will listen to me when I feel the need to explain a rather difficult point I have come across in my course of studies. And I want a wife who will type my papers for me when I have written them.

I want a wife who will take care of the details of my social life. When my wife and I are invited out by friends, I want a wife who will take care of the babysitting arrangements. When I meet people at school that I like and want to entertain, I want a wife who will have the house clean, will prepare a special meal, serve it to me and my friends, and not interrupt when I talk about the things that interest me and my friends. I want a wife who will have arranged that the children are fed and ready for bed before my guests arrive so that the children do not bother us. I want a wife who takes care of the needs of my guests so that they feel comfortable, who makes sure that they have an ashtray, that they are passed the hors d'oeuvres, that they are offered a second helping of the food, that their wine glasses are replenished when necessary, that their coffee is served to them as they like it. And I want a wife who knows that sometimes I need a night out by myself.

I want a wife who is sensitive to my sexual needs, a wife who makes love passionately and eagerly when I feel like it, a wife who makes sure that I am satisfied. And, of course, I want a wife who will not demand sexual attention when I am not in the mood for it. I want a wife who assumes the complete responsibility for birth control, because I do not want more children. I want a wife who will remain sexually faithful to me so that I do not have to clutter up my intellectual life with jealousies. And I want a wife who understands that *my* sexual needs may entail more than strict adherence to monogamy. I must, after all, be able to relate to people as fully as possible.

If, by chance, I find another person more suitable as a wife than the wife I already have, I want the liberty to replace my present wife with another one. Naturally, I will expect a fresh, new life; my wife will take the children and be solely responsible for them so that I am left free.

When I am through with school and have a job, I want my wife to quit working and remain at home so that my wife can more fully and completely take care of a wife's duties.

10   My God, who *wouldn't* want a wife?   10

Questions on Meaning

1. Do you know any wives such as Brady describes? Describe one of them. If Brady's description seems unrealistic, describe a more realistic wife.
2. Does Brady seem to claim that she is such a wife herself? Explain your answer with evidence from the essay.
3. At first the essay seems to deplore a double standard. Does it really? What is the theme of the essay about male/female differences?

Questions on Rhetorical Strategy and Style

1. Satire commonly uses exaggeration both for humorous effect and to make a point. Analyze the exaggeration you see in this essay and explain how it enriches the reading experience.
2. What is the effect of Brady's use of great detail throughout the essay, including such things as filling the guests' wine glasses and taking the children to the zoo? Find other examples of detail to support your opinion.
3. If you substituted the word "husband" for "wife" throughout the essay, how would a contemporary reader react?

Writing Assignments

1. Judy Brady has said she was discouraged from continuing her education and thus married and became a wife. How much has the role of wife changed since the late 1950s and early 1960s, when she was in college? Comment on the extent to which this essay still has meaning to a contemporary reader.
2. Consider what characteristics you desire (or expect) most from a spouse or life partner. Try to differentiate between essential qualities and other abilities or traits that would make your life easier or more pleasant. Consider also whether the other person might desire or expect the same or different characteristics from you. Then write an essay in which you compare and contrast these two sets of characteristics.

Autobiographical Notes

James Baldwin

James Baldwin (1924–1987) was born in poverty in the Harlem district of New York City, where he lived until he was eighteen. From age fourteen to seventeen he was a revivalist minister, manifesting a religious intensity seen in much of his work. After high school he worked various jobs in Greenwich Village while studying and writing on his own. He then moved to Paris for eight years, and thereafter much of his life was spent back and forth between New York and Europe. In the early 1960s Baldwin worked in the civil rights movement. At the time the following essay was written, in 1963, Baldwin had already written and published several successful novels, and he continued writing until his death in France. His novels include Go Tell It on the Mountain *(1953)*, Giovanni's Room *(1956)*, and Another Country *(1967)*. His best-known collections of essays are* Notes of a Native Son *(1955)*, Nobody Knows My Name *(1961)*, and The Fire Next Time. *His play* Blues for Mister Charley *(1964) is equally powerful. In the following autobiographical sketch written midway through his career, one can see several of Baldwin's great themes as he analyzes his early life in the context of his heritage and American society.*

I was born in Harlem thirty-one years ago. I began plotting novels at about the time I learned to read. The story of my childhood is the usual bleak fantasy, and we can dismiss it with the restrained observation that I certainly would not consider living it again. In those days my mother was given to the exasperating and mysterious habit of having babies. As they were born, I took them over with one hand and held a book with the other. The children probably suffered, though they have since been kind enough to deny it, and in this way I read *Uncle Tom's Cabin* and *A Tale of Two Cities* over and over and over again; in this way, in fact, I read just about everything I could get my hands on—except the Bible, probably because it was the only book I was encouraged to read. I must also confess that I wrote—a great deal—and my first professional triumph, in any case, the first effort of mine to be seen in print, occurred at the age of twelve or thereabouts, when a short story I had written about the Spanish revolution won some sort of prize in an extremely short-lived church newspaper. I remember the story was censored by the lady editor, though I don't remember why, and I was outraged.

Also wrote plays, and songs, for one of which I received a letter of congratulations from Mayor La Guardia, and poetry, about which the less said, the better. My mother was delighted by all these goings-on, but my father wasn't; he wanted me to be a preacher. When I was fourteen I became a preacher, and when I was seventeen I stopped. Very shortly thereafter I left home. For God knows how long I struggled with the world of commerce and industry—I guess they would say they struggled with *me*—and when I was about twenty-one I had enough done of a novel to get a Saxton Fellowship. When I was twenty-two the fellowship was over, the novel turned out to be unsalable, and I started waiting on tables in a Village restaurant and writing book reviews—mostly, as it turned out, about the Negro problem, concerning which the color of my skin made me automatically an expert. Did another book, in company with photographer Theodore Pelatowski, about the storefront churches in Harlem. This book met exactly the same fate as my first—fellowship, but no sale. (It was a Rosenwald Fellowship.) By the time I was twenty-four I had decided to stop reviewing books about the Negro problem—which, by this time, was only slightly less horrible in print than it was in life—and I packed my bags and went to France, where I finished, God knows how, *Go Tell It on the Mountain.*

Any writer, I suppose, feels that the world into which he was born is nothing less than a conspiracy against the cultivation of his talent—which attitude certainly has a great deal to support it. On the other hand, it is only because the world looks on his talent with such a frightening indifference that the artist is compelled to make his talent important. So that any writer, looking back over even so short a span of time as I am here forced to assess, finds that the things which hurt him and the things which helped him cannot be divorced from each other; he could be helped in a certain way only because he was hurt in a certain way; and his help is simply to be enabled to move from one conundrum to the next—one is tempted to say that he moves from one disaster to the next. When one begins looking for influences one finds them by the score. I haven't thought much about my own, not enough anyway; I hazard that the King James Bible, the rhetoric of the store-front church, something ironic and violent and perpetually understated in Negro speech—and something of Dickens' love for bravura—have something to do with me today; but I wouldn't stake my life on it. Likewise, innumerable people have helped me in many ways; but finally, I suppose, the most difficult (and most rewarding) thing in my life has been the fact that I was born a Negro and was forced, therefore, to effect some kind of truce with this reality. (Truce, by the way, is the best one can hope for.)

One of the difficulties about being a Negro writer (and this is not special pleading, since I don't mean to suggest that he has it worse than anybody else) is that the Negro problem is written about so widely. The bookshelves groan under the weight of information, and everyone therefore considers himself informed. And this information, furthermore, operates usually (generally, popularly) to reinforce traditional attitudes. Of traditional attitudes there are only two—For or Against—and I, personally, find it difficult to say which attitude has caused me the most pain. I am speaking as a writer; from a social point of view I am perfectly aware that the change from ill-will to good-will, however motivated, however imperfect, however expressed, is better than no change at all.

5   But it is part of the business of the writer—as I see it—to examine attitudes, to go beneath the surface, to tap the source. From this point of view the Negro problem is nearly inaccessible. It is not only written about so widely; it is written about so badly. It is quite possible to say that the price a Negro pays for becoming articulate is to find himself, at length, with nothing to be articulate about. ("You taught me language," says Caliban to Prospero, "and my profit on't is I know how to curse.") Consider: the tremendous social activity that this problem generates imposes on whites and Negroes alike the necessity

of looking forward, of working to bring about a better day. This is fine, it keeps the waters troubled; it is all, indeed, that has made possible the Negro's progress. Nevertheless, social affairs are not generally speaking the writer's prime concern, whether they ought to be or not; it is absolutely necessary that he establish between himself and these affairs a distance which will allow, at least, for clarity, so that before he can look forward in any meaningful sense, he must first be allowed to take a long look back. In the context of the Negro problem neither whites nor blacks, for excellent reasons of their own, have the faintest desire to look back; but I think that the past is all that makes the present coherent, and further, that the past will remain horrible for exactly as long as we refuse to assess it honestly.

I know, in any case, that the most crucial time in my own development came when I was forced to recognize that I was a kind of bastard of the West; when I followed the line of my past I did not find myself in Europe but in Africa. And this meant that in some subtle way, in a really profound way, I brought to Shakespeare, Bach, Rembrandt, to the stones of Paris, to the cathedral at Chartres, and to the Empire State Building, a special attitude. These were not really my creations, they did not contain my history; I might search in them in vain forever for any reflection of myself. I was an interloper; this was not my heritage. At the same time I had no other heritage which I could possibly hope to use—I had certainly been unfitted for the jungle or the tribe. I would have to appropriate these white centuries. I would have to make them mine—I would have to accept my special attitude, my special place in this scheme—otherwise I would have no place in *any* scheme. What was the most difficult was the fact that I was forced to admit something I had always hidden from myself, which the American Negro has had to hide from himself as the price of his public progress; that I hated and feared white people. This did not mean that I loved black people; on the contrary, I despised them, possibly because they failed to produce Rembrandt. In effect, I hated and feared the world. And this meant, not only that I thus gave the world an altogether murderous power over me, but also that in such a self-destroying limbo I could never hope to write.

One writes out of one thing only—one's own experience. Everything depends on how relentlessly one forces from this experience the last drop, sweet or bitter, it can possibly give. This is the only real concern of the artist, to recreate out of the disorder of life that order which

BALDWIN | AUTOBIOGRAPHICAL NOTES

is art. The difficulty then, for me, of being a Negro writer was the fact that I was, in effect, prohibited from examining my own experience too closely by the tremendous demands and the very real dangers of my social situation.

I don't think the dilemma outlined above is uncommon. I do think, since writers work in the disastrously explicit medium of language, that it goes a little way towards explaining why, out of the enormous resources of Negro speech and life, and despite the example of Negro music, prose written by Negroes has been generally speaking so pallid and so harsh. I have not written about being a Negro at such length because I expect that to be my only subject, but only because it was the gate I had to unlock before I could hope to write about anything else. I don't think that the Negro problem in America can be even discussed coherently without bearing in mind its context; its context being the history, traditions, customs, the moral assumptions and preoccupations of the country; in short, the general social fabric. Appearances to the contrary, no one in America escapes its effects and everyone in America bears some responsibility for it. I believe this the more firmly because it is the overwhelming tendency to speak of this problem as though it were a thing apart. But in the work of Faulkner, in the general attitude and certain specific passages in Robert Penn Warren, and, most significantly, in the advent of Ralph Ellison, one sees the beginnings—at least—of a more genuinely penetrating search. Mr. Ellison, by the way, is the first Negro novelist I have ever read to utilize in language, and brilliantly, some of the ambiguity and irony of Negro life.

About my interests: I don't know if I have any, unless the morbid desire to own a sixteen-millimeter camera and make experimental movies can be so classified. Otherwise, I love to eat and drink—it's my melancholy conviction that I've scarcely ever had enough to eat (this is because it's *impossible* to eat enough if you're worried about the next meal)—and I love to argue with people who do not disagree with me too profoundly, and I love to laugh. I do *not* like bohemia, or bohemians, I do not like people whose principal aim is pleasure, and I do not like people who are *earnest* about anything. I don't like people who like me because I'm a Negro; neither do I like people who find in the same accident grounds for contempt. I love America more than any other country in the world, and, exactly for this reason, I insist on the right to criticize her perpetually. I think all theories are suspect,

11

that the finest principles may have to be modified, or may even be pul-
verized by the demands of life, and that one must find, therefore, one's
own moral center and move through the world hoping that this center will guide one aright. I consider that I have many responsibilities,
but none greater than this: to last, as Hemingway says, and get my
work done.

10   I want to be an honest man and a good writer. 10

Questions on Meaning

1. Explain this statement by Baldwin: "The difficulty then, for me, of being a Negro writer was the fact that I was, in effect, prohibited from examining my own experience too closely by the tremendous demands and the very real dangers of my social situation." What are those demands and dangers?
2. Why does Baldwin feel a writer needs to understand his or her heritage? How does Baldwin define his own heritage?
3. What does Baldwin mean when he says that "the most difficult (and most rewarding) thing in my life has been the fact that I was born a Negro and was forced, therefore, to effect some kind of truce with reality"?

Questions on Rhetorical Strategy and Style

1. Baldwin's style in this essay includes a tendency to make sweeping statements with great effect and then move on rather than dwell on them with examples or extensive development. An example of this is his statement, "The story of my childhood is the usual bleak fantasy, and we can dismiss it with the restrained observation that I certainly would not consider living it again." Find another example like this. What is the larger effect throughout the essay of such statements?
2. As Baldwin relates his life, he is also defining what it means to be a writer. Reread the essay and note all the passages about writers. Assemble these into a definition.

Writing Assignments

1. Baldwin comments that "the past will remain horrible for exactly as long as we refuse to assess it honestly." In this case Baldwin is referring in part to the Negro's past—to slavery and discrimination—but is also making a general observation. What other examples can you cite from American history of something horrible? How would, or could, an honest evaluation diminish its horror?
2. Baldwin says he has the right to criticize America because he loves this country. At the other extreme is the "America—love it or leave it" attitude that arose during the Vietnam War, with the implication that if one finds fault with America, one can always go live somewhere else instead of criticizing the country. Where do

you stand on this question about criticizing the country? Is criticism healthy for a country or not? Can it ever go too far? Write an essay in which you argue for a specific position on this issue.

3. The closing of Baldwin's essay associates his desires to be honest and a good writer. How does good writing in part depend on being honest, even when writing fiction? How would you define "honesty" beyond the simple meaning of being factually accurate? Write an essay in which you explore the relationship of honesty and writing.

Learning to Read and Write

Frederick Douglass

Frederick Douglass (1817–1895)—abolitionist, author, and the first black American to become a prominent public figure—was born into slavery near Tuckahoe, Maryland. As a youth, Douglass worked as a household servant, a field hand, and a shipyard apprentice. In 1838, after several failed attempts to escape (for which he received beatings), he successfully reached New York. He took the surname "Douglass" and eventually settled in New Bedford, Massachusetts. In 1841, the Massachusetts Anti-Slavery League, impressed by his great oratory skills, hired Douglass to help promote the abolition of slavery. Douglass bought his freedom in 1847, using money contributed both by Americans and by sympathizers in England, where he had fled to preserve his freedom. For the next 13 years, Douglass edited the abolitionist periodical North Star *(changed to* Frederick Douglass's Paper *in 1851). During the Civil War, Douglass urged President Lincoln to emancipate the slaves and helped recruit black troops. After the war, he held a series of government posts, including Assistant Secretary to the Santo Domingo Commission, Marshall of the District of Columbia, District Recorder of Deeds, and Ambassador to Haiti. This essay, which comes from Douglass's autobiography,* Narrative of the Life of Frederick Douglass, an American Slave *(1845), reveals the guile and determination that Douglass employed to teach himself to read. As you read the words of a former slave, written more than a century ago, think of how closed the world was to Douglass, yet how he recognized that literacy could help open the door.*

I lived in Master Hugh's family about seven years. During this time, I succeeded in learning to read and write. In accomplishing this, I was compelled to resort to various stratagems. I had no regular teacher. My mistress, who had kindly commenced to instruct me, had, in compliance with the advice and direction of her husband, not only ceased to instruct, but had set her face against my being instructed by any one else. It is due, however, to my mistress to say of her, that she did not adopt this course of treatment immediately. She at first lacked the depravity indispensable to shutting me up in mental darkness. It was at least necessary for her to have some training in the exercise of irresponsible power, to make her equal to the task of treating me as though I were a brute.

My mistress was, as I have said, a kind and tender-hearted woman; and in the simplicity of her soul she commenced, when I first went to live with her, to treat me as she supposed one human being ought to treat another. In entering upon the duties of a slaveholder, she did not seem to perceive that I sustained to her the relation of a mere chattel, and that for her to treat me as a human being was not only wrong, but dangerously so. Slavery proved as injurious to her as it did to me. When I went there, she was a pious, warm, and tender-hearted woman. There was no sorrow or suffering for which she had not a tear. She had bread for the hungry, clothes for the naked, and comfort for every mourner that came within her reach. Slavery soon proved its ability to divest her of these heavenly qualities. Under its influence, the tender heart became stone, and the lamb-like disposition gave way to one of tiger-like fierceness. The first step in her downward course was in her ceasing to instruct me. She now commenced to practise her husband's precepts. She finally became even more violent in her opposition than her husband himself. She was not satisfied with simply doing as well as he had commanded; she seemed anxious to do better. Nothing seemed to make her more angry than to see me with a newspaper. She seemed to think that here lay the danger. I have had her rush at me with a face made all up of fury, and snatch from me a newspaper, in a manner that fully revealed her apprehension. She was an apt woman; and a little experience soon demonstrated, to her satisfaction, that education and slavery were incompatible with each other.

From this time I was most narrowly watched. If I was in a separate room any considerable length of time, I was sure to be suspected of having a book, and was at once called to give an account of myself. All this, however, was too late. The first step had been taken. Mistress, in teaching me the alphabet, had given me the *inch*, and no precaution could prevent me from taking the *ell.*

The plan which I adopted, and the one by which I was most successful, was that of making friends of all the little white boys whom I met in the street. As many of these as I could, I converted into teachers. With their kindly aid, obtained at different times and in different places, I finally succeeded in learning to read. When I was sent on errands, I always took my book with me, and by going one part of my errand quickly, I found time to get a lesson before my return. I used also to carry bread with me, enough of which was always in the house, and to which I was always welcome; for I was much better off in this regard than many of the poor white children in our neighborhood. This bread I used to bestow upon the hungry little urchins, who, in return, would give me that more valuable bread of knowledge. I am strongly tempted to give the names of two or three of those little boys, as a testimonial of the gratitude and affection I bear them; but prudence forbids;—not that it would injure me, but it might embarrass them; for it is almost an unpardonable offense to teach slaves to read in this Christian country. It is enough to say of the dear little fellows, that they lived on Philpot Street, very near Durgin and Bailey's shipyard. I used to talk this matter of slavery over with them. I would sometimes say to them, I wished I could be as free as they would be when they got to be men. "You will be free as soon as you are twenty-one, *but I am a slave for life!* Have not I as good a right to be free as you have?" These words used to trouble them; they would express for me the liveliest sympathy, and console me with the hope that something would occur by which I might be free.

5   I was now about twelve years old, and the thought of being *a slave*   5 *for life* began to bear heavily upon my heart. Just about this time, I got hold of a book entitled "The Columbian Orator." Every opportunity I got, I used to read this book. Among much of other interesting matter, I found in it a dialogue between a master and his slave. The slave was represented as having run away from his master three times. The dialogue represented the conversation which took place between them, when the slave was retaken the third time. In this dialogue, the whole argument in behalf of slavery was brought forward by the master, all of which was disposed of by the slave. The slave was made to

say some very smart as well as impressive things in reply to his master—things which had the desired though unexpected effect; for the conversation resulted in the voluntary emancipation of the slave on the part of the master.

In the same book, I met with one of Sheridan's mighty speeches on and in behalf of Catholic emancipation. These were choice documents to me. I read them over and over again with unabated interest. They gave tongue to interesting thoughts of my own soul, which had frequently flashed through my mind, and died away for want of utterance. The moral which I gained from the dialogue was the power of truth over the conscience of even a slaveholder. What I got from Sheridan was a bold denunciation of slavery, and a powerful vindication of human rights. The reading of these documents enabled me to utter my thoughts, and to meet the arguments brought forward to sustain slavery; but while they relieved me of one difficulty, they brought on another even more painful than the one of which I was relieved. The more I read, the more I was led to abhor and detest my enslavers. I could regard them in no other light than a band of successful robbers, who had left their homes, and gone to Africa, and stolen us from our homes, and in a strange land reduced us to slavery. I loathed them as being the meanest as well as the most wicked of men. As I read and contemplated the subject, behold! that very discontentment which Master Hugh had predicted would follow my learning to read had already come, to torment and sting my soul to unutterable anguish. As I writhed under it, I would at times feel that learning to read had been a curse rather than a blessing. It had given me a view of my wretched condition, without the remedy. It opened my eyes to the horrible pit, but to no ladder upon which to get out. In moments of agony, I envied my fellow-slaves for their stupidity. I have often wished myself a beast. I preferred the condition of the meanest reptile to my own. Any thing, no matter what, to get rid of thinking! It was this everlasting thinking of my condition that tormented me. There was no getting rid of it. It was pressed upon me by every object within sight or hearing, animate or inanimate. The silver trump of freedom had roused my soul to eternal wakefulness. Freedom now appeared, to disappear no more forever. It was heard in every sound, and seen in every thing. It was ever present to torment me with a sense of my wretched condition. I saw nothing without seeing it, I heard nothing without hearing it, and felt nothing without feeling it. It looked from every star, it smiled in every calm, breathed in every wind, and moved in every storm.

I often found myself regretting my own existence, and wishing myself dead; and but for the hope of being free, I have no doubt but that I should have killed myself, or done something for which I should have been killed. While in this state of mind, I was eager to hear any one speak of slavery. I was a ready listener. Every little while, I could hear something about the abolitionists. It was some time before I found what the word meant. It was always used in such connections as to make it an interesting word to me. If a slave ran away and succeeded in getting clear, or if a slave killed his master, set fire to a barn, or did any thing very wrong in the mind of a slaveholder, it was spoken of as the fruit of *abolition*. Hearing the word in this connection very often, I set about learning what it meant. The dictionary afforded me little or no help. I found it was "the act of abolishing," but then I did not know what was to be abolished. Here I was perplexed. I did not dare to ask any one about its meaning, for I was satisfied that it was something they wanted me to know very little about. After a patient waiting, I got one of our city papers, containing an account of the number of petitions from the north, praying for the abolition of slavery in the District of Columbia, and of the slave trade between the States. From this time I understood the words *abolition* and *abolitionist,* and always drew near when that word was spoken, expecting to hear something of importance to myself and fellow-slaves. The light broke in upon me by degrees. I went one day down on the wharf of Mr. Waters; and seeing two Irishmen unloading a scow of stone, I went, unasked, and helped them. When we had finished, one of them came to me and asked me if I were a slave. I told him I was. He asked, "Are ye a slave for life?" I told him that I was. The good Irishman seemed to be deeply affected by the statement. He said to the other that it was a pity so fine a little fellow as myself should be a slave for life. He said it was a shame to hold me. They both advised me to run away to the north; that I should find friends there, and that I should be free. I pretended not to be interested in what they said, and treated them as if I did not understand them; for I feared they might be treacherous. White men have been known to encourage slaves to escape, and then, to get the reward, catch them and return them to their masters. I was afraid that these seemingly good men might use me so; but I nevertheless remembered their advice, and from that time I resolved to run away. I looked forward to a time at which it would be safe for me to escape. I was too young to think of doing so immediately; besides, I wished to learn how to write, as I might have occasion to write my own pass. I consoled myself with the hope that I should one day find a good chance. Meanwhile, I would learn to write.

The idea as to how I might learn to write was suggested to me by being in Durgin and Bailey's ship-yard, and frequently seeing the ship carpenters, after hewing, and getting a piece of timber ready for use, write on the timber the name of that part of the ship for which it was intended. When a piece of timber was intended for the larboard side, it would be marked thus—"L." When a piece was for the starboard side, it would be marked thus—"S." A piece for the larboard side forward, would be marked thus—"L. F." When a piece was for starboard side forward, it would be marked thus—"S. F." For larboard aft, it would be marked thus—"L. A." For starboard aft, it would be marked thus—"S. A." I soon learned the names of these letters, and for what they were intended when placed upon a piece of timber in the shipyard. I immediately commenced copying them, and in a short time was able to make the four letters named. After that, when I met with any boy who I knew could write, I would tell him I could write as well as he. The next word would be, "I don't believe you. Let me see you try it." I would then make the letters which I had been so fortunate as to learn, and ask him to beat that. In this way I got a good many lessons in writing, which it is quite possible I should never have gotten in any other way. During this time, my copy-book was the board fence, brick wall, and pavement; my pen and ink was a lump of chalk. With these, I learned mainly how to write. I then commenced and continued copying the Italics in Webster's Spelling Book, until I could make them all without looking on the book. By this time, my little Master Thomas had gone to school, and learned how to write, and had written over a number of copy-books. These had been brought home, and shown to some of our near neighbors, and then laid aside. My mistress used to go to class meeting at the Wilk Street meetinghouse every Monday afternoon, and leave me to take care of the house. When left thus, I used to spend the time in writing in the spaces left in Master Thomas's copy-book, copying what he had written. I continued to do this until I could write a hand very similar to that of Master Thomas. Thus, after a long, tedious effort for years, I finally succeeded in learning how to write.

Questions on Meaning

1. Douglass stated that by teaching him the alphabet, his mistress had "given me the *inch,* and no precaution could prevent me from taking the *ell.*" What did he mean by that statement? If you are not certain, look up the English/European definition of the word "ell." What expression would a writer most often use today to convey that meaning?
2. From reading *The Columbian Orator,* Douglass learned some invaluable lessons about the power of education and the ability to express oneself intelligently. What is the *moral* lesson that he attributes to this book?
3. What is the single word that gave Douglass hope, that made him believe that there was a way out of his slavery? What is the irony about learning this word that delayed his revelation?

Questions on Rhetorical Strategy and Style

1. What is the primary rhetorical strategy used in this essay? Give examples of two other rhetorical strategies also used.
2. Although Douglass is sparing with dates, this essay is vaguely chronological. Read through the essay again and see if you can determine how old he was when he began working as a servant, when he apprenticed at the boatyard, and when he "finally succeeded in learning how to write." Does Douglass's inattention to dates affect the impact of the essay?

Writing Assignments

1. As Douglass learned more about slavery, he came to despise slaveholders and what they were doing to his people. In time, he would come to realize that the discontent his knowledge gave him was why his master did not want him to become educated. This is a common theme in oppression: Keep the oppressed from gaining a foothold, be it through wisdom or material possessions. Research how white South Africa oppressed black South Africans during Apartheid. What parallels can you draw between oppression in South Africa and the oppression experienced by Douglass?
2. As Douglass became more literate and more aware of his plight as a slave, he sometimes felt that "learning to read had been a curse

rather than a blessing." Write an essay about something you have learned that you later wished you did not know. Did your enlightenment eventually enrich your life, or has it continued to torment you? Has it made you a less curious person? What lesson did you learn from this experience?

3. In the second paragraph, Douglass explains how his mistress "did not perceive" how to act as a slaveowner and thus acted contrary to her position by treating Douglass with kindness. Later, in the fourth paragraph, he describes how other boys who had befriended him might be embarrassed if identified. Think of a time when you have crossed an invisible barrier of class, race, education, or wealth to treat someone with equality. Perhaps you had a friend in high school who your parents did not feel was "your kind," or maybe you have become friends with someone in college whom other college acquaintances look down upon. Write an essay describing the reactions of others to your relationship with this person and how his or her reactions, in turn, have affected this relationship. Did the barrier damage your relationship with this person or strengthen your resolve?

Workers

Richard Rodriguez

Richard Rodriguez (1944–) was born in San Francisco. A child of Mexican immigrants, Rodriguez spoke Spanish until he went to a Catholic school at age 6. As a youth, he delivered newspapers and worked as a gardener. Rodriguez received a B.A. from Stanford University, an M.A. from Columbia University, and a Ph.D. in English Renaissance literature from the University of California at Berkeley, and attended the Warburg Institute in London on a Fulbright fellowship. A noted prose stylist, Rodriguez has worked as a teacher, journalist, and educational consultant, in addition to writing, lecturing, and appearing frequently on the Public Broadcast System (PBS) program, The MacNeil-Lehrer News Hour. *Rodriguez's books include* Hunger of Memory: The Education of Richard Rodriguez *(1982), a collection of autobiographical essays;* Mexico's Children *(1990); and* Days of Obligation: An Argument With My Mexican Father *(1992), which was nominated for a National Book Award. In addition, he has been published in* The American Scholar, Change, College English, Harper's, Mother Jones, Reader's Digest, *and* Time. *Not unfamiliar with controversy, Rodriguez often speaks out against affirmative action and bilingual education. The following essay, which appeared in* Hunger of Memory, *reveals lessons Rodriguez learned about his choices in life and Mexican migrant workers who have none.*

1   It was at Stanford, one day near the end of my senior year, that a friend told me about a summer construction job he knew was available. I was quickly alert. Desire uncoiled within me. My friend said that he knew I had been looking for summer employment.

From *Hunger of Memory.* Published by David A. Godine. Copyright © 1982 by Richard Rodriguez.

He knew I needed some money. Almost apologetically he explained: It was something I probably wouldn't be interested in, but a friend of his, a contractor, needed someone for the summer to do menial jobs. There would be lots of shoveling and raking and sweeping. Nothing too hard. But nothing more interesting either. Still, the pay would be good. Did I want it? Or did I know someone who did?

I did. Yes, I said, surprised to hear myself say it.

In the weeks following, friends cautioned that I had no idea how hard physical labor really is. ("You only *think* you know what it is like to shovel for eight hours straight.") Their objections seemed to me challenges. They resolved the issue. I became happy with my plan. I decided, however, not to tell my parents. I wouldn't tell my mother because I could guess her worried reaction. I would tell my father only after the summer was over, when I could announce that, after all, I did know what "real work" is like.

The day I met the contractor (a Princeton graduate, it turned out), he asked me whether I had done any physical labor before. "In high school, during the summer," I lied. And although he seemed to regard me with skepticism, he decided to give me a try. Several days later, expectant, I arrived at my first construction site. I would take off my shirt to the sun. And at last grasp desired sensation. No longer afraid. At last become like a *bracero.* "We need those tree stumps out of here by tomorrow," the contractor said. I started to work.

5   I labored with excitement that first morning—and all the days   5 after. The work was harder than I could have expected. But it was never as tedious as my friends had warned me it would be. There was too much physical pleasure in the labor. Especially early in the day, I would be most alert to the sensations of movement and straining. Beginning around seven each morning (when the air was still damp but the scent of weeds and dry earth anticipated the heat of the sun), I would feel my body resist the first thrusts of the shovel. My arms, tightened by sleep, would gradually loosen; after only several minutes, sweat would gather in beads on my forehead and then—a short while later—I would feel my chest silky with sweat in the breeze. I would return to my work. A nervous spark of pain would fly up my arm and settle to burn like an ember in the thick of my shoulder. An hour, two passed. Three. My whole body would assume regular movements; my shoveling would be described by identical, even movements. Even later in the day, my enthusiasm for primitive sensation would survive

25

the heat and the dust and the insects pricking my back. I would strain wildly for sensation as the day came to a close. At three-thirty, quitting time, I would stand upright and slowly let my head fall back, luxuriating in the feeling of tightness relieved.

Some of the men working nearby would watch me and laugh. Two or three of the older men took the trouble to teach me the right way to use a pick, the correct way to shovel. "You're doing it wrong, too fucking hard," one man scolded. Then proceeded to show me—what persons who work with their bodies all their lives quickly learn—the most economical way to use one's body in labor.

"Don't make your back do so much work," he instructed. I stood impatiently listening, half listening, vaguely watching, then noticed his work-thickened fingers clutching the shovel. I was annoyed. I wanted to tell him that I enjoyed shoveling the wrong way. And I didn't want to learn the right way. I wasn't afraid of back pain. I liked the way my body felt sore at the end of the day.

I was about to, but, as it turned out, I didn't say a thing. Rather it was at that moment I realized that I was fooling myself if I expected a few weeks of labor to gain me admission to the world of the laborer. I would not learn in three months what my father had meant by "real work." I was not bound to this job; I could imagine its rapid conclusion. For me the sensations were to be feared. Fatigue took a different toll on their bodies—and minds.

It was, I know, a simple insight. But it was with this realization that I took my first step that summer toward realizing something even more important about the "worker." In the company of carpenters, electricians, plumbers, and painters at lunch, I would often sit quietly, observant. I was not shy in such company. I felt easy, pleased by the knowledge that I was casually accepted, my presence taken for granted by men (exotics) who worked with their hands. Some days the younger men would talk and talk about sex, and they would howl at women who drove by in cars. Other days the talk at lunchtime was subdued; men gathered in separate groups. It depended on who was around. There were rough, good-natured workers. Others were quiet. The more I remember that summer, the more I realize that there was no single *type* of worker. I am embarrassed to say I had not expected such diversity. I certainly had not expected to meet, for example, a plumber who was an abstract painter in his off hours and admired the work of Mark Rothko. Nor did I expect to meet so many workers with college diplomas. (They were the ones who were not surprised that I intended to enter graduate school in the fall.) I suppose what I really want to say here is painfully obvious, but I must say it nevertheless: The men of that summer were middle-class Americans. They certainly didn't constitute an oppressed society. Carefully completing their work sheets; talking about the fortunes of local football teams; planning Las Vegas vacations; comparing the gas mileage of various makes of campers—they were not *los pobres* my mother had spoken about.

10 On two occasions, the contractor hired a group of Mexican aliens. They were employed to cut down some trees and haul off debris. In all, there were six men of varying age. The youngest in his late twenties; the oldest (his father?) perhaps sixty years old. They came and they left in a single old truck. Anonymous men. They were never introduced to the other men at the site. Immediately upon their arrival, they would follow the contractor's directions, start working—rarely resting—seemingly driven by a fatalistic sense that work which had to be done was best done as quickly as possible.

I watched them sometimes. Perhaps they watched me. The only time I saw them pay me much notice was one day at lunchtime when I was laughing with the other men. The Mexicans sat apart when they ate, just as they worked by themselves. Quiet. I rarely heard them say much to each other. All I could hear were their voices calling out sharply to one another, giving directions. Otherwise, when they stood briefly resting, they talked among themselves in voices too hard to overhear.

The contractor knew enough Spanish, and the Mexicans—or at least the oldest of them, their spokesman—seemed to know enough English to communicate. But because I was around, the contractor decided one day to make me his translator. (He assumed I could speak Spanish.) I did what I was told. Shyly I went over to tell the Mexicans that the *patrón* wanted them to do something else before they left for the day. As I started to speak, I was afraid with my old fear that I would be unable to pronounce the Spanish words. But it was a simple instruction I had to convey. I could say it in phrases.

The dark sweating faces turned toward me as I spoke. They stopped their work to hear me. Each nodded in response. I stood there. I wanted to say something more. But what could I say in Spanish, even if I could have pronounced the words right? Perhaps I just wanted to engage them in small talk, to be assured of their confidence, our familiarity. I thought for a moment to ask them where in Mexico they were from. Something like that. And maybe I wanted to tell them (a lie, if need be) that my parents were from the same part of Mexico.

I stood there.

15   Their faces watched me. The eyes of the man directly in front of 15
me moved slowly over my shoulder, and I turned to follow his glance toward *el patrón* some distance away. For a moment I felt swept up by that glance into the Mexicans' company. But then I heard one of them returning to work. And then the others went back to work. I left them without saying anything more.

When they had finished, the contractor went over to pay them in cash. (He later told me that he paid them collectively—"for the job," though he wouldn't tell me their wages. He said something quickly about the good rate of exchange "in their own country.") I can still hear the loudly confident voice he used with the Mexicans. It was the sound of the *gringo* I had heard as a very young boy. And I can still hear the quiet, indistinct sounds of the Mexican, the oldest, who replied. At hearing that voice I was sad for the Mexicans. Depressed by their vulnerability. Angry at myself. The adventure of the summer seemed suddenly ludicrous. I would not shorten the distance I felt from *los pobres* with a few weeks of physical labor. I would not become like them. They were different from me.

After that summer, a great deal—and not very much really—changed in my life. The curse of physical shame was broken by the sun; I was no longer ashamed of my body. No longer would I deny myself the pleasing sensations of my maleness. During those years when middle-class black Americans began to assert with pride, "Black is beautiful," I was able to regard my complexion without shame. I am today darker than I ever was as a boy. I have taken up the middle-class sport of long-distance running. Nearly every day now I run ten or fifteen miles, barely clothed, my skin exposed to the California winter rain and wind or the summer sun of late afternoon. The torso, the soccer player's calves and thighs, the arms of the twenty-year-old I never was, I possess now in my thirties. I study the youthful parody shape in the mirror: the stomach lipped tight by muscle; the shoulders rounded by chin-ups; the arms veined strong. This man. A man. I meet him. He laughs to see me, what I have become.

The dandy. I wear double-breasted Italian suits and custom-made English shoes. I resemble no one so much as my father—the man

28

pictured in those honeymoon photos. At that point in life when he abandoned the dandy's posture, I assume it. At the point when my parents would not consider going on vacation, I register at the Hotel Carlyle in New York and the Plaza Athenée in Paris. I am as taken by the symbols of leisure and wealth as they were. For my parents, however, those symbols became taunts, reminders of all they could not achieve in one lifetime. For me those same symbols are reassuring reminders of public success. I tempt vulgarity to be reassured. I am filled with the gaudy delight, the monstrous grace of the nouveau riche.

In recent years I have had occasion to lecture in ghetto high schools. There I see students of remarkable style and physical grace. (One can see more dandies in such schools than one ever will find in middle-class high schools.) There is not the look of casual assurance I saw students at Stanford display. Ghetto girls mimic high-fashion models. Their dresses are of bold, forceful color; their figures elegant, long; the stance theatrical. Boys wear shirts that grip at their overdeveloped muscular bodies. (Against a powerless future, they engage images of strength.) Bad nutrition does not yet tell. Great disappointment, fatal to youth, awaits them still. For the moment, movements in school hallways are dancelike, a procession of postures in a sexual masque. Watching them, I feel a kind of envy. I wonder how different my adolescence would have been had I been free. . . . But no, it is my parents I see—their optimism during those years when they were entertained by Italian grand opera.

20   The registration clerk in London wonders if I have just been to   20 Switzerland. And the man who carries my luggage in New York guesses the Caribbean. My complexion becomes a mark of my leisure. Yet no one would regard my complexion the same way if I entered such hotels through the service entrance. That is only to say that my complexion assumes its significance from the context of my life. My skin, in itself, means nothing. I stress the point because I know there are people who would label me "disadvantaged" because of my color. They make the same mistake I made as a boy, when I thought a disadvantaged life was circumscribed by particular occupations. That summer I worked in the sun may have made me physically indistinguishable from the Mexicans working nearby. (My skin was actually darker because, unlike them, I worked without wearing a shirt. By late August my hands were probably as tough as theirs.) But I was not one

of *los pobres*. What made me different from them was an attitude of *mind,* my imagination of myself.

I do not blame my mother for warning me away from the sun when I was young. In a world where her brother had become an old man in his twenties because he was dark, my complexion was something to worry about. "Don't run in the sun," she warns me today. I run. In the end, my father was right—though perhaps he did not know how right or why—to say that I would never know what real work is. I will never know what he felt at his last factory job. If tomorrow I worked at some kind of factory, it would go differently for me. My long education would favor me. I could act as a public person—able to defend my interests, to unionize, to petition, to speak up—to challenge and demand. (I will never know what real work is.) I will never know what the Mexicans knew, gathering their shovels and ladders and saws.

Their silence stays with me now. The wages those Mexicans received for their labor were only a measure of their disadvantaged condition. Their silence is more telling. They lack a public identity. They remain profoundly alien. Persons apart. People lacking a union obviously, people without grounds. They depend upon the relative good will or fairness of their employers each day. For such people, lacking a better alternative, it is not such an unreasonable risk.

Their silence stays with me. I have taken these many words to describe its impact. Only: the quiet. Something uncanny about it. Its compliance. Vulnerability. Pathos. As I heard their truck rumbling away, I shuddered, my face mirrored with sweat. I had finally come face to face with *los pobres.*

Questions on Meaning

1. What does manual labor symbolize to Rodriguez? Why do you feel he wanted to be a laborer so much that he would lie to get the job? When does he realize that he will never truly be a manual laborer?
2. What does Rodriguez mean when he states that he is not one of *los pobres* because of an "attitude of mind"? Reread the paragraph directly before the break and the next-to-the-last paragraph. How could the Mexican laborers he describes formulate such an attitude?
3. What does Rodriguez's complexion symbolize? Why? What would it symbolize if the conditions of his life were different, if "I entered hotels through the service entrance"?

Questions on Rhetorical Strategy and Style

1. Rodriguez uses comparison and contrast to show the differences between himself and the workers he first encounters, then between himself and the alien Mexicans. What are some of the differences between these two worker groups? Why don't they intermingle?
2. Find where Rodriguez inserts narrative segments in the essay. How do these narratives accentuate the differences between himself and the laborers?
3. Rodriguez spices the essay with sensory descriptions, such as "the air was still damp but the scent of weeds and dry earth anticipated the heat of the sun." Mark other passages that created strong imagery as you read the essay. Analyze their effects in the essay.

Writing Assignments

1. Rodriguez describes the alien Mexican laborers as "anonymous" and states that they lack a public destiny. Describe an experience you have had when you felt anonymous—perhaps the only person from your ethnic group in a class, the new member of a close-knit sports team, or a new person in an office. What were your feelings toward the group? How did they react to you? Did you try to overcome the feeling of anonymity; if so, how?

2. The fact that Rodriguez's job is temporary influences his feelings about himself and the other laborers. Write an essay about an experience you have had when your time was clearly limited, while everyone else was there to stay. You might describe a summer job, as Rodriguez did, or a school you attended for a semester before you transferred out, or even an apartment where you lived temporarily while waiting for your own place. Explain how your temporary status affected your relationship with those with whom you interacted.

Stereotyping of Arabs by the U.S. Ensures Years of Turmoil

Edward Said

*Edward Said (1935–2003) was a distinguished Professor
of Literature at Columbia University in New York. His
most famous work,* Orientalism *(1978) forms an important background for postcolonial studies. Said calls into
question the underlying assumptions that form the foundation of Orientalist thinking. A rejection of Orientals
entails a rejection of biological generalizations, cultural
constructions of people, and racial and religious prejudices.
For Said, Orientals can be found in American people's
attitudes toward Arabs. Most recently, he published the*
Edward Said Reader *(2000), which contains much of his
writings. In 2000, he also published* The End of the
Peace Process: Oslo and After. *Born in Jerusalem, he
was an advocate of the Palestinian cause. In this selection,
from the* Los Angeles Times, *Said is concerned that the
United States and Israel have a blind eye—an Orientalist's
view—denying Arabs the right to self-determination.*

1   The great modern empires have never been held together only   1
by military power. Britain ruled the vast territories of India
with only a few thousand colonial officers and a few more
thousand troops, many of them Indians. France did the same in
North Africa and Indochina, the Dutch in Indonesia, the Portuguese
and Belgians in Africa. The key element was imperial perspective, that

way of looking at a distant foreign reality by subordinating it in one's gaze, constructing its history from one's own point of view, seeing its people as subjects whose fate can be decided by what distant administrators think is best for them. From such willful perspectives ideas develop, including the theory that imperialism is a benign and necessary thing.

For a while this worked, as many local leaders believed—mistakenly—that cooperating with the imperial authority was the only way. But because the dialectic between the imperial perspective and the local one is adversarial and impermanent, at some point the conflict between ruler and ruled becomes uncontainable and breaks out into colonial war, as happened in Algeria and India. We are still a long way from that moment in American rule over the Arab and Muslim world because, over the last century, pacification through unpopular local rulers has so far worked.

At least since World War II, American strategic interests in the Middle East have been, first, to ensure supplies of oil and, second, to guarantee at enormous cost the strength and domination of Israel over its neighbors.

Every empire, however, tells itself and the world that it is unlike all other empires, that its mission is not to plunder and control but to educate and liberate. These ideas are by no means shared by the people who inhabit that empire, but that hasn't prevented the U.S. propaganda and policy apparatus from imposing its imperial perspective on Americans, whose sources of information about Arabs and Islam are woefully inadequate.

5   Several generations of Americans have come to see the Arab world mainly as a dangerous place, where terrorism and religious fanaticism are spawned and where a gratuitous anti-Americanism is inculcated in the young by evil clerics who are anti-democratic and virulently anti-Semitic.

In the United States, "Arabists" are under attack. Simply to speak Arabic or to have some sympathetic acquaintance with the vast Arab cultural tradition has been made to seem a threat to Israel. The media runs the vilest racist stereotypes about Arabs—see, for example, a piece by Cynthia Ozick in *The Wall Street Journal* in which she speaks of Palestinians as having "reared children unlike any other children, removed from ordinary norms and behaviors" and of Palestinian culture as "the life force traduced, cultism raised to a sinister spiritualism."

Americans are sufficiently blind that when a Middle Eastern leader emerges whom our leaders like—the shah of Iran or Anwar Sadat—it is assumed that he is a visionary who does things our way not because he understands the game of imperial power (which is to survive by humoring the regnant authority) but because he is moved by principles that we share.

Almost a quarter of a century after his assassination, Sadat is a forgotten and unpopular man in his own country because most Egyptians regard him as having served the United States first, not Egypt. The same is true of the shah in Iran. That Sadat and the shah were followed in power by rulers who are less palatable to the United States indicates not that Arabs are fanatics, but that the distortions of imperialism produce further distortions, inducing extreme forms of resistance and political self-assertion.

The Palestinians are considered to have reformed themselves by allowing Mahmoud Abbas, rather than the terrible Yasser Arafat, to be their leader. But "reform" is a matter of imperial interpretation. Israel and the United States regard Arafat as an obstacle to the settlement they wish to impose on the Palestinians, a settlement that would obliterate Palestinian demands and allow Israel to claim, falsely, that it has atoned for its "original sin."

Never mind that Arafat—whom I have criticized for years in the Arabic and Western media—is still universally regarded as the legitimate Palestinian leader. He was legally elected and has a level of popular support that no other Palestinian approaches, least of all Abbas, a bureaucrat and longtime Arafat subordinate. And never mind that there is now a coherent Palestinian opposition, the Independent National Initiative; it gets no attention because the U.S. and the Israeli establishment wish for a compliant interlocutor who is in no position to make trouble. As to whether the Abbas arrangement can work, that is put off to another day. This is shortsightedness indeed—the blind arrogance of the imperial gaze. The same pattern is repeated in the official U.S. view of Iraq, Saudi Arabia, Egypt and the other Arab states.

Underlying this perspective is a long-standing view—the Orientalist view—that denies Arabs their right to national self-determination because they are considered incapable of logic, unable to tell the truth and fundamentally murderous.

Since Napoleon's invasion of Egypt in 1798, there has been an uninterrupted imperial presence based on these premises throughout the Arab world, producing untold misery—and some benefits, it is true. But so accustomed have Americans become to their own ignorance and the blandishments of U.S. advisers such as Bernard Lewis and Fouad Ajami, who have directed their venom against the Arabs in every possible way, that we somehow think that what we do is correct because "that's the way the Arabs are." That this happens also to be an Israeli dogma shared uncritically by the neo-conservatives who are at the heart of the Bush administration simply adds fuel to the fire.

We are in for many more years of turmoil and misery in the Middle East, where one of the main problems is, to put it as plainly as possible, U.S. power. What the United States refuses to see clearly it can hardly hope to remedy.

Questions on Meaning

1. A key term in this essay is imperialism. How does the author define this term? What does he mean by "the imperial gaze" and what is its distorting effect on perceptions of the Arab states?
2. In the author's opinion, how have the United States and Israel used their imperial perspective to exercise control over Palestine and to keep it from achieving self-determination?
3. The author implies that U.S. policy in the Middle East is likely to fail. What is your opinion of this? How do you deem the status of the war on terrorism?

Questions on Rhetorical Strategy and Style

1. In the very beginning of the essay the author distinguishes between military power and imperial perspective. What is the significance of these two concepts and how does the author's use of them establish his agenda?
2. Frequently, an author will advance an argument by refuting someone else's ideas. Why do you suppose this author chooses to criticize Ozick's published statement from *The Wall Street Journal*? Why does he quote it rather than merely make reference to it?
3. While the author insists that Arafat is "the legitimate Palestine leader," he also makes it known that he has been a critic of him. Why does he point this out? In what way does it improve his credibility?

Writing Assignments

1. Write an essay in which you describe a mix (visual and textual) of media representations of Arabs, in order to test the author's assertion that the "sources of information about Arabs and Islam are woefully inadequate." What images of and perspectives on Middle Eastern people have you discovered?
2. Every day the news carries stories and reports about the conflict over Palestine. However, to understand this conflict, the author seems to suggest, we must look beyond daily news items to

appreciate the complex nature of this conflict. Write an anno-
tated bibliography of sources dealing the tensions in Palestine. In
your bibliography, consult a variety of sources and perspectives
on the problem.

Professions for Women

Virginia Woolf

Virginia Woolf (1882–1941) was born in London. She was educated at home by her father, a well-known writer and scholar. As a young woman, she became a member of the Bloomsbury Group of writers and artists in London. In 1912, she wed author and publisher Leonard Woolf, another member of the Bloomsbury Group; together they set up Hogarth Press, which published much of her work. Woolf, who suffered from depression throughout her life, committed suicide in her late fifties. Woolf's publications include the novels Mrs. Dalloway *(1925),* To the Lighthouse *(1927), and* The Waves *(1931) and the essay collections* A Room of One's Own *(1920) and* The Death of the Moth and Other Essays *(1948). Known for her impressionistic, stream-of-consciousness style, Woolf is a dominant force in English literature. This essay, written as a speech that Woolf presented to the Women's Service League in 1931, presents Woolf's view of employment hurdles facing women.*

1   When your secretary invited me to come here, she told me that your Society is concerned with the employment of women and she suggested that I might tell you something about my own professional experiences. It is true I am a woman; it is true I am employed; but what professional experiences have I had? It is difficult to say. My profession is literature; and in that profession there are fewer experiences for women than in any other, with the exception of the stage—fewer, I mean, that are peculiar to women. For the road was cut many years ago—by Fanny Burney, by Aphra Behn,

by Harriet Martineau, by Jane Austen, by George Eliot—many famous women, and many more unknown and forgotten, have been before me, making the path smooth, and regulating my steps. Thus, when I came to write, there were very few material obstacles in my way. Writing was a reputable and harmless occupation. The family peace was not broken by the scratching of a pen. No demand was made upon the family purse. For ten and sixpence one can buy paper enough to write all the plays of Shakespeare—if one has a mind that way. Pianos and models, Paris, Vienna and Berlin, masters and mistresses, are not needed by a writer. The cheapness of writing paper is, of course, the reason why women have succeeded as writers before they have succeeded in the other professions.

But to tell you my story—it is a simple one. You have only got to figure to yourselves a girl in a bedroom with a pen in her hand. She had only to move that pen from left to right—from ten o'clock to one. Then it occurred to her to do what is simple and cheap enough after all—to slip a few of those pages into an envelope, fix a penny stamp in the corner, and drop the envelope into the red box at the corner. It was thus that I became a journalist; and my effort was rewarded on the first day of the following month—a very glorious day it was for me—by a letter from an editor containing a cheque for one pound ten shillings and sixpence. But to show you how little I deserve to be called a professional woman, how little I know of the struggles and difficulties of such lives, I have to admit that instead of spending that sum upon bread and butter, rent, shoes and stockings, or butcher's bills, I went out and bought a cat—a beautiful cat, a Persian cat, which very soon involved me in bitter disputes with my neighbors.

What could be easier than to write articles and to buy Persian cats with the profits? But wait a moment. Articles have to be about something. Mine, I seem to remember, was about a novel by a famous man. And while I was writing this review, I discovered that if I were going to review books I should need to do battle with a certain phantom. And the phantom was a woman, and when I came to know her better I called her after the heroine of a famous poem, "The Angel in the House." It was she who used to come between me and my paper when I was writing reviews. It was she who bothered me and wasted my time and so tormented me that at last I killed her. You who come of a younger and happier generation may not have heard of her—you may not know what I mean by the Angel in the House. I will describe her as shortly as I can. She was intensely sympathetic. She was immensely charming. She was utterly unselfish. She excelled in the difficult arts of family life. She sacrificed herself daily. If there was chicken, she took the leg; if there was a draught she sat in it—in short she was so constituted that she never had a mind or a wish of her own, but preferred to sympathize always with the minds and wishes of others. Above all—I need not say it—she was pure. Her purity was supposed to be her chief beauty—her blushes, her great grace. In those days—the last of Queen Victoria—every house had its Angel. And when I came to write I encountered her with the very first words. The shadow of her wings fell on my page; I heard the rustling of her skirts in the room. Directly, that is to say, I took my pen in hand to review that novel by a famous man, she slipped behind me and whispered: "My dear, you are a young woman. You are writing about a book that has been written by a man. Be sympathetic; be tender; flatter; deceive; use all the arts and wiles of our sex. Never let anybody guess that you have a mind of your own. Above all, be pure." And she made as if to guide my pen. I now record the one act for which I take some credit to myself, though the credit rightly belongs to some excellent ancestors of mine who left me a certain sum of money—shall we say five hundred pounds a year?—so that it was not necessary for me to depend solely on charm for my living. I turned upon her and caught her by the throat. I did my best to kill her. My excuse, if I were to be had up in a court of law, would be that I acted in self-defence. Had I not killed her she would have killed me. She would have plucked the heart out of my writing. For, as I found, directly I put pen to paper, you cannot review even a novel without having a mind of your own, without expressing what you think to be the truth about human relations, morality, sex. And all these questions, according to the Angel in the House, cannot be dealt with freely and openly by women; they must charm, they must conciliate, they must— to put it bluntly—tell lies if they are to succeed. Thus, whenever I felt the shadow of her wing or the radiance of her halo upon my page, I took up the inkpot and flung it at her. She died hard. Her fictitious nature was of great assistance to her. It is far harder to kill a phantom than a reality. She was always creeping back when I thought I had despatched her. Though I flatter myself that I killed her in the end, the struggle was severe; it took much time that had better have been spent upon learning Greek grammar; or in roaming the world in search of adventures. But it was a real experience; it was an experience that was bound to befall all women writers at that time. Killing the Angel in the House was part of the occupation of a woman writer.

But to continue my story. The Angel was dead; what then remained? You may say that what remained was a simple and common object—a young woman in a bedroom with an inkpot. In other words, now that she had rid herself of falsehood, that young woman had only to be herself. Ah, but what is "herself"? I mean, what is a woman? I assure you, I do not know. I do not believe that you know. I do not believe that anybody can know until she has expressed herself in all the arts and professions open to human skill. That indeed is one of the reasons why I have come here—out of respect for you, who are in process of showing us by your experiments what a woman is, who are in process of providing us, by your failures and successes, with that extremely important piece of information.

5   But to continue the story of my professional experiences. I made one pound ten and six by my first review; and I bought a Persian cat with the proceeds. Then I grew ambitious. A Persian cat is all very well, I said; but a Persian cat is not enough. I must have a motor car. And it was thus that I became a novelist—for it is a very strange thing that people will give you a motor car if you will tell them a story. It is a still stranger thing that there is nothing so delightful in the world as telling stories. It is far pleasanter than writing reviews of famous novels. And yet, if I am to obey your secretary and tell you my professional experiences as a novelist, I must tell you about a very strange experience that befell me as a novelist. And to understand it you must try first to imagine a novelist's state of mind. I hope I am not giving away professional secrets if I say that a novelist's chief desire is to be as unconscious as possible. He has to induce in himself a state of perpetual lethargy. He wants life to proceed with the utmost quiet and regularity. He wants to see the same faces, to read the same books, to do the same things day after day, month after month, while he is writing, so that nothing may break the illusion in which he is living—so that nothing may disturb or disquiet the mysterious nosings about, feelings round, darts, dashes and sudden discoveries of that very shy and illusive spirit, the imagination. I suspect that this state is the same both for men and women. Be that as it may, I want you to imagine me writing a novel in a state of trance. I want you to figure to yourself a girl sitting with a pen in her hand, which for minutes, and indeed for hours, she never dips into the inkpot. The image that comes

to my mind when I think of this girl is the image of a fisherman lying sunk in dreams on the verge of a deep lake with a rod held out over the water. She was letting her imagination sweep unchecked round every rock and cranny of the world that lies submerged in the depths of our unconscious being. Now came the experience, the experience that I believe to be far commoner with women writers than with men. The line raced through the girl's fingers. Her imagination had rushed away. It had sought the pools, the depths, the dark places where the largest fish slumber. And then there was a smash. There was an explosion. There was foam and confusion. The imagination had dashed itself against something hard. The girl was roused from her dream. She was indeed in a state of the most acute and difficult distress. To speak without figure she had thought of something, something about the body, about the passions which it was unfitting for her as a woman to say. Men, her reason told her, would be shocked. The consciousness of what men will say of a woman who speaks the truth about her passions had roused her from her artist's state of unconsciousness. She could write no more. The trance was over. Her imagination could work no longer. This I believe to be a very common experience with women writers—they are impeded by the extreme conventionality of the other sex. For though men sensibly allow themselves great freedom in these respects, I doubt that they realize or can control the extreme severity with which they condemn such freedom in women.

These then were two very genuine experiences of my own. These were two of the adventures of my professional life. The first—killing the Angel in the House—I think I solved. She died. But the second, telling the truth about my own experiences as a body, I do not think I solved. I doubt that any woman has solved it yet. The obstacles against her are still immensely powerful—and yet they are very difficult to define. Outwardly, what is simpler than to write books? Outwardly, what obstacles are there for a woman rather than for a man? Inwardly, I think, the case is very different: she has still many ghosts to fight, many prejudices to overcome. Indeed it will be a long time still, I think, before a woman can sit down to write a book without finding a phantom to be slain, a rock to be dashed against. And if this is so in literature, the freest of all professions for women, how is it in the new professions which you are now for the first time entering?

Those are the questions that I should like, had I time, to ask you. And indeed, if I have laid stress upon these professional experiences of mine, it is because I believe that they are, though in different forms, yours also. Even when the path is nominally open—when there is nothing to prevent a woman from being a doctor, a lawyer, a civil servant—there are many phantoms and obstacles, as I believe, looming in her way. To discuss and define them is, I think, of great value and importance; for thus only can the labour be shared, the difficulties be solved. But besides this, it is necessary also to discuss the ends and the aims for which we are fighting, for which we are doing battle with these formidable obstacles. Those aims cannot be taken for granted; they must be perpetually questioned and examined. The whole position, as I see it—here in this hall surrounded by women practicing for the first time in history I know not how many different professions— is one of extraordinary interest and importance. You have won rooms of your own in the house hitherto exclusively owned by men. You are able, though not without great labor and effort, to pay the rent. You are earning your five hundred pounds a year. But this freedom is only a beginning; the room is your own, but it is still bare. It has to be furnished; it has to be decorated; it has to be shared. How are you going to furnish it, how are you going to decorate it? With whom are you going to share it, and upon what terms? These, I think, are questions of the utmost importance and interest. For the first time in history you are able to ask them; for the first time you are able to decide for yourselves what the answers should be. Willingly would I stay and discuss those questions and answers—but not tonight. My time is up; and I must cease.

Questions on Meaning

1. What does Woolf's "angel in the house" symbolize? Why did she feel she must kill her? Explain why you feel Woolf did or did not kill the angel.
2. Why was writing a "harmless" profession for a woman in Woolf's day? What does that tell you about the place of women in society at this time? Accordingly, what socioeconomic slice of life did women represent then?
3. What was your reaction to the closing paragraph of the essay of Woolf's speech? How would *you* have concluded it?

Questions on Rhetorical Strategy and Style

1. How persuasive is Woolf's argument that women writers face different obstacles than men? Find where she uses example to reinforce her argument. Would those examples still stand today?
2. What was your reaction when Woolf suddenly switched from first person to the male third-person pronoun "he," and then back to first person when she was discussing her trance experience as a novelist. Why do you think she used the male pronoun?
3. Imagine Woolf—a woman who did not have to earn a salary to cover her room and board—standing before the Women's Service League, an organization of "women practicing for the first time in history many different professions." What does the tone of her talk tell you about how she related to this group? How do you think they reacted to her words?

Writing Assignments

1. Think of other occupations in which women today still must contend with "angels in the house," such as doctors, engineers, executives, laborers, and mechanics. How are these occupational prejudices perpetuated? Suggest some techniques for overcoming them.
2. Write an essay about your experience with "angels"—either an angel you have experienced or an angel your mother, sister, aunt, or another woman you know—has had to contend with. Describe how the angel stifles the subject of your essay and how your subject reacts. (She may not even know the angel is there.) Does she try to kill the angel? Is she successful?

Roberto Acuna, Migrant Farm Worker

Studs Terkel

Studs Terkel (1912–2008) was born in New York and graduated from the University of Chicago in 1934. In his long career he was a civil servant, an actor, and a movie house manager. He worked in radio in the 1930s and, from 1949–1953, produced a television program called "Stud's Place." In the 1950s he ran afoul of Senator Joseph McCarthy and the House Un-American Activities Committee, which subsequently led to the show's cancellation. In 1967 he published Division Street: America, *a book based on oral histories. In 1974 he published one of his best-known books, titled* Working: People Talk about What They Do All Day and How They Feel about What They Do. *This was followed by such works as* American Dreams: Lost and Found *(1980);* The Great Divide: Second Thoughts on the American Dream *(1988);* My American Century *(1997); and* Hope Dies Last: Keeping the Faith in Difficult Times *(2003). Terkel was nominated for the National Book Award and received the Peabody Broadcasting Award. He also won the Pulitzer Prize in 1985 for* The Good War: An Oral History of WWII, *and a National Book Critics Circle Lifetime Achievement Award. The following selection from* Working *reflects Terkel's considerable skill with the art of the interview and his understanding of the lives of everyday citizens.*

1   I walked out of the fields two years ago. I saw the need to change   1
the California feudal system, to change the lives of farm workers,
to make these huge, corporations feel they're not above anybody. I
am thirty-four years old and I try to organize for the United Farm
Workers of America.

*His hands are calloused and each of his thumbnails is singularly cut.
"If you're picking lettuce, the thumbnails fall off cause they're banged on
the box. Your hands get swollen. You can't slow down because the foreman
sees you're so many boxes behind and you'd better get on. But people
would help each other. If you're feeling bad that day, somebody who's feeling pretty good would help. Any people that are suffering have to stick
together, whether they like it or riot, whether they be black, brown,
or pink."*

According to Mom, I was born on a cotton sack out in the fields,
'cause she had no money to go to the hospital. When I was a child, we
used to migrate from California to Arizona and back and forth. The
things I saw shaped my life. I remember when we used to go out and
pick carrots and onions, the whole family, We tried to scratch a livin'
out of the ground. I saw my parents cry out in despair, even though
we had the whole family working. At the time, they were paying
sixty-two and a half cents an hour. The average income must have
been fifteen hundred dollars, maybe two thousand.[1]

This was supplemented by child labor. During those years, the
growers used to have a Pick-Your-Harvest Week. They would get all
the migrant kids out of school and have 'em out there pickin' the
crops at peak harvest time. A child was off that week and when he
went back to school, he got a little gold star. They would make it
seem like something civic to do.

5   We'd pick everything: lettuce, carrots, onions, cucumbers, cauli-   5
flower, broccoli, tomatoes—all the salads you could make out of vegetables, we picked 'em. Citrus fruits, watermelons—you name it.
We'd be in Salinas about four months. From there we'd go down into
the Imperial Valley. From there we'd go to picking citrus. It was like a
cycle. We'd follow the seasons.

After my dad died, my mom would come home and she'd go into
her tent and I would go into ours. We'd roughhouse and everything
and then we'd go into the tent where Mom was sleeping and I'd see
her crying. When I asked her why she was crying she never gave me
an answer. All she said was things would get better. She retired

a beaten old lady with a lot of dignity. That day she thought would be better never came for her.

"One time, my mom was in bad need of money, so she got a part-time evening job in a restaurant. I'd be helping her. All the growers would come in and they'd be laughing, making nasty remarks, and make passes at her. I used to go out there and kick 'em and my mom told me to leave 'em alone, she could handle 'em. But they would embarrass her and she would cry.

"My mom was a very proud woman. She brought us up without any help from nobody. She kept the family strong. They say that a family that prays together stays together. I say that a family that works together stays together—because of the suffering, My mom couldn't speak English too good. Or much Spanish, for that matter. She wasn't educated. But she knew some prayers and she used to make us say them. That's another thing: when I see the many things in this world and this country, I could tear the churches apart. I never saw a priest out in the fields trying to help people. Maybe in these later years they're doing it. But it's always the church taking from the people.

"We were once asked by the church to bring vegetables to make it a successful bazaar. After we got the stuff there, the only people havin' a good time were the rich people because they were the only ones that were buyin' the stuff . . ."

10 I'd go barefoot to school. The bad thing was they used to laugh at us, 10
the Anglo kids. They would laugh because we'd bring tortillas and frijoles to lunch. They would have their nice little compact lunch boxes with cold milk in their thermos and they'd laugh at us because all we had was dried tortillas. Not only would they laugh at us, but the kids would pick fights, My older brother used to do most of the fighting for us and he'd come home with black eyes all the time.

What really hurt is when we had to go on welfare. Nobody knows the erosion of man's dignity. They used to have a label of canned goods that said, "U.S. Commodities, Not to be sold or exchanged." Nobody knows how proud it is to feel when you bought canned goods with your own money.

"I wanted to be accepted. It must have been in sixth grade. It was just before the Fourth of July. They were trying out students for this patriotic play. I wanted to do Abe Lincoln, so I learned the Gettysburg Address inside and out. I'd be out in the fields pickin' the crops and I'd be memorizin'. I was the only one who didn't have to read the part, 'cause I learned it. The *part was given to a girl who was a grower's daughter. She had to read it out of a book, but they said she had better diction, I was very disappointed. I quit about eighth grade,*

"Any time anybody'd talk to me about politics, about civil rights, I would ignore it. It's a very degrading thing because you can't express yourself. They wanted us to speak English in the school classes. We'd put out a real effort. I would get into a lot of fights because I spoke Spanish and they couldn't understand it. I was punished. I was kept after school for not speaking English."

We used to have our own tents on the truck. Most migrants would live in the tents that were already there in the fields, put up by the company. We got one for ourselves, secondhand, but it was ours. Anglos used to laugh at us, "Here comes the carnival," they'd say. We couldn't keep our clothes clean, we couldn't keep nothing clean, because we'd go by the dirt roads and the dust. We'd stay outside the town.

15   I never did want to go to town because it was a very bad thing for   15 me. We used to go to the small stores, even though we got clipped more. If we went to the other stores, they would laugh at us. They would always point at us with a finger. We'd go to town maybe every two weeks to get what we needed. Everybody would walk in a bunch. We were afraid. (Laughs.) We sang to keep our spirits up. We joked about our poverty. This one guy would say, "When I get to be rich, I'm gonna marry an Anglo woman, so I can be accepted into society." The other guy would say, "When I get rich I'm gonna marry a Mexican woman, so I can go to that Anglo society of yours and see them hang you for marrying an Anglo." Our world was around the fields.

I started picking crops when I was eight. I couldn't do much, but every little bit counts. Every time I would get behind on my chores, I would get a carrot thrown at me by my parents. I would daydream: If I were a millionaire, I would buy all these ranches and give them back to the people. I would picture my mom living in one area all the time and being admired by all the people in the community. All of a sudden I'd be rudely awaken by a broken carrot in my back. That would bust your whole dream apart and you'd work for a while and come back to daydreaming.

We used to work early, about four o'clock in the morning. We'd pick the harvest until about six. Then we'd run home and get into our supposedly clean clothes and run all the way to school because we'd be late. By the time we got to school, we'd be all tuckered out.

Around maybe eleven o'clock, we'd be dozing off. Our teachers would send notes to the house telling Mom that we were inattentive. The only thing I'd make fairly good grades on was spelling. I couldn't do anything else. Many times we never did our homework, because we were out in the fields. The teachers couldn't understand that. I would get whacked there also.

School would end maybe four o'clock. We'd rush home again, change clothes, go back to work until seven, seven thirty at night. That's not counting the weekends. On Saturday and Sunday, we'd be there from four thirty in the morning until about seven thirty in the evening. This is where we made the money, those two days. We all worked.

I would carry boxes for my mom to pack the carrots in. I would pull the carrots out and she would sort them into different sizes. I would get water for her to drink. When you're picking tomatoes, the boxes are heavy. They weigh about thirty pounds. They're dropped very hard on the trucks so they have to be sturdy.

20   The hardest work would be thinning and hoeing with a short-   20 handled hoe. The fields would be about a half a mile long. You would be bending and stooping all day. Sometimes you would have hard ground and by the time you got home, your hands would be full of calluses. And you'd have a backache. Sometimes I wouldn't have dinner or anything. I'd just go home and fall asleep and wake up just in time to go out to the fields again.

I remember when we just got into California from Arizona to pick up the carrot harvest. It was very cold and very windy out in the fields. We just had a little old blanket for the four of us kids in the tent. We were freezin' our tail off. So I stole two brand-new blankets that belonged to a grower, When we got under those blankets it was nice and comfortable. Somebody saw me. The next morning the grower told my mom he'd turn us in unless we gave him back his blankets—sterilized. So my mom and I and my kid brother went to the river and cut some wood and made a fire and boiled the water and she scrubbed the blankets. She hung them out to dry, ironed them, and sent them back to the grower. We got a spanking for that.

I remember this labor camp that was run by the city. It was a POW camp for German soldiers. They put families in there and it would have barbed wire all around it. If you were out after ten o'clock at night, you couldn't get back in until the next day at four in the

50

morning. We didn't know the rules. Nobody told us. We went to visit some relatives. We got back at about ten thirty and they wouldn't let us in. So we slept in the pickup outside the gate. In the morning, they let us in, we had a fast breakfast and went back to work in the fields.[2]

The grower would keep the families apart, hoping they'd fight against each other. He'd have three or four camps and he'd have the people over here pitted against the people over there. For jobs. He'd give the best crops to the people he thought were the fastest workers. This way he kept us going harder and harder, competing.

When I was sixteen, I had my first taste as a foreman. Handling braceros, aliens, that came from Mexico to work. They'd bring these people to work over here and then send them back to Mexico after the season was over. My job was to make sure they did a good job and pushin' 'em even harder. I was a company man, yes. My parents needed money and I wanted to make sure they were proud of me. A foreman is recognized. I was very naive. Even though I was pushing the workers, I knew their problems. They didn't know how to write, so I would write letters home for them. I would take 'em to town, buy their clothes, outside of the company stores. They had paid me $1.10 an hour. The farm workers' wage was raised to eighty-two and a half cents. But even the braceros were making more money than me, because they were working piecework. I asked for more money. The manager said, "If you don't like it you can quit." I quit and joined the Marine Corps.

25   *I joined the Marine Corps at seventeen. I was very mixed up.* 25
I wanted to become a first-class citizen. I wanted to be accepted and I was very proud of my uniform. My mom didn't want to sign the papers, but she knew I had to better myself and maybe I'd get an education in the services.

"*I did many jobs. I took a civil service exam and was very proud when I passed. Most of the others were college kids. There were only three Chicanos in the group of sixty. I got a job as a correctional officer in a state prison. I quit after eight months because I couldn't take the misery I saw. They wanted me to use a rubber hose on some of the prisoners— mostly Chicanos and blacks. I couldn't do it. They called me chicken-livered because I didn't want to hit nobody. They constantly harassed me after that. I didn't quit because I was afraid of them but because they were trying to make me into a mean man. I couldn't see it. This was Soledad State Prison.*"

I began to see how everything was so wrong. When growers can have an intricate watering system to irrigate their crops but they can't have running water inside the houses of workers. Veterinarians tend to the needs of domestic animals but they can't have medical care for the workers. They can have land subsidies for the growers but they can't have adequate unemployment compensation for the workers. They treat him like a farm implement. In fact, they treat their implements better and their domestic animals better. They have heat and insulated barns for the animals but the workers live in beat-up shacks with no heat at all.

Illness in the fields is 120 percent higher than the average rate for industry. It's mostly back trouble, rheumatism and arthritis, because the damp weather and the cold. Stoop labor is very hard on a person. Tuberculosis is high. And now because of the pesticides, we have many respiratory diseases.

The University of California at Davis has government experiments with pesticides and chemicals. To get a bigger crop each year. They haven't any regard as to what safety precautions are needed. In 1964 or '65, an airplane was spraying these chemicals on the fields. Spraying rigs they're called. Flying low, the wheels got tangled on the fence wire. The pilot got up, dusted himself off, and got a drink of water. He died of convulsions. The ambulance attendants got violently sick because of the pesticides he had on his person. A little girl was playing around a sprayer. She stuck her tongue on it. She died instantly.

30 These pesticides affect the farm worker through the lungs. He 30 breathes it in. He gets no compensation. All they do is say he's sick. They don't investigate the cause.

There were times when I felt I couldn't take it any more. It was 105 in the shade and I'd see endless rows of lettuce and I felt my back hurting . . . I felt the frustration of not being able to get out of the fields. I was getting ready to jump any foreman who looked at me cross-eyed. But until two years ago, my world was still very small.

I would read all these things in the papers about Cesar Chavez and I would denounce him because I still had that thing about becoming a first-class patriotic citizen. In Mexicali they would pass out leaflets and I would throw 'em away. I never participated. The grape boycott didn't affect me much because I was in lettuce. It wasn't until Chavez came to Salinas, where I was working in the fields, that

I saw what a beautiful man he was. I went to this rally. I still intended to stay with the company. But something—I don't know—I was close to the workers. They couldn't speak English and wanted me to be their spokesman in favor of going on strike. I don't know—I just got caught up with it all, the beautiful feeling of solidarity.

You'd see the people on the picket lines at four in the morning, at the camp fires, heating up beans and coffee and tortillas. It gave me a sense of belonging. These were my own people and they wanted change. I knew this is what I was looking for. I just didn't know it before.

My mom had always wanted me to better myself. I wanted to better myself because of her. Now when the strikes started, I told her I was going to join the union and the whole movement. I told her I was going to work without pay. She said she was proud of me. (His eyes glisten. A long, long pause.) See, I told her I wanted to be with my people. If I were a company man, nobody would like me any more. I had to belong to somebody and this was it right here. She said, "I pushed you in your early years to try to better yourself and get a social position. But I see that's not the answer. I know I'll be proud of you."

35   All kinds of people are farm workers, not just Chicanos. Filipinos 35 started the strike. We have Puerto Ricans and Appalachians too, Arabs, some Japanese, some Chinese. At one time they used us against each other. But now they can't and they're scared, the growers. They can organize conglomerates. Yet when we try organization to better our lives, they are afraid. Suffering people never dreamed it could be different. Cesar Chavez tells them this and they grasp the idea—and this is what scares the growers.

Now the machines are coming in. It takes skill to operate them. But anybody can be taught. We feel migrant workers should be given the chance. They got one for grapes. They got one for lettuce. They have cotton machines that took jobs away from thousands of farm workers. The people wind up in the ghettos of the city, their culture, their families, their unity destroyed.

We're trying to stipulate it in our contract that the company will not use any machinery without the consent of the farm workers. So we can make sure the people being replaced by the machines will know how to operate the machines.

Working in the fields is not in itself a degrading job. It's hard, but if you're given regular hours, better pay, decent housing, unemployment and medical compensation, pension plans—we have a very relaxed way of living. But the growers don't recognize us as persons. That's the worst thing, the way they treat you. Like we have no brains. Now we see they have no brains. They have only a wallet in their head. The more you squeeze it, the more they cry out.

If we had proper compensation we wouldn't have to be working seventeen hours a day and following the crops. We could stay in one area and it would give us roots. Being a migrant, it tears the family apart. You get in debt. You leave the area penniless. The children are the ones hurt the most. They go to school three months in one place and then on to another. No sooner do they make friends, they are uprooted again. Right here, your childhood is taken away. So when they grow up, they're looking for this childhood they have lost.

40 If people could see—in the winter, ice on the fields. We'd be on 40 our knees all day long. We'd build fires and warm up real fast and go back onto the ice. We'd be picking watermelons in 105 degrees all day long. When people have melons or cucumber or carrots or lettuce, they don't know how they got on their table and the consequences to the people who picked it. If I had enough money, I would take busloads of people out to the fields and into the labor camps. Then they'd know how that fine salad got on their table.

End Notes

1. "Today, because of our struggles, the pay is up to two dollars an hour. Yet we know that is not enough."
2. "Since we started organizing, this camp has been destroyed. They started building housing on it."

Questions on Meaning

1. As the interview opens, Acuna refers to the feudal system that controlled the lives of migrant workers. In what ways is the system feudal?
2. Why does Acuna seem bitter toward the church?
3. Acuna speaks several times of the need for acceptance. What effort did he make to achieve it?
4. What would take place in the POW camp for German soldiers?
5. Who was Cesar Chavez and how did he help the plight of the migrant farm worker?

Questions on Rhetorical Strategy and Style

1. How has Terkel shaped his interview with Acuna to achieve his goal in reaching the reader?
2. Why does Terkel include Acuna's information about pesticides? How did you react to it?
3. What is the purpose of the account of the POW camp? What does it add to the interview?

Writing Assignments

1. Terkel is a highly skilled interviewer. His approach is to leave himself largely out of the text so that the interviewee can speak for him or herself. Conduct an interview with someone of interest to you. Prepare your questions ahead of time with an idea for what you would like to learn about this person and why.
2. Write a report on the history of the United Farm Workers from its inception to the present day. How has it served to improve conditions for migrant workers?

And Our Flag was Still There

Barbara Kingsolver

Poet, novelist, and essayist, Barbara Kingsolver is one of the most prolific and versatile writers of our time. She currently has fourteen books in print, and she regularly writes for major periodicals like the New York Times. *Blending her love of the natural world, her scientific training, and her talent as a writer, Kingsolver has been compared to Thoreau on more than one occasion. Here, though, she turns her attention to what it means to be an American. The three attacks on September 11, 2001, left an indelible mark on Americans, and in this essay Kingsolver writes about one layer of that experience. To learn more about her, visit her official website:* www.kingsolver.com

1   My daughter came home from kindergarten and announced, "Tomorrow we all have to wear red, white and blue."

"Why?" I asked, trying not to sound wary.

"For all the people that died when the airplanes hit the buildings."

I fear the sound of saber-rattling, dread that not just my taxes but even my children are being dragged to the cause of death in the wake of death. I asked quietly, "Why not wear black, then? Why the colors of the flag, what does that mean?"

5   "It means we're a country. Just all people together."

So we sent her to school in red, white and blue, because it felt to her like something she could do to help people who are hurting. And because my wise husband put a hand on my arm and said, "You can't let hateful people steal the flag from us."

He didn't mean terrorists, he meant Americans. Like the man in a city near us who went on a rampage crying "I'm an American" as he shot at foreign-born neighbors, killing a gentle Sikh man in a turban and terrifying every brown- skinned person I know. Or the talk-radio hosts, who are viciously bullying a handful of members of Congress for airing sensible skepticism at a time when the White House was announcing preposterous things in apparent self-interest, such as the "revelation" that terrorists had aimed to hunt down Air Force One with a hijacked commercial plane. Rep. Barbara Lee cast the House's only vote against handing over virtually unlimited war powers to one man that a whole lot of us didn't vote for. As a consequence, so many red-blooded Americans have now threatened to kill her, she has to have additional bodyguards.

Patriotism seems to be falling to whoever claims it loudest, and we're left struggling to find a definition in a clamor of reaction. This is what I'm hearing: Patriotism opposes the lone representative of democracy who was brave enough to vote her conscience instead of following an angry mob. (Several others have confessed they wanted to vote the same way, but chickened out.) Patriotism threatens free speech with death. It is infuriated by thoughtful hesitation, constructive criticism of our leaders and pleas for peace. It despises people of foreign birth who've spent years learning our culture and contributing their talents to our economy. It has specifically blamed homosexuals, feminists and the American Civil Liberties Union. In other words, the American flag stands for intimidation, censorship, violence, bigotry, sexism, homophobia, and shoving the Constitution through a paper shredder? Who are we calling terrorists here? Outsiders can destroy airplanes and buildings, but it is only we, the people, who have the power to demolish our own ideals.

It's a fact of our culture that the loudest mouths get the most airplay, and the loudmouths are saying now that in times of crisis it is treasonous to question our leaders. Nonsense. That kind of thinking let fascism grow out of the international depression of thc 1930s. In critical times, our leaders need most to be influenced by the moderating force of dissent. That is the basis of democracy, in sickness and in health, and especially when national choices are difficult, and bear grave consequences.

It occurs to me that my patriotic duty is to recapture my flag from the men now waving it in the name of jingoism and censorship. This isn't easy for me.

The last time I looked at a flag with unambiguous pride, I was 13. Right after that, Vietnam began teaching me lessons in ambiguity, and the lessons have kept coming. I've learned of things my government has done to the world that made me direly ashamed. I've been further alienated from my flag by people who waved it at me declaring I should love it or leave it. I search my soul and find I cannot love killing for any reason. When I look at the flag, I see it illuminated by the rocket's red glare.

This is why the warmongers so easily gain the upper hand in the patriot game: Our nation was established with a fight for independence, so our iconography grew out of war. Our national anthem celebrates it; our language of patriotism is inseparable from a battle cry. Our every military campaign is still launched with phrases about men dying for the freedoms we hold dear, even when this is impossible to square with reality. In the Persian Gulf War we rushed to the aid of Kuwait, a monarchy in which women enjoyed approximately the same rights as a 19th century American slave. The values we fought for and won there are best understood, I think, by oil companies. Meanwhile, a country of civilians was devastated, and remains destroyed.

Stating these realities does not violate the principles of liberty, equality, and freedom of speech; it exercises them, and by exercise we grow stronger. I would like to stand up for my flag and wave it over a few things I believe in, including but not limited to the protection of dissenting points of view. After 225 years, I vote to retire the rocket's red glare and the bullet wound as obsolete symbols of Old Glory. We desperately need a new iconography of patriotism. I propose we rip stripes of cloth from the uniforms of public servants who rescued the injured and panic-stricken, remaining at their post until it fell down on them. The red glare of candles held in vigils everywhere as peace-loving people pray for the bereaved, and plead for compassion and restraint. The blood donated to the Red Cross. The stars of film and theater and music who are using their influence to raise money for recovery. The small hands of schoolchildren collecting pennies, toothpaste, teddy bears, anything they think might help the kids who've lost their moms and dads.

My town, Tucson, Ariz., has become famous for a simple gesture in which some 8,000 people wearing red, white or blue T-shirts assembled themselves in the shape of a flag on a baseball field and had their photograph taken from above. That picture has begun to turn up everywhere, but we saw it first on our newspaper's front page. Our family stood in silence for a minute looking at that photo of a human flag, trying to know what to make of it. Then my teenage daughter, who has a quick mind for numbers and a sensitive heart, did an interesting thing. She laid her hand over a quarter of the picture, leaving visible more or less 6,000 people, and said, "That many are dead." We stared at what that looked like–all those innocent souls, multi-colored and packed into a conjoined destiny–and shuddered at the one simple truth behind all the noise, which is that so many beloved people have suddenly gone from us. That is my flag, and that's what it means: We're all just people together.

Questions on Meaning

1. What is Kingsolver's main point in this essay? Does she make the point explicitly or implicitly?
2. What does the term "jingoism" mean, and how does the use of the word relate to Kingsolver's overall point?
3. How does Kingsolver define patriotism in this piece? Does she offer more than one definition? How do you define patriotism?

Questions on Rhetorical Strategy and Style

1. What rhetorical modes does Kingsolver use to develop this essay? Which mode do you find to be most effective?
2. What is Kingsolver's predominant tone? What words or phrases does she use that help you to identify the tone?
3. Read over Kingsolver's introduction and her conclusion. How does she link them? Do you think her strategy is effective?

Writing Assignments

1. In paragraph thirteen, Kingsolver declares that "we need a new iconography of patriotism." Write an essay in which you propose the iconography that best represents your concept of patriotism.
2. Write an essay in which you compare and contrast Kingsolver's idea of patriotism with that of your own.

Education and Language

Talking Back

bell hooks

bell hooks (1952–), the pseudonym of Gloria Watkins, was born in Kentucky. She received a B.A. from Stanford University and a Ph.D. from the University of California, Santa Cruz. An advocate for African-American women in the feminist movement as well as a critic of the white male-dominated U.S. power structure, hooks has taught at Oberlin College and Yale University. Her books include Ain't I a Woman: Black Women and Feminism *(1981),* Feminist Theory: From Margin to Center *(1984),* Talking Back: Thinking Feminist, Thinking Black *(1989),* Yearning: Race, Gender, and Cultural Politics *(1990),* Breaking Bread: Insurgent Black Intellectual Life *(1992),* Black Looks: Race and Representation *(1992),* Outlaw Culture *(1994),* Teaching to Transgress: Education as the Practice of Freedom *(1994),* Reel to Real: Race, Sex, and Class at the Movies *(1996), and* Remembering Rapture *(1999). hooks describes her confrontations throughout life with rules of speech—and the role of silence—in this excerpt from* Talking Back.

1   In the world of the southern black community I grew up in, "back talk" and "talking back" meant speaking as an equal to an authority figure. It meant daring to disagree and sometimes it just meant having an opinion. In the "old school," children were meant to be seen and not heard. My great-grandparents, grandparents, and parents were all from the old school. To make yourself heard if you were a child was to invite punishment, the back-hand lick, the slap across the face that would catch you unaware, or the feel of switches stinging your arms and legs.

To speak then when one was not spoken to was a courageous act—an act of risk and daring. And yet it was hard not to speak in warm rooms where heated discussions began at the crack of dawn, women's voices filling the air, giving orders, making threats, fussing. Black men may have excelled in the art of poetic preaching in the male-dominated church, but in the church of the home, where the everyday rules of how to live and how to act were established, it was black women who preached. There, black women spoke in a language so rich, so poetic, that it felt to me like being shut off from life, smothered to death if one were not allowed to participate.

It was in that world of woman talk (the men were often silent, often absent) that was born in me the craving to speak, to have a voice, and not just any voice but one that could be identified as belonging to me. To make my voice, I had to speak, to hear myself talk—and talk I did—darting in and out of grown folks' conversations and dialogues, answering questions that were not directed at me, endlessly asking questions, making speeches. Needless to say, the punishments for these acts of speech seemed endless. They were intended to silence me—the child—and more particularly the girl child. Had I been a boy, they might have encouraged me to speak believing that I might someday be called to preach. There was no "calling" for talking girls, no legitimized rewarded speech. The punishments I received for "talking back" were intended to suppress all possibility that I would create my own speech. That speech was to be suppressed so that the "right speech of womanhood" would emerge.

Within feminist circles, silence is often seen as the sexist "right speech of womanhood"—the sign of woman's submission to patriarchal authority. This emphasis on woman's silence may be an accurate remembering of what has taken place in the households of women from WASP backgrounds in the United States, but in black communities (and diverse ethnic communities), women have not been silent. Their voices can be heard. Certainly for black women, our struggle has not been to emerge from silence into speech but to change the nature and direction of our speech, to make a speech that compels listeners, one that is heard.

Our speech, "the right speech of womanhood," was often the soliloquy, the talking into thin air, the talking to ears that do not hear you—the talk that is simply not listened to. Unlike the black male preacher whose speech was to be heard, who was to be listened to, whose words were to be remembered, the voices of black women—giving orders, making threats, fussing—could be tuned out, could become a kind of background music, audible but not acknowledged as significant speech. Dialogue—the sharing of speech and recognition—took place not between mother and child or mother and male authority figure but among black women. I can remember watching fascinated as our mother talked with her mother, sisters, and women friends. The intimacy and intensity of their speech—the satisfaction they received from talking to one another, the pleasure, the joy. It was in this world of woman speech, loud talk, angry words, women with tongues quick and sharp, tender sweet tongues, touching our world with their words, that I made speech my birthright—and the right to voice, to authorship, a privilege I would not be denied. It was in that world and because of it that I came to dream of writing, to write.

Writing was a way to capture speech, to hold onto it, keep it close. And so I wrote down bits and pieces of conversations, confessing in cheap diaries that soon fell apart from too much handling, expressing the intensity of my sorrow, the anguish of speech—for I was always saying the wrong thing, asking the wrong questions. I could not confine my speech to the necessary corners and concerns of life. I hid these writings under my bed, in pillow stuffings, among faded underwear. When my sisters found and read them, they ridiculed and mocked me—poking fun. I felt violated, ashamed, as if the secret parts of my self had been exposed, brought into the open, and hung like newly clean laundry, out in the air for everyone to see. The fear of exposure, the fear that one's deepest emotions and innermost thoughts will be dismissed as mere nonsense, felt by so many young girls keeping diaries, holding and hiding speech, seems to me now one of the barriers that women have always needed and still need to destroy so that we are no longer pushed into secrecy or silence.

Despite my feelings of violation, of exposure, I continued to speak and write, choosing my hiding places well, learning to destroy work when no safe place could be found. I was never taught absolute silence, I was taught that it was important to speak but to talk a talk that was in itself a silence. Taught to speak and yet beware of the betrayal of too much heard speech, I experienced intense confusion and deep anxiety in my efforts to speak and write. Reciting poems at Sunday afternoon church service might be rewarded. Writing a poem (when one's time could be "better" spent sweeping, ironing, learning to cook) was luxurious activity, indulged in at the expense of others. Questioning authority, raising issues that were not deemed appropriate subjects, brought pain, punishments—like telling mama I wanted to die before her because I could not live without her—that was crazy talk, crazy speech, the kind that would lead you to end up in a mental institution. "Little girl," I would be told, "if you don't stop all this crazy talk and crazy acting you are going to end up right out there at Western State."

Madness, not just physical abuse, was the punishment for too much talk if you were female. Yet even as this fear of madness haunted me, hanging over my writing like a monstrous shadow, I could not stop the words, making thought, writing speech. For this terrible madness which I feared, which I was sure was the destiny of daring women born to intense speech (after all, the authorities emphasized this point daily), was not as threatening as imposed silence, as suppressed speech.

Safety and sanity were to be sacrificed if I was to experience defiant speech. Though I risked them both, deep-seated fears and anxieties characterized my childhood days. I would speak but I would not ride a bike, play hardball, or hold the gray kitten. Writing about the ways we are traumatized in our growing-up years, psychoanalyst Alice Miller makes the point in *For Your Own Good* that it is not clear why childhood wounds become for some folk an opportunity to grow, to move forward rather than backward in the process of self-realization. Certainly, when I reflect on the trials of my growing-up years, the many punishments, I can see now that in resistance I learned to be vigilant in the nourishment of my spirit, to be tough, to courageously protect that spirit from forces that would break it.

10   While punishing me, my parents often spoke about the necessity 10
of breaking my spirit. Now when I ponder the silences, the voices that are not heard, the voices of those wounded and/or oppressed individuals who do not speak or write, I contemplate the acts of persecution, torture—the terrorism that breaks spirits, that makes creativity impossible. I write these words to bear witness to the primacy of resistance struggle in any situation of domination (even within family life); to the strength and power that emerges from sustained resistance and the profound conviction that these forces can be healing, can protect us from dehumanization and despair.

These early trials, wherein I learned to stand my ground, to keep my spirit intact, came vividly to mind after I published *Ain't I A Woman* and the book was sharply and harshly criticized. While I had expected a climate of critical dialogue, I was not expecting a critical avalanche that had the power in its intensity to crush the spirit, to push one into silence. Since that time, I have heard stories about black women, about women of color, who write and publish (even when the work is quite successful) having nervous breakdowns, being made mad because they cannot bear the harsh responses of family, friends, and unknown critics, or becoming silent, unproductive. Surely, the absence of a humane critical response has tremendous impact on the writer from any oppressed, colonized group who endeavors to speak. For us, true speaking is not solely an expression of creative power; it is an act of resistance, a political gesture that challenges politics of domination that would render us nameless and voiceless. As such, it is a courageous act—as such, it represents a threat. To those who wield oppressive power, that which is threatening must necessarily be wiped out, annihilated, silenced.

Recently, efforts by black women writers to call attention to our work serve to highlight both our presence and absence. Whenever I peruse women's bookstores, I am struck not by the rapidly growing body of feminist writing by black women, but by the paucity of available published material. Those of us who write and are published remain few in number. The context of silence is varied and multidimensional. Most obvious are the ways racism, sexism, and class exploitation act to suppress and silence. Less obvious are the inner struggles, the efforts made to gain the necessary confidence to write, to re-write, to fully develop craft and skill—and the extent to which such efforts fail.

Although I have wanted writing to be my life-work since childhood, it has been difficult for me to claim "writer" as part of that which identifies and shapes my everyday reality. Even after publishing books, I would often speak of wanting to be a writer as though these works did not exist. And though I would be told, "you are a writer," I was not yet ready to fully affirm this truth. Part of myself was still held captive by domineering forces of history, of familial life that had charted a map of silence, of right speech. I had not completely let go of the fear of saying the wrong thing, of being punished. Somewhere in the deep recesses of my mind, I believed I could avoid both responsibility and punishment if I did not declare myself a writer.

One of the many reasons I chose to write using the pseudonym bell hooks, a family name (mother to Sarah Oldham, grandmother to Rosa Bell Oldham, great-grandmother to me), was to construct a writer-identity that would challenge and subdue all impulses leading me away from speech into silence. I was a young girl buying bubble gum at the corner store when I first really heard the full name bell hooks. I had just "talked back" to a grown person. Even now I can recall the surprised look, the mocking tones that informed me I must be kin to bell hooks—a sharp-tongued woman, a woman who spoke her mind, a woman who was not afraid to talk back. I claimed this legacy of defiance, of will, of courage, affirming my link to female ancestors who were bold and daring in their speech. Unlike my bold and daring mother and grandmother, who were not supportive of talking back, even though they were assertive and powerful in their speech, bell hooks as I discovered, claimed, and invented her was my ally, my support.

15   That initial act of talking back outside the home was empowering. It was the first of many acts of defiant speech that would make it possible for me to emerge as an independent thinker and writer. In retrospect, "talking back" became for me a rite of initiation, testing my courage, strengthening my commitment, preparing me for the days ahead—the days when writing, rejection notices, periods of silence, publication, ongoing development seem impossible but necessary.

Moving from silence into speech is for the oppressed, the colonized, the exploited, and those who stand and struggle side by side a gesture of defiance that heals, that makes new life and new growth possible. It is that act of speech, of "talking back," that is no mere gesture of empty words, that is the expression of our movement from object to subject—the liberated voice.

Questions on Meaning

1. How does hooks define "back talk" and "talking back"? How does she describe her reaction to her first act of "talking back" outside her house?
2. What does hooks mean by "true speak"? Who is the "us" she is referring to when she discusses "true speak"?
3. Even though hooks learned as a young girl that writing was her life, why has she had such a difficult time accepting that she *is* a writer? How has her "map of silence" affected her ability to grow into her role as a writer?

Questions on Rhetorical Strategy and Style

1. How does hooks compare and contrast "silence" with "speech"? What are the various "contexts" of silence that she reveals—from quieting the "girl child" to suppressing the expression of women to talking a talk that is silence to the "right speech of womanhood"? What examples does she provide to illustrate the differences between silence and speech?
2. How does she compare and contrast the woman talk of black women with the talk of black men? The talk of black women and other women of color with the talk of white women? Explain how your experience confirms or contradicts these observations.

Writing Assignments

1. What has been your experience when you have spoken out or expressed yourself (perhaps in writing) in terms that might offend some people. What kind of criticism have you received? How has it affected you? Has it affected your subsequent "talking out": did it silence you or increase your resolve to continue to express yourself?
2. Write an essay comparing and contrasting "talking back" (as hooks defines it) with rudeness and disrespect. When is a comment by a child to an adult applauded as a forthright child speaking up for what is right, and when is it criticized as being contentious, argumentative, or nasty? Is it possible to create *rules* of speech? How do language, mannerisms, and context affect whether a spoken word is "acceptable" or "unacceptable"?

Three Days to See

Helen Keller

Helen Keller (1880–1968) was born in Tuscumbia, Alabama. As a result of illness, she lost her senses of sight and hearing at 19 months. Taught to speak, read, and write by Anne Sullivan (her teacher and lifelong companion), Keller graduated from Radcliffe (1904) with honors at age 24 and became a distinguished lecturer and writer and a symbol of personal strength and perseverance. Her autobiography, The Story of My Life *(1902), was made into the award-winning film,* The Miracle Worker *(1959). Other books by Keller include* Optimism *(1903),* The World I Live In *(1908), and* Out of the Dark *(1913). In this essay, Keller describes what she would do if she had sight for just three days.*

1 All of us have read thrilling stories in which the hero had only a limited and specified time to live. Sometimes it was as long as a year; sometimes as short as twenty-four hours. But always we were interested in discovering just how the doomed man chose to spend his last days or his last hours. I speak, of course, of free men who have a choice, not condemned criminals whose sphere of activities is strictly delimited.

Such stories set us thinking, wondering what we should do under similar circumstances. What events, what experiences, what associations should we crowd into those last hours as mortal beings? What happiness should we find in reviewing the past, what regrets?

Sometimes I have thought it would be an excellent rule to live each day as if we should die tomorrow. Such an attitude would emphasize sharply the values of life. We should live each day with a gentleness, a vigor, and a keenness of appreciation which are often lost when time stretches before us in the constant panorama of more days and months and years to come. There are those, of course, who would adopt the epicurean motto of "Eat, drink, and be merry," but most people would be chastened by the certainty of impending death.

In stories, the doomed hero is usually saved at the last minute by some stroke of fortune, but almost always his sense of values is changed. He becomes more appreciative of the meaning of life and its permanent spiritual values. It has often been noted that those who live, or have lived, in the shadow of death bring a mellow sweetness to everything they do.

Most of us, however, take life for granted. We know that one day we must die, but usually we picture that day as far in the future. When we are in buoyant health, death is all but unimaginable. We seldom think of it. The days stretch out in an endless vista. So we go about our petty tasks, hardly aware of our listless attitude toward life.

The same lethargy, I am afraid, characterizes the use of all our faculties and senses. Only the deaf appreciate hearing, only the blind realize the manifold blessings that lie in sight. Particularly does this observation apply to those who have lost sight and hearing in adult life. But those who have never suffered impairment of sight or hearing seldom make the fullest use of these blessed faculties. Their eyes and ears take in all sights and sounds hazily, without concentration and with little appreciation. It is the same old story of not being grateful for what we have until we lose it, of not being conscious of health until we are ill.

I have often thought it would be a blessing if each human being were stricken blind and deaf for a few days at some time during his early adult life. Darkness would make him more appreciative of sight; silence would teach him the joys of sound.

Now and then I have tested my seeing friends to discover what they see. Recently I was visited by a very good friend who had just returned from a long walk in the woods, and I asked her what she had observed. "Nothing in particular," she replied. I might have been incredulous had I not been accustomed to such responses, for long ago I became convinced that the seeing see little.

How was it possible, I asked myself, to walk for an hour through the woods and see nothing worthy of note? I who cannot see find hundreds of things to interest me through mere touch. I feel the delicate symmetry of a leaf. I pass my hands lovingly about the smooth skin of a silver birch, or the rough shaggy bark of a pine. In spring I touch the branches of trees hopefully in search of a bud, the first sign of awakening Nature after her winter's sleep. I feel the delightful, velvety texture of a flower, and discover its remarkable convolutions; and something of the miracle of Nature is revealed to me. Occasionally, if I am fortunate, I place my hand gently on a small tree and feel the happy quiver of a bird in full song. I am delighted to have the cool waters of a brook rush through my open fingers. To me a lush carpet of pine needles or spongy grass is more welcome than the most luxurious Persian rug. To me the pageant of seasons is a thrilling and unending drama, the action of which streams through my finger tips.

10   At times my heart cries out with longing to see all these things. If   10
I can get so much pleasure from mere touch, how much more beauty must be revealed by sight. Yet, those who have eyes apparently see little. The panorama of color and action which fills the world is taken for granted. It is human, perhaps, to appreciate little that which we have and to long for that which we have not, but it is a great pity that in the world of light the gift of sight is used only as a mere convenience rather than as a means of adding fullness to life.

If I were the president of a university I should establish a compulsory course in "How to Use Your Eyes." The professor would try to show his pupils how they could add joy to their lives by really seeing what passes unnoticed before them. He would try to awake their dormant and sluggish faculties.

Perhaps I can best illustrate by imagining what I should most like to see if I were given the use of my eyes, say, for just three days. And while I am imagining, suppose you, too, set your mind to work on the problem of how you would use your own eyes if you had only three more days to see. If with the oncoming darkness of the third night you knew that the sun would never rise for you again, how would you spend those three precious intervening days? What would you most want to let your gaze rest upon?

I, naturally, should want most to see the things which have become dear to me through my years of darkness. You, too, would want to let your eyes rest long on the things that have become dear to you so that you could take the memory of them with you into the night that loomed before you.

If by some miracle I were granted three seeing days, to be followed by a relapse into darkness, I should divide the period into three parts.

15   On the first day, I should want to see the people whose kindness   15
and gentleness and companionship have made my life worth living. First I should like to gaze long upon the face of my dear teacher,

Mrs. Anne Sullivan Macy, who came to me when I was a child and opened the outer world to me. I should want not merely to see the outline of her face, so that I could cherish it in my memory, but to study that face and find in it the living evidence of the sympathetic tenderness and patience with which she accomplished the difficult task of my education. I should like to see in her eyes that strength of character which has enabled her to stand firm in the face of difficulties, and that compassion for all humanity which she has revealed to me so often.

I do not know what it is to see into the heart of a friend through that "window of the soul," the eye. I can only "see" through my finger tips the outline of a face. I can detect laughter, sorrow, and many other obvious emotions. I know my friends from the feel of their faces. But I cannot really picture their personalities by touch. I know their personalities, of course, through other means, through the thoughts they express to me, through whatever of their actions are revealed to me. But I am denied that deeper understanding of them which I am sure would come through sight of them, through watching their reactions to various expressed thoughts and circumstances, through noting the immediate and fleeting reactions of their eyes and countenance.

Friends who are near to me I know well, because through the months and years they reveal themselves to me in all their phases; but of casual friends I have only an incomplete impression, an impression gained from a handclasp, from spoken words which I take from their lips with my finger tips, or which they tap into the palm of my hand.

How much easier, how much more satisfying it is for you who can see to grasp quickly the essential qualities of another person by watching the subtleties of expression, the quiver of a muscle, the flutter of a hand. But does it ever occur to you to use your sight to see into the inner nature of a friend or acquaintance? Do not most of you seeing people grasp casually the outward features of a face and let it go at that?

For instance, can you describe accurately the faces of five good friends? Some of you can, but many cannot. As an experiment, I have questioned husbands of long standing about the color of their wives' eyes, and often they express embarrassed confusion and admit that they do not know. And, incidentally, it is a chronic complaint of wives that their husbands do not notice new dresses, new hats, and changes in household arrangements.

20   The eyes of seeing persons soon become accustomed to the rou- 20
tine of their surroundings, and they actually see only the startling and
spectacular. But even in viewing the most spectacular sights the eyes
are lazy. Court records reveal every day how inaccurately "eyewit-
nesses" see. A given event will be "seen" in several different ways by as
many witnesses. Some see more than others, but few see everything
that is within the range of their vision.

Oh, the things that I should see if I had the power of sight for just
three days!

The first day would be a busy one. I should call to me all my dear
friends and look long into their faces, imprinting upon my mind the
outward evidences of the beauty that is within them. I should let my
eyes rest, too, on the face of a baby, so that I could catch a vision of
the eager, innocent beauty which precedes the individual's consciousness of the conflicts which life develops.

And I should like to look into the loyal, trusting eyes of my
dogs—the grave, canny little Scottie, Darkie, and the stalwart, understanding Great Dane, Helga, whose warm, tender, and playful friendships are so comforting to me.

On that busy first day I should also view the small simple things
of my home. I want to see the warm colors in the rugs under my feet,
the pictures on the walls, the intimate trifles that transform a house
into home. My eyes would rest respectfully on the books in raised type
which I have read, but they would be more eagerly interested in the
printed books which seeing people can read, for during the long night
of my life the books I have read and those which have been read to
me have built themselves into a great shining lighthouse, revealing to
me the deepest channels of human life and the human spirit.

25   In the afternoon of that first seeing day, I should take a long walk 25
in the woods and intoxicate my eyes on the beauties of the world of
Nature, trying desperately to absorb in a few hours the vast splendor
which is constantly unfolding itself to those who can see. On the way
home from my woodland jaunt my path would lie near a farm so that
I might see the patient horses plowing in the field (perhaps I should
see only a tractor!) and the serene content of men living close to the
soil. And I should pray for the glory of a colorful sunset.

When dusk had fallen, I should experience the double delight of
being able to see by artificial light, which the genius of man has created to extend the power of his sight when Nature decrees darkness.

In the night of that first day of sight, I should not be able to sleep, so full would be my mind of the memories of the day.

The next day—the second day of sight—I should arise with the dawn and see the thrilling miracle by which night is transformed into day. I should behold with awe the magnificent panorama of light with which the sun awakens the sleeping earth.

This day I should devote to a hasty glimpse of the world, past and present. I should want to see the pageant of man's progress, the kaleidoscope of the ages. How can so much be compressed into one day? Through the museums, of course. Often I have visited the New York Museum of Natural History to touch with my hands many of the objects there exhibited, but I have longed to see with my eyes the condensed history of the earth and its inhabitants displayed there— animals and the races of men pictured in their native environment; gigantic carcasses of dinosaurs and mastodons which roamed the earth long before man appeared, with his tiny stature and powerful brain, to conquer the animal kingdom; realistic presentations of the processes of evolution in animals, in man, and in the implements which man has used to fashion for himself a secure home on this planet; and a thousand and one other aspects of natural history.

30 I wonder how many readers of this article have viewed this 30 panorama of the face of living things as pictured in that inspiring museum. Many, of course, have not had the opportunity, but I am sure that many who *have* had the opportunity have not made use of it. There, indeed, is a place to use your eyes. You who see can spend many fruitful days there, but I, with my imaginary three days of sight, could only take a hasty glimpse, and pass on.

My next stop would be the Metropolitan Museum of Art, for just as the Museum of Natural History reveals the material aspects of the world, so does the Metropolitan show the myriad facets of the human spirit. Throughout the history of humanity the urge to artistic expression has been almost as powerful as the urge for food, shelter, and procreation. And here, in the vast chambers of the Metropolitan Museum, is unfolded before me the spirit of Egypt, Greece, and Rome, as expressed in their art. I know well through my hands the sculptured gods and goddesses of the ancient Nile-land. I have felt copies of Parthenon friezes, and I have sensed the rhythmic beauty of charging Athenian warriors. Apollos and Venuses and the Winged Victory of

Samothrace are friends of my finger tips. The gnarled, bearded features of Homer are dear to me, for he, too, knew blindness.

My hands have lingered upon the living marble of Roman sculpture as well as that of later generations. I have passed my hands over a plaster cast of Michelangelo's inspiring and heroic Moses; I have sensed the power of Rodin; I have been awed by the devoted spirit of Gothic wood carving. These arts which can be touched have meaning for me, but even they were meant to be seen rather than felt, and I can only guess at the beauty which remains hidden from me. I can admire the simple lines of a Greek vase, but its figured decorations are lost to me.

So on this, my second day of sight, I should try to probe into the soul of man through his art. The things I knew through touch I should now see. More splendid still, the whole magnificent world of painting would be opened to me, from the Italian Primitives, with their serene religious devotion, to the Moderns, with their feverish visions. I should look deep into the canvases of Raphael, Leonardo da Vinci, Titian, Rembrandt. I should want to feast my eyes upon the warm colors of Veronese, study the mysteries of El Greco, catch a new vision of Nature from Corot. Oh, there is so much rich meaning and beauty in the art of the ages for you who have eyes to see!

Upon my short visit to this temple of art I should not be able to review a fraction of that great world of art which is open to you. I should be able to get only a superficial impression. Artists tell me that for a deep and true appreciation of art one must educate the eye. One must learn through experience to weigh the merits of line, of composition, of form and color. If I had eyes, how happily would I embark upon so fascinating a study! Yet I am told that, to many of you who have eyes to see, the world of art is a dark night, unexplored and unilluminated.

35 It would be with extreme reluctance that I should leave the Metropolitan Museum, which contains the key to beauty—a beauty so neglected. Seeing persons, however, do not need a Metropolitan to find this key to beauty. The same key lies waiting in smaller museums, and in books on the shelves of even small libraries. But naturally, in my limited time of imaginary sight, I should choose the place where the key unlocks the greatest treasures in the shortest time. 35

The evening of my second day of sight I should spend at a theater or at the movies. Even now I often attend theatrical performances of all sorts, but the action of the play must be spelled into my hand by a companion. But how I should like to see with my own eyes the fascinating figure of Hamlet, or the gusty Falstaff amid colorful Elizabethan trappings! How I should like to follow each movement of the graceful Hamlet, each strut of the hearty Falstaff! And since I could see only one play, I should be confronted by a many-horned dilemma, for there are scores of plays I should want to see. You who have eyes can see any you like. How many of you, I wonder, when you gaze at a play, a movie, or any spectacle, realize and give thanks for the miracle of sight which enables you to enjoy its color, grace, and movement?

I cannot enjoy the beauty of rhythmic movement except in a sphere restricted to the touch of my hands. I can envision only dimly the grace of a Pavlova, although I know something of the delight of rhythm, for often I can sense the beat of music as it vibrates through the floor. I can well imagine that cadenced motion must be one of the most pleasing sights in the world. I have been able to gather something of this by tracing with my fingers the lines in sculptured marble; if this static grace can be so lovely, how much more acute must be the thrill of seeing grace in motion.

One of my dearest memories is of the time when Joseph Jefferson allowed me to touch his face and hands as he went through some of the gestures and speeches of his beloved Rip Van Winkle. I was able to catch thus a meager glimpse of the world of drama, and I shall never forget the delight of that moment. But, oh, how much I must miss, and how much pleasure you seeing ones can derive from watching and hearing the interplay of speech and movement in the unfolding of a dramatic performance! If I could see only one play, I should know how to picture in my mind the action of a hundred plays which I have read or had transferred to me through the medium of the manual alphabet.

So, through the evening of my second imaginary day of sight, the great figures of dramatic literature would crowd sleep from my eyes.

40   The following morning, I should again greet the dawn, anxious 40
to discover new delights, for I am sure that, for those who have eyes which really see, the dawn of each day must be a perpetually new revelation of beauty.

This, according to the terms of my imagined miracle, is to be my third and last day of sight. I shall have no time to waste in regrets or longings; there is too much to see. The first day I devoted to my friends, animate and inanimate. The second revealed to me the history of man and Nature. Today I shall spend in the workaday world of the present, amid the haunts of men going about the business of life. And where can one find so many activities and conditions of men as in New York? So the city becomes my destination.

I start from my home in the quiet little suburb of Forest Hills, Long Island. Here, surrounded by green lawns, trees, and flowers, are neat little houses, happy with the voices and movements of wives and children, havens of peaceful rest for men who toil in the city. I drive across the lacy structure of steel which spans the East River, and I get a new and startling vision of the power and ingenuity of the mind of man. Busy boats chug and scurry about the river—racy speed boats, stolid, snorting tugs. If I had long days of sight ahead, I should spend many of them watching the delightful activity upon the river.

I look ahead, and before me rise the fantastic towers of New York, a city that seems to have stepped from the pages of a fairy story. What an awe-inspiring sight, these glittering spires, these vast banks of stone and steel—structures such as the gods might build for themselves! This animated picture is a part of the lives of millions of people every day. How many, I wonder, give it so much as a second glance? Very few, I fear. Their eyes are blind to this magnificent sight because it is so familiar to them.

I hurry to the top of one of those gigantic structures, the Empire State Building, for there, a short time ago, I "saw" the city below through the eyes of my secretary. I am anxious to compare my fancy with reality. I am sure I should not be disappointed in the panorama spread out before me, for to me it would be a vision of another world.

Now I begin my rounds of the city. First, I stand at a busy corner, merely looking at people, trying by sight of them to understand something of their lives. I see smiles, and I am happy. I see serious determination, and I am proud. I see suffering, and I am compassionate.

I stroll down Fifth Avenue. I throw my eyes out of focus so that I see no particular object but only a seething kaleidoscope of color. I am certain that the colors of women's dresses moving in a throng must be a gorgeous spectacle of which I should never tire. But perhaps if I had sight I should be like most other women—too interested in styles and the cut of individual dresses to give much attention to the splendor of color in the mass. And I am convinced, too, that I should become an inveterate window shopper, for it must be a delight to the eye to view the myriad articles of beauty on display.

From Fifth Avenue, I make a tour of the city—to Park Avenue, to the slums, to factories, to parks where children play. I take a stay-at-home trip abroad by visiting the foreign quarters. Always my eyes are open wide to all the sights of both happiness and misery so that I may probe deep and add to my understanding of how people work and live. My heart is full of the images of people and things. My eye passes lightly over no single trifle; it strives to touch and hold closely each thing its gaze rests upon. Some sights are pleasant, filling the heart with happiness; but some are miserably pathetic. To these latter I do not shut my eyes, for they, too, are part of life. To close the eye on them is to close the heart and mind.

My third day of sight is drawing to an end. Perhaps there are many serious pursuits to which I should devote the few remaining hours, but I am afraid that on the evening of that last day I should again run away to the theater, to a hilariously funny play, so that I might appreciate the overtones of comedy in the human spirit.

At midnight my temporary respite from blindness would cease, and permanent night would close in on me again. Naturally in those three short days I should not have seen all I wanted to see. Only when darkness had again descended upon me should I realize how much I had left unseen. But my mind would be so crowded with glorious memories that I should have little time for regrets. Thereafter the touch of every object would bring a glowing memory of how that object looked.

50 Perhaps this short outline of how I should spend three days of 50 sight does not agree with the program you would set for yourself if you knew that you were about to be stricken blind. I am, however, sure that if you actually faced that fate your eyes would open to things you had never seen before, storing up memories for the long night ahead. You would use your eyes as never before. Everything you saw would become dear to you. Your eyes would touch and embrace every object that came within your range of vision. Then, at last, you would really see, and a new world of beauty would open itself before you.

I who am blind can give one hint to those who see—one admonition to those who would make full use of the gift of sight: Use your eyes as if tomorrow you would be stricken blind. And the same method can be applied to the other senses. Hear the music of voices, the song of a bird, the mighty strains of an orchestra, as if you would be stricken deaf tomorrow. Touch each object you want to touch as if tomorrow your tactile sense would fail. Smell the perfume of flowers, taste with relish each morsel, as if tomorrow you could never smell and taste again. Make the most of every sense; glory in the facts of pleasure and beauty which the world reveals to you through the several means of contact which Nature provides. But of all the senses, I am sure that sight must be the most delightful.

Questions on Meaning

1. Into what three distinct phases does Keller divide her imaginary three days of sight? Why would she spend all of her time in and around New York City?
2. How does Keller get to know her friends? What various emotions can she detect through the sense of touch? How does she "hear" what people have to say? What does she miss about her friends because she cannot see?
3. What single admonition would Keller give people about their senses? Which sense does she believe is the "most delightful"?

Questions on Rhetorical Strategy and Style

1. Keller provides numerous examples in her narrative of what she would want to see in her three days of sight, what she would want to take back with her "into the night." Which of these examples works best for you? Why?
2. To illustrate her contention that most sighted people "seldom make the fullest use of their blessed faculties," Keller relates a sighted friend's description of a walk in the woods. How does she compare and contrast what this friend saw on her walk to what she imagines she would see? How much of what Keller describes would *you* be able to sense—such as the bark on different types of trees or a bud on a twig?
3. Throughout her narrative, Keller provides descriptions that most sighted persons would not normally think of, such as the "splendor of color in the mass" on Fifth Avenue. Find other descriptive passages in which she perceives a scene differently than you might. How do you think her perspective differs from the perspective of a sighted person?

Writing Assignments

1. Describe what you would do if you learned that you had only a week more to see. How would your activities change if you learned you had only a week more to *live*?
2. Read about Keller's life and learn how she learned to communicate. What techniques did she use to "hear"? What tools are available to a person with hearing and vision impairment today that could have helped Keller?

3. Write an essay describing the elements of your life that you take for granted—things that are important to you but that you do not give much thought to. What would happen if you lost some of the these pleasures—good health, food, clothing, shelter, intelligence, material possessions, etc.?

No Name Woman

Maxine Hong Kingston

Maxine Hong Kingston (1940–) was born in Stockton, California. One of eight children—two born in China, Kingston and the others born in the United States— Kingston spent her youth with many Chinese immigrants. Her first language was Chinese, and she was exposed from birth to the rich oral traditions of the Chinese culture. Kingston entered the University of California at Berkeley on scholarship as an engineering major, but quickly switched to English literature. She received a B. A. (1962) and a teaching certificate (1965), and spent many years teaching in Hawaii. The recipient of both the National Book Critics Circle Award and the American Book Award, Kingston has written widely on life as a Chinese-American. Her books include The Woman Warrior: Memoirs of a Girlhood Among Ghosts *(1976),* China Men *(1980), and* Tripmaster Monkey: His Fake Book *(1989). Kingston's works are imbued with Chinese culture and reflect the rhythm of Chinese-American speech. In this essay, the first chapter of* The Woman Warrior, *Kingston confronts the ghost of her aunt and tries to save her from disgrace and the punishment of silence.*

1   "You must not tell anyone," my mother said, "what I am about to tell you. In China your father had a sister who killed herself. She jumped into the family well. We say that your father has all brothers because it is as if she had never been born.

"In 1924 just a few days after our village celebrated seventeen hurry-up weddings—to make sure that every young man who went 'out on the road' would responsibly come home—your father and his brothers and your grandfather and his brothers and your aunt's new husband sailed for America, the Gold Mountain. It was your grandfather's last trip. Those lucky enough to get contracts waved good-bye from the decks. They fed and guarded the stowaways and helped them off in Cuba, New York, Bali, Hawaii. 'We'll meet in California next year,' they said. All of them sent money home.

"I remember looking at your aunt one day when she and I were dressing; I had not noticed before that she had such a protruding melon of a stomach. But I did not think, 'She's pregnant,' until she began to look like other pregnant women, her shirt pulling and the white tops of her black pants showing. She could not have been pregnant, you see, because her husband had been gone for years. No one said anything. We did not discuss it. In early summer she was ready to have the child, long after the time when it could have been possible.

"The village had also been counting. On the night the baby was to be born the villagers raided our house. Some were crying. Like a great saw, teeth strung with lights, files of people walked zigzag across our land, tearing the rice. Their lanterns doubled in the disturbed black water, which drained away through the broken bunds. As the villagers closed in, we could see that some of them, probably men and women we knew well, wore white masks. The people with long hair hung it over their faces. Women with short hair made it stand up on end. Some had tied white bands around their foreheads, arms, and legs.

5 "At first they threw mud and rocks at the house. Then they threw   5 eggs and began slaughtering our stock. We could hear the animals scream their deaths—the roosters, the pigs, a last great roar from the ox. Familiar wild heads flared in our night windows; the villagers encircled us. Some of the faces stopped to peer at us, their eyes rushing like searchlights. The hands flattened against the panes, framed heads, and left red prints.

"The villagers broke in the front and the back doors at the same time, even though we had not locked the doors against them. Their knives dripped with the blood of our animals. They smeared blood on the doors and walls. One woman swung a chicken, whose throat she had slit, splattering blood in red arcs about her. We stood together in the middle of our house, in the family hall with the pictures and tables of the ancestors around us, and looked straight ahead.

"At that time the house had only two wings. When the men came back, we would build two more to enclose our courtyard and a third one to begin a second courtyard. The villagers rushed through both wings, even your grandparents' rooms, to find your aunt's, which was also mine until the men returned. From this room a new wing for one of the younger families would grow. They ripped up her clothes and shoes and broke her combs, grinding them underfoot. They tore her work from the loom. They scattered the cooking fire and rolled the new weaving in it. We could hear them in the kitchen breaking our bowls and banging the pots. They overturned the great waist-high earthenware jugs; duck eggs, pickled fruits, vegetables burst out and mixed in acrid torrents. The old woman from the next field swept a broom through the air and loosed the spirits-of-the-broom over our heads. 'Pig.' 'Ghost.' 'Pig,' they sobbed and scolded while they ruined our house.

"When they left, they took sugar and oranges to bless themselves. They cut pieces from the dead animals. Some of them took bowls that were not broken and clothes that were not torn. Afterward we swept up the rice and sewed it back up into sacks. But the smells from the spilled preserves lasted. Your aunt gave birth in the pigsty that night. The next morning when I went for the water, I found her and the baby plugging up the family well.

"Don't let your father know that I told you. He denies her. Now that you have started to menstruate, what happened to her could happen to you. Don't humiliate us. You wouldn't like to be forgotten as if you had never been born. The villagers are watchful."

Whenever she had to warn us about life, my mother told stories that ran like this one, a story to grow up on. She tested our strength to establish realities. Those in the emigrant generations who could not reassert brute survival died young and far from home. Those of us in the first American generations have had to figure out how the invisible world the emigrants built around our childhoods fit in solid America.

The emigrants confused the gods by diverting their curses, misleading them with crooked streets and false names. They must try to confuse their offspring as well, who, I suppose, threaten them in similar ways—always trying to get things straight, always trying to name the unspeakable. The Chinese I know hide their names; sojourners take new names when their lives change and guard their real names with silence.

Chinese-Americans, when you try to understand what things in you are Chinese, how do you separate what is peculiar to childhood, to poverty, insanities, one family, your mother who marked your growing with stories, from what is Chinese? What is Chinese tradition and what is the movies?

If I want to learn what clothes my aunt wore, whether flashy or ordinary, I would have to begin, "Remember Father's drowned-in-the-well sister?" I cannot ask that. My mother has told me once and for all the useful parts. She will add nothing unless powered by Necessity, a riverbank that guides her life. She plants vegetable gardens rather than lawns; she carries the odd-shaped tomatoes home from the fields and eats food left for the gods.

Whenever we did frivolous things, we used up energy; we flew high kites. We children came up off the ground over the melting cones our parents brought home from work and the American movie on New Year's Day—*Oh, You Beautiful Doll* with Betty Grable one year, and *She Wore a Yellow Ribbon* with John Wayne another year. After the one carnival ride each, we paid in guilt; our tired father counted his change on the dark walk home.

15   Adultery is extravagance. Could people who hatch their own   15
chicks and eat the embryos and the heads for delicacies and boil the feet in vinegar for party food, leaving only the gravel, eating even the gizzard lining—could such people engender a prodigal aunt? To be a woman, to have a daughter in starvation time was a waste enough. My aunt could not have been the lone romantic who gave up everything for sex. Women in the old China did not choose. Some man had commanded her to lie with him and be his secret evil. I wonder whether he masked himself when he joined the raid on her family.

Perhaps she encountered him in the fields or on the mountain where the daughters-in-law collected fuel. Or perhaps he first noticed her in the market-place. He was not a stranger because the village housed no strangers. She had to have dealings with him other than sex. Perhaps he worked an adjoining field, or he sold her the cloth for the dress she sewed and wore. His demand must have surprised, then terrified her. She obeyed him; she always did as she was told.

When the family found a young man in the next village to be her husband, she stood tractably beside the best rooster, his proxy, and promised before they met that she would be his forever. She was lucky that he was her age and she would be the first wife, an advantage secure now. The night she first saw him, he had sex with her. Then he left for America. She had almost forgotten what he looked like. When she tried to envision him, she only saw the black and white face in the group photograph the men had had taken before leaving.

The other man was not, after all, much different from her husband. They both gave orders: she followed. "If you tell your family, I'll beat you. I'll kill you. Be here again next week." No one talked sex, ever. And she might have separated the rapes from the rest of living if only she did not have to buy her oil from him or gather wood in the same forest. I want her fear to have lasted just as long as rape lasted so that the fear could have been contained. No drawn-out fear. But women at sex hazarded birth and hence lifetimes. The fear did not stop but permeated everywhere. She told the man, "I think I'm pregnant." He organized the raid against her.

On nights when my mother and father talked about their life back home, sometimes they mentioned an "outcast table" whose business they still seemed to be settling, their voices tight. In a commensal tradition, where food is precious, the powerful older people made wrongdoers eat alone. Instead of letting them start separate new lives like the Japanese, who could become samurais and geishas, the Chinese family, faces averted but eyes glowering sideways, hung on to the offenders and fed them leftovers. My aunt must have lived in the same house as my parents and eaten at an outcast table. My mother spoke about the raid as if she had seen it, when she and my aunt, a daughter-in-law to a different household, should not have been living together at all. Daughters-in-law lived with their husbands' parents, not their own; a synonym for marriage in Chinese is "taking a daughter-in-law." Her husband's parents could have sold her, mortgaged her, stoned her. But they had sent her back to her own mother and father, a mysterious act hinting at disgraces not told me. Perhaps they had thrown her out to deflect the avengers.

20   She was the only daughter; her four brothers went with her father,   20 husband, and uncles "out on the road" and for some years became western men. When the goods were divided among the family, three of the brothers took land, and the youngest, my father, chose an education. After my grandparents gave their daughter away to her husband's family, they had dispensed all the adventure and all the property. They expected her alone to keep the traditional ways, which her brothers, now among the barbarians, could fumble without detection. The heavy, deep-rooted women were to maintain the past against the flood, safe for returning. But the rare urge west had fixed upon our family, and so my aunt crossed boundaries not delineated in space.

The work of preservation demands that the feelings playing about in one's guts not be turned into action. Just watch their passing like

84

cherry blossoms. But perhaps my aunt, my forerunner, caught in a slow life, let dreams grow and fade and after some months or years went toward what persisted. Fear at the enormities of the forbidden kept her desires delicate, wire and bone. She looked at a man because she liked the way the hair was tucked behind his ears, or she liked the question-mark line of a long torso curving at the shoulder and straight at the hip. For warm eyes or a soft voice or a slow walk—that's all— a few hairs, a line, a brightness, a sound, a pace, she gave up family. She offered us up for a charm that vanished with tiredness, a pigtail that didn't toss when the wind died. Why, the wrong lighting could erase the dearest thing about him.

It could very well have been, however, that my aunt did not take subtle enjoyment of her friend, but, a wild woman, kept rollicking company. Imagining her free with sex doesn't fit, though. I don't know any women like that, or men either. Unless I see her life branching into mine, she gives me no ancestral help.

To sustain her being in love, she often worked at herself in the mirror, guessing at the colors and shapes that would interest him, changing them frequently in order to hit on the right combination. She wanted him to look back.

On a farm near the sea, a woman who tended her appearance reaped a reputation for eccentricity. All the married women blunt-cut their hair in flaps about their ears or pulled it back in tight buns. No nonsense. Neither style blew easily into heart-catching tangles. And at their weddings they displayed themselves in their long hair for the last time. "It brushed the backs of my knees," my mother tells me. "It was braided, and even so, it brushed the backs of my knees."

At the mirror my aunt combed individuality into her bob. A bun could have been contrived to escape into black streamers blowing in the wind or in quiet wisps about her face, but only the older women in our picture album wear buns. She brushed her hair back from her forehead, tucking the flaps behind her ears. She looped a piece of thread, knotted into a circle between her index fingers and thumbs, and ran the double strand across her forehead. When she closed her fingers as if she were making a pair of shadow geese bite, the string twisted together catching the little hairs. Then she pulled the thread away from her skin, ripping the hairs out neatly, her eyes watering from the needles of pain. Opening her fingers, she cleaned the thread, then rolled it along her hairline and the tops of her eyebrows. My mother did the same to me and my sisters and herself. I used to believe that the expression "caught by the short hairs" meant a captive held with a depilatory string. It especially hurt at the temples, but my mother said we were lucky we didn't have to have our feet bound when we were seven. Sisters used to sit on their beds and cry together, she said, as their mothers or their slave removed the bandages for a few minutes each night and let the blood gush back into their veins. I hope that the man my aunt loved appreciated a smooth brow, that he wasn't just a tits-and-ass man.

Once my aunt found a freckle on her chin, at a spot that the almanac said predestined her for unhappiness. She dug it out with a hot needle and washed the wound with peroxide.

More attention to her looks than these pullings of hairs and pickings at spots would have caused gossip among the villagers. They owned work clothes and good clothes, and they wore good clothes for feasting the new seasons. But since a woman combing her hair hexes beginnings, my aunt rarely found an occasion to look her best. Women looked like great sea snails—the corded wood, babies, and laundry they carried were the whorls on their backs. The Chinese did not admire a bent back; goddesses and warriors stood straight. Still there must have been a marvelous freeing of beauty when a worker laid down her burden and stretched and arched.

Such commonplace loveliness, however, was not enough for my aunt. She dreamed of a lover for the fifteen days of New Year's, the time for families to exchange visits, money, and food. She plied her secret comb. And sure enough she cursed the year, the family, the village, and herself.

Even as her hair lured her imminent lover, many other men looked at her. Uncles, cousins, nephews, brothers would have looked, too, had they been home between journeys. Perhaps they had already been restraining their curiosity, and they left, fearful that their glances, like a field of nesting birds, might be startled and caught. Poverty hurt, and that was their first reason for leaving. But another, final reason for leaving the crowded house was the never-said.

30 She may have been unusually beloved, the precious only daugh- 30
ter, spoiled and mirror gazing because of the affection the family lavished on her. When her husband left, they welcomed the chance to take her back from the in-laws; she could live like the little daughter for just a while longer. There are stories that my grandfather was

different from other people, "crazy ever since the little Jap bayoneted him in the head." He used to put his naked penis on the dinner table, laughing. And one day he brought home a baby girl, wrapped up inside his brown western-style greatcoat. He had traded one of his sons, probably my father, the youngest, for her. My grandmother made him trade back. When he finally got a daughter of his own, he doted on her. They must have all loved her, except perhaps my father, the only brother who never went back to China, having once been traded for a girl.

Brothers and sisters, newly men and women, had to efface their sexual color and present plain miens. Disturbing hair and eyes, a smile like no other, threatened the ideal of five generations living under one roof. To focus blurs, people shouted face to face and yelled from room to room. The immigrants I know have loud voices, unmodulated to American tones even after years away from the village where they called their friendships out across the fields. I have not been able to stop my mother's screams in public libraries or over telephones. Walking erect (knees straight, toes pointed forward, not pigeon-toed, which is Chinese-feminine) and speaking in an inaudible voice, I have tried to turn myself American-feminine. Chinese communication was loud, public. Only sick people had to whisper. But at the dinner table, where the family members came nearest one another, no one could talk, not the outcasts nor any eaters. Every word that falls from the mouth is a coin lost. Silently they gave and accepted food with both hands. A preoccupied child who took his bowl with one hand got a sideways glare. A complete moment of total attention is due everyone alike. Children and lovers have no singularity here, but my aunt used a secret voice, a separate attentiveness.

She kept the man's name to herself throughout her labor and dying; she did not accuse him that he be punished with her. To save her inseminator's name she gave silent birth.

He may have been somebody in her own household, but intercourse with a man outside the family would have been no less abhorrent. All the village were kinsmen, and the titles shouted in loud country voices never let kinship be forgotten. Any man within visiting distance would have been neutralized as a lover—"brother," "younger brother," "older brother"—one hundred and fifteen relationship titles. Parents researched birth charts probably not so much to assure good fortune as to circumvent incest in a population that has but one hundred surnames. Everybody has eight million relatives. How useless then sexual mannerisms, how dangerous.

As if it came from an atavism deeper than fear, I used to add "brother" silently to boys' names. It hexed the boys, who would or would not ask me to dance, and made them less scary and as familiar and deserving of benevolence as girls.

35   But, of course, I hexed myself also—no dates. I should have stood 35 up, both arms waving, and shouted out across libraries, "Hey, you! Love me back." I had no idea, though, how to make attraction selective, how to control its direction and magnitude. If I made myself American-pretty so that the five or six Chinese boys in the class fell in love with me, everyone else—the Caucasian, Negro, and Japanese boys—would too. Sisterliness, dignified and honorable, made much more sense.

Attraction eludes control so stubbornly that whole societies designed to organize relationships among people cannot keep order, not even when they bind people to one another from childhood and raise them together. Among the very poor and the wealthy, brothers married their adopted sisters, like doves. Our family allowed some romance, paying adult brides' prices and providing dowries so that their sons and daughters could marry strangers. Marriage promises to turn strangers into friendly relatives—a nation of siblings.

In the village structure, spirits shimmered among the live creatures, balanced and held in equilibrium by time and land. But one human being flaring up into violence could open up a black hole, a maelstrom that pulled in the sky. The frightened villagers, who depended on one another to maintain the real, went to my aunt to show her a personal, physical representation of the break she had made in the "roundness." Misallying couples snapped off the future, which was to be embodied in true offspring. The villagers punished her for acting as if she could have a private life, secret and apart from them.

If my aunt had betrayed the family at a time of large grain yields and peace, when many boys were born, and wings were being built on many houses, perhaps she might have escaped such severe punishment. But the men—hungry, greedy, tired of planting in dry soil, cuckolded—had had to leave the village in order to send food-money home. There were ghost plagues, bandit plagues, wars with the Japanese, floods. My Chinese brother and sister had died of an unknown sickness. Adultery, perhaps only a mistake during good times, became a crime when the village needed food.

The round moon cakes and round doorways, the round tables of graduated size that fit one roundness inside another, round windows and rice bowls—these talismans had lost their power to warn this family of the law: a family must be whole, faithfully keeping the descent line by having sons to feed the old and the dead, who in turn look after the family. The villagers came to show my aunt and her lover-in-hiding a broken house. The villagers were speeding up the circling of events because she was too shortsighted to see that her infidelity had already harmed the village, that waves of consequences would return unpredictably, sometimes in disguise, as now, to hurt her. This roundness had to be made coin-sized so that she would see its circumference: punish her at the birth of her baby. Awaken her to the inexorable. People who refused fatalism because they could invent small resources insisted on culpability. Deny accidents and wrest fault from the stars.

40

After the villagers left, their lanterns now scattering in various directions toward home, the family broke their silence and cursed her. "Aiaa, we're going to die. Death is coming. Death is coming. Look what you've done. You've killed us. Ghost! Dead ghost! Ghost! You've never been born." She ran out into the fields, far enough from the house so that she could no longer hear their voices, and pressed herself against the earth, her own land no more. When she felt the birth coming, she thought that she had been hurt. Her body seized together. "They've hurt me too much," she thought. "This is gall, and it will kill me." With forehead and knees against the earth, her body convulsed and then relaxed. She turned on her back, lay on the ground. The black well of sky and stars went out and out and out forever; her body and her complexity seemed to disappear, without home, without a companion, in eternal cold and silence. An agoraphobia rose in her, speeding higher and higher, bigger and bigger; she would not be able to contain it; there would be no end to fear.

Flayed, unprotected against space, she felt pain return, focusing her body. This pain chilled her—a cold, steady kind of surface pain. Inside, spasmodically, the other pain, the pain of the child, heated her. For hours she lay on the ground, alternately body and space. Sometimes a vision of normal comfort obliterated reality: she saw the family in the evening gambling at the dinner table, the young people massaging their elders' backs. She saw them congratulating one another, high joy on the mornings the rice shoots came up. When these pictures burst, the stars drew yet further apart. Black space opened.

She got to her feet to fight better and remembered that old-fashioned women gave birth in their pigsties to fool the jealous, pain-dealing gods, who do not snatch piglets. Before the next spasms could stop her, she ran to the pigsty, each step a rushing out into emptiness. She climbed over the fence and knelt in the dirt. It was good to have a fence enclosing her, a tribal person alone.

Laboring, this woman who had carried her child as a foreign growth that sickened her every day, expelled it at last. She reached down to touch the hot, wet, moving mass, surely smaller than anything human, and could feel that it was human after all—fingers, toes, nails, nose. She pulled it up on to her belly, and it lay curled there, butt in the air, feet precisely tucked one under the other. She opened her loose shirt and buttoned the child inside. After resting, it squirmed and thrashed and she pushed it up to her breast. It turned its head this way and that until it found her nipple. There, it made little snuffling noises. She clenched her teeth at its preciousness, lovely as a young calf, a piglet, a little dog.

She may have gone to the pigsty as a last act of responsibility: she would protect this child as she had protected its father. It would look after her soul, leaving supplies on her grave. But how would this tiny child without family find her grave when there would be no marker for her anywhere, neither in the earth nor the family hall? No one would give her a family hall name. She had taken the child with her into the wastes. At its birth the two of them had felt the same raw pain of separation, a wound that only the family pressing tight could close. A child with no descent line would not soften her life but only trail after her, ghost-like, begging her to give it purpose. At dawn the villagers on their way to the fields would stand around the fence and look.

45 Full of milk, the little ghost slept. When it awoke, she hardened 45
her breasts against the milk that crying loosens. Toward morning she picked up the baby and walked to the well.

Carrying the baby to the well shows loving. Otherwise abandon it. Turn its face into the mud. Mothers who love their children take them along. It was probably a girl; there is some hope of forgiveness for boys.

"Don't tell anyone you had an aunt. Your father does not want to hear her name. She has never been born." I have believed that sex was unspeakable and words so strong and fathers so frail that "aunt" would do my father mysterious harm. I have thought that my family, having settled among immigrants who had also been their neighbors in the ancestral land, needed to clean their name, and a wrong word would incite the kinspeople even here. But there is more to this silence: they want me to participate in her punishment. And I have.

In the twenty years since I heard this story I have not asked for details nor said my aunt's name; I do not know it. People who can comfort the dead can also chase after them to hurt them further—a reverse ancestor worship. The real punishment was not the raid swiftly inflicted by the villagers, but the family's deliberately forgetting her. Her betrayal so maddened them, they saw to it that she would suffer forever, even after death. Always hungry, always needing, she would have to beg food from other ghosts, snatch and steal it from those whose living descendants give them gifts. She would have to fight the ghosts massed at crossroads for the buns a few thoughtful citizens leave to decoy her away from village and home so that the ancestral spirits could feast unharassed. At peace, they could act like gods, not ghosts, their descent lines providing them with paper suits and dresses, spirit money, paper houses, paper automobiles, chicken, meat, and rice into eternity—essences delivered up in smoke and flames, steam and incense rising from each rice bowl. In an attempt to make the Chinese care for people outside the family, Chairman Mao encourages us now to give our paper replicas to the spirits of outstanding soldiers and workers, no matter whose ancestors they may be. My aunt remains forever hungry. Goods are not distributed evenly among the dead.

My aunt haunts me—her ghost drawn to me because now, after fifty years of neglect, I alone devote pages of paper to her, though not origamied into houses and clothes. I do not think she always means me well. I am telling on her, and she was a spite suicide, drowning herself in the drinking water. The Chinese are always very frightened of the drowned one, whose weeping ghost, wet hair hanging and skin bloated, waits silently by the water to pull down a substitute.

Questions on Meaning

1. Why did Kingston's mother tell her this story? Why did her mother demand that she never tell anyone? What did her mother fear might happen if Kingston did mention her aunt's name?
2. Describe how extended families grew through marriage in the society in which Kingston's parents were brought up. How did the structure of a family's house indicate the size of a family and the number of generations living together?
3. Women were clearly subordinate in the society in which Kingston's parents were reared. Find five statements that describe the roles of women in Chinese society at that time.

Questions on Rhetorical Strategy and Style

1. Kingston's skillful use of the narrative writing strategy reflects the oral tradition that she learned from her parents and from the generations of immigrants with whom she lived. Reread the essay, noting how she weaves hypotheses about her aunt into the story she was told by her mother. Mark where she shifts from simply retelling a family story to letting her imagination elaborate this tragic tale.
2. What does Kingston's tone tell you about her feelings toward her relatives and their culture? As a Chinese-American with American roots and a rich Chinese heritage, how accepting is she of the cultural differences she reveals in the essay?
3. At the middle of Kingston's mother's story is an infant, the most helpless and innocent character in the essay. How does Kingston make you feel about this child? Why does she call the baby "it"? What were your thoughts when she suddenly stated, "It was probably a girl"?

Writing Assignments

1. Throughout time, almost every family has housed a ghost, or ghosts—perhaps that shiftless uncle who shows up unannounced to eat, sleep, and embarrass the family, or a mentally handicapped sibling institutionalized since childhood whom everyone tries to forget. Identify such a person in your family or extended family. Why is the person treated as though he or she never existed? What

rationalizations does your family go through to cover up or deny this person's existence? How did Kingston's essay affect your impression of your relative?

2. As she develops her scenarios for her aunt's pregnancy, Kingston first describes her aunt as having been raped, but then depicts her as having taken a lover. Her aunt, silenced by society, can lend no clues. What normally goes through your mind when you encounter an unmarried pregnant woman? Do you assume she was in a relationship that fell apart, was having an affair, didn't use birth control, or perhaps was raped? What impact did Kingston's essay have on your views of out-of-wedlock pregnancy?

3. Write an essay about a "story to grow on" that a family member or a friend, teacher, or other acquaintance has told you. Provide enough background to explain why the story was noteworthy to the story teller and then describe your reaction. Explain how the story has changed in meaning as you have gotten older, as your experiences have changed your perception of its message.

Sex, Lies, and Conversation

Deborah Tannen

Deborah Tannen (1945–), born in Brooklyn, New York, received her Ph.D. in linguistics from the University of California, Berkeley and teaches at Georgetown University. Her research into how people communicate has brought her critical and popular acclaim, and she has appeared on several television programs and has written for The New York Times, *the* Washington Post, *and* Vogue. *Her book* That's Not What I Meant *(1987) analyzes the effects of conversational styles on relationships.* You Just Don't Understand *(1990), in which the following selection was included, examines differences in how men and women converse.* Talking From 9 to 5 *(1994) resulted from her research into conversational styles in work settings and their impact on how work is performed and who gets ahead. The following essay, which first appeared in* The New York Times, *is based on her scientific study of the conversational patterns of men and women and how differences in these styles lead to misinterpretation, tension, and sometimes divorce.*

1   I was addressing a small gathering in a suburban Virginia living room—a women's group that had invited men to join them. Throughout the evening, one man had been particularly talkative, frequently offering ideas and anecdotes, while his wife sat silently beside him on the couch. Toward the end of the evening, I commented that women frequently complain that their husbands don't talk to them. This man quickly concurred. He gestured toward his wife and said, "She's the talker in our family." The room burst into laughter;

the man looked puzzled and hurt. "It's true," he explained. "When I come home from work I have nothing to say. If she didn't keep the conversation going, we'd spend the whole evening in silence."

This episode crystallizes the irony that although American men tend to talk more than women in public situations, they often talk less at home. And this pattern is wreaking havoc with marriage.

The pattern was observed by political scientist Andrew Hacker in the late '70s. Sociologist Catherine Kohler Riessman reports in her new book *Divorce Talk* that most of the women she interviewed—but only a few of the men—gave lack of communication as the reason for their divorces. Given the current divorce rate of nearly 50 percent, that amounts to millions of cases in the United States every year—a virtual epidemic of failed conversation.

In my own research, complaints from women about their husbands most often focused not on tangible inequities such as having given up the chance for a career to accompany a husband to his, or doing far more than their share of daily life-support work like cleaning, cooking, social arrangements and errands. Instead, they focused on communication: "He doesn't listen to me," "He doesn't talk to me." I found, as Hacker observed years before, that most wives want their husbands to be, first and foremost, conversational partners, but few husbands share this expectation of their wives.

5   In short, the image that best represents the current crisis is the   5
stereotypical cartoon scene of a man sitting at the breakfast table with a newspaper held up in front of his face, while a woman glares at the back of it, wanting to talk.

Linguistic Battle of the Sexes

How can women and men have such different impressions of communication in marriage? Why the widespread imbalance in their interests and expectations?

In the April [1990] issue of *American Psychologist,* Stanford University's Eleanor Maccoby reports the results of her own and others' research showing that children's development is most influenced by the social structure of peer interactions. Boys and girls tend to play with children of their own gender, and their sex-separate groups have different organizational structures and interactive norms.

I believe these systematic differences in childhood socialization make talk between women and men like cross-cultural communication,

heir to all the attraction and pitfalls of that enticing but difficult en-
terprise. My research on men's and women's conversations uncovered
patterns similar to those described for children's groups.

For women, as for girls, intimacy is the fabric of relationships, and
talk is the thread from which it is woven. Little girls create and maintain friendships by exchanging secrets; similarly, women regard conversation as the cornerstone of friendship. So a woman expects her
husband to be a new and improved version of a best friend. What is
important is not the individual subjects that are discussed but the
sense of closeness, of a life shared, that emerges when people tell their
thoughts, feelings, and impressions.

10   Bonds between boys can be as intense as girls', but they are based   10
less on talking, more on doing things together. Since they don't assume
talk is the cement that binds a relationship, men don't know what kind
of talk women want, and they don't miss it when it isn't there.

Boys' groups are larger, more inclusive, and more hierarchical, so
boys must struggle to avoid the subordinate position in the group.
This may play a role in women's complaints that men don't listen to
them. Some men really don't like to listen, because being the listener
makes them feel one-down, like a child listening to adults or an em-
ployee to a boss.

But often when women tell men, "You aren't listening," and the
men protest, "I am," the men are right. The impression of not listening results from misalignments in the mechanics of conversation. The
misalignment begins as soon as a man and a woman take physical positions. This became clear when I studied videotapes made by psychologist Paul Dorval of children and adults talking to their same-sex
best friends. I found that at every age, the girls and women faced each
other directly, their eyes anchored on each other's faces. At every age,
the boys and men sat at angles to each other and looked elsewhere in
the room, periodically glancing at each other. They were obviously at-
tuned to each other, often mirroring each other's movements. But the
tendency of men to face away can give women the impression they
aren't listening even when they are. A young woman in college was
frustrated: Whenever she told her boyfriend she wanted to talk to him,
he would lie down on the floor, close his eyes, and put his arm over
his face. This signaled to her, "He's taking a nap." But he insisted he
was listening extra hard. Normally, he looks around the room, so he
is easily distracted. Lying down and covering his eyes helped him concentrate on what she was saying.

Analogous to the physical alignment that women and men take in conversation is their topical alignment. The girls in my study tended to talk at length about one topic, but the boys tended to jump from topic to topic. The second-grade girls exchanged stories about people they knew. The second-grade boys teased, told jokes, noticed things in the room and talked about finding games to play. The sixth-grade girls talked about problems with a mutual friend. The sixth-grade boys talked about fifty-five different topics, none of which extended over more than a few turns.

Listening to Body Language

Switching topics is another habit that gives women the impression men aren't listening, especially if they switch to a topic about themselves. But the evidence of the tenth-grade boys in my study indicates otherwise. The tenth-grade boys sprawled across their chairs with bodies parallel and eyes straight ahead, rarely looking at each other. They looked as if they were riding in a car, staring out the windshield. But they were talking about their feelings. One boy was upset because a girl had told him he had a drinking problem, and the other was feeling alienated from all his friends.

15 Now, when a girl told a friend about a problem, the friend responded by asking probing questions and expressing agreement and understanding. But the boys dismissed each other's problems. Todd assured Richard that his drinking was "no big problem" because "sometimes you're funny when you're off your butt." And when Todd said he felt left out, Richard responded, "Why should you? You know more people than me."

Women perceive such responses as belittling and unsupportive. But the boys seemed satisfied with them. Whereas women reassure each other by implying, "You shouldn't feel bad because I've had similar experiences," men do so by implying, "You shouldn't feel bad because your problems aren't so bad."

There are even simpler reasons for women's impression that men don't listen. Linguist Lynette Hirschman found that women make more listener-noise, such as "mhm," "uhuh," and "yeah," to show "I'm with you." Men, she found, more often give silent attention. Women who expect a stream of listener-noise interpret silent attention as no attention at all.

97

Women's conversational habits are as frustrating to men as men's are to women. Men who expect silent attention interpret a stream of listener-noise as overreaction or impatience. Also, when women talk to each other in a close, comfortable setting, they often overlap, finish each other's sentences and anticipate what the other is about to say. This practice, which I call "participatory listenership," is often perceived by men as interruption, intrusion, and lack of attention.

A parallel difference caused a man to complain about his wife, "She just wants to talk about her own point of view. If I show her another view, she gets mad at me." When most women talk to each other, they assume a conversationalist's job is to express agreement and support. But many men see their conversational duty as pointing out the other side of an argument. This is heard as disloyalty by women, and refusal to offer the requisite support. It is not that women don't want to see other points of view, but that they prefer them phrased as suggestions and inquiries rather than as direct challenges.

20   In his book *Fighting for Life,* Walter Ong points out that men use   20
"agonistic," or warlike, oppositional formats to do almost anything; thus discussion becomes debate, and conversation becomes a competitive sport. In contrast, women see conversation as a ritual means of establishing rapport. If Jane tells a problem and June says she has a similar one, they walk away feeling closer to each other. But this attempt at establishing rapport can backfire when used with men. Men take too literally women's ritual "troubles talk," just as women mistake men's ritual challenges for real attack.

The Sounds of Silence

These differences begin to clarify why women and men have such different expectations about communication in marriage. For women, talk creates intimacy. Marriage is an orgy of closeness: you can tell your feelings and thoughts, and still be loved. Their greatest fear is being pushed away. But men live in a hierarchical world, where talk maintains independence and status. They are on guard to protect themselves from being put down and pushed around.

This explains the paradox of the talkative man who said of his silent wife, "She's the talker." In the public setting of a guest lecture, he felt challenged to show his intelligence and display his understanding of the lecture. But at home, where he has nothing to prove and no one to defend against, he is free to remain silent. For his wife, being home means she is free from the worry that something she says might offend someone, or spark disagreement, or appear to be showing off; at home she is free to talk.

The communication problems that endanger marriage can't be fixed by mechanical engineering. They require a new conceptual framework about the role of talk in human relationships. Many of the psychological explanations that have become second nature may not be helpful, because they tend to blame either women (for not being assertive enough) or men (for not being in touch with their feelings). A sociolinguistic approach by which male-female conversation is seen as cross-cultural communication allows us to understand the problem and forge solutions without blaming either party.

Once the problem is understood, improvement comes naturally, as it did to the young woman and her boyfriend who seemed to go to sleep when she wanted to talk. Previously, she had accused him of not listening, and he had refused to change his behavior, since that would be admitting fault. But then she learned about and explained to him the differences in women's and men's habitual ways of aligning themselves in conversation. The next time she told him she wanted to talk, he began, as usual, by lying down and covering his eyes. When the familiar negative reaction bubbled up, she reassured herself that he really was listening. But then he sat up and looked at her. Thrilled, she asked why. He said, "You like me to look at you when we talk, so I'll try to do it." Once he saw their differences as cross-cultural rather than right and wrong, he independently altered his behavior.

25 Women who feel abandoned and deprived when their husbands 25 won't listen to or report daily news may be happy to discover their husbands trying to adapt once they understand the place of small talk in women's relationships. But if their husbands don't adapt, the women may still be comforted that for men, this is not a failure of intimacy. Accepting the difference, the wives may look to their friends or family for that kind of talk. And husbands who can't provide it shouldn't feel their wives have made unreasonable demands. Some couples will still decide to divorce, but at least their decisions will be based on realistic expectations.

In these times of resurgent ethnic conflicts, the world desperately needs cross-cultural understanding. Like charity, successful cross-cultural communication should begin at home.

Questions on Meaning

1. What do men generally want out of conversation? What do women want?
2. Describe the differences between men and women in physical position and behavior during conversation with others of the same sex. What are the differences in how men and women speak?
3. Does Tannen argue that men and women should both try to change so that there are no differences anymore in conversational styles? If so, why? If not, what is her solution?

Questions on Rhetorical Strategy and Style

1. Examine how Tannen uses the rhetorical strategy of comparison and contrast to describe and explain the differences between men and women. How balanced is her analysis?
2. Tannen also uses examples to support and develop her points about how men and women communicate differently. Without rereading, how many different examples can you recall about such differences?
3. At the end of the essay Tannen switches from an emphasis that has been mostly descriptive to one that briefly argues a position. Evaluate the effectiveness of her concluding argument about how men and women should try to understand each other and adapt. What might make her argument stronger?

Writing Assignments

1. Tannen writes of couples who have apparently been married at least a little while, but whose problems are moving them toward divorce. Speculate about a topic she does not discuss: how couples might act and converse differently when they are first dating and forming a relationship. If their conversational styles are the same even early on, enough to cause divorce later on, how do they overcome these problems at first and get married? Or if you think people's conversational styles change after they have been married a while, what causes that change?
2. Tannen generalizes about communication differences between all males and females, even though she writes primarily about married couples. How much do you think her observations apply to single people in your own age group? Go to a place where you can

easily observe apparently single people near your age. Observe at least three conversations: one between two males, one between two females, and one between a male and a female. Take note of behaviors such as physical position, the amount of eye contact, how long each person seems to speak, and so on. Then write an essay presenting your findings.

The Library Card

Richard Wright

Richard Wright (1908–1960) was born on a plantation in Natchez, Mississippi. When he was young, his family was frequently displaced as his mother moved about looking for work. Eventually his family dissolved and Wright spent time in a number of orphanages and foster homes. At age 15, Wright took off on his own, supporting himself with odd jobs. In 1943 he moved to Chicago and later joined the Federal Writer's Project. A member of the "radical left," Wright published in such publications as the Daily Worker, Left Front, *and* New Masses, *in addition to more mainstream publications, such as* Harper's. *His first novel,* Uncle Tom's Children: Four Novellas *(1938) won him the critical acclaim that led to a Guggenheim Fellowship. His novel* Native Son *(1940) became a classic in American literature. Other books by Wright include* Eight Men *(1940),* Black Boy *(1945),* The Outsider *(1953),* Black Power *(1954), and* The Long Dream *(1958). In 1946, Wright emigrated to France. In this essay, an excerpt from* Black Boy, *Wright reveals how his introduction to books both expanded his intellectual horizons and revealed the limits imposed on him by the American South of the 1920s.*

1   One morning I arrived early at work and went into the bank lobby where the Negro porter was mopping. I stood at a counter and picked up the Memphis *Commercial Appeal* and began my free reading of the press. I came finally to the editorial page and saw an article dealing with one H. L. Mencken. I knew by hearsay that he was the editor of the *American Mercury,* but aside from that I

knew nothing about him. The article was a furious denunciation of Mencken, concluding with one hot, short sentence: Mencken is a fool.

I wondered what on earth this Mencken had done to call down upon him the scorn of the South. The only people I had ever heard denounced in the South were Negroes, and this man was not a Negro. Then what ideas did Mencken hold that made a newspaper like the *Commercial Appeal* castigate him publicly? Undoubtedly he must be advocating ideas that the South did not like. Were there, then, people other than Negroes who criticized the South? I knew that during the Civil War the South had hated northern whites, but I had not encountered such hate during my life. Knowing no more of Mencken than I did at that moment, I felt a vague sympathy for him. Had not the South, which had assigned me the role of a non-man, cast at him its hardest words?

Now, how could I find out about this Mencken? There was a huge library near the riverfront, but I knew that Negroes were not allowed to patronize its shelves any more than they were the parks and playgrounds of the city. I had gone into the library several times to get books for the white men on the job. Which of them would now help me to get books? And how could I read them without causing concern to the white men with whom I worked? I had so far been successful in hiding my thoughts and feelings from them, but I knew that I would create hostility if I went about this business of reading in a clumsy way.

I weighed the personalities of the men on the job. There was Don, a Jew; but I distrusted him. His position was not much better than mine and I knew that he was uneasy and insecure; he had always treated me in an offhand, bantering way that barely concealed his contempt. I was afraid to ask him to help me to get books; his frantic desire to demonstrate a racial solidarity with the whites against Negroes might make him betray me.

Then how about the boss? No, he was a Baptist and I had the suspicion that he would not be quite able to comprehend why a black boy would want to read Mencken. There were other white men on the job whose attitudes showed clearly that they were Kluxers or sympathizers, and they were out of the question.

There remained only one man whose attitude did not fit into an anti-Negro category, for I had heard the white men refer to him as a "Pope lover." He was an Irish Catholic and was hated by the white Southerners. I knew that he read books, because I had got him volumes from the library several times. Since he, too, was an object of hatred, I felt that he might refuse me but would hardly betray me. I hesitated, weighing and balancing the imponderable realities.

One morning I paused before the Catholic fellow's desk.

"I want to ask you a favor," I whispered to him.

"What is it?"

"I want to read. I can't get books from the library. I wonder if you'd let me use your card?"

He looked at me suspiciously.

"My card is full most of the time," he said.

"I see," I said and waited, posing my question silently.

"You're not trying to get me into trouble, are you, boy?" he asked, staring at me.

"Oh, no, sir."

"What book do you want?"

"A book by H. L. Mencken."

"Which one?"

"I don't know. Has he written more than one?"

"He has written several."

"I didn't know that."

"What makes you want to read Mencken?"

"Oh, I just saw his name in the newspaper," I said.

"It's good of you to want to read," he said. "But you ought to read the right things."

I said nothing. Would he want to supervise my reading?

"Let me think," he said. "I'll figure out something."

I turned from him and he called me back. He stared at me quizzically.

"Richard, don't mention this to the other white men," he said.

"I understand," I said. "I won't say a word."

A few days later he called me to him.

"I've got a card in my wife's name," he said. "Here's mine."

"Thank you, sir."

"Do you think you can manage it?"

"I'll manage fine," I said.

"If they suspect you, you'll get in trouble," he said.

"I'll write the same kind of notes to the library that you wrote when you sent me for books," I told him. "I'll sign your name."

He laughed.

"Go ahead. Let me see what you get," he said.

That afternoon I addressed myself to forging a note. Now, what were the names of books written by H. L. Mencken? I did not know any of them. I finally wrote what I thought would be a foolproof note: *Dear Madam: Will you please let this nigger boy*—I used the word "nigger" to make the librarian feel that I could not possibly be the author of the note—*have some books by H. L. Mencken?* I forged the white man's name.

40   I entered the library as I had always done when on errands for whites, but I felt that I would somehow slip up and betray myself. I doffed my hat, stood a respectful distance from the desk, looked as unbookish as possible, and waited for the white patrons to be taken care of. When the desk was clear of people, I still waited. The white librarian looked at me.

"What do you want, boy?"

As though I did not possess the power of speech, I stepped forward and simply handed her the forged note, not parting my lips.

"What books by Mencken does he want?" she asked.

"I don't know, ma'am," I said, avoiding her eyes.

45   "Who gave you this card?"

"Mr. Falk," I said.

"Where is he?"

"He's at work, at the M——Optical Company," I said. "I've been in here for him before."

"I remember," the woman said. "But he never wrote notes like this."

50   Oh, God, she's suspicious. Perhaps she would not let me have the books? If she had turned her back at that moment, I would have ducked out the door and never gone back. Then I thought of a bold idea.

"You can call him up, ma'am," I said, my heart pounding.

"You're not using these books, are you?" she asked pointedly.

"Oh, no, ma'am. I can't read."

"I don't know what he wants by Mencken," she said under her breath.

55   I knew now that I had won; she was thinking of other things and the race question had gone out of her mind. She went to the shelves. Once or twice she looked over her shoulder at me, as though she was still doubtful. Finally she came forward with two books in her hand.

"I'm sending him two books," she said. "But tell Mr. Falk to come in next time, or send me the names of the books he wants. I don't know what he wants to read."

I said nothing. She stamped the card and handed me the books. Not daring to glance at them, I went out of the library, fearing that the woman would call me back for further questioning. A block away from the library I opened one of the books and read a title: *A Book of Prefaces*. I was nearing my nineteenth birthday and I did not know how to pronounce the word "preface." I thumbed the pages and saw strange words and strange names. I shook my head, disappointed. I looked at the other book; it was called *Prejudices*. I knew what that word meant; I had heard it all my life. And right off I was on guard against Mencken's books. Why would a man want to call a book *Prejudices*? The word was so stained with all my memories of racial hate that I could not conceive of anybody using it for a title. Perhaps I had made a mistake about Mencken? A man who had prejudices must be wrong.

When I showed the books to Mr. Falk, he looked at me and frowned.

"That librarian might telephone you," I warned him.

"That's all right," he said. "But when you're through reading those books, I want you to tell me what you get out of them."

That night in my rented room, while letting the hot water run over my can of pork and beans in the sink, I opened *A Book of Prefaces* and began to read. I was jarred and shocked by the style, the clear, clean, sweeping sentences. Why did he write like that? And how did one write like that? I pictured the man as a raging demon, slashing with his pen, consumed with hate, denouncing everything American, extolling everything European or German, laughing at the weaknesses of people, mocking God, authority. What was this? I stood up, trying to realize what reality lay behind the meaning of the words. . . . Yes, this man was fighting, fighting with words. He was using words as a weapon, using them as one would use a club. Could words be weapons? Well, yes, for here they were. Then, maybe, perhaps, I could use them as a weapon? No. It frightened me. I read on and what amazed me was not what he said, but how on earth anybody had the courage to say it.

Occasionally I glanced up to reassure myself that I was alone in the room. Who were these men about whom Mencken was talking so passionately? Who was Anatole France? Joseph Conrad? Sinclair Lewis, Sherwood Anderson, Dostoevski, George Moore, Gustave Flaubert, Maupassant, Tolstoy, Frank Harris, Mark Twain, Thomas Hardy, Arnold Bennett, Stephen Crane, Zola, Norris, Gorky, Bergson,

Ibsen, Balzac, Bernard Shaw, Dumas, Poe, Thomas Mann, O. Henry, Dreiser, H. G. Wells, Gogol, T. S. Eliot, Gide, Baudelaire, Edgar Lee Masters, Stendhal, Turgenev, Huneker, Nietzsche, and scores of others? Were these men real? Did they exist or had they existed? And how did one pronounce their names?

I ran across many words whose meanings I did not know, and I either looked them up in a dictionary or, before I had a chance to do that, encountered the word in a context that made its meaning clear. But what strange world was this? I concluded the book with the conviction that I had somehow overlooked something terribly important in life. I had once tried to write, had once reveled in feeling, had let my crude imagination roam, but the impulse to dream had been slowly beaten out of me by experience. Now it surged up again and I hungered for books, new ways of looking and seeing. It was not a matter of believing or disbelieving what I read, but of feeling something new, of being affected by something that made the look of the world different.

As dawn broke I ate my pork and beans, feeling dopey, sleepy. I went to work, but the mood of the book would not die; it lingered, coloring everything I saw, heard, did. I now felt that I knew what the white men were feeling. Merely because I had read a book that had spoken of how they lived and thought, I identified myself with that book. I felt vaguely guilty. Would I, filled with bookish notions, act in a manner that would make the whites dislike me?

65   I forged more notes and my trips to the library became frequent.   65
Reading grew into a passion. My first serious novel was Sinclair Lewis's *Main Street*. It made me see my boss, Mr. Gerald, and identify him as an American type. I would smile when I saw him lugging his golf bags into the office. I had always felt a vast distance separating me from the boss, and now I felt closer to him, though still distant. I felt now that I knew him, that I could feel the very limits of his narrow life. And this had happened because I had read a novel about a mythical man called George F. Babbitt.

The plots and stories in the novels did not interest me so much as the point of view revealed. I gave myself over to each novel without reserve, without trying to criticize it; it was enough for me to see and feel something different. And for me, everything was something different. Reading was like a drug, a dope. The novels created moods in which I lived for days. But I could not conquer my sense of guilt, my feeling that the white men around me knew that I was changing, that I had begun to regard them differently.

Whenever I brought a book to the job, I wrapped it in newspaper—
a habit that was to persist for years in other cities and under other circumstances. But some of the white men pried into my packages when
I was absent and they questioned me.

"Boy, what are you reading those books for?"

"Oh, I don't know, sir."

70 "That's deep stuff you're reading, boy." 70

"I'm just killing time, sir."

"You'll addle your brains if you don't watch out."

I read Dreiser's *Jennie Gerhardt* and *Sister Carrie* and they revived
in me a vivid sense of my mother's suffering; I was overwhelmed. I
grew silent, wondering about the life around me. It would have been
impossible for me to have told anyone what I derived from these novels, for it was nothing less than a sense of life itself. All my life had
shaped me for the realism, the naturalism of the modern novel, and I
could not read enough of them.

Steeped in new moods and ideas, I bought a ream of paper and
tried to write; but nothing would come, or what did come was flat beyond telling. I discovered that more than desire and feeling were necessary to write and I dropped the idea. Yet I still wondered how it was
possible to know people sufficiently to write about them. Could I ever
learn about life and people? To me, with my vast ignorance, my Jim
Crow station in life, it seemed a task impossible of achievement. I now
knew what being a Negro meant. I could endure the hunger. I had
learned to live with hate. But to feel that there were feelings denied
me, that the very breath of life itself was beyond my reach, that more
than anything else hurt, wounded me. I had a new hunger.

75 In buoying me up, reading also cast me down, made me see what 75
was possible, what I had missed. My tension returned, new, terrible,
bitter, surging, almost too great to be contained. I no longer *felt* that
the world about me was hostile, killing; I *knew* it. A million times I
asked myself what I could do to save myself, and there were no answers. I seemed forever condemned, ringed by walls.

I did not discuss my reading with Mr. Falk, who had lent me his
library card; it would have meant talking about myself and that would
have been too painful. I smiled each day, fighting desperately to maintain my old behavior, to keep my disposition seemingly sunny. But
some of the white men discerned that I had begun to brood.

"Wake up there, boy!" Mr. Olin said one day.

"Sir!" I answered for the lack of a better word.

"You act like you've stolen something," he said.

80   I laughed in the way I knew he expected me to laugh, but I re-   80
solved to be more conscious of myself, to watch my every act, to guard
and hide the new knowledge that was dawning within me.

If I went north, would it be possible for me to build a new life
then? But how could a man build a life upon vague, unformed yearnings? I wanted to write and I did not even know the English language.
I bought English grammars and found them dull. I felt that I was getting a better sense of the language from novels than from grammars.
I read hard, discarding a writer as soon as I felt that I had grasped his
point of view. At night the printed page stood before my eyes in sleep.

Mrs. Moss, my landlady, asked me one Sunday morning: "Son,
what is this you keep on reading?"

"Oh, nothing. Just novels."

"What you get out of 'em?"

85   "I'm just killing time," I said.   85

"I hope you know your own mind," she said in a tone which implied that she doubted if I had a mind.

I knew of no Negroes who read the books I liked and I wondered
if any Negroes ever thought of them. I knew that there were Negro
doctors, lawyers, newspapermen, but I never saw any of them. When
I read a Negro newspaper I never caught the faintest echo of my preoccupation in its pages. I felt trapped and occasionally, for a few days,
I would stop reading. But a vague hunger would come over me for
books, books that opened up new avenues of feeling and seeing, and
again I would forge another note to the white librarian. Again I would
read and wonder as only the naive and unlettered can read and wonder, feeling that I carried a secret, criminal burden about with me
each day.

That winter my mother and brother came and we set up house-
keeping, buying furniture on the installment plan, being cheated and
yet knowing no way to avoid it. I began to eat warm food and to my
surprise found that regular meals enabled me to read faster. I may have
lived through many illnesses and survived them, never suspecting that
I was ill. My brother obtained a job and we began to save toward the
trip north, plotting our time, setting tentative dates for departure. I
told none of the white men on the job that I was planning to go north;
I knew that the moment they felt I was thinking of the North they
would change toward me. It would have made them feel that I did not
like the life I was living, and because my life was completely condi-

tioned by what they said or did, it would have been tantamount to challenging them.

I could calculate my chances for life in the South as a Negro fairly clearly now.

90   I could fight the southern whites by organizing with other Ne- 90 groes, as my grandfather had done. But I knew that I could never win that way; there were many whites and there were but few blacks. They were strong and we were weak. Outright black rebellion could never win. If I fought openly I would die and I did not want to die. News of lynchings were frequent.

I could submit and live the life of a genial slave, but that was impossible. All of my life had shaped me to live by my own feelings and thoughts. I could make up to Bess and marry her and inherit the house. But that, too, would be the life of a slave; if I did that, I would crush to death something within me, and I would hate myself as much as I knew the whites already hated those who had submitted. Neither could I ever willingly present myself to be kicked, as Shorty had done. I would rather have died than do that.

I could drain off my restlessness by fighting with Shorty and Harrison. I had seen many Negroes solve the problem of being black by transferring their hatred of themselves to others with a black skin and fighting them. I would have to be cold to do that, and I was not cold and I could never be.

I could, of course, forget what I had read, thrust the whites out of my mind, forget them; and find release from anxiety and longing in sex and alcohol. But the memory of how my father had conducted himself made that course repugnant. If I did not want others to violate my life, how could I voluntarily violate it myself?

I had no hope whatever of being a professional man. Not only had I been so conditioned that I did not desire it, but the fulfillment of such an ambition was beyond my capabilities. Well-to-do Negroes lived in a world that was almost as alien to me as the world inhabited by whites.

95   What, then, was there? I held my life in my mind, in my con- 95 sciousness each day, feeling at times that I would stumble and drop it, spill it forever. My reading had created a vast sense of distance between me and the world in which I lived and tried to make a living, and that sense of distance was increasing each day. My days and nights were one long, quiet, continuously contained dream of terror, tension, and anxiety. I wondered how long I could bear it.

Questions on Meaning

1. If you did not know when this essay was published, what words used by Wright would help you identify the time period? What would happen if a black writer used these words today? What about a white writer?
2. What amazed Wright about Mencken? What did the first Mencken book teach Wright about writing?
3. What does Wright mean by his "Jim Crow station in life"?

Questions on Rhetorical Strategy and Style

1. How does Wright use causation to show how his book knowledge changed his view of the white men he worked for? What kind of power did Wright gain from this knowledge? How did it affect his whites bosses' perception of him?
2. Compare and contrast how reading both inspired and depressed Wright. What frustrations did reading cause him? Why did he become tense and bitter?
3. Find where Wright analyzes his options as a southern black. What would you have done in his shoes? How many of these options apply today to blacks in America?

Writing Assignments

1. Describe something you learned from personal research (e.g., books, lectures, or the Internet) that had a significant impact on your life—such as something to do with a hobby, travel, religion, or politics. How were you introduced to this new knowledge? How did you satisfy your quest for more knowledge? How has it altered other aspects of your life?
2. Wright mentions that some of the white men he worked with were "Kluxers," a reference to the Ku Klux Klan. Research this organization and its roots. Typically who were members of the Klan? What are the current activities of the organization?
3. Wright had few if any real black role models. Although he knew that "Negro" professionals existed, he never saw them. Write an essay on the importance of successful minority role models for minority youths to achieve success. How would you recommend getting minority teachers, journalists, engineers, doctors, and other professionals involved with youth programs? What could you do as a college student (even if you are not a member of a minority group)?

A Homemade Education

Malcolm X

Malcolm X (1925–1965), a noted political activist and writer, was born Malcolm Little in Omaha, Nebraska. The son of Earl Little, a Baptist minister who supported the back-to-Africa movement of the 1920s, Malcolm experienced as a child the violence of the Ku Klux Klan and its agencies. After his father was murdered by the Ku Klux Klan and his mother, Louise Little, was committed to a mental institution, Malcolm, in only eighth grade, quit school and drifted to the streets. Jailed for burglary in 1946, Malcolm taught himself the importance of reading and education and converted to the religion of Islam through the Black Muslim Movement led by Elijah Muhammad. When he was released from prison in 1953, Malcolm took his new name "X" signifying "the unknown" and began speaking on behalf of the Black Muslim Movement, pressing for black separatism and the use of self-defense. In 1964, following a trip to Mecca, Malcolm X began advocating for all religions and races and he founded the Organization of Afro-American Unity. A feud that developed over his desire to unify the races and free blacks in America resulted in his assassination by unnamed assassins at the Audubon Ballroom in Harlem, N.Y. on February 21, 1965. Malcolm X's story was told in the early 1990s in the biographical movie by director Spike Lee. His writing includes The Autobiography of Malcolm X *(1965, written with Alex Haley),* Malcolm X Talks to Young People *(1969) and* Malcolm X on Afro-

American Unity (1970). This essay, published in his autobiography, explains how reading in prison created his passionate thirst for education

1   It was because of my letters that I happened to stumble upon starting to acquire some kind of a homemade education.

I became increasingly frustrated at not being able to express what I wanted to convey in letters that I wrote, especially those to Mr. Elijah Muhammad. In the street, I had been the most articulate hustler out there—I had commanded attention when I said something. But now, trying to write simple English, I not only wasn't articulate, I wasn't even functional. How would I sound writing in slang, the way I would say it, something such as, "Look, daddy, let me pull your coat about a cat, Elijah Muhammad—"

Many who today hear me somewhere in person, or on television, or those who read something I've said, will think I went to school far beyond the eighth grade. This impression is due entirely to my prison studies.

It had really begun back in the Charlestown Prison, when Bimbi first made me feel envy of his stock of knowledge. Bimbi had always taken charge of any conversations he was in, and I had tried to emulate him. But every book I picked up had few sentences which didn't contain anywhere from one to nearly all of the words that might as well have been in Chinese. When I just skipped those words, of course, I really ended up with little idea of what the book said. So I had come to the Norfolk Prison Colony still going through only book-reading motions. Pretty soon, I would have quit even these motions, unless I had received the motivation that I did.

5   I saw that the best thing I could do was get hold of a dictionary— to study, to learn some words. I was lucky enough to reason also that I should try to improve my penmanship. It was sad. I couldn't even write in a straight line. It was both ideas together that moved me to request a dictionary along with some tablets and pencils from the Norfolk Prison Colony school.

I spent two days just riffling uncertainly through the dictionary's pages. I'd never realized so many words existed! I didn't know *which* words I needed to learn. Finally, just to start some kind of action, I began copying.

In my slow, painstaking, ragged handwriting, I copied into my tablet everything printed on that first page, down to the punctuation marks.

I believe it took me a day. Then, aloud, I read back, to myself, everything I'd written on the tablet. Over and over, aloud, to myself, I read my own handwriting.

I woke up the next morning, thinking about those words—immensely proud to realize that not only had I written so much at one time, but I'd written words that I never knew were in the world. Moreover, with a little effort, I also could remember what many of these words meant. I reviewed the words whose meanings I didn't remember. Funny thing, from the dictionary first page right now, that "aardvark" springs to my mind. The dictionary had a picture of it, a long-tailed, long-eared, burrowing African mammal, which lives off termites caught by sticking out its tongue as an anteater does for ants.

10 I was so fascinated that I went on—I copied the dictionary's next page. And the same experience came when I studied that. With every succeeding page, I also learned of people and places and events from history. Actually the dictionary is like a miniature encyclopedia. Finally the dictionary's A section had filled a whole tablet—and I went on into the B's. That was the way I started copying what eventually became the entire dictionary. It went a lot faster after so much practice helped me to pick up handwriting speed. Between what I wrote in my tablet, and writing letters, during the rest of my time in prison I would guess I wrote a million words.

I suppose it was inevitable that as my word-base broadened, I could for the first time pick up a book and read and now begin to understand what the book was saying. Anyone who has read a great deal can imagine the new world that opened. Let me tell you something: from then until I left that prison, in every free moment I had, if I was not reading in the library, I was reading on my bunk. You couldn't have gotten me out of books with a wedge. Between Mr. Muhammad's teachings, my correspondence, my visitors—usually Ella and Reginald—and my reading of books, months passed without my even thinking about being imprisoned. In fact, up to then, I never had been so truly free in my life.

The Norfolk Prison Colony's library was in the school building. A variety of classes was taught there by instructors who came from such places as Harvard and Boston universities. The weekly debates between inmate teams were also held in the school building. You would be astonished to know how worked up convict debaters and audiences would get over subjects like "Should Babies Be Fed Milk?"

Available on the prison library's shelves were books on just about every general subject. Much of the big private collection that Parkhurst had willed to the prison was still in crates and boxes in the back of the library—thousands of old books. Some of them looked ancient: covers faded; old-time parchment-looking binding. Parkhurst, I've mentioned, seemed to have been principally interested in history and religion. He had the money and the special interest to have a lot of books that you wouldn't have in general circulation. Any college library would have been lucky to get that collection.

As you can imagine, especially in a prison where there was heavy emphasis on rehabilitation, an inmate was smiled upon if he demonstrated an unusually intense interest in books. There was a sizable number of well-read inmates, especially the popular debaters. Some were said by many to be practically walking encyclopedias. They were almost celebrities. No university would ask any student to devour literature as I did when this new world opened to me, of being able to read and *understand.*

I read more in my room than in the library itself. An inmate who was known to read a lot could check out more than the permitted maximum number of books. I preferred reading in the total isolation of my own room.

When I had progressed to really serious reading, every night at about ten P.M. I would be outraged with the "lights out." It always seemed to catch me right in the middle of something engrossing.

Fortunately, right outside my door was a corridor light that cast a glow into my room. The glow was enough to read by, once my eyes adjusted to it. So when "lights out" came, I would sit on the floor where I could continue reading in that glow.

At one-hour intervals the night guards paced past every room. Each time I heard the approaching footsteps, I jumped into bed and feigned sleep. And as soon as the guard passed, I got back out of bed onto the floor area of that light-glow, where I would read for another fifty-eight minutes—until the guard approached again. That went on until three or four every morning. Three or four hours of sleep a night was enough for me. Often in the years in the streets I had slept less than that.

The teachings of Mr. Muhammad stressed how history had been "whitened"—when white men had written history books, the black man simply had been left out. Mr. Muhammad couldn't have said anything that would have struck me much harder. I had never forgotten how when my class, me and all of those whites, had studied seventh-grade United States history back in Mason, the history of the Negro had been covered in one paragraph, and the teacher had gotten a big laugh with his joke, "Negroes' feet are so big that when they walk, they leave a hole in the ground."

20   This is one reason why Mr. Muhammad's teachings spread so   20
swiftly all over the United States, among *all* Negroes, whether or not they became followers of Mr. Muhammad. The teachings ring true—to every Negro. You can hardly show me a black adult in America—or a white one, for that matter—who knows from the history books anything like the truth about the black man's role. In my own case, once I heard of the "glorious history of the black man," I took special pains to hunt in the library for books that would inform me on details about black history.

I can remember accurately the very first set of books that really impressed me. I have since bought that set of books and I have it at home for my children to read as they grow up. It's called *Wonders of the World*. It's full of pictures of archeological finds, statues that depict, usually, non-European people.

I found books like Will Durant's *Story of Civilization*. I read H.G. Wells' *Outline of History*. *Souls of Black Folk* by W.E.B. Du Bois gave me a glimpse into the black people's history before they came to this country. Carter G. Woodson's *Negro History* opened my eyes about black empires before the black slave was brought to the United States, and the early Negro struggles for freedom.

J.A. Rogers' three volumes of *Sex and Race* told about race-mixing before Christ's time; about Aesop being a black man who told fables; about Egypt's Pharaohs; about the great Coptic Christian Empires; about Ethiopia, the earth's oldest continuous black civilization, as China is the oldest continuous civilization.

Mr. Muhammad's teaching about how the white man had been created led me to *Findings in Genetics* by Gregor Mendel. (The dictionary's G section was where I had learned what "genetics" meant.) I really studied this book by the Austrian monk. Reading it over and over, especially certain sections, helped me to understand that if you started with a black man, a white man could be produced; but starting with a white man, you never could produce a black man—because the white chromosome is recessive. And since no one disputes that there was but one Original Man, the conclusion is clear.

25   During the last year or so, in the *New York Times,* Arnold Toynbee used the word "bleached" in describing the white man. (His words were: "White [i.e. bleached] human beings of North European origin. . . .") Toynbee also referred to the European geographic area as only a peninsula of Asia. He said there is no such thing as Europe. And if you look at the globe, you will see for yourself that America is only an extension of Asia. (But at the same time Toynbee is among those who have helped to bleach history. He has written that Africa was the only continent that produced no history. He won't write that again. Every day now, the truth is coming to light.)

I never will forget how shocked I was when I began reading about slavery's total horror. It made such an impact upon me that it later became one of my favorite subjects when I became a minister of Mr. Muhammad's. The world's most monstrous crime, the sin and the blood on the white man's hands, are almost impossible to believe. Books like the one by Frederick Olmstead opened my eyes to the horrors suffered when the slave was landed in the United States. The European woman, Fannie Kimball, who had married a Southern white slaveowner, described how human beings were degraded. Of course I read *Uncle Tom's Cabin.* In fact, I believe that's the only novel I have ever read since I started serious reading.

Parkhurst's collection also contained some bound pamphlets of the Abolitionist Anti-Slavery Society of New England. I read descriptions of atrocities, saw those illustrations of black slave women tied up and flogged with whips; of black mothers watching their babies being dragged off, never to be seen by their mothers again; of dogs after slaves, and of the fugitive slave catchers, evil white men with whips and clubs and chains and guns. I read about the slave preacher Nat Turner, who put the fear of God into the white slavemaster. Nat Turner wasn't going around preaching pie-in-the-sky and "nonviolent" freedom for the black man. There in Virginia one night in 1831, Nat and seven other slaves started out at his master's home and through the night they went from one plantation "big house" to the next, killing, until by the next morning 57 white people were dead and Nat had about 70 slaves following him. White people, terrified for their lives, fled from their homes, locked themselves up in public buildings, hid in the woods, and some even left the state. A small army of soldiers took two months to catch and hang Nat Turner. Somewhere I have read where Nat Turner's example is said to have inspired John Brown to invade Virginia and attack Harper's Ferry nearly thirty years later, with thirteen white men and five Negroes.

I read Herodotus, "the father of History," or, rather, I read about him. And I read the histories of various nations, which opened my eyes gradually, then wider and wider, to how the whole world's white men had indeed acted like devils, pillaging and raping and bleeding and draining the whole world's non-white people. I remember, for instance, books such as Will Durant's *The Story of Oriental Civilization,* and Mahatma Gandhi's accounts of the struggle to drive the British out of India.

Book after book showed me how the white man had brought upon the world's black, brown, red, and yellow peoples every variety of the sufferings of exploitation. I saw how since the sixteenth century, the so-called "Christian trader" white man began to ply the seas in his lust for Asian and African empires, and plunder, and power. I read, I saw, how the white man never has gone among the non-white peoples bearing the Cross in the true manner and spirit of Christ's teachings—meek, humble, and Christlike.

30 I perceived, as I read, how the collective white man had been 30 actually nothing but a piratical opportunist who used Faustian machinations to make his own Christianity his initial wedge in criminal conquests. First, always "religiously," he branded "heathen" and "pagan" labels upon ancient non-white cultures and civilizations. The stage thus set, he then turned upon his non-white victims his weapons of war.

I read how, entering India—half a *billion* deeply religious brown people—the British white man, by 1759, through promises, trickery and manipulations, controlled much of India through Great Britain's East India Company. The parasitical British administration kept tentacling out to half of the subcontinent. In 1857, some of the desperate people of India finally mutinied—and, excepting the African slave trade, nowhere has history recorded any more unnecessary bestial and ruthless human carnage than the British suppression of the nonwhite Indian people.

Over 115 million African blacks—close to the 1930s population of the United States—were murdered or enslaved during the slave trade. And I read how when the slave market was glutted, the cannibalistic white powers of Europe next carved up, as their colonies, the richest areas of the black continent. And Europe's chancelleries for the next century played a chess game of naked exploitation and power from Cape Horn to Cairo.

Ten guards and the warden couldn't have torn me out of those books. Not even Elijah Muhammad could have been more eloquent than those books were in providing indisputable proof that the collective white man had acted like a devil in virtually every contact he had with the world's collective non-white man. I listen today to the radio, and watch television, and read the headlines about the collective white man's fear and tension concerning China. When the white man professes ignorance about why the Chinese hate him so, my mind can't help flashing back to what I read, there in prison, about how the blood forebears of this same white man raped China at a time when China was trusting and helpless. Those original white "Christian traders" sent into China millions of pounds of opium. By 1839, so many of the Chinese were addicts that China's desperate government destroyed twenty thousand chests of opium. The first Opium War was promptly declared by the white man. Imagine! Declaring *war* upon someone who objects to being narcotized! The Chinese were severely beaten, with Chinese-invented gunpowder.

The Treaty of Nanking made China pay the British white man for the destroyed opium: forced open China's major ports to British trade; forced China to abandon Hong Kong; fixed China's import tariffs so low that cheap British articles soon flooded in, maiming China's industrial development.

After a second Opium War, the Tientsin Treaties legalized the ravaging opium trade, legalized a British-French-American control of China's customs. China tried delaying that Treaty's ratification; Peking was looted and burned.

"Kill the foreign white devils!" was the 1901 Chinese war cry in the Boxer Rebellion. Losing again, this time the Chinese were driven from Peking's choicest areas. The vicious, arrogant white man put up the famous signs, "Chinese and dogs not allowed."

Red China after World War II closed its doors to the Western white world. Massive Chinese agricultural, scientific, and industrial efforts are described in a book that *Life* magazine recently published. Some observers inside Red China have reported that the world never has known such a hate-white campaign as is now going on in this non-white country where, present birthrates continuing, in fifty more years Chinese will be half the earth's population. And it seems that some Chinese chickens will soon come home to roost, with China's recent successful nuclear tests.

Let us face reality. We can see in the United Nations a new world order being shaped, along color lines—an alliance among the non-white nations. America's U.N. Ambassador Adlai Stevenson complained not long ago that in the United Nations "a skin game" was being played. He was right. He was facing reality. A "skin game" *is* being played. But Ambassador Stevenson sounded like Jesse James accusing the marshal of carrying a gun. Because who in the world's history ever has played a worse "skin game" than the white man?

Mr. Muhammad, to whom I was writing daily, had no idea of what a new world had opened up to me through my efforts to document his teachings in books.

40 When I discovered philosophy, I tried to touch all the landmarks 40 of philosophical development. Gradually, I read most of the old philosophers, Occidental and Oriental. The Oriental philosophers were the ones I came to prefer; finally, my impression was that most Occidental philosophy had largely been borrowed from the Oriental thinkers. Socrates, for instance, traveled in Egypt. Some sources even say that Socrates was initiated into some of the Egyptian mysteries. Obviously Socrates got some of his wisdom among the East's wise men.

I have often reflected upon the new vistas that reading opened to me. I knew right there in prison that reading had changed forever the course of my life. As I see it today, the ability to read awoke inside me some long dormant craving to be mentally alive. I certainly wasn't seeking any degree, the way a college confers a status symbol upon its students. My homemade education gave me, with every additional book that I read, a little bit more sensitivity to the deafness, dumbness, and blindness that was afflicting the black race in America. Not long ago, an English writer telephoned me from London, asking questions. One was, "What's your alma mater?" I told him, "Books." You will never catch me with a free fifteen minutes in which I'm not studying something I feel might be able to help the black man.

Yesterday I spoke in London, and both ways on the plane across the Atlantic I was studying a document about how the United Nations proposes to insure the human rights of the oppressed minorities of the world. The American black man is the world's most shameful case of minority oppression. What makes the black man think of himself as only an internal United States issue is just a catch-phrase, two words, "civil rights." How is the black man going to get "civil rights" before first he wins his *human* rights? If the American black man will start thinking about his *human* rights, and then start thinking of himself as part of one of the world's great peoples, he will see he has a case for the United Nations.

I can't think of a better case! Four hundred years of black blood and sweat invested here in America, and the white man still has the black man begging for what every immigrant fresh off the ship can take for granted the minute he walks down the gangplank.

But I'm digressing. I told the Englishman that my alma mater was books, a good library. Every time I catch a plane, I have with me a book that I want to read—and that's a lot of books these days. If I weren't out here every day battling the white man, I could spend the rest of my life reading, just satisfying my curiosity—because you can hardly mention anything I'm not curious about. I don't think anybody ever got more out of going to prison than I did. In fact, prison enabled me to study far more intensively than I would have if my life had gone differently and I had attended some college. I imagine that one of the biggest troubles with colleges is there are too many distractions, too much panty-raiding, fraternities, and boola-boola and all of that. Where else but in a prison could I have attacked my ignorance by being able to study intensely sometimes as much as fifteen hours a day?

Questions on Meaning

1. What inspired Malcolm X to continue his education independently? What was he trying to accomplish? How did he teach himself?
2. Explain why Malcolm X believed that white people were "devils."
3. Which philosophical concepts most appealed to Malcolm X? Cite evidence of his philosophical bent from his writing.

Questions on Rhetorical Strategy and Style:

1. Malcolm X employs a clear narrative style in this essay. Identify places in the essay where example, description, and persuasion are also used.
2. What does Malcolm X's narrative style reveal about his character and his motivations? If he were alive today, would you be drawn to him? Explain why he would or would not be a compelling figure.

Writing Assignments:

1. Research illiteracy in the United States along race, age, and income lines. Does this information surprise you? Identify some of the aspects of today's world that make it difficult for illiterate and uneducated persons to improve their lot. What programs could be implemented to help these people?
2. Malcolm X learned from his mentor, Elijah Muhammad, how history had been whitened. In the years since Malcolm X wrote this essay, many people, people of color and whites alike, have awakened to the deceit of history. As a result, Black Studies and other programs dedicated to nonwhite ethnic groups have emerged in academia. Have these programs successfully changed the roles assigned to people of color and whites by historians? Interview two or three instructors who teach history, and then write an essay on the state of whitened history today. Use examples from current teaching materials to support your arguments.
3. Unfortunately, white supremacy still exists in many areas. Research white supremacy activities in the United States today. Do these movements have more or fewer members now than during the 1960s? Describe how Malcolm X might address white supremacy organizations and such individuals today.

4. Try to appreciate the ignorance that Malcolm X felt when he was in prison, trying to communicate on various levels of intellect in his letters, with only an eighth grade education and street slang. Go to your library, select a narrowly focused, highly technical, scientific journal from a discipline that you have no familiarity with, and read an article. Then write an essay describing the hurdles you would face if you were asked to paraphrase that article—terminology, historical perspective, background, comparative topics, controversy, etc.

I Think, Therefore IM

Jennifer Lee

*Jennifer Lee (1976–) was born in New York City. She grad-
uated from Harvard University in 1999 with a degree in
mathematics and economics. While at Harvard she spent a
year at Beijing University on a fellowship studying international relations. Lee has received a scholarship from the
Asian American Journalism Association and has interned at*
The Boston Globe, The New York Times, Newsday, The
Wall Street Journal, *and* The Washington Post. *She joined
the staff of* The New York Times *in 2001 as a technology
reporter and began writing for the Metro section the next
year. The following selection on instant-messaging language
originally appeared in the* Times *in September 2002.*

1 **E**ach September Jacqueline Harding prepares a classroom presentation on the common writing mistakes she sees in her students'
work.

Ms. Harding, an eighth-grade English teacher at Viking Middle
School in Guernee, Ill., scribbles the words that have plagued generations of school children across her whiteboard:

There. Their. They're.
Your. You're.
To. Too. Two.
Its. It's.

This September, she has added a new list: u, r, ur, b4, wuz, cuz, 2.

When she asked her students how many of them used shortcuts
like them in their writing, Ms. Harding said, she was not surprised
when most of them raised their hands. This, after all, is their online

lingua franca: English adapted for the spitfire conversational style of Internet instant messaging.

Ms. Harding, who has seen such shortcuts creep into student papers over the last two years, said she gave her students a warning: "If I see this in your assignments, I will take points off."

"Kids should know the difference," said Ms. Harding, who decided to address this issue head-on this year. "They should know where to draw the line between formal writing and conversational writing."

As more and more teenagers socialize online, middle school and high school teachers like Ms. Harding are increasingly seeing a breezy form of Internet English jump from e-mail into schoolwork. To their dismay, teachers say that papers are being written with shortened words, improper capitalization and punctuation, and characters like &, $ and @.

Teachers have deducted points, drawn red circles and tsk-tsked at their classes. Yet the errant forms continue. "It stops being funny after you repeat yourself a couple of times," Ms. Harding said.

But teenagers, whose social life can rely as much these days on text communication as the spoken word, say that they use instant-messaging shorthand without thinking about it. They write to one another as much as they write in school, or more.

"You are so used to abbreviating things, you just start doing it unconsciously on schoolwork and reports and other things," said Eve Brecker, 15, a student at Montclair High School in New Jersey.

Ms. Brecker once handed in a midterm exam riddled with instant-messaging shorthand. "I had an hour to write an essay on *Romeo and Juliet,*" she said. "I just wanted to finish before my time was up. I was writing fast and carelessly. I spelled 'you' 'u.'" She got a C.

Even terms that cannot be expressed verbally are making their way into papers. Melanie Weaver was stunned by some of the term papers she received from a 10th-grade class she recently taught as part of an internship. "They would be trying to make a point in a paper, they would put a smiley face in the end," said Ms. Weaver, who teaches at Alvernia College in Reading, PA. "If they were presenting an argument and they needed to present an opposite view, they would put a frown."

As Trisha Fogarty, a sixth-grade teacher at Houlton Southside School in Houlton, Maine, puts it, today's students are "Generation Text."

Almost 60 percent of the online population under age 17 uses instant messaging, according to Nielsen/NetRatings. In addition to cellphone text messaging, Weblogs and e-mail, it has become a popular means of flirting, setting up dates, asking for help with homework and keeping in contact with distant friends. The abbreviations are a natural outgrowth of this rapid-fire style of communication.

"They have a social life that centers around typed communication," said Judith S. Donath, a professor at the Massachusetts Institute of Technology's Media Lab who has studied electronic communication. "They have a writing style that has been nurtured in a teenage social milieu."

15   Some teachers see the creeping abbreviations as part of a continuing assault of technology on formal written English. Others take it more lightly, saying that it is just part of the larger arc of language evolution.

"To them it's not wrong," said Ms. Harding, who is 28. "It's acceptable because it's in their culture. It's hard enough to teach them the art of formal writing. Now we've got to overcome this new instant-messaging language."

Ms. Harding noted that in some cases the shorthand isn't even shorter. "I understand 'cuz,' but what's with the 'wuz'? It's the same amount of letters as 'was,' so what's the point?" she said.

Deborah Bova, who teaches eighth-grade English at Raymond Park Middle School in Indianapolis, thought her eyesight was failing several years ago when she saw the sentence "B4 we perform, ppl have 2 practice" on a student assignment.

"I thought, 'My God, what is this?' " Ms. Bova said. "Have they lost their minds?"

20   The student was summoned to the board to translate the sentence into standard English: "Before we perform, people have to practice." She realized that the students thought she was out of touch. "It was like 'Get with it, Bova,' " she said. Ms. Bova had a student type up a reference list of translations for common instant-messaging expressions. She posted a copy on the bulletin board by her desk and took another one home to use while grading.

Students are sometimes unrepentant.

"They were astonished when I began to point these things out to them," said Henry Assetto, a social studies teacher at Twin Valley High School in Elverson, Pa. "Because I am a history teacher, they did not think a history teacher would be checking up on their grammar or their spelling," said Mr. Assetto, who has been teaching for 34 years.

But Montana Hodgen, 16, another Montclair student, said she was so accustomed to instant-messaging abbreviations that she often read right past them. She proofread a paper last year only to get it returned with the messaging abbreviations circled in red.

"I was so used to reading what my friends wrote to me on Instant Messenger that I didn't even realize that there was something wrong," she said. She said her ability to separate formal and informal English declined the more she used instant messages. "Three years ago, if I had seen that, I would have been 'What is that?'"

The spelling checker doesn't always help either, students say. For one, Microsoft Word's squiggly red spell-check lines don't appear beneath single letters and numbers such as u, r, c, 2 and 4. Nor do they catch words which have numbers in them such as "l8r" and "b4" by default.

Teenagers have essentially developed an unconscious "accent" in their typing, Professor Donath said. "They have gotten facile at typing and they are not paying attention."

Teenagers have long pushed the boundaries of spoken language, introducing words that then become passe with adult adoption. Now teenagers are taking charge and pushing the boundaries of written language. For them, expressions like "oic" (oh I see), "nm" (not much), "jk" (just kidding) and "lol" (laughing out loud), "brb" (be right back), "ttyl" (talk to you later) are as standard as conventional English.

"There is no official English language," said Jesse Sheidlower, the North American editor of the *Oxford English Dictionary*. "Language is spread not because anyone dictates any one thing to happen. The decisions are made by the language and the people who use the language."

Some teachers find the new writing style alarming. "First of all, it's very rude, and it's very careless," said Lois Moran, a middle school English teacher at St. Nicholas School in Jersey City.

"They should be careful to write properly and not to put these little codes in that they are in such a habit of writing to each other," said Ms. Moran, who has lectured her eighth-grade class on such mistakes.

Others say that the instant-messaging style might simply be a fad, something that students will grow out of. Or they see it as an opportunity to teach students about the evolution of language.

"I turn it into a very positive teachable moment for kids in the class," said Erika V. Karres, an assistant professor at the University of North Carolina at Chapel Hill who trains student teachers. She shows students how English has evolved since Shakespeare's time. "Imagine Langston Hughes's writing in quick texting instead of 'Langston writing,' " she said. "It makes teaching and learning so exciting."

Other teachers encourage students to use messaging shorthand to spark their thinking processes. "When my children are writing first drafts, I don't care how they spell anything, as long as they are writing," said Ms. Fogarty, the sixth-grade teacher from Houlton, Maine. "If this lingo gets their thoughts and ideas onto paper quicker, the more power to them." But during editing and revising, she expects her students to switch to standard English.

Ms. Bova shares the view that instant-messaging language can help free up their creativity. With the help of students, she does not even need the cheat sheet to read the shorthand anymore.

35   "I think it's a plus," she said. "And I would say that with a + sign."   35

Questions on Meaning

1. What are the social and technological conditions that have shaped cyberlingo vocabulary and its uses?
2. What does the term "lingua franca" mean? How does it capture the full significance of the text messaging style of young people?
3. Why, in your opinion, are adults frequently appalled when students use an informal or unconventional style in their writing?

Questions on Rhetorical Strategy and Style

1. Why does Lee open her article with the words Ms. Harding puts on the board each September? What is she trying to suggest to her readers?
2. How does the article adhere to the conventions of the newspaper journalism? Does the writer remain balanced and objective? Explain how.
3. Why does the writer quote the editor of the *Oxford English Dictionary?*

Writing Assignments

1. Why do teachers often seem fussy, and even offended, by their students' use of language? Why are they so insistent about the conventions of standard, edited English? Write an essay that explains to your teachers your experience trying to learn these conventions, and why your language is necessary to your sense of identity.
2. Try the exercise used by Erika Karres, the teacher at the University of North Carolina. Take a poem or any piece of writing and translate it into a quick text version. How does the meaning of it change?

Rights and Responsibilities

The Declaration of Independence

Thomas Jefferson

Thomas Jefferson (1743–1826) was born in Virginia in a well-to-do land-owning family. He graduated from the College of William and Mary and then studied law. When he was elected at age 26 to the Virginia legislature, he had already begun forming his revolutionary views. As a delegate to the Second Continental Congress in 1775, he was the principal writer of the Declaration of Independence, which was adopted on July 4, 1776. After the Revolution he was Governor of Virginia from 1775 to 1777. From then until 1801, when he was elected the third President of the United States, Jefferson served in various federal positions, including secretary of state and ambassador to France. Jefferson was influential as an advocate of democracy in the early years of the United States, although his ideas were more typical of the eighteenth century "enlightened man" than original. The Declaration of Independence shows his ideas and style as well as those of the times and remains not merely an important historical document but also an eloquent statement of the founding principles of this country.

1   When in the course of human events, it becomes necessary for one people to dissolve the political bands which have connected them with another, and to assume among the powers of the earth, the separate and equal station to which the Laws of Nature and of Nature's God entitle them, a decent respect to the opinions of mankind requires that they should declare the causes which impel them to the separation.

We hold these truths to be self-evident, that all men are created equal, that they are endowed by their Creator with certain inalienable rights, that among these are life, liberty, and the pursuit of happiness. That to secure these rights, governments are instituted among men, deriving their just powers from the consent of the governed. That whenever any form of government becomes destructive of these ends, it is the right of the people to alter or to abolish it, and to institute new government, laying its foundation on such principles and organizing its powers in such form, as to them shall seem most likely to effect their safety and happiness. Prudence, indeed, will dictate that governments long established should not be changed for light and transient causes; and accordingly all experience hath shown, that mankind are more disposed to suffer, while evils are sufferable, than to right themselves by abolishing the forms to which they are accustomed. But when a long train of abuses and usurpations, pursuing invariably the same object, evinces a design to reduce them under absolute despotism, it is their right, it is their duty, to throw off such government, and to provide new guards for their future security. Such has been the patient sufferance of these Colonies; and such is now the necessity which constrains them to alter their former systems of government. The history of the present King of Great Britain is a history of repeated injuries and usurpations, all having in direct object the establishment of an absolute tyranny over these States. To prove this, let facts be submitted to a candid world.

He has refused his assent to laws, the most wholesome and necessary for the public good.

He has forbidden his Governors to pass laws of immediate and pressing importance, unless suspended in their operation till his assent should be obtained; and when so suspended, he has utterly neglected to attend to them.

5 He has refused to pass other laws for the accommodation of large 5 districts of people, unless those people would relinquish the right of representation in the legislature, a right inestimable to them and formidable to tyrants only.

He has called together legislative bodies at places unusual, uncomfortable, and distant from the depository of their public records, for the sole purpose of fatiguing them into compliance with his measures.

He has dissolved representative houses repeatedly, for opposing with manly firmness his invasions on the rights of the people.

He has refused for a long time, after such dissolutions, to cause others to be elected; whereby the legislative powers, incapable of annihilation, have returned to the people at large for their exercise; the State remaining in the meantime exposed to all the dangers of invasion from without and convulsions within.

He has endeavoured to prevent the population of these states; for that purpose obstructing the laws for naturalization of foreigners; refusing to pass others to encourage their migration hither, and raising the conditions of new appropriations of lands.

10   He has obstructed the administration of justice, by refusing his assent to laws for establishing judiciary powers.

He has made judges dependent on his will alone, for the tenure of their offices, and the amount and payment of their salaries.

He has erected a multitude of new offices, and sent hither swarms of officers to harass our people, and eat out their substance.

He has kept among us, in times of peace, standing armies without the consent of our legislatures.

He has affected to render the military independent of and superior to the civil power.

15   He has combined with others to subject us to a jurisdiction foreign of our constitution, and unacknowledged by our laws; giving his assent to their acts of pretended legislation:

For quartering large bodies of armed troops among us:

For protecting them, by a mock trial, from punishment for any murders which they should commit on the inhabitants of these States:

For cutting off our trade with all parts of the world:

For imposing taxes on us without our consent:

20   For depriving us in many cases of the benefits of trial by jury:

For transporting us beyond seas to be tried for pretended offences:

For abolishing the free system of English laws in a neighbouring Province, establishing therein an arbitrary government, and enlarging its boundaries so as to render it at once an example and fit instrument for introducing the same absolute rule into these Colonies:

For taking away our Charters, abolishing our most valuable laws, and altering fundamentally the forms of our governments:

For suspending our own legislatures, and declaring themselves invested with power to legislate for us in all cases whatsoever.

25   He has abdicated government here, by declaring us out of his protection and waging war against us.

He has plundered our seas, ravaged our coasts, burnt our towns, and destroyed the lives of our people.

He is at this time transporting large armies of foreign mercenaries to complete the works of death, desolation, and tyranny, already begun with circumstances of cruelty and perfidy scarcely paralleled in the most barbarous ages, and totally unworthy the head of a civilized nation.

He has constrained our fellow citizens taken captive on the high seas to bear arms against their country, to become the executioners of their friends and brethren, or to fall themselves by their hands.

He has excited domestic insurrections amongst us, and has endeavoured to bring on the inhabitants of our frontiers, the merciless Indian savages, whose known rule of warfare, is an undistinguished destruction of all ages, sexes, and conditions.

30   In every stage of these oppressions we have petitioned for redress   30
in the most humble terms: our repeated petitions have been answered only by repeated injury. A prince whose character is thus marked by every act which may define a tyrant is unfit to be the ruler of a free people.

Nor have we been wanting in attention to our British brethren. We have warned them from time to time of attempts by their legislature to extend an unwarrantable jurisdiction over us. We have reminded them of the circumstances of our emigration and settlement here. We have appealed to their native justice and magnanimity, and we have conjured them by the ties of our common kindred to disavow these usurpations, which would inevitably interrupt our connections and correspondence. They too have been deaf to the voice of justice and of consanguinity. We must, therefore, acquiesce in the necessity, which denounces our separation, and hold them, as we hold the rest of mankind, enemies in war, in peace friends.

We, therefore, the Representatives of the United States of America, in General Congress assembled, appealing to the Supreme Judge of the world for the rectitude of our intentions, do, in the name, and by authority of the good people of these Colonies, solemnly publish and declare, That these United Colonies are, and of right ought to be, Free and Independent States; that they are absolved from all allegiance to the British Crown, and that all political connection between them and the state of Great Britain, is and ought to be totally dissolved; and that as Free and Independent States, they have full power to levy war, conclude peace, contract alliances, establish commerce, and to do all other acts and things which Independent States may of right do. And for the support of this declaration, with a firm reliance on the protection of Divine Providence, we mutually pledge to each other our lives, our fortunes, and our sacred honor.

Questions on Meaning

1. Most readers will recall the historical purpose of the Declaration of Independence, but unless you've had cause to read it in recent years you've probably forgotten much of its substance. As you just read it, what feelings did it evoke? What aspects had you forgotten? What is your impression of it now as a work of literature rather than as a historical document?
2. To whom is the Declaration of Independence addressed? What leads you to that conclusion?
3. Explain in your own words Jefferson's justification for democratic government.

Questions on Rhetorical Strategy and Style

1. The Declaration frequently uses dramatic language such as "sent hither swarms of officers to harass our people" and "plundered our seas, ravaged our coasts, burnt our towns, and destroyed the lives of our people." Find several other examples of similar powerful language. What is the purpose of such language in this document?
2. Note that the part of the Declaration that enumerates the long list of "facts . . . submitted to a candid world" comprises the greatest part of its length. Why is that?
3. Jefferson uses the rhetorical strategy of persuasion, to craft the Declaration. Identify at least two aspects of persuasion in this writing and explain their effect.

Writing Assignments

1. "Pursuit of happiness" is a phrase much used in the two centuries since it was written. Think about what that phrase implies about a government's power over people. Write an essay in which you define the right to pursue happiness in the modern world. Make sure you clarify with examples both what that right should guarantee and what it should not guarantee.
2. If the Colonies were justified in declaring their independence from what they saw as an oppressive England, were the Southern states also justified in declaring their independence when they seceded from the Union (thus beginning the Civil War)? Do some basic research if necessary to understand both situations, and then write an essay building your argument by comparing and contrasting these two situations.

The Gettysburg Address

Abraham Lincoln

Abraham Lincoln (1809–1865) was the sixteenth president of the United States. He was born in a log cabin in Kentucky and grew up in Indiana and Illinois. At the age of 26 he entered the Illinois state legislature and 12 years later was elected to the U.S. House of Representatives. Through the 1850s he increasingly became a spokesman for the antislavery cause, resulting in his nomination for President in 1860. Soon after becoming president, Southern states seceded and formed the Confederacy, precipitating the Civil War as the Union attempted to maintain the United States as one nation. In 1862 Lincoln delivered the "Emancipation Proclamation," which focused the Civil War on the issue of slavery. He delivered the Gettysburg Address in 1863 to dedicate a cemetery in Pennsylvania for soldiers who had died there in battle. Shortly after the end of the Civil War in 1865, Lincoln was assassinated by John Wilkes Booth, a Southern fanatic. "The Gettysburg Address" is Lincoln's best-known writing, combining his simple, homespun, yet eloquent language with a statesmen's oratory and his own moral vision.

1   Four score and seven years ago our fathers brought forth on this continent, a new nation, conceived in Liberty, and dedicated to the proposition that all men are created equal.

Now we are engaged in a great civil war, testing whether that nation, or any nation so conceived and so dedicated, can long endure. We are met on a great battlefield of that war. We have come to dedicate a portion of that field, as a final resting place for those who here gave their lives that that nation might live. It is altogether fitting and proper that we should do this.

But, in a larger sense, we can not dedicate—we can not consecrate—we can not hallow—this ground. The brave men, living and dead, who struggled here, have consecrated it, far above our poor power to add or detract. The world will little note nor long remember what we say here, but it can never forget what they did here. It is for us the living, rather, to be dedicated here to the unfinished work which they who fought here have thus far so nobly advanced. It is rather for us to be here dedicated to the great task remaining before us—that from these honored dead we take increased devotion to that cause for which they gave the last full measure of devotion—that we here highly resolve that these dead shall not have died in vain—that this nation, under God, shall have a new birth of freedom—and that government of the people, by the people, for the people, shall not perish from the earth.

Questions on Meaning

1. What exactly do you think Lincoln means by the phrase "created equal"?
2. What is the "new birth of freedom" referred to at the end of the Address?

Questions on Rhetorical Strategy and Style

1. Note how many times Lincoln uses the word "dedicate." What is the effect of this repetition? Comment on the shift in meaning from dedicating the cemetery to dedicating ourselves to "the great task remaining."
2. How would you describe the tone and style of phrases such as "Four score and seven years ago," "brought forth on this continent," and "of the people, by the people, for the people"?
3. Read the "Address" aloud. What characteristics do you discover that suggest it was in fact written originally to be spoken aloud?

Writing Assignments

1. What relevance does "The Gettysburg Address" still have for us today?
2. The rhetorical strategy of definition is used in "The Gettysburg Address" to explore the concepts of freedom and equality for the nation as a whole. Choose a different abstract term, either positive or negative, that you think characterizes some aspect of modern American society, and write a brief essay using definition and description to explore that concept.

Brown et al. *v.* Board of Education of Topeka et al.

Earl Warren

Earl Warren (1891–1974), the fourteenth Chief Justice of the United States Supreme Court, was born in Los Angeles and grew up in the town of Bakersfield, California. Interested in criminal law since childhood, Warren earned a J.D. degree from the School of Jurisprudence at the University of California at Berkeley in 1914. He entered government service six years later, after a brief period in private practice in the San Francisco Bay area. A moderate republican, Warren used his success as district attorney for Alameda County to win the governorship of California in 1942, a post he held until 1950. His single foray into national politics occurred when he became John Dewey's running mate in the 1948 presidential election. Harry Truman won that race by a narrow margin.

Warren was appointed Chief Justice by President Dwight D. Eisenhower in 1953. For the next 16 years, he presided over what has come to be known as one of the most liberal, activist courts in U.S. history. He issued his opinion on Brown v. the Board of Education of Topeka, Kansas *only after lengthy deliberations in which he used his diplomatic skills to build consensus within the previously divided Court. Scholars agree that the* Brown *decision would not have had nearly as much impact on the burgeoning Civil Rights movement had it not been unanimous. The wording of the opinion itself, below,*

"Brown et al *v.* Board of Education of Topeka et al." by Earl Warren, *347 U.S. 483,* May 17, 1954.

reveals Warren's ability to reason carefully and convincingly.

These cases come to us from the states of Kansas, South Carolina, Virginia, and Delaware. They are premised on different facts and different local conditions, but a common legal question justifies their consideration together in this consolidated opinion.[1]

In each of the cases, minors of the Negro race, through their legal representatives, seek the aid of the courts in obtaining admission to the public schools of their community on a nonsegregated basis. In each instance, they had been denied admission to schools attended by white children under laws requiring or permitting segregation according to race. This segregation was alleged to deprive the plaintiffs of the equal protection of the laws under the Fourteenth Amendment. In each of the cases other than the Delaware case, a three-judge federal District Court denied relief to the plaintiffs on the so-called "separate but equal" doctrine announced by this Court in *Plessy* v. *Ferguson*, 163 U.S. 537. Under that doctrine, equality of treatment is accorded when the races are provided substantially equal facilities, even though these facilities be separate. In the Delaware case, the Supreme Court of Delaware adhered to that doctrine, but ordered that the plaintiffs be admitted to the white schools because of their superiority to the Negro schools.

The plaintiffs contend that segregated public schools are not "equal" and cannot be made "equal," and that hence they are deprived of the equal protection of the laws. Because of the obvious importance of the question presented, the Court took jurisdiction.[2] Argument was heard in the 1952 Term, and reargument was heard this Term on certain questions propounded by the Court.[3]

Reargument was largely devoted to the circumstances surrounding the adoption of the Fourteenth Amendment in 1868. It covered exhaustively consideration of the amendment in Congress, ratification by the states, then-existing practices in racial segregation, and the views of proponents and opponents of the amendment. This discussion and our own investigation convince us that, although these sources cast some light, it is not enough to resolve the problem with which we are faced. At best, they are inconclusive. The most avid proponents of the postwar amendments undoubtedly intended them to remove all legal distinctions among "all persons born or naturalized in the United States." Their opponents, just as certainly, were antagonistic to both the letter and the spirit of the amendments and wished them to have the most limited effect. What others in Congress and the state legislatures had in mind cannot be determined with any degree of certainty.

An additional reason for the inconclusive nature of the amendment's history, with respect to segregated schools, is the status of public education at that time.[4] In the South, the movement toward free common schools, supported by general taxation, had not yet taken hold. Education of white children was largely in the hands of private groups. Education of Negroes was almost nonexistent, and practically all of the race were illiterate. In fact, any education of Negroes was forbidden by law in some states. Today, in contrast, many Negroes have achieved outstanding success in the arts and sciences as well as in the business and professional world. It is true that public-school education at the time of the amendment had advanced further in the North, but the effect of the amendment on Northern states was generally ignored in the congressional debates.

Even in the North, the conditions of public education did not approximate those existing today. The curriculum was usually rudimentary; ungraded schools were common in rural areas; the school term was but three months a year in many states; and compulsory school attendance was virtually unknown. As a consequence, it is not surprising that there should be so little in the history of the Fourteenth Amendment relating to its intended effect on public education.

In the first cases in this Court construing the Fourteenth Amendment, decided shortly after its adoption, the Court interpreted it as proscribing all state-imposed discriminations against the Negro race.[5] The doctrine of "separate but equal" did not make its appearance in this Court until 1896 in the case of *Plessy* v. *Ferguson, supra,* involving not education but transportation.[6] American courts have since labored with the doctrine for over half a century.

In this Court there have been six cases involving the "separate but equal" doctrine in the field of public education.[7] In *Cumming* v. *County Board of Education*, 175 U.S. 528, and *Gong Lum* v. *Rice*, 275

U. S. 78, the validity of the doctrine itself was not challenged.[8] In more recent cases, all on the graduate-school level, inequality was found in that specific benefits enjoyed by white students were denied to Negro students of the same educational qualifications. *Missouri ex rel. Gaines* v. *Canada,* 305 U. S. 337; *Sipuel* v. *Oklahoma,* 332 U. S. 631; *Sweatt* v. *Painter,* 339 U. S. 629; *McLaurin* v. *Oklahoma State Regents,* 339 U. S. 637. In none of these cases was it necessary to reexamine the doctrine to grant relief to the Negro plaintiff. And in *Sweatt* v. *Painter, supra,* the Court expressly reserved decision on the question whether *Plessy* v. *Ferguson* should be held inapplicable to public education.

In the instant cases, that question is directly presented. Here, unlike *Sweatt* v. *Painter,* there are findings below that the Negro and white schools involved have been equalized, or are being equalized, with respect to buildings, curricula, qualifications and salaries of teachers, and other "tangible" factors.[9] Our decision, therefore, cannot turn on merely a comparison of these tangible factors in the Negro and white schools involved in each of the cases. We must look instead to the effect of segregation itself on public education.

10   In approaching this problem, we cannot turn the clock back to   10 1868 when the amendment was adopted, or even to 1896 when *Plessy* v. *Ferguson* was written. We must consider public education in the light of its full development and its present place in American life throughout the nation. Only in this way can it be determined if segregation in public schools deprives these plaintiffs of the equal protection of the laws.

Today, education is perhaps the most important function of state and local governments. Compulsory school-attendance laws and the great expenditures for education both demonstrate our recognition of the importance of education to our democratic society. It is required in the performance of our most basic public responsibilities, even service in the armed forces. It is the very foundation of good citizenship. Today it is a principal instrument in awakening the child to cultural values, in preparing him for later professional training, and in helping him to adjust normally to his environment. In these days, it is doubtful that any child may reasonably be expected to succeed in life if he is denied the opportunity of an education. Such an opportunity, where the state has undertaken to provide it, is a right which must be made available to all on equal terms.

We come then to the question presented: Does segregation of children in public schools solely on the basis of race, even though the physical facilities and other "tangible" factors may be equal, deprive the children of the minority group of equal educational opportunities? We believe that it does.

In *Sweatt* v. *Painter, supra,* in finding that a segregated law school for Negroes could not provide them equal educational opportunities, this Court relied in large part on "those qualities which are incapable of objective measurement but which make for greatness in a law school." In *McLaurin* v. *Oklahoma State Regents, supra,* the Court, in requiring that a Negro admitted to a white graduate school be treated like all other students, again resorted to intangible considerations: ". . . his ability to study, to engage in discussions and exchange views with other students, and, in general, to learn his profession." Such considerations apply with added force to children in grade and high schools. To separate them from others of similar age and qualifications solely because of their race generates a feeling of inferiority as to their status in the community that may affect their hearts and minds in a way unlikely ever to be undone. The effect of this separation on their educational opportunities was well stated by a finding in the Kansas case by a court which nevertheless felt compelled to rule against the Negro plaintiffs:

> Segregation of white and colored children in public schools has a detrimental effect upon the colored children. The impact is greater when it has the sanction of the law; for the policy of separating the races is usually interpreted as denoting the inferiority of the Negro group. A sense of inferiority affects the motivation of a child to learn. Segregation with the sanction of law therefore, has a tendency to [retard] the educational and mental development of Negro children and to deprive them of some of the benefits they would receive in a racial[ly] integrated school system.[10]

Whatever may have been the extent of psychological knowledge at the time of *Plessy* v. *Ferguson,* this finding is amply supported by modern authority.[11] Any language in *Plessy* v. *Ferguson* contrary to this finding is rejected.

We conclude that in the field of public education the doctrine of "separate but equal" has no place. Separate educational facilities are inherently unequal. Therefore, we hold that the plaintiffs and others similarly situated for whom the actions have been brought are, by reason of the segregation complained of, deprived of the equal protection of the laws guaranteed by the Fourteenth Amendment. This disposition makes unnecessary any discussion whether such segregation also violates the due process clause of the Fourteenth Amendment.[12]

Because these are class actions, because of the wide applicability of this decision, and because of the great variety of local conditions, the formulation of decrees in these cases presents problems of considerable complexity. On reargument, the consideration of appropriate relief was necessarily subordinated to the primary question—the constitutionality of segregation in public education. We have now announced that such segregation is a denial of the equal protection of the laws. In order that we may have the full assistance of the parties in formulating decrees, the cases will be restored to the docket, and the parties are requested to present further argument on Questions 4 and 5 previously propounded by the Court for the reargument this Term.[13] The attorney general of the United States is again invited to participate. The attorneys general of the states requiring or permitting segregation in public education will also be permitted to appear as *amici curiae* upon request to do so by Sept. 15, 1954, and submission of briefs by Oct. 1, 1954.[14]

Endnotes

1. In the Kansas case, *Brown* v. *Board of Education*, the plaintiffs are Negro children of elementary-school age residing in Topeka. They brought this action in the United States District Court for the District of Kansas to enjoin enforcement of a Kansas statute which permits, but does not require, cities of more than 15,000 population to maintain separate school facilities for Negro and white students. Kan. Gen. Stat. Sec. 72-1724 (1949). Pursuant to that authority, the Topeka Board of Education elected to establish segregated elementary schools. Other public schools in the community, however, are operated on a nonsegregated basis. The three-judge District Court, convened under 28 U.S.C. Sec. 2281 and 2284, found that segregation in public education has a detrimental effect upon Negro children, but denied relief on the ground that the Negro and white schools were substantially equal with respect to buildings, transportation, curricula, and educational qualifications of teachers. 98 F. Supp. 797. The case is here on direct appeal under 28 U.S.C. Sec. 1253.

In the South Carolina case, *Briggs* v. *Elliott,* the plaintiffs are Negro children of both elementary and high-school age residing in Clarendon County. They brought this action in the United Stares District Court for the Eastern District of South Carolina to enjoin enforcement of provisions in the state constitution and statutory code which require the segregation of Negroes and whites in public schools. S.C. Const., Art. XI, Sec. 7; S.C. Code Sec. 5377 (1942). The three-judge District Court, convened tinder 28 U.S.C. Sec. 2281 and 2284, denied the requested relief. The court found that the Negro schools were inferior to the white schools and ordered the defendants to begin immediately to equalize the facilities. But the court sustained the validity of the contested provisions and denied the plaintiffs admission to the white schools during in the equalization program. 98 F. Supp. 529. This Court vacated the District Court's judgment and remanded the case for the purpose of obtaining the court's views on a report filed by the defendants concerning the progress made in the equalization program. 342 U.S. 350. On remand, the District Court found that substantial equality had been achieved except for buildings and that the defendants were proceeding to rectify this inequality as well. 103 F. Supp. 920. The case is again here on direct appeal under 28 U.S.C. Sec. 1253.

In the Virginia case, *Davis* v. *County School Board,* the plaintiffs are Negro children of high-school age residing in Prince Edward County. They brought this action in the United States District Court for the Eastern District of Virginia to enjoin enforcement of provisions in the state constitution and statutory code which require the segregation of Negroes and whites in public schools. Va. Const., Sec. 140; Va. Code Sec. 22–221 (1950). The three-judge District Court, convened under 28 U.S.C. Sec. 2281 and 2284, denied the requested relief. The court found the Negro school inferior in physical plant, curricula, and transportation, and ordered the defendants forthwith to provide substantially equal curricula and transportation and to "proceed with all reasonable diligence and dispatch to remove" the inequality in physical plant. But, as in the South Carolina case, the court sustained the validity of the contested provisions and denied the plaintiffs admission to the white schools during the equalization program. 103 F. Supp. 337. The case is here on direct appeal under 28 U.S.C. Sec. 1253.

In the Delaware case, *Gebhart* v. *Belton,* the plaintiffs are Negro children of both elementary and high-school age residing in New Castle County. They brought this action in the Delaware Court of Chancery to enjoin enforcement of provisions in the state constitution and statutory code which require the segregation of Negroes and whites in public schools. Del. Const., Art X, Sec. 2; Del. Rev. Code Sec. 2631 (1935). The chancellor gave judgment for the plaintiffs and ordered their immediate admission to schools previously attended only by white children on the ground that the Negro schools were inferior with respect to teacher training, pupil-teacher ratio, extracurricular activities, physical plant, and time and distance involved in travel. 87 A. 2d 862. The chancellor also found that segregation itself results in an inferior education for Negro children (see note 10, *infra*), but did not rest his decision on that ground. *Id.,* at 865. The chancellor's decree was affirmed by the Supreme Court of Delaware, which intimated, however, that the defendants might be able to obtain a modification of the decree after equalization of the Negro and white schools had been accomplished. 91 A. 2nd 137, 152. The defendants, contending only that the Delaware courts had erred in ordering the immediate admission of the Negro plaintiffs to the white schools, applied to this Court for certiorari. The writ was granted, 344 U.S. 891. The plaintiffs, who were successful below, did not submit a cross-petition.

2. 344 U.S. 1, 141, 891.

3. 345 U.S. 972. The attorney general of the United States participated both Terms as *amicus curiae.*

4. For a general study of the development of public education prior to the amendment, see Butts and Cremin, *A History of Education in American Culture* (1953), Pts. 1, 11; Cubberley, *Public Education in the United States* (1934 ed.), cc. II–XII. School practices current at the time of the adoption of the Fourteenth Amendment are described in Butts and Cremin, *supra,* at 269–275; Cubberley, *supra,* at 288–339, 408–431; Knight, *Public Education in the South* (1922), cc. VIII, IX. See also H. Ex. Doc. No. 315, 41st Cong., 2nd Sess. (1871). Although the demand for free public schools followed substantially the same pattern in both the North and the South, the development in the South did not begin to gain momentum until about 1850, some twenty years after that in the North. The reasons for the somewhat slower development in the South (*e.g.,* the rural character of the South and the different regional attitudes toward state assistance) are well explained in Cubberley, *supra,* at 408–423, In the country as a whole, but particularly in the South, the war virtually stopped all progress in public education. *Id.,* at 427–428. The low status of Negro education in all sections of the country, both before and immediately after the war, is described in Beale, *A History of Freedom of Teaching in American Schools* (1941), 112–132, 175–195. Compulsory school-attendance laws were not generally adopted until after the ratification of the Fourteenth Amendment, and it was not until 1918 that such laws were in force in all the states. Cubberley, *supra,* at 563–565.

5. *Slaughter-House Cases,* 16 Wall. 36, 67–72 (1873); *Strauder* v. *West Virginia,* 100 U. S. 303, 307–308 (1880): "It ordains that no state shall deprive any person of life, liberty, or property, without due process of law, or

deny to any person within its jurisdiction the equal protection of the laws. What is this but declaring that the law in the states shall be the same for the black as for the white; that all persons, whether colored or white, shall stand equal before the laws of the states, and, in regard to the colored race, for whose protection the amendment was primarily designed, that no discrimination shall be made against them by law because of their color? The words of the amendment, it is true, are prohibitory, but they contain a necessary implication of a positive immunity, or right, most valuable to the colored race—the right to exemption from unfriendly legislation against them distinctively as colored—exemption from legal discriminations, implying inferiority in civil society, lessening the security of their enjoyment of the rights which others enjoy, and discriminations which are steps toward reducing them to the condition of a subject race." See also *Virginia* v. *Rives*, 100 U.S. 313, 318 (1880); *Ex parte Virginia*, 100 U.S. 339, 344–345 (1880).

6. The doctrine apparently originated in *Roberts* v. *City of Boston*, 59 Mass. 198, 206 (1850), upholding school segregation against attack as being violative of a state constitutional guarantee of equality. Segregation in Boston public schools was eliminated in 1855. Mass. Acts 1855, c. 256. But elsewhere in the North, segregation in public education has persisted in some communities until recent years. It is apparent that such segregation has long been nationwide problem, not merely one of sectional concern.

7. See also *Berta College* v. *Kentucky*, 211 U.S. 45 (1908).

8. In the *Cumming* case, Negro taxpayers sought an injunction requiring the defendant school board to discontinue the operation of a high school for white children until the board resumed operation of a high school for Negro children. Similarly, in the *Gong Lum* case, the plaintiff, a child of Chinese descent, contended only that state authorities had misapplied the doctrine by classifying him with Negro children and requiring him to attend a Negro school.

9. In the Kansas case, the court below found substantial equality as to all such factors. 98 F. Supp. 797, 798. In the South Carolina case, the court below found that the defendants were proceeding "promptly and in good faith to comply with the court's decree." 103 F. Supp. 920, 921. In the Virginia case, the court below noted that the equalization program was already "afoot and progressing" (103 F. Supp. 337, 341); since then, we have been advised, in the Virginia attorney general's brief on reargument, that the program has now been completed. In the Delaware case, the court below similarly noted that the state's equalization program was well under way. 91 A. 2d 137, 149.

10. A similar finding was made in the Delaware case: "I conclude from the testimony that, in our Delaware society, state-imposed segregation in education itself results in the Negro children, as a class, receiving educational opportunities which are substantially inferior to those available to white children otherwise similarly situated." 87 A. 2d 862, 865,

11. K. B. Clark, *Effect of Prejudice and Discrimination on Personality Development* (Midcentury White House Conference on Children and Youth, 1950); Witmer and Kotinsky, *Personality in the Making* (1952), c. VI; Deutscher and Chein, "The Psychological Effects of Enforced Segregation: A Survey of Social Science Opinion," *26 J. Psychol.* 259 (1948); Chein, "What are the Psychological Effects of Segregation Under Conditions of Equal Facilities?" 3 *Int. J. Opinion and Attitude Res.* 229 (1949); Brameld, *Educational Costs, in Discrimination and National Welfare* (MacIver, ed., 1949), 44–48; Frazier, *The Negro in the United States* (1949), 674–681. And see generally Myrdal, *An American Dilemma* (1944).

12. See *Bolling* v. *Sharpe, post,* p. 497, concerning the due process clause of the Fifth Amendment.

13. "4. Assuming it is decided that segregation in public Schools violates the Fourteenth Amendment

"*(a)* would a decree necessarily follow providing that, within the limits set by normal geographic school districting, Negro children should forthwith be admitted to schools of their choice, or

"*(b)* may this Court, in the exercise of its equity powers, permit an effective gradual adjustment to be brought about from existing segregated systems to a system not based on color distinctions?

"5. On the assumption on which questions 4 *(a)* and *(b)* are based, and assuming further that this Court will exercise its equity powers to the end described in question 4 *(b)*,

"*(a)* should this Court formulate detailed decrees in these cases;

"*(b)* if so, what specific issues should the decrees reach;

"*(c)* should this Court appoint a special master to hear evidence with a view to recommending specific terms for such decrees;

"*(d)* should this Court remand to the courts of first instance with directions to frame decrees in these cases, and if so what general directions should the decrees of this Court include and what procedures should the courts of first instance follow in arriving at the specific terms of more detailed decrees?"

14. See Rule 42, Revised Rules of this Court (effective July 1, 1954).

Questions on Meaning

1. According to the Court, why was it impossible to speculate as to whether the Fourteenth Amendment (granting equal protection of the law to African-Americans) was intended to apply to public education?
2. In your own words, explain the Court's reasoning with regard to the relevance of *Plessy* v. *Ferguson* (1896) to this case. Do you agree with the Court's assessment of the importance of education? Why or why not?
3. According to the Court, why was separation "inherently un-equal"? On what basis did the Court come to this conclusion?

Questions on Rhetorical Strategy and Style

1. Effective persuasion often depends on appeals to precedent and authority. Choose an example of each from this document and ex-plain its significance to the Court's decision.
2. The decision that there was a cause-and-effect relationship be-tween segregated schools and black students' academic success. How did the Court demonstrate that relationship? How signifi-cant was the establishment of this relationship to the Court's conclusions?
3. On what basis did the Court compare its decision to the Four-teenth Amendment and the *Plessy* v. *Ferguson* case? How impor-tant were these distinctions to the *Brown* decision?

Writing Assignments

1. Write a summary of the *Brown* v. *Board of Education* decision. In it, explain the case's key features to the average citizen.
2. Research the *Plessy* v. *Ferguson* decision, and write a paper com-paring it to *Brown*. Focus on the ways in which each case reflected the period in which it was heard.
3. The *Brown* case stimulated debate throughout the second half of the twentieth century. Look up one of the controversies resulting from the case—for example, the integration of Central High School in Little Rock, Arkansas; the school busing crisis in

Boston; the *Bakke* reverse discrimination case against the University of California at Berkeley; or affirmative action in education. Write a paper highlighting the central issues involved in the controversy.

The Perils of Indifference

Elie Wiesel

Elie Wiesel (1928–) was born in the village of Sighet in Romania to a religious Jewish family. In 1944 his life changed when his family was deported by the Nazis to Auschwitz, where his father died in 1945. After the camp was liberated by the Allied forces, Wiesel spent a few years in a French orphanage. In 1948 he entered the Sorbonne and began writing for the newspaper L'arche. *In 1954 he made the decision to write about the Holocaust, which led to the publication of his first book,* Night *(1958), followed by* Jews of Silence *(1966). In 1963 he became a U.S. citizen. In 1978 he was appointed chair of the Presidential Commission on the Holocaust, which led to the American memorial monument to the victims of Nazi oppression during World War II. In 1985 Wiesel received the Congressional Gold Medal of Achievement. The following year he received the Nobel Peace Prize. He has written numerous books dealing with the Holocaust, hatred, racism, genocide, and faith, including* Sages and Dreamers *(1991), and his memoir* All Rivers Run to the Sea *(1995). In the following speech he addresses Congress and the President about the need for vigilance in the face of evil.*

1   Mr. President, Mrs. Clinton, members of Congress, Ambassador Holbrooke, Excellencies, friends:

Fifty-four years ago to the day, a young Jewish boy from a small town in the Carpathian Mountains woke up, not far from Goethe's beloved Weimar, in a place of eternal infamy called Buchenwald. He was finally free, but there was no joy in his heart. He thought there never would be again. Liberated a day earlier by American soldiers, he remembers their rage at what they saw. And even if he lives to be a very old man, he will always be grateful to them for that rage, and also for their compassion. Though he did not understand their language, their eyes told him what he needed to know—that they, too, would remember, and bear witness.

And now, I stand before you, Mr. President—Commander-in-Chief of the army that freed me, and tens of thousands of others—and I am filled with a profound and abiding gratitude to the American people. Gratitude is a word that I cherish. Gratitude is what defines the humanity of the human being. And I am grateful to you, Hillary, or Mrs. Clinton, for what you said, and for what you are doing for children in the world, for the homeless, for the victims of injustice, the victims of destiny and society. And I thank all of you for being here.

We are on the threshold of a new century, a new millennium. What will the legacy of this vanishing century be? How will it be remembered in the new millennium? Surely it will be judged, and judged severely, in both moral and metaphysical terms. These failures have cast a dark shadow over humanity: two World Wars, countless civil wars, the senseless chain of assassinations (Gandhi, the Kennedys, Martin Luther King, Sadat, Rabin), bloodbaths in Cambodia and Nigeria, India and Pakistan, Ireland and Rwanda, Eritrea and Ethiopia, Sarajevo and Kosovo; the inhumanity in the gulag and the tragedy of Hiroshima. And, on a different level, of course, Auschwitz and Treblinka. So much violence; so much indifference.

5   What is indifference? Etymologically, the word means "no difference." A strange and unnatural state in which the lines blur between light and darkness, dusk and dawn, crime and punishment, cruelty and compassion, good and evil. What are its courses and inescapable consequences? Is it a philosophy? Is there a philosophy of indifference conceivable? Can one possibly view indifference as a virtue? Is it necessary at times to practice it simply to keep one's sanity, live normally, enjoy a fine meal and a glass of wine, as the world around us experiences harrowing upheavals?

Of course, indifference can be tempting—more than that, seductive. It is so much easier to look away from victims. It is so much easier to avoid such rude interruptions to our work, our dreams, our hopes.

It is, after all, awkward, troublesome, to be involved in another person's pain and despair. Yet, for the person who is indifferent, his or her neighbor are of no consequence. And, therefore, their lives are meaningless. Their hidden or even visible anguish is of no interest. Indifference reduces the Other to an abstraction.

Over there, behind the black gates of Auschwitz, the most tragic of all prisoners were the "Muselmanner," as they were called. Wrapped in their torn blankets, they would sit or lie on the ground, staring vacantly into space, unaware of who or where they were—strangers to their surroundings. They no longer felt pain, hunger, thirst. They feared nothing. They felt nothing. They were dead and did not know it.

Rooted in our tradition, some of us felt that to be abandoned by humanity then was not the ultimate. We felt that to be abandoned by God was worse than to be punished by Him. Better an unjust God than an indifferent one. For us to be ignored by God was a harsher punishment than to be a victim of His anger. Man can live far from God—not outside God. God is wherever we are. Even in suffering? Even in suffering.

In a way, to be indifferent to that suffering is what makes the human being inhuman. Indifference, after all, is more dangerous than anger and hatred. Anger can at times be creative. One writes a great poem, a great symphony. One does something special for the sake of humanity because one is angry at the injustice that one witnesses. But indifference is never creative. Even hatred at times may elicit a response. You fight it. You denounce it. You disarm it.

10 Indifference elicits no response. Indifference is not a response. In- 10 difference is not a beginning; it is an end. And, therefore, indifference is always the friend of the enemy, for it benefits the aggressor—never his victim, whose pain is magnified when he or she feels forgotten. The political prisoner in his cell, the hungry children, the homeless refugees—not to respond to their plight, not to relieve their solitude by offering them a spark of hope is to exile them from human memory. And in denying their humanity, we betray our own.

Indifference, then, is not only a sin, it is a punishment.

And this is one of the most important lessons of this outgoing century's wide-ranging experiments in good and evil.

In the place that I come from, society was composed of three simple categories: the killers, the victims, and the bystanders. During the darkest of times, inside the ghettoes and death camps—and I'm glad that Mrs. Clinton mentioned that we are now commemorating that event, that period, that we are now in the Days of Remembrance—but then, we felt abandoned, forgotten. All of us did.

And our only miserable consolation was that we believed that Auschwitz and Treblinka were closely guarded secrets; that the leaders of the free world did not know what was going on behind those black gates and barbed wire; that they had no knowledge of the war against the Jews that Hitler's armies and their accomplices waged as part of the war against the Allies. If they knew, we thought, surely those leaders would have moved heaven and earth to intervene. They would have spoken out with great outrage and conviction. They would have bombed the railways leading to Birkenau, just the railways, just once.

15   And now we knew, we learned, we discovered that the Pentagon 15
knew, the State Department knew. And the illustrious occupant of the White House then, who was a great leader—and I say it with some anguish and pain, because, today is exactly 54 years marking his death—Franklin Delano Roosevelt died on April the 12th, 1945. So he is very much present to me and to us. No doubt, he was a great leader. He mobilized the American people and the world, going into battle, bringing hundreds and thousands of valiant and brave soldiers in America to fight fascism, to fight dictatorship, to fight Hitler. And so many of the young people fell in battle. And, nevertheless, his image in Jewish history—I must say it—his image in Jewish history is flawed.

The depressing tale of the *St. Louis* is a case in point. Sixty years ago, its human cargo—nearly 1,000 Jews—was turned back to Nazi Germany. And that happened after the Kristallnacht, after the first state sponsored pogrom, with hundreds of Jewish shops destroyed, synagogues burned, thousands of people put in concentration camps. And that ship, which was already in the shores of the United States, was sent back. I don't understand. Roosevelt was a good man, with a heart. He understood those who needed help. Why didn't he allow these refugees to disembark? A thousand people—in America, the great country, the greatest democracy, the most generous of all new nations in modern history. What happened? I don't understand. Why the indifference, on the highest level, to the suffering of the victims?

155

But then, there were human beings who were sensitive to our tragedy. Those non-Jews, those Christians, that we call the "Righteous Gentiles," whose selfless acts of heroism saved the honor of their faith. Why were they so few? Why was there a greater effort to save SS murderers after the war than to save their victims during the war? Why did some of America's largest corporations continue to do business with Hitler's Germany until 1942? It has been suggested, and it was documented, that the Wehrmacht could not have conducted its invasion of France without oil obtained from American sources. How is one to explain their indifference?

And yet, my friends, good things have also happened in this traumatic century: the defeat of Nazism, the collapse of communism, the rebirth of Israel on its ancestral soil, the demise of apartheid, Israel's peace treaty with Egypt, the peace accord in Ireland. And let us remember the meeting, filled with drama and emotion, between Rabin and Arafat that you, Mr. President, convened in this very place. I was here and I will never forget it.

And then, of course, the joint decision of the United States and NATO to intervene in Kosovo and save those victims, those refugees, those who were uprooted by a man, whom I believe that because of his crimes, should be charged with crimes against humanity.

20 But this time, the world was not silent. This time, we do respond. 20 This time, we intervene.

Does it mean that we have learned from the past? Does it mean that society has changed? Has the human being become less indifferent and more human? Have we really learned from our experiences? Are we less insensitive to the plight of victims of ethnic cleansing and other forms of injustices in places near and far? Is today's justified intervention in Kosovo, led by you, Mr. President, a lasting warning that never again will the deportation, the terrorization of children and their parents, be allowed anywhere in the world? Will it discourage other dictators in other lands to do the same?

What about the children? Oh, we see them on television, we read about them in the papers, and we do so with a broken heart. Their fate is always the most tragic, inevitably. When adults wage war, children perish. We see their faces, their eyes. Do we hear their pleas? Do we feel their pain, their agony? Every minute one of them dies of disease, violence, famine.

Some of them—so many of them—could be saved.

And so, once again, I think of the young Jewish boy from the Carpathian Mountains. He has accompanied the old man I have become throughout these years of quest and struggle. And together we walk towards the new millennium, carried by profound fear and extraordinary hope.

Questions on Meaning

1. Wiesel defines indifference as a "strange and unnatural state." What is your definition? How can indifference be unnatural?
2. What does the author mean by "Better an unjust God than an indifferent one"? How does this relate to the way various theologies explanation why bad things happen to good people?
3. How aware were you that the United States knew about the concentration camps? Explain what you understand about that time in history.

Questions on Rhetorical Strategy and Style

1. How does the tone of Wiesel's speech acknowledge or account for the significance of the day? Why does he open with a personal recollection?
2. What is the rhetorical purpose of referring to the "new millennium [and] the legacy of this vanishing century"? What is the metaphoric significance of "vanishing" in this context?
3. The speech essentially offers an extended definition of indifference. Describe how that definition develops over the course of the occasion.

Writing Assignments

1. Wiesel refers to more recent examples of genocide, such as in Rwanda and Kosovo. Write an essay explaining what occurred in these places and why.
2. Toward the end of his speech, Wiesel asks whether we have learned from the past. "Has the human being become less indifferent and more human?" Write an essay in which you respond to this question. What is your answer?

A Vindication of the Rights of Woman

Mary Wollstonecraft

Mary Wollstonecraft (1759–1797) was born in London, England. Wollstonecraft worked as a teacher, governess, translator, and literary advisor. A very early feminist, she wrote Thoughts on the Education of Daughters *(1787) and* A Vindication of the Rights of Women *(1792). In this essay, Wollstonecraft argues that providing women with the opportunity to improve their minds is in the best interests of both men and women.*

M y own sex, I hope, will excuse me, if I treat them like ratio-
nal creatures, instead of flattering their *fascinating* graces, and viewing them as if they were in a state of perpetual childhood, unable to stand alone. I earnestly wish to point out in what true dignity and human happiness consists—I wish to persuade women to endeavor to acquire strength, both of mind and body, and to convince them that the soft phrases, susceptibility of heart, delicacy of sentiment, and refinement of taste, are almost synonymous with epithets of weakness, and that those beings who are only the objects of pity and that kind of love, which has been termed its sister, will soon become objects of contempt.

Dismissing, then, those pretty feminine phrases, which the men condescendingly use to soften our slavish dependence, and despising that weak elegancy of mind, exquisite sensibility, and sweet docility of manners, supposed to be the sexual characteristics of the weaker vessel, I wish to show that elegance is inferior to virtue, that the first object of laudable ambition is to obtain a character as a human being, regardless of the distinction of sex; and that secondary views should be brought to this simple touchstone.

This is a rough sketch of my plan; and should I express my conviction with the energetic emotions that I feel whenever I think of the subject, the dictates of experience and reflection will be felt by some of my readers. Animated by this important object, I shall disdain to cull my phrases or polish my style; I aim at being useful, and sincerity will render me unaffected; for, wishing rather to persuade by the force of my arguments, than dazzle by the elegance of my language, I shall not waste my time in rounding periods, or in fabricating the turgid bombast of artificial feelings, which, coming from the head, never reach the heart. I shall be employed about things, not words! and, anxious to render my sex more respectable members of society, I shall try to avoid that flowery diction which has slided from essays into novels, and from novels into familiar letters and conversation.

These pretty superlatives, dropping glibly from the tongue, vitiate the taste, and create a kind of sickly delicacy that runs away from simple unadorned truth; and a deluge of false sentiments and overstretched feelings, stifling the natural emotions of the heart, render the domestic pleasures insipid, that ought to sweeten the exercise of those severe duties, which educate a rational and immortal being for a nobler field of action.

5   The education of women has, of late, been more attended to than   5 formerly; yet they are still reckoned a frivolous sex, and ridiculed or pitied by the writers who endeavor by satire or instruction to improve them. It is acknowledged that they spend many of the first years of their lives in acquiring a smattering of accomplishments; meanwhile strength of body and mind are sacrificed to libertine notions of beauty, to the desire of establishing themselves—the only way women can rise in the world—by marriage. And this desire making mere animals of them, when they marry they act as such children may be expected to act—they dress; they paint, and nickname God's creatures. Surely these weak beings are only fit for a seraglio!—Can they be expected to govern a family with judgment, or take care of the poor babes whom they bring into the world?

If then it can be fairly deduced from the present conduct of the sex, from the prevalent fondness for pleasure which takes place of ambition, and those nobler passions that open and enlarge the soul; that the instruction which women have hitherto received has only tended, with the constitution of civil society, to render them insignificant objects of desire—mere propagators of fools!—if it can be proved that in aiming to accomplish them, without cultivating their understandings, they are taken out of their sphere of duties, and made ridiculous and useless when the short-lived bloom of beauty is over, I presume that *rational* men will excuse me for endeavoring to persuade them to become more masculine and respectable.

Indeed the word masculine is only a bugbear: there is little reason to fear that women will acquire too much courage or fortitude; for their apparent inferiority with respect to bodily strength, must render them, in some degree, dependent on men in the various relations of life; but why should it be increased by prejudices that give a sex to virtue, and confound simple truths with sensual reveries?

Women are, in fact, so much degraded by mistaken notions of female excellence, that I do not mean to add a paradox when I assert, that this artificial weakness produces a propensity to tyrannize, and gives birth to cunning, the natural opponent of strength, which leads them to play off those contemptible infantine airs that undermine esteem even whilst they excite desire. Let men become more chaste and modest, and if women do not grow wiser in the same ratio, it will be clear that they have weaker understandings. It seems scarcely necessary to say, that I now speak of the sex in general. Many individuals have more sense than their male relatives; and, as nothing preponderates where there is a constant struggle for an equilibrium, without it has naturally more gravity, some women govern their husbands without degrading themselves, because intellect will always govern.

Questions on Meaning

1. What is the self-image that Wollstonecraft feels most women have? What do most women see as the only way they might "rise in the world"?
2. What does Wollstonecraft's comment, "the prevalent fondness for pleasure which takes place of ambition" tell you about her opinion of other women? Find other statements that reveal her feelings about how most women conduct themselves.
3. How does Wollstonecraft explain the statement, "this artificial weakness produces a propensity to tyrannize"? Why is this a paradox? How does Wollstonecraft feel that women should respond to the prevailing image of being the "weaker" sex?

Questions on Rhetorical Strategy and Style

1. Describe the tone of Wollstonecraft's essay. How is her writing style reflected in her concluding sentence?
2. Although Wollstonecraft stated that she wished to "persuade by the force of my arguments" rather than "dazzle by the elegance of my language," she nonetheless shapes her argument with well-crafted descriptions of the stereotypical attributes of women, such as women being "in a state of perpetual childhood, unable to stand alone." Which of her descriptive phrases has the greatest impact on her essay? Which might also be used in feminist writing today?

Writing Assignments

1. Many of the stereotypes of women noted by Wollstonecraft remain today, particularly in advertising. Find examples of advertising that promote the "weaker sex" image and describe why this practice is or is not offensive to you. Why do you think advertisers continue to use this type of material?
2. By and large, men still receive more pay than women for the same work. Research current salary data and evaluate the discrepancy between the sexes. For what types of work (i.e., professions) and what positions (i.e., laborer, professional, executive, etc.) do men still tend to receive more pay than women for the same work? Write an essay on the current state of pay inequality. What would you suggest should be done to create an equitable workplace?

from The World as I See It

Albert Einstein

Many consider Albert Einstein (1879–1955) to be the father of modern science. At age five Einstein was greatly moved by his father's pocket compass, recalling that it left a "deep and lasting impression" on his mind. This early fascination with the physical world would lead Einstein into a prolific career in the field of theoretical physics. Although born in Germany, Einstein spent much of his adult life in Switzerland, where he earned a degree in physics and mathematics. Following his graduation, Einstein quickly set to work on some of his most remarkable discoveries. Einstein's theories of relativity, developed in his mid-20s, mark a shift in our understanding of space, time, gravity and the nature of light. While dismissed by many notable physicists at the turn of the century, Einstein's work slowly gained more support, and in 1922 he was awarded the Nobel Prize in Physics. In 1999 Time *magazine named Einstein its "Person of the Century." To this day, Einstein's contributions to science remain a lasting legacy as they continue to shape the way we view our place in this "expanding universe."*

1   "How strange is the lot of us mortals! Each of us is here for a brief sojourn; for what purpose he knows not, though he sometimes thinks he senses it. But without deeper reflection one knows from daily life that one exists for other people–first of all for those upon whose smiles and well-being our own happiness is wholly dependent, and then for the many, unknown to us, to whose destinies we are bound by the ties of sympathy. A hundred times

Reprinted from *The World As I See It* (2001), Citadel Press.

every day I remind myself that my inner and outer life are based on the labors of other men, living and dead, and that I must exert myself in order to give in the same measure as I have received and am still receiving...

"I have never looked upon ease and happiness as ends in themselves–this critical basis I call the ideal of a pigsty. The ideals that have lighted my way, and time after time have given me new courage to face life cheerfully, have been Kindness, Beauty, and Truth. Without the sense of kinship with men of like mind, without the occupation with the objective world, the eternally unattainable in the field of art and scientific endeavors, life would have seemed empty to me. The trite objects of human efforts–possessions, outward success, luxury–have always seemed to me contemptible.

"My passionate sense of social justice and social responsibility has always contrasted oddly with my pronounced lack of need for direct contact with other human beings and human communities. I am truly a 'lone traveler' and have never belonged to my country, my home, my friends, or even my immediate family, with my whole heart; in the face of all these ties, I have never lost a sense of distance and a need for solitude..."

"My political ideal is democracy. Let every man be respected as an individual and no man idolized. It is an irony of fate that I myself have been the recipient of excessive admiration and reverence from my fellow-beings, through no fault, and no merit, of my own. The cause of this may well be the desire, unattainable for many, to understand the few ideas to which I have with my feeble powers attained through ceaseless struggle. I am quite aware that for any organization to reach its goals, one man must do the thinking and directing and generally bear the responsibility. But the led must not be coerced, they must be able to choose their leader. In my opinion, an autocratic system of coercion soon degenerates; force attracts men of low morality... The really valuable thing in the pageant of human life seems to me not the political state, but the creative, sentient individual, the personality; it alone creates the noble and the sublime, while the herd as such remains dull in thought and dull in feeling.

5   "This topic brings me to that worst outcrop of herd life, the   5
military system, which I abhor... This plague-spot of civilization
ought to be abolished with all possible speed. Heroism on command, senseless violence, and all the loathsome nonsense that goes
by the name of patriotism—how passionately I hate them!

"The most beautiful experience we can have is the mysterious.
It is the fundamental emotion that stands at the cradle of true art
and true science. Whoever does not know it and can no longer
wonder, no longer marvel, is as good as dead, and his eyes are
dimmed. It was the experience of mystery—even if mixed with
fear—that engendered religion. A knowledge of the existence of
something we cannot penetrate, our perceptions of the profound-
est reason and the most radiant beauty, which only in their most
primitive forms are accessible to our minds: it is this knowledge
and this emotion that constitute true religiosity. In this sense, and
only this sense, I am a deeply religious man... I am satisfied with
the mystery of life's eternity and with a knowledge, a sense, of the
marvelous structure of existence—as well as the humble attempt to
understand even a tiny portion of the Reason that manifests itself
in nature."

Questions on Meaning

1. Why does Einstein begin this essay with the exclamatory sentence,
    "How strange is the lot of us mortals!"? What is the definition of
    "lot" in this context, and why does he consider it to be so strange?

2. In paragraph 2, Einstein outlines his own personal values and
    beliefs. In other words, he describes to us his worldview. What
    does he value above all else? What values does he view as
    "contemptible"?

3. This essay seems to be a personal manifesto of sorts as it attempts
    to address what motivates Einstein to "exert" himself in his
    research and his life. What role does mystery play in Einstein's
    life? Why does he say that mystery "is the fundamental emotion
    that stands at the cradle of true art and science"?

Questions on Rhetorical Strategy and Style

1. Near the end of his essay, Einstein says he hates "the military system." How does his emotional word choice, especially his choice of adjectives, in this section of the essay work to support his own feelings of such a political system?

2. Even though this is very much a personal essay wherein Einstein remarks on his own values, beliefs and desires, he repeatedly tries to connect his own values to the values of all human beings. How does Einstein use shifts in perspective (i.e., first person singular to first person plural) to make his own values appear universal? How does the use of first person plural work to strengthen his own personal belief system?

Writing Assignments

1. Einstein stated that the ideals that motivated his life and work were "Kindness, Beauty and Truth." What two ideals have guided you throughout your life? Write an essay that describes why these particular ideals have, in Einstein's words, "given [you] new courage to face life cheerfully."

2. Einstein's work was driven by the power of mystery: "[Mystery] is the fundamental emotion that stands at the cradle of true art and science." Write an essay describing how the work of scientists, or artists, is fueled by seemingly unanswerable questions. How might the unknown be inspirational for people working in these fields?

Nobel Lecture
Albert Gore

As a soldier, a senator, and a vice-president, Al Gore (1948–) has spent the bulk of his life in public service. After an unsuccessful bid for president in 2000, Gore gave his undivided attentions to a cause he had been passionate about for years: the environment. In 2006 he followed up his bestselling treatise on the environment, Earth in the Balance *(1992), with a book and documentary entitled* An Inconvenient Truth. *His efforts on behalf of the environment earned him the prestigious Nobel Peace Prize in 2007. Below is his lecture to the commission that granted him the prize.*

Your Majesties, Your Royal Highnesses, Honorable members of the Norwegian Nobel Committee, Excellencies, Ladies and gentlemen.

I have a purpose here today. It is a purpose I have tried to serve for many years. I have prayed that God would show me a way to accomplish it.

Sometimes, without warning, the future knocks on our door with a precious and painful vision of what might be. One hundred and nineteen years ago, a wealthy inventor read his own obituary, mistakenly published years before his death. Wrongly believing the inventor had just died, a newspaper printed a harsh judgment of his life's work, unfairly labeling him "The Merchant of Death" because of his invention–dynamite. Shaken by this condemnation, the inventor made a fateful choice to serve the cause of peace.

Seven years later, Alfred Nobel created this prize and the others that bear his name.

Reprinted by permission of the Nobel Foundation.

5   Seven years ago tomorrow, I read my own political obituary in a   5
judgment that seemed to me harsh and mistaken–if not premature.
But that unwelcome verdict also brought a precious if painful gift: an
opportunity to search for fresh new ways to serve my purpose.

Unexpectedly, that quest has brought me here. Even though I fear
my words cannot match this moment, I pray what I am feeling in my
heart will be communicated clearly enough that those who hear me will
say, "We must act."

The distinguished scientists with whom it is the greatest honor of
my life to share this award have laid before us a choice between two
different futures–a choice that to my ears echoes the words of an
ancient prophet: "Life or death, blessings or curses. Therefore, choose
life, that both thou and thy seed may live."

We, the human species, are confronting a planetary emergency–a
threat to the survival of our civilization that is gathering ominous and
destructive potential even as we gather here. But there is hopeful news as
well: we have the ability to solve this crisis and avoid the worst–though
not all–of its consequences, if we act boldly, decisively and quickly.

However, despite a growing number of honorable exceptions, too many
of the world's leaders are still best described in the words Winston
Churchill applied to those who ignored Adolf Hitler's threat: "They go
on in strange paradox, decided only to be undecided, resolved to be
irresolute, adamant for drift, solid for fluidity, all powerful to be
impotent."

10   So today, we dumped another 70 million tons of global-warming   10
pollution into the thin shell of atmosphere surrounding our planet, as
if it were an open sewer. And tomorrow, we will dump a slightly
larger amount, with the cumulative concentrations now trapping
more and more heat from the sun.

As a result, the earth has a fever. And the fever is rising. The
experts have told us it is not a passing affliction that will heal by itself.
We asked for a second opinion. And a third. And a fourth. And the
consistent conclusion, restated with increasing alarm, is that something basic is wrong.

We are what is wrong, and we must make it right.

Last September 21, as the Northern Hemisphere tilted away from
the sun, scientists reported with unprecedented distress that the

North Polar ice cap is "falling off a cliff." One study estimated that it could be completely gone during summer in less than 22 years. Another new study, to be presented by U.S. Navy researchers later this week, warns it could happen in as little as 7 years.

Seven years from now.

15 In the last few months, it has been harder and harder to misinterpret the signs that our world is spinning out of kilter. Major cities in North and South America, Asia and Australia are nearly out of water due to massive droughts and melting glaciers. Desperate farmers are losing their livelihoods. Peoples in the frozen Arctic and on low-lying Pacific islands are planning evacuations of places they have long called home. Unprecedented wildfires have forced a half million people from their homes in one country and caused a national emergency that almost brought down the government in another. Climate refugees have migrated into areas already inhabited by people with different cultures, religions, and traditions, increasing the potential for conflict. Stronger storms in the Pacific and Atlantic have threatened whole cities. Millions have been displaced by massive flooding in South Asia, Mexico, and 18 countries in Africa. As temperature extremes have increased, tens of thousands have lost their lives. We are recklessly burning and clearing our forests and driving more and more species into extinction. The very web of life on which we depend is being ripped and frayed.

We never intended to cause all this destruction, just as Alfred Nobel never intended that dynamite be used for waging war. He had hoped his invention would promote human progress. We shared that same worthy goal when we began burning massive quantities of coal, then oil and methane.

Even in Nobel's time, there were a few warnings of the likely consequences. One of the very first winners of the Prize in chemistry worried that, "We are evaporating our coal mines into the air." After performing 10,000 equations by hand, Svante Arrhenius calculated that the earth's average temperature would increase by many degrees if we doubled the amount of CO_2 in the atmosphere.

Seventy years later, my teacher, Roger Revelle, and his colleague, Dave Keeling, began to precisely document the increasing CO_2 levels day by day. Contrast by scientific documentation

But unlike most other forms of pollution, CO_2 is invisible, tasteless, and odorless—which has helped keep the truth about what it is doing to our climate out of sight and out of mind. Moreover, the catastrophe now threatening us is unprecedented—and we often confuse the unprecedented with the improbable.

20   We also find it hard to imagine making the massive changes that are now necessary to solve the crisis. And when large truths are genuinely inconvenient, whole societies can, at least for a time, ignore them. Yet as George Orwell reminds us: "Sooner or later a false belief bumps up against solid reality, usually on a battlefield."

In the years since this prize was first awarded, the entire relationship between humankind and the earth has been radically transformed. And still, we have remained largely oblivious to the impact of our cumulative actions.

Indeed, without realizing it, we have begun to wage war on the earth itself. Now, we and the earth's climate are locked in a relationship familiar to war planners: "Mutually assured destruction."

More than two decades ago, scientists calculated that nuclear war could throw so much debris and smoke into the air that it would block life-giving sunlight from our atmosphere, causing a "nuclear winter." Their eloquent warnings here in Oslo helped galvanize the world's resolve to halt the nuclear arms race.

Now science is warning us that if we do not quickly reduce the global warming pollution that is trapping so much of the heat our planet normally radiates back out of the atmosphere, we are in danger of creating a permanent "carbon summer."

25   As the American poet Robert Frost wrote, "Some say the world will end in fire; some say in ice." Either, he notes, "would suffice."

But neither need be our fate. It is time to make peace with the planet.

We must quickly mobilize our civilization with the urgency and resolve that has previously been seen only when nations mobilized for war. These prior struggles for survival were won when leaders found words at the 11th hour that released a mighty surge of courage, hope and readiness to sacrifice for a protracted and mortal challenge.

These were not comforting and misleading assurances that the threat was not real or imminent; that it would affect others but not ourselves; that ordinary life might be lived even in the presence of extraordinary threat; that Providence could be trusted to do for us what we would not do for ourselves.

No, these were calls to come to the defense of the common future. They were calls upon the courage, generosity and strength of entire peoples, citizens of every class and condition who were ready to stand against the threat once asked to do so. Our enemies in those times calculated that free people would not rise to the challenge; they were, of course, catastrophically wrong.

30   Now comes the threat of climate crisis—a threat that is real, rising,   30
imminent, and universal. Once again, it is the 11th hour. The penalties for ignoring this challenge are immense and growing, and at some near point would be unsustainable and unrecoverable. For now we still have the power to choose our fate, and the remaining question is only this: Have we the will to act vigorously and in time, or will we remain imprisoned by a dangerous illusion?

Mahatma Gandhi awakened the largest democracy on earth and forged a shared resolve with what he called "Satyagraha"—or "truth force."

In every land, the truth—once known—has the power to set us free.

Truth also has the power to unite us and bridge the distance between "me" and "we," creating the basis for common effort and shared responsibility.

There is an African proverb that says, "If you want to go quickly, go alone. If you want to go far, go together." We need to go far, quickly.

35   We must abandon the conceit that individual, isolated, private
actions are the answer. They can and do help. But they will not take   35
us far enough without collective action. At the same time, we must ensure that in mobilizing globally, we do not invite the establishment of ideological conformity and a new lock-step "ism."

That means adopting principles, values, laws, and treaties that release creativity and initiative at every level of society in multifold responses originating concurrently and spontaneously.

This new consciousness requires expanding the possibilities inherent in all humanity. The innovators who will devise a new way to harness the sun's energy for pennies or invent an engine that's carbon negative may live in Lagos or Mumbai or Montevideo. We must ensure that entrepreneurs and inventors everywhere on the globe have the chance to change the world.

When we unite for a moral purpose that is manifestly good and true, the spiritual energy unleashed can transform us. The generation that defeated fascism throughout the world in the 1940s found, in rising to meet their awesome challenge, that they had gained the moral authority and long-term vision to launch the Marshall Plan, the United Nations, and a new level of global cooperation and fore-sight that unified Europe and facilitated the emergence of democracy and prosperity in Germany, Japan, Italy and much of the world. One of their visionary leaders said, "It is time we steered by the stars and not by the lights of every passing ship."

In the last year of that war, you gave the Peace Prize to a man from my hometown of 2000 people, Carthage, Tennessee. Cordell Hull was described by Franklin Roosevelt as the "Father of the United Nations." He was an inspiration and hero to my own father, who followed Hull in the Congress and the U.S. Senate and in his commitment to world peace and global cooperation.

40 My parents spoke often of Hull, always in tones of reverence and 40 admiration. Eight weeks ago, when you announced this prize, the deep-est emotion I felt was when I saw the headline in my hometown paper that simply noted I had won the same prize that Cordell Hull had won. In that moment, I knew what my father and mother would have felt were they alive.

Just as Hull's generation found moral authority in rising to solve the world crisis caused by fascism, so too can we find our greatest opportunity in rising to solve the climate crisis. In the Kanji characters used in both Chinese and Japanese, "crisis" is written with two symbols, the first meaning "danger," the second "opportunity." By facing and removing the danger of the climate crisis, we have the opportunity to gain the moral authority and vision to vastly increase our own capacity to solve other crises that have been too long ignored.

We must understand the connections between the climate crisis and the afflictions of poverty, hunger, HIV-Aids and other pan-demics. As these problems are linked, so too must be their solutions. We must begin by making the common rescue of the global environ-ment the central organizing principle of the world community.

Fifteen years ago, I made that case at the "Earth Summit" in Rio de Janeiro. Ten years ago, I presented it in Kyoto. This week, I will urge the delegates in Bali to adopt a bold mandate for a treaty that establishes a universal global cap on emissions and uses the market in emissions trading to efficiently allocate resources to the most effective opportunities for speedy reductions.

45   This treaty should be ratified and brought into effect everywhere   45
in the world by the beginning of 2010–two years sooner than presently contemplated. The pace of our response must be accelerated to match the accelerating pace of the crisis itself.

Heads of state should meet early next year to review what was accomplished in Bali and take personal responsibility for addressing this crisis. It is not unreasonable to ask, given the gravity of our circumstances, that these heads of state meet every three months until the treaty is completed.

We also need a moratorium on the construction of any new generating facility that burns coal without the capacity to safely trap and store carbon dioxide.

And most important of all, we need to put a *price* on carbon–with a CO2 tax that is then rebated back to the people, progressively, according to the laws of each nation, in ways that shift the burden of taxation from employment to pollution. This is by far the most effective and simplest way to accelerate solutions to this crisis.

The world needs an alliance–especially of those nations that weigh heaviest in the scales where earth is in the balance. I salute Europe and Japan for the steps they've taken in recent years to meet the challenge, and the new government in Australia, which has made solving the climate crisis its first priority.

But the outcome will be decisively influenced by two nations that are now failing to do enough: the United States and China. While India is also growing fast in importance, it should be absolutely clear that it is the two largest CO2 emitters–most of all, my own country–that will need to make the boldest moves, or stand accountable before history for their failure to act.

50   Both countries should stop using the other's behavior as an   50
excuse for stalemate and instead develop an agenda for mutual survival in a shared global environment.

These are the last few years of decision, but they can be the first years of a bright and hopeful future if we do what we must. No one should believe a solution will be found without effort, without cost, without change. Let us acknowledge that if we wish to redeem squandered time and speak again with moral authority, then these are the hard truths:

The way ahead is difficult. The outer boundary of what we currently believe is feasible is still far short of what we actually must do. Moreover, between here and there, across the unknown, falls the shadow.

That is just another way of saying that we have to expand the boundaries of what is possible. In the words of the Spanish poet, Antonio Machado, "Pathwalker, there is no path. You must make the path as you walk."

We are standing at the most fateful fork in that path. So I want to end as I began, with a vision of two futures–each a palpable possibility–and with a prayer that we will see with vivid clarity the necessity of choosing between those two futures, and the urgency of making the right choice now.

55 The great Norwegian playwright, Henrik Ibsen, wrote, "One of 55 these days, the younger generation will come knocking at my door."

The future is knocking at our door right now. Make no mistake, the next generation *will* ask us one of two questions. Either they will ask: "What were you thinking; why didn't you act?"

Or they will ask instead: "How did you find the moral courage to rise and successfully resolve a crisis that so many said was impossible to solve?"

We have everything we need to get started, save perhaps political will, but political will is a renewable resource.

So let us renew it, and say together: "We have a purpose. We are many. For this purpose we will rise, and we will act."

Questions on Meaning

1. Gore's lecture is persuasive in nature. What is his main point and what kinds of evidence does he use to support it? Is the evidence convincing?
2. Who is Alfred Nobel, and why does Gore spend so much time likening himself to Nobel?

Questions on Rhetorical Strategy and Style

1. Who is the intended audience for Gore's lecture? In what ways does he gear the lecture toward that audience?

2. What organizational strategies does Gore use?
3. Gore incorporates a good deal of personal information in his lecture. Why does he do so, and is it a rhetorically effective strategy?

Writing Assignments

1. In paragraph 35, Gore declares that "we must abandon the conceit that individual, isolated, private actions are the answer." Yet, Gore's lecture is essentially a call to action. Write an essay in which you describe what you, one reader, could do in response to his call to action.
2. Read Elie Wiesel's "The Perils of Indifference." Write an essay in which you compare these two pieces in terms of their respective messages and rhetorical strategies.

Activists and Leaders

Inaugural Address

Barack Obama

Barack Obama (1961–) was born in Honolulu, Hawaii, and spent most of his childhood there. At 18, he moved to Los Angeles to attend Occidental College, but two years later he transferred to Columbia University. After college, he found his way to Chicago, where he worked as a community organizer. Obama left Chicago long enough to earn a law degree from Harvard Law School, and then he returned to practice law. He eventually served in the Illinois State Senate and U.S. Senate. His Democratic National Convention keynote speech and the publication of his autobiography, Dreams from My Father: A Story of Race and Inheritance, *both in 2004, proved pivotal to his political future. On January 20, 2009, Obama was inaugurated as the 44th president of the United States.*

1   PRESIDENT BARACK OBAMA: Thank you. Thank you.   1

CROWD: Obama! Obama! Obama! Obama!

My fellow citizens: I stand here today humbled by the task before us, grateful for the trust you have bestowed, mindful of the sacrifices borne by our ancestors.

I thank President Bush for his service to our nation...

(APPLAUSE)

5   ... as well as the generosity and cooperation he has shown throughout   5
this transition.

Forty-four Americans have now taken the presidential oath.

The words have been spoken during rising tides of prosperity and the
still waters of peace. Yet, every so often the oath is taken amidst gathering clouds and raging storms. At these moments, America has carried on not simply because of the skill or vision of those in high
office, but because We the People have remained faithful to the ideals
of our forebears, and true to our founding documents.

So it has been. So it must be with this generation of Americans.

That we are in the midst of crisis is now well understood. Our nation
is at war against a far-reaching network of violence and hatred. Our
economy is badly weakened, a consequence of greed and irresponsi-
bility on the part of some but also our collective failure to make hard
choices and prepare the nation for a new age.

10   Homes have been lost, jobs shed, businesses shuttered. Our health   10
care is too costly, our schools fail too many, and each day brings further evidence that the ways we use energy strengthen our adversaries
and threaten our planet.

These are the indicators of crisis, subject to data and statistics. Less
measurable, but no less profound, is a sapping of confidence across
our land; a nagging fear that America's decline is inevitable, that the
next generation must lower its sights.

Today I say to you that the challenges we face are real, they are serious
and they are many. They will not be met easily or in a short span of
time. But know this America: They will be met.

(APPLAUSE)

On this day, we gather because we have chosen hope over fear, unity
of purpose over conflict and discord.

On this day, we come to proclaim an end to the petty grievances and false promises, the recriminations and worn-out dogmas that for far too long have strangled our politics.

15 We remain a young nation, but in the words of Scripture, the time   15
has come to set aside childish things. The time has come to reaffirm our enduring spirit; to choose our better history; to carry forward that precious gift, that noble idea, passed on from generation to generation: the God-given promise that all are equal, all are free, and all deserve a chance to pursue their full measure of happiness.

(APPLAUSE)

In reaffirming the greatness of our nation, we understand that greatness is never a given. It must be earned. Our journey has never been one of shortcuts or settling for less.

It has not been the path for the faint-hearted, for those who prefer leisure over work, or seek only the pleasures of riches and fame.

Rather, it has been the risk-takers, the doers, the makers of things—some celebrated, but more often men and women obscure in their labor—who have carried us up the long, rugged path towards prosperity and freedom.

For us, they packed up their few worldly possessions and traveled across oceans in search of a new life. For us, they toiled in sweatshops and settled the West, endured the lash of the whip and plowed the hard earth.

20 For us, they fought and died in places Concord and Gettysburg; Nor-   20
mandy and Khe Sanh.

Time and again these men and women struggled and sacrificed and worked till their hands were raw so that we might live a better life. They saw America as bigger than the sum of our individual ambitions; greater than all the differences of birth or wealth or faction.

This is the journey we continue today. We remain the most prosperous, powerful nation on Earth. Our workers are no less productive than when this crisis began. Our minds are no less inventive, our goods and services no less needed than they were last week or last month or last year. Our capacity remains undiminished. But our time of standing pat, of protecting narrow interests and putting off unpleasant decisions–that time has surely passed.

Starting today, we must pick ourselves up, dust ourselves off, and begin again the work of remaking America.

(APPLAUSE)

For everywhere we look, there is work to be done.

25 The state of our economy calls for action: bold and swift. And we will act not only to create new jobs but to lay a new foundation for growth.

We will build the roads and bridges, the electric grids and digital lines that feed our commerce and bind us together.

We will restore science to its rightful place and wield technology's wonders to raise health care's quality...

(APPLAUSE)

... and lower its costs.

We will harness the sun and the winds and the soil to fuel our cars and run our factories. And we will transform our schools and colleges and universities to meet the demands of a new age.

30 All this we can do. All this we will do.

Now, there are some who question the scale of our ambitions, who suggest that our system cannot tolerate too many big plans. Their memories are short, for they have forgotten what this country has already done, what free men and women can achieve when imagination is joined to common purpose and necessity to courage.

What the cynics fail to understand is that the ground has shifted beneath them, that the stale political arguments that have consumed us for so long, no longer apply.

The question we ask today is not whether our government is too big or too small, but whether it works, whether it helps families find jobs at a decent wage, care they can afford, a retirement that is dignified.

35 Where the answer is yes, we intend to move forward. Where the answer is no, programs will end.

And those of us who manage the public's dollars will be held to account, to spend wisely, reform bad habits, and do our business in the light of day, because only then can we restore the vital trust between a people and their government.

Nor is the question before us whether the market is a force for good or ill. Its power to generate wealth and expand freedom is unmatched.

But this crisis has reminded us that without a watchful eye, the market can spin out of control. The nation cannot prosper long when it favors only the prosperous.

The success of our economy has always depended not just on the size of our gross domestic product, but on the reach of our prosperity; on the ability to extend opportunity to every willing heart—not out of charity, but because it is the surest route to our common good.

(APPLAUSE)

40 As for our common defense, we reject as false the choice between our safety and our ideals.

Our founding fathers faced with perils that we can scarcely imagine, drafted a charter to assure the rule of law and the rights of man, a charter expanded by the blood of generations.

Those ideals still light the world, and we will not give them up for expedience's sake.

And so, to all other peoples and governments who are watching today, from the grandest capitals to the small village where my father was born: know that America is a friend of each nation and every man, woman and child who seeks a future of peace and dignity, and we are ready to lead once more.

(APPLAUSE)

45   Recall that earlier generations faced down fascism and communism   45 not just with missiles and tanks, but with the sturdy alliances and enduring convictions.

They understood that our power alone cannot protect us, nor does it entitle us to do as we please. Instead, they knew that our power grows through its prudent use. Our security emanates from the justness of our cause; the force of our example; the tempering qualities of humility and restraint.

We are the keepers of this legacy, guided by these principles once more, we can meet those new threats that demand even greater effort, even greater cooperation and understanding between nations. We'll begin to responsibly leave Iraq to its people and forge a hard- earned peace in Afghanistan.

With old friends and former foes, we'll work tirelessly to lessen the nuclear threat and roll back the specter of a warming planet.

We will not apologize for our way of life nor will we waver in its defense.

And for those who seek to advance their aims by inducing terror and slaughtering innocents, we say to you now that, "Our spirit is stronger and cannot be broken. You cannot outlast us, and we will defeat you."

(APPLAUSE)

50 For we know that our patchwork heritage is a strength, not a weakness. 50

We are a nation of Christians and Muslims, Jews and Hindus, and nonbelievers. We are shaped by every language and culture, drawn from every end of this Earth.

And because we have tasted the bitter swill of civil war and segregation and emerged from that dark chapter stronger and more united, we cannot help but believe that the old hatreds shall someday pass; that the lines of tribe shall soon dissolve; that as the world grows smaller, our common humanity shall reveal itself; and that America must play its role in ushering in a new era of peace.

To the Muslim world, we seek a new way forward, based on mutual interest and mutual respect.

To those leaders around the globe who seek to sow conflict or blame their society's ills on the West, know that your people will judge you on what you can build, not what you destroy.

55 To those... 55

(APPLAUSE)

To those who cling to power through corruption and deceit and the silencing of dissent, know that you are on the wrong side of history, but that we will extend a hand if you are willing to unclench your fist.

(APPLAUSE)

To the people of poor nations, we pledge to work alongside you to make your farms flourish and let clean waters flow; to nourish starved bodies and feed hungry minds.

And to those nations like ours that enjoy relative plenty, we say we can no longer afford indifference to the suffering outside our borders, nor can we consume the world's resources without regard to effect. For the world has changed, and we must change with it.

As we consider the road that unfolds before us, we remember with humble gratitude those brave Americans who, at this very hour, patrol far-off deserts and distant mountains. They have something to tell us, just as the fallen heroes who lie in Arlington whisper through the ages.

60 We honor them not only because they are guardians of our liberty, 60
but because they embody the spirit of service: a willingness to find meaning in something greater than themselves.

And yet, at this moment, a moment that will define a generation, it is precisely this spirit that must inhabit us all.

For as much as government can do and must do, it is ultimately the faith and determination of the American people upon which this nation relies.

It is the kindness to take in a stranger when the levees break; the self-lessness of workers who would rather cut their hours than see a friend lose their job which sees us through our darkest hours.

It is the firefighter's courage to storm a stairway filled with smoke, but also a parent's willingness to nurture a child, that finally decides our fate.

65 Our challenges may be new, the instruments with which we meet 65
them may be new, but those values upon which our success depends, honesty and hard work, courage and fair play, tolerance and curiosity, loyalty and patriotism—these things are old.

These things are true. They have been the quiet force of progress throughout our history.

What is demanded then is a return to these truths. What is required of us now is a new era of responsibility–a recognition, on the part of every American, that we have duties to ourselves, our nation and the world, duties that we do not grudgingly accept but rather seize gladly, firm in the knowledge that there is nothing so satisfying to the spirit, so defining of our character than giving our all to a difficult task.

This is the price and the promise of citizenship.

This is the source of our confidence: the knowledge that God calls on us to shape an uncertain destiny.

70 This is the meaning of our liberty and our creed, why men and 70 women and children of every race and every faith can join in celebration across this magnificent mall. And why a man whose father less than 60 years ago might not have been served at a local restaurant can now stand before you to take a most sacred oath.

(APPLAUSE)

So let us mark this day in remembrance of who we are and how far we have traveled.

In the year of America's birth, in the coldest of months, a small band of patriots huddled by dying campfires on the shores of an icy river.

The capital was abandoned. The enemy was advancing. The snow was stained with blood.

At a moment when the outcome of our revolution was most in doubt, the father of our nation ordered these words be read to the people:

"Let it be told to the future world that in the depth of winter, when nothing but hope and virtue could survive, that the city and the country, alarmed at one common danger, came forth to meet it."

75 America, in the face of our common dangers, in this winter of our 75
hardship, let us remember these timeless words; with hope and
virtue, let us brave once more the icy currents, and endure what
storms may come; let it be said by our children's children that when
we were tested we refused to let this journey end, that we did not
turn back nor did we falter; and with eyes fixed on the horizon and
God's grace upon us, we carried forth that great gift of freedom and
delivered it safely to future generations.

Thank you. God bless you.

(APPLAUSE)

And God bless the United States of America.

(APPLAUSE)

Questions on Meaning

1. When President Obama says, "This is the price and the promise of citizenship," to what is he referring? What point is Obama making about the responsibilities of the American citizen?
2. In paragraph 15, President Obama references scripture saying, "[T]he time has come to set aside childish things." What "things" is he making reference to? Why does he feel we must set them aside?
3. What qualities of the political climate and outgoing administration is President Obama most critical of?

Questions on Rhetorical Strategy and Style

1. The speech often utilizes figurative language. Identify three examples, and analyze and evaluate why and how effectively Obama uses them.

2. In paragraph 10, Obama catalogues the difficulties the country is facing: "Homes have been lost; jobs shed; businesses shuttered. Our health care is too costly; our schools fail too many." Do you agree with some critics that Obama's tone is gratuitously bleak? What purpose might he have for cataloguing these difficult circumstances?

3. Obama alludes to several national catastrophes and wars without naming them explicitly. Find three examples, and comment on why you think he references them indirectly.

Writing Assignments

1. Imagine that you were given the opportunity to address the country and express your opinions about the current state of our nation and where we should be headed. Write your own brief speech that, like Obama's, utilizes figurative language to vividly convey your ideas.

2. Imagine President Obama sent you this text as a draft before he made the speech on Inauguration Day and asked for your feedback. Write a letter to President Obama in response. What points do you agree with? What do you disagree with and why? What important issues has Obama left out?

The Power of Nonviolence

Mahatma Gandhi

Few individuals have made as great an impact on the world as Mohandas Karamchand Gandhi. Born on October 2, 1869, in the province of Porbandar, India, Mohandas Gandhi came to be known as Mahatma (Great Soul) Gandhi. Trained as a lawyer and raised in the Hindu faith, Gandhi used his education and his spiritual beliefs to help free the oppressed. For most of his adult life and up until his death in 1948, Gandhi worked to liberate people from various tyrannies, but he is probably most well known for his role in helping free India from British rule in 1947. In the following passage, Gandhi defines the concept that guided his civic activism.

Nonviolence in its dynamic condition means conscious suffering. It does not mean meek submission to the will of the evil-doer, but it means the pitting of one's whole soul against the will of the tyrant. Working under this law of our being, it is possible for a single individual to defy the whole might of an unjust empire to save his honour, his religion, his soul and lay the foundation for that empire's fall or its regeneration.

Active Force

The nonviolence of my conception is a more active and more real fighting against wickedness than retaliation whose very nature is to increase wickedness. I contemplate a mental and, therefore, a moral opposition to immoralities. I seek entirely to blunt the edge of the tyrant's sword, not by putting up against it a sharper-edged weapon, but by disappointing his expectation that I would be offering physical resistance. The resistance of the soul that I should offer instead would elude him. It would at first dazzle him, and at last compel recognition from him, which recognition would not humiliate him but would uplift him. It may be urged that this again is an ideal state. And so it is. The propositions from which I have drawn my arguments are as true as Euclid's definitions, which are none the less true because in practice we are unable to even draw Euclid's line on a blackboard. But even a geometrician finds it impossible to get on without bearing in mind Euclid's definitions. Nor may we...dispense with the fundamental propositions on which the doctrine of Satyagraha is based.

I admit that the strong will rob the weak and that it is sin to be weak. But this is said of the soul in man, not of the body. If it be said of the body, we could never be free from the sin of weakness. But the strength of soul can defy a whole world in arms against it. This strength is open to the weakest in body.

Nonviolence is the greatest force at the disposal of mankind. It is mightier than the mightiest weapon of destruction devised by the ingenuity of man. Destruction is not the law of the humans. Man lives freely by his readiness to die, if need be, at the hands of his brother, never by killing him. Every murder or other injury, no matter for what cause, committed or inflicted on another is a crime against humanity.

Nonviolence is like radium in its action. An infinitesimal quantity of it embedded in a malignant growth acts continuously, silently and ceaselessly till it has transformed the whole mass of the diseased tissue into a healthy one. Similarly, even a little of true nonviolence acts in a silent, subtle, unseen way and leavens the whole society.

Matchless Bravery

An armed soldier relies on his weapons for his strength. Take away from him his weapons—his gun or his sword—and he generally becomes helpless. But a person who has truly realized the principle of nonviolence has the God-given strength for his weapon and the world has not known anything that can match it.

A small body of determined spirits fired by an unquenchable faith in their mission can alter the course of history.

Nonviolence of the strong is any day stronger than that of the bravest soldier fully armed or a whole host.

Exercise in Faith

The hardest metal yields to sufficient heat. Even so the hardest heart must melt before sufficiency of the heat of nonviolence. And there is no limit to the capacity of nonviolence to generate heat.

Every action is a resultant of a multitude of forces even of a contrary nature. There is no waste of energy. So we learn in the books on mechanics. This is equally true of human actions. The difference is that in the one case we generally know the forces at work, and when we do, we can mathematically foretell the resultant. In the case of human actions, they result from a concurrence of forces of most of which we have no knowledge. But our ignorance must not be made to serve the cause of disbelief in the power of these forces. Rather is our ignorance a cause for greater faith. And nonviolence being the mightiest force in the world and also the most elusive in its working, it demands the greatest exercise of faith. Even as we believe in God in faith, so have we to believe in nonviolence in faith.

Violence like water, when it has an outlet, rushes forward furiously with an overwhelming force. Nonviolence cannot act madly. It is the essence of discipline. But, when it is set going, no amount of violence can crush it. For full play, it requires unsullied purity and an unquenchable faith...

A Science

Ahimsa is a science. The word 'failure' has no place in the vocabulary of science. Failure to obtain the expected result is often the precursor to further discoveries.

If the function of himsa is to devour all it comes across, the function of ahimsa is to rush into the mouth of himsa. In an atmosphere of ahimsa one has no scope to put his ahimsa to the test. It can be tested only in the face of himsa.

Violence can only be effectively met by nonviolence. This is an old, established truth...that the weapon of violence, even if it was the atom bomb, became useless when matched against nonviolence. That very few understand how to wield this mighty weapon is true. It requires a lot of understanding and strength of mind. It is unlike what is needed in military schools and colleges. The difficulty one experiences in meeting himsa with ahimsa arises from weakness of mind.

The Deed, not Doer

15 'Hate the sin and not the sinner' is a precept which, though easy 15 enough to understand, is rarely practised, and that is why the poison of hatred spreads in the world.

This ahimsa is the basis of the search for truth. I am realizing every day that the search is vain unless it is founded on ahimsa as the basis. It is quite proper to resist and attack a system, but to resist and attack its author is tantamount to resisting and attacking oneself. For we are all tarred with the same brush, and are children of one and the same creator, and as such, the divine powers within us are infinite. To slight a single human being is to slight those divine powers, and thus to harm not only that Being but with Him the whole world.

Man and his deed are two distinct things. Whereas a good deed should call forth approbation and a wicked deed disapprobation, the doer of the deed, whether good or wicked, always deserves respect or pity as the case may be.

Those who seek to destroy men rather than manners adopt the latter and become worse than those whom they destroy under the mistaken belief that the manners will die with the men. They do not know the root of the evil.

It is the acid test of nonviolence that, in a nonviolent conflict, there is no rancour left behind, and in the end the enemies are converted into friends. That was my experience in South Africa, with General Smuts. He started with being my bitterest opponent and critic. Today he is my warmest friend.

20 The principal implication of ahimsa is that the ahimsa in us 20 ought to soften and not to stiffen our opponents' attitude to us; it ought to melt him; it ought to strike a responsive chord in his heart.

As ahimsa-ites, can you say that you practice genuine ahimsa? Can you say that you receive the arrows of the opponent on your bare breasts without returning them? Can you say that you are not angry, that you are not perturbed by his criticism?

By reason of life-long practice of ahimsa, I claim to be an expert in it, though very imperfect. Speaking in absolute terms, the more

I practice it the clearer I see how far I am from the full expression of ahimsa in my life. It is his ignorance of this, the greatest duty of man in the world, which makes him say that in this age nonviolence has little scope in the face of violence, whereas I make bold to say that in this age of the Atom Bomb unadulterated nonviolence is the only force that can confound all the tricks put together of violence.

Questions on Meaning

1. Who is Euclid and why does Gandhi reference him?
2. Define the following Sanskrit terms: himsa, ahimsa, and Satyagraha. Why is each term important to understanding Gandhi's points?
3. What does Gandhi mean when he writes in paragraph 11 that "nonviolence cannot act madly"?

Questions on Rhetorical Strategy and Style

1. What distinct strategies does Gandhi use to define the concept of nonviolence? Which strategies are most effective? Why?
2. Why does Gandhi use headings in this short piece? Is the use of headings effective?
3. In paragraph 21, Gandhi asks the reader three questions. Why does he do so? Does he answer these questions?

Writing Assignments

1. Choose a philosophical concept like freedom, and write an essay in which you define the concept. Instead of relying on research, use the same definition strategies that Gandhi uses.
2. Using only Gandhi's treatise and Martin Luther King's "Letter from Birmingham Jail," write an essay in which you define the concept of nonviolence.
3. In paragraph 7, Gandhi asserts, "A small body of determined spirits fired by an unquenchable faith in their mission can alter the course of history." Write an essay in which you illustrate the truth of his statement by giving examples from your own life and/or from events in your family/community/city/country.

Letter from Birmingham Jail

Martin Luther King, Jr.

Martin Luther King, Jr. (1929–1968) was born in Atlanta, Georgia. The son and grandson of Baptist ministers, he attended Moorhouse College, Crozer Theological Seminary, and Boston University where he received a Ph.D. (1955) and met his future wife, Coretta Scott. King's active involvement in the civil rights movement began in 1955, when he led a boycott of segregated buses in Montgomery, Alabama. From the mid 1950s until he was shot and killed in Memphis, Tennessee, while supporting striking city workers, King organized boycotts, sit-ins, mass demonstrations, and other protest activities. As a black civil rights leader, King was arrested, jailed, stoned, stabbed, and beaten; his house was bombed; he was placed under secret surveillance by Federal Bureau of Investigation (FBI) director J. Edgar Hoover; and in 1966 he was awarded the Nobel Peace Prize. Through his leadership—always underscored by his nonviolent beliefs—King's name has become synonymous with the watersheds of the civil rights movement in the United States: Rosa Parks; the Southern Christian Leadership Conference (which King founded); Selma, Alabama; the Civil Rights Act; the Voting Rights Act; and the 1963 civil rights march on Washington, D. C. His published works include Strength to Love *(1963) and* Conscience for Change *(1967). This essay—published in a revised form in* Why We Can't Wait *(1964)—is King's stern response to eight clergymen from Alabama who were asking civil rights activists to give up public demonstrations in Birmingham, Alabama, and turn to the courts. Read the clergymen's public statement first, then King's detailed rebuttal (printed here as it appeared originally). Keep in mind that King wrote these words four months before he delivered his famous "I Have a Dream" speech during the August 1963 civil rights march on Washington; after long years of activism, he was clearly impatient with the slow progress of the civil rights movement.*

Public Statement by Eight Alabama Clergymen

(April 12, 1963)

1   We the undersigned clergymen are among those who, in January, issued "An Appeal for Law and Order and Common Sense," in dealing with racial problems in Alabama. We expressed understanding that honest convictions in racial matters could properly be pursued in the courts, but urged that decisions of those courts should in the meantime be peacefully obeyed.

Since that time there had been some evidence of increased forbearance and a willingness to face facts. Responsible citizens have undertaken to work on various problems which cause racial friction and unrest. In Birmingham, recent public events have given indication that we all have opportunity for a new constructive and realistic approach to racial problems.

However, we are now confronted by a series of demonstrations by some of our Negro citizens, directed and led in part by outsiders. We recognize the natural impatience of people who feel that their hopes are slow in being realized. But we are convinced that these demonstrations are unwise and untimely.

We agree rather with certain local Negro leadership which has called for honest and open negotiation of racial issues in our area. And we believe this kind of facing of issues can best be accomplished by citizens of our own metropolitan area, white and Negro, meeting with their knowledge and experience of the local situation. All of us need to face that responsibility and find proper channels for its accomplishment.

5   Just as we formerly pointed out that "hatred and violence have no   5
sanction in our religious and political traditions," we also point out
that such actions as incite to hatred and violence, however technically
peaceful those actions may be, have not contributed to the resolution
of our local problems. We do not believe that these days of new hope
are days when extreme measures are justified in Birmingham.

We commend the community as a whole, and the local news
media and law enforcement officials in particular, on the calm manner in which these demonstrations have been handled. We urge the
public to continue to show restraint should the demonstrations continue, and the law enforcement officials to remain calm and continue
to protect our city from violence.

We further strongly urge our own Negro community to withdraw
support from these demonstrations, and to unite locally in working
peacefully for a better Birmingham. When rights are consistently denied, a cause should be pressed in the courts and in negotiations
among local leaders, and not in the streets. We appeal to both our
white and Negro citizenry to observe the principles of law and order
and common sense.

Signed by:

C.C. J. CARPENTER, D.D., LL.D., *Bishop of Alabama*
JOSEPH A. DURICK, D.D., *Auxiliary Bishop, Diocese of*
    Mobile, Birmingham
RABBI MILTON L. GRAFMAN, *Temple Emanu-El,*
    Birmingham, Alabama
BISHOP PAUL HARDIN, *Bishop of the Alabama-West Florida*
    Conference of the Methodist Church
BISHOP NOLAN B. HARMON, *Bishop of the North Alabama*
    Conference of the Methodist Church
GEORGE M. MURRAY, D.D., LL.D., *Bishop Coadjutor,*
    Episcopal Diocese of Alabama
EDWARD V. RAMAGE, *Moderator, Synod of the Alabama*
    Presbyterian Church in the United States
EARL STALLINGS, *Pastor, First Baptist Church, Birmingham,*
    Alabama

Letter from Birmingham Jail

MARTIN LUTHER KING, JR.
Birmingham City Jail
April 16, 1963

Bishop C. C. J. Carpenter
Bishop Joseph A. Durick
Rabbi Milton L. Grafman
Bishop Paul Hardin
Bishop Nolan B. Harmon
The Rev. George M. Murray
The Rev. Edward V. Ramage
The Rev. Earl Stallings

My dear Fellow Clergymen,

While confined here in the Birmingham City Jail, I came across your recent statement calling our present activities "unwise and untimely." Seldom, if ever, do I pause to answer criticism of my work and ideas. If I sought to answer all of the criticisms that cross my desk, my secretaries would be engaged in little else in the course of the day and I would have no time for constructive work. But since I feel that you are men of genuine good will and your criticisms are sincerely set forth, I would like to answer your statement in what I hope will be patient and reasonable terms.

I think I should give the reason for my being in Birmingham, since you have been influenced by the argument of "outsiders coming in." I have the honor of serving as president of the Southern Christian Leadership Conference, an organization operating in every Southern state with headquarters in Atlanta, Georgia. We have some eighty-five affiliate organizations all across the South—one being the Alabama Christian Movement for Human Rights. Whenever necessary and possible we share staff, educational, and financial resources with our affiliates. Several months ago our local affiliate here in Birmingham invited us to be on call to engage in a nonviolent direct action program if such were deemed necessary. We readily consented, and when the hour came we lived up to our promises. So I, along with several members of my staff, am here, because I was invited here. I am here because I have basic organizational ties here.

10 But more basically, I am in Birmingham because injustice is here. 10 Just as the eighth century prophets left their little villages and carried their "thus saith the Lord" far beyond the boundaries of their home town, and just as the Apostle Paul left his little village of Tarsus and carried the gospel of Jesus Christ to practically every hamlet and city of the Greco-Roman world, I too am compelled to carry the gospel of freedom beyond my particular home town. Like Paul, I must constantly respond to the Macedonian call for aid.

Moreover, I am cognizant of the interrelatedness of all communities and states. I cannot sit idly by in Atlanta and not be concerned about what happens in Birmingham. Injustice anywhere is a threat to justice everywhere. We are caught in an inescapable network of mutuality, tied in a single garment of destiny. Whatever affects one directly affects all indirectly. Never again can we afford to live with the narrow, provincial "outside agitator" idea. Anyone who lives inside the United States can never be considered an outsider anywhere in this country.

You deplore the demonstrations that are presently taking place in Birmingham. But I am sorry that your statement did not express a similar concern for the conditions that brought the demonstrations into being. I am sure that each of you would want to go beyond the superficial social analyst who looks merely at effects, and does not grapple with underlying causes. I would not hesitate to say that it is unfortunate that so-called demonstrations are taking place in Birmingham at this time, but I would say in more emphatic terms that it is even more unfortunate that the white power structure of this city left the Negro community with no other alternative.

In any nonviolent campaign there are four basic steps: (1) collection of the facts to determine whether injustices are alive; (2) negotiation; (3) self-purification; and (4) direct action. We have gone through all of these steps in Birmingham. There can be no gainsaying of the fact that racial injustice engulfs this community. Birmingham is probably the most thoroughly segregated city in the United States. Its ugly record of police brutality is known in every section of this country. Its unjust treatment of Negroes in the courts is a notorious reality. There have been more unsolved bombings of Negro homes and churches in Birmingham than any city in this nation. These are the hard, brutal, and unbelievable facts. On the basis of these conditions, Negro leaders sought to negotiate with the city fathers. But the political leaders consistently refused to engage in good faith negotiation.

Then came the opportunity last September to talk with some of the leaders of the economic community. In these negotiating sessions certain promises were made by the merchants—such as the promise to remove the humiliating racial signs from the stores. On the basis of these promises Rev. Shuttlesworth and the leaders of the Alabama Christian Movement for Human Rights agreed to call a moratorium on any type of demonstrations. As the weeks and months unfolded we realized that we were the victims of a broken promise. The signs remained. As in so many experiences of the past we were confronted with blasted hopes, and the dark shadow of a deep disappointment settled upon us. So we had no alternative except that of preparing for direct action, whereby we would present our very bodies as a means of laying our case before the conscience of the local and national community. We were not unmindful of the difficulties involved. So we decided to go through a process of self-purification. We started having workshops on nonviolence and repeatedly asked ourselves the questions, "Are you able to accept blows without retaliating?" "Are you able to endure the ordeals of jail?"

15   We decided to set our direct action program around the Easter   15 season, realizing that with the exception of Christmas, this was the largest shopping period of the year. Knowing that a strong economic withdrawal program would be the by-product of direct action, we felt that this was the best time to bring pressure on the merchants for the needed changes. Then it occurred to us that the March election was ahead, and so we speedily decided to postpone action until after election day. When we discovered that Mr. Connor was in the run-off, we decided again to postpone so that the demonstrations could not be used to cloud the issues. At this time we agreed to begin our nonviolent witness the day after the run-off.

This reveals that we did not move irresponsibly into direct action. We too wanted to see Mr. Connor defeated; so we went through postponement after postponement to aid in this community need. After this we felt that direct action could be delayed no longer.

You may well ask, "Why direct action? Why sit-ins, marches, etc.? Isn't negotiation a better path?" You are exactly right in your call for negotiation. Indeed, this is the purpose of direct action. Nonviolent direct action seeks to create such a crisis and establish such creative tension that a community that has constantly refused to negotiate is forced to confront the issue. It seeks so to dramatize the issue that it can no longer be ignored. I just referred to the creation of tension as a part of the work of the nonviolent resister. This may sound rather shocking. But I must confess that I am not afraid of the word tension. I have earnestly worked and preached against violent tension, but there is a type of constructive nonviolent tension that is necessary for growth. Just as Socrates felt that it was necessary to create a tension in the mind so that individuals could rise from the bondage of myths and half-truths to the unfettered realm of creative analysis and objective appraisal, we must see the need of having nonviolent gadflies to create the kind of tension in society that will help men rise from the dark depths of prejudice and racism to the majestic heights of understanding and brotherhood. So the purpose of the direct action is to create a situation so crisis-packed that it will inevitably open the door to negotiation. We, therefore, concur with you in your call for negotiation. Too long has our beloved Southland been bogged down in the tragic attempt to live in monologue rather than dialogue.

One of the basic points in your statement is that our acts are untimely. Some have asked, "Why didn't you give the new administration time to act?" The only answer that I can give to this inquiry is that the new administration must be prodded about as much as the outgoing one before it acts. We will be sadly mistaken if we feel that the election of Mr. Boutwell will bring the millennium to Birmingham. While Mr. Boutwell is much more articulate and gentle than Mr. Connor, they are both segregationists dedicated to the task of maintaining the status quo. The hope I see in Mr. Boutwell is that he will be reasonable enough to see the futility of massive resistance to desegregation. But he will not see this without pressure from the devotees of civil rights. My friends, I must say to you that we have not made a single gain in civil rights without determined legal and nonviolent pressure. History is the long and tragic story of the fact that privileged groups seldom give up their privileges voluntarily. Individuals may see the moral light and voluntarily give up their unjust posture; but as Reinhold Niebuhr has reminded us, groups are more immoral than individuals.

We know through painful experience that freedom is never voluntarily given by the oppressor; it must be demanded by the oppressed. Frankly I have never yet engaged in a direct action movement that was "well timed," according to the timetable of those who have not suffered unduly from the disease of segregation. For years now I have heard the word "Wait!" It rings in the ear of every Negro with a piercing familiarity. This "wait" has almost always meant "never." It has been a tranquilizing thalidomide, relieving the emotional stress for a moment, only to give birth to an ill-formed infant of frustration. We must come to see with the distinguished jurist of yesterday that "justice too long delayed is justice denied." We have waited for more than three hundred and forty years for our constitutional and God-given rights. The nations of Asia and Africa are moving with jet-like speed toward the goal of political independence, and we still creep at horse and buggy pace toward the gaining of a cup of coffee at a lunch counter.

20   I guess it is easy for those who have never felt the stinging darts 20 of segregation to say wait. But when you have seen vicious mobs lynch your mothers and fathers at will and drown your sisters and brothers at whim; when you have seen hate filled policemen curse, kick, brutalize, and even kill your black brothers and sisters with impunity; when you see the vast majority of your twenty million Negro brothers smothering in an air-tight cage of poverty in the midst of an affluent society; when you suddenly find your tongue twisted and your speech stammering as you seek to explain to your six-year-old daughter why she can't go to the public amusement park that has just been advertised on television, and see tears welling up in her little eyes when she is told that Funtown is closed to colored children, and see the depressing clouds of inferiority begin to form in her little mental sky, and see her begin to distort her little personality by unconsciously developing a bitterness toward white people; when you have to concoct an answer for a five-year-old son asking in agonizing pathos: "Daddy, why do white people treat colored people so mean?"; when you take a cross country drive and find it necessary to sleep night after night in the uncomfortable corners of your automobile because no motel will accept you; when you are humiliated day in and day out by nagging signs reading "white" and "colored"; when your first name becomes "nigger" and your middle name becomes "boy" (however old you are) and your last name becomes "John," and when your wife and mother are never given the respected title "Mrs."; when you are harried by day and haunted by night by the fact that you are a Negro, living constantly at tip-toe stance never quite knowing what to expect next, and plagued with inner fears and outer resentments; when you are forever

fighting a degenerating sense of "nobodiness";——then you will understand why we find it difficult to wait. There comes a time when the cup of endurance runs over, and men are no longer willing to be plunged into an abyss of injustice where they experience the bleakness of corroding despair. I hope, sirs, you can understand our legitimate and unavoidable impatience.

You express a great deal of anxiety over our willingness to break laws. This is certainly a legitimate concern. Since we so diligently urge people to obey the Supreme Court's decision of 1954 outlawing segregation in the public schools, it is rather strange and paradoxical to find us consciously breaking laws. One may well ask, "How can you advocate breaking some laws and obeying others?" The answer is found in the fact that there are two types of laws. There are *just* laws and there are *unjust* laws. I would be the first to advocate obeying just laws. One has not only a legal but moral responsibility to obey just laws. Conversely, one has a moral responsibility to disobey unjust laws. I would agree with Saint Augustine that "An unjust law is no law at all."

Now what is the difference between the two? How does one determine when a law is just or unjust? A just law is a man-made code that squares with the moral law or the law of God. An unjust law is a code that is out of harmony with the moral law. To put it in the terms of Saint Thomas Aquinas, an unjust law is a human law that is not rooted in eternal and natural law. Any law that uplifts human personality is just. Any law that degrades human personality is unjust. All segregation statutes are unjust because segregation distorts the soul and damages the personality. It gives the segregator a false sense of superiority and the segregated a false sense of inferiority. To use the words of Martin Buber, the great Jewish philosopher, segregation substitutes an "I-it" relationship for the "I-thou" relationship, and ends up relegating persons to the status of things. So segregation is not only politically, economically, and sociologically unsound, but it is morally wrong and sinful. Paul Tillich has said that sin is separation. Isn't segregation an existential expression of man's tragic separation, an expression of his awful estrangement, his terrible sinfulness? So I can urge men to obey the 1954 decision of the Supreme Court because it is morally right, and I can urge them to disobey segregation ordinances because they are morally wrong.

Let us turn to a more concrete example of just and unjust laws. An unjust law is a code that a majority inflicts on a minority that is not binding on itself. This is *difference* made legal. On the other hand a just law is a code that a majority compels a minority to follow that it is willing to follow itself. This is *sameness* made legal.

Let me give another explanation. An unjust law is a code inflicted upon a minority which that minority had no part in enacting or creating because they did not have the unhampered right to vote. Who can say the legislature of Alabama which set up the segregation laws was democratically elected? Throughout the state of Alabama all types of conniving methods are used to prevent Negroes from becoming registered voters and there are some counties without a single Negro registered to vote despite the fact that the Negro constitutes a majority of the population. Can any law set up in such a state be considered democratically structured?

25 These are just a few examples of unjust and just laws. There are 25 some instances when a law is just on its face but unjust in its application. For instance, I was arrested Friday on a charge of parading without a permit. Now there is nothing wrong with an ordinance which requires a permit for a parade, but when the ordinance is used to preserve segregation and to deny citizens the First Amendment privilege of peaceful assembly and peaceful protest, then it becomes unjust.

I hope you can see the distinction I am trying to point out. In no sense do I advocate evading or defying the law as the rabid segregationist would do. This would lead to anarchy. One who breaks an unjust law must do it *openly, lovingly* (not hatefully as the white mothers did in New Orleans when they were seen on television screaming "nigger, nigger, nigger") and with a willingness to accept the penalty. I submit that an individual who breaks a law that conscience tells him is unjust, and willingly accepts the penalty by staying in jail to arouse the conscience of the community over its injustice, is in reality expressing the very highest respect for law.

Of course there is nothing new about this kind of civil disobedience. It was seen sublimely in the refusal of Shadrach, Meshach, and Abednego to obey the laws of Nebuchadnezzar because a higher moral law was involved. It was practiced superbly by the early Christians who were willing to face hungry lions and the excruciating pain of chopping blocks, before submitting to certain unjust laws of the Roman Empire. To a degree academic freedom is a reality today because Socrates practiced civil disobedience.

We can never forget that everything Hitler did in Germany was "legal" and everything the Hungarian freedom fighters did in Hungary was "illegal." It was "illegal" to aid and comfort a Jew in Hitler's Germany. But I am sure that, if I had lived in Germany during that time, I would have aided and comforted my Jewish brothers even though it was illegal. If I lived in a communist country today where certain principles dear to the Christian faith are suppressed, I believe I would openly advocate disobeying those antireligious laws.

I must make two honest confessions to you, my Christian and Jewish brothers. First I must confess that over the last few years I have been gravely disappointed with the white moderate. I have almost reached the regrettable conclusion that the Negroes' great stumbling block in the stride toward freedom is not the White Citizens' "Counciler" or the Ku Klux Klanner, but the white moderate who is more devoted to "order" than to justice; who prefers a negative peace which is the absence of tension to a positive peace which is the presence of justice; who constantly says "I agree with you in the goal you seek, but I can't agree with your methods of direct action;" who paternalistically feels that he can set the timetable for another man's freedom; who lives by the myth of time and who constantly advises the Negro to wait until a "more convenient season." Shallow understanding from people of good will is more frustrating than absolute misunderstanding from people of ill will. Lukewarm acceptance is much more bewildering than outright rejection.

30   I had hoped that the white moderate would understand that law   30
and order exist for the purpose of establishing justice, and that when they fail to do this they become the dangerously structured dams that block the flow of social progress. I had hoped that the white moderate would understand that the present tension in the South is merely a necessary phase of the transition from an obnoxious negative peace, where the Negro passively accepted his unjust plight, to a substance-filled positive peace, where all men will respect the dignity and worth of human personality. Actually, we who engage in nonviolent direct action are not the creators of tension. We merely bring to the surface the hidden tension that is already alive. We bring it out in the open where it can be seen and dealt with. Like a boil that can never be cured as long as it is covered up but must be opened with all its pus-flowing ugliness to the natural medicines of air and light, injustice must likewise be exposed, with all of the tension its exposing creates, to the light

KING | LETTER FROM BIRMINGHAM JAIL

of human conscience and the air of national opinion before it can be cured.

In your statement you asserted that our actions, even though peaceful, must be condemned because they precipitate violence. But can this assertion be logically made? Isn't this like condemning the robbed man because his possession of money precipitated the evil act of robbery? Isn't this like condemning Socrates because his unswerving commitment to truth and his philosophical delvings precipitated the misguided popular mind to make him drink the hemlock? Isn't this like condemning Jesus because His unique God consciousness and never-ceasing devotion to His will precipitated the evil act of crucifixion? We must come to see, as federal courts have consistently affirmed, that it is immoral to urge an individual to withdraw his efforts to gain his basic constitutional rights because the quest precipitates violence. Society must protect the robbed and punish the robber.

I had also hoped that the white moderate would reject the myth of time. I received a letter this morning from a white brother in Texas which said: "All Christians know that the colored people will receive equal rights eventually, but is it possible that you are in too great of a religious hurry? It has taken Christianity almost 2,000 years to accomplish what it has. The teachings of Christ take time to come to earth." All that is said here grows out of a tragic misconception of time. It is the strangely irrational notion that there is something in the very flow of time that will inevitably cure all ills. Actually time is neutral. It can be used either destructively or constructively. I am coming to feel that the people of ill will have used time much more effectively than the people of good will. We will have to repent in this generation not merely for the vitriolic words and actions of the bad people, but for the appalling silence of the good people. We must come to see that human progress never rolls in on wheels of inevitability. It comes through the tireless efforts and persistent work of men willing to be co-workers with God, and without this hard work time itself becomes an ally of the forces of social stagnation.

We must use time creatively, and forever realize that the time is always ripe to do right. Now is the time to make real the promise of democracy, and transform our pending national elegy into a creative psalm of brotherhood. Now is the time to lift our national policy from the quicksand of racial injustice to the solid rock of human dignity.

You spoke of our activity in Birmingham as extreme. At first I was rather disappointed that fellow clergymen would see my nonviolent efforts as those of the extremist. I started thinking about the fact that I stand in the middle of two opposing forces in the Negro community. One is a force of complacency made up of Negroes who, as a result of long years of oppression, have been so completely drained of self-respect and a sense of "somebodiness" that they have adjusted to segregation, and of a few Negroes in the middle class who, because of a degree of academic and economic security, and because at points they profit by segregation, have unconsciously become insensitive to the problems of the masses. The other force is one of bitterness and hatred and comes perilously close to advocating violence. It is expressed in the various black nationalist groups that are springing up over the nation, the largest and best known being Elijah Muhammad's Muslim movement. This movement is nourished by the contemporary frustration over the continued existence of racial discrimination. It is made up of people who have lost faith in America, who have absolutely repudiated Christianity, and who have concluded that the white man is an incurable "devil." I have tried to stand between these two forces saying that we need not follow the "do-nothingism" of the complacent or the hatred and despair of the black nationalist. There is the more excellent way of love and nonviolent protest. I'm grateful to God that, through the Negro church, the dimension of nonviolence entered our struggle. If this philosophy had not emerged I am convinced that by now many streets of the South would be flowing with floods of blood. And I am further convinced that if our white brothers dismiss us as "rabble rousers" and "outside agitators"—those of us who are working through the channels of nonviolent direct action—and refuse to support our nonviolent efforts, millions of Negroes, out of frustration and despair, will seek solace and security in black nationalist ideologies, a development that will lead inevitably to a frightening racial nightmare.

35   Oppressed people cannot remain oppressed forever. The urge for 35 freedom will eventually come. This is what has happened to the American Negro. Something within has reminded him of his birthright of freedom; something without has reminded him that he can gain it. Consciously and unconsciously, he has been swept in by what the Germans call the *Zeitgeist*, and with his black brothers of Africa, and his brown and yellow brothers of Asia, South America, and the

Caribbean, he is moving with a sense of cosmic urgency toward the promised land of racial justice. Recognizing this vital urge that has engulfed the Negro community, one should readily understand public demonstrations. The Negro has many pent-up resentments and latent frustrations. He has to get them out. So let him march sometime; let him have his prayer pilgrimages to the city hall; understand why he must have sit-ins and freedom rides. If his repressed emotions do not come out in these nonviolent ways, they will come out in ominous expressions of violence. This is not a threat; it is a fact of history. So I have not said to my people, "Get rid of your discontent." But I have tried to say that this normal and healthy discontent can be channeled through the creative outlet of nonviolent direct action. Now this approach is being dismissed as extremist. I must admit that I was initially disappointed in being so categorized.

But as I continued to think about the matter I gradually gained a bit of satisfaction from being considered an extremist. Was not Jesus an extremist in love? "Love your enemies, bless them that curse you, pray for them that despitefully use you." Was not Amos an extremist for justice— "Let justice roll down like waters and righteousness like a mighty stream." Was not Paul an extremist for the gospel of Jesus Christ— "I bear in my body the marks of the Lord Jesus." Was not Martin Luther an extremist— "Here I stand; I can do none other so help me God." Was not John Bunyan an extremist— "I will stay in jail to the end of my days before I make a butchery of my conscience." Was not Abraham Lincoln an extremist— "This nation cannot survive half slave and half free." Was not Thomas Jefferson an extremist— "We hold these truths to be self evident that all men are created equal." So the question is not whether we will be extremist but what kind of extremist will we be. Will we be extremists for hate or will we be extremists for love? Will we be extremists for the preservation of injustice or will we be extremists for the cause of justice? In that dramatic scene on Calvary's hill three men were crucified. We must never forget that all three were crucified for the same crime—the crime of extremism. Two were extremists for immorality, and thus fell below their environment. The other, Jesus Christ, was an extremist for love, truth, and goodness, and thereby rose above His environment. So, after all, maybe the South, the nation, and the world are in dire need of creative extremists.

I had hoped that the white moderate would see this. Maybe I was too optimistic. Maybe I expected too much. I guess I should have realized that few members of a race that has oppressed another race can understand or appreciate the deep groans and passionate yearnings of those that have been oppressed, and still fewer have the vision to see that injustice must be rooted out by strong, persistent, and determined action. I am thankful, however, that some of our white brothers have grasped the meaning of this social revolution and committed themselves to it. They are still all too small in quantity, but they are big in quality. Some like Ralph McGill, Lillian Smith, Harry Golden, and James Dabbs have written about our struggle in eloquent, prophetic, and understanding terms. Others have marched with us down nameless streets of the South. They have languished in filthy, roach-infested jails, suffering the abuse and brutality of angry policemen who see them as "dirty nigger lovers." They, unlike so many of their moderate brothers and sisters, have recognized the urgency of the moment and sensed the need for powerful "action" antidotes to combat the disease of segregation.

Let me rush on to mention my other disappointment. I have been so greatly disappointed with the white Church and its leadership. Of course there are some notable exceptions. I am not unmindful of the fact that each of you has taken some significant stands on this issue. I commend you, Rev. Stallings, for your Christian stand on this past Sunday, in welcoming Negroes to your worship service on a nonsegregated basis. I commend the Catholic leaders of this state for integrating Springhill College several years ago.

But despite these notable exceptions I must honestly reiterate that I have been disappointed with the Church. I do not say that as one of those negative critics who can always find something wrong with the Church. I say it as a minister of the gospel, who loves the Church; who was nurtured in its bosom; who has been sustained by its spiritual blessings and who will remain true to it as long as the cord of life shall lengthen.

40   I had the strange feeling when I was suddenly catapulted into the 40 leadership of the bus protest in Montgomery several years ago that we would have the support of the white Church. I felt that the white ministers, priests, and rabbis of the South would be some of our strongest allies. Instead, some have been outright opponents, refusing to understand the

freedom movement and misrepresenting its leaders; all too many others have been more cautious than courageous and have remained silent behind the anesthetizing security of stained glass windows.

In spite of my shattered dreams of the past, I came to Birmingham with the hope that the white religious leadership of the community would see the justice of our cause and, with deep moral concern, serve as the channel through which our just grievances could get to the power structure. I had hoped that each of you would understand. But again I have been disappointed.

I have heard numerous religious leaders of the South call upon their worshippers to comply with a desegregation decision because it is the law, but I have longed to hear white ministers say follow this decree because integration is morally right and the Negro is your brother. In the midst of blatant injustices inflicted upon the Negro, I have watched white churches stand on the sideline and merely mouth pious irrelevancies and sanctimonious trivialities. In the midst of a mighty struggle to rid our nation of racial and economic injustice, I have heard so many ministers say, "Those are social issues with which the Gospel has no real concern," and I have watched so many churches commit themselves to a completely otherworldly religion which made a strange distinction between body and soul, the sacred and the secular.

So here we are moving toward the exit of the twentieth century with a religious community largely adjusted to the status quo, standing as a tail light behind other community agencies rather than a headlight leading men to higher levels of justice.

I have travelled the length and breadth of Alabama, Mississippi, and all the other Southern states. On sweltering summer days and crisp autumn mornings I have looked at her beautiful churches with their spires pointing heavenward. I have beheld the impressive outlay of her massive religious education buildings. Over and over again I have found myself asking: "Who worships here? Who is their God? Where were their voices when the lips of Governor Barnett dripped with words of interposition and nullification? Where were they when Governor Wallace gave the clarion call for defiance and hatred? Where were their voices of support when tired, bruised, and weary Negro men and women decided to rise from the dark dungeons of complacency to the bright hills of creative protest?"

45 Yes, these questions are still in my mind. In deep disappointment, 45 I have wept over the laxity of the Church. But be assured that my tears

have been tears of love. There can be no deep disappointment where there is not deep love. Yes, I love the Church; I love her sacred walls. How could I do otherwise? I am in the rather unique position of being the son, the grandson, and the great grandson of preachers. Yes, I see the Church as the body of Christ. But, oh! How we have blemished and scarred that body through social neglect and fear of being non-conformists.

There was a time when the Church was very powerful. It was during that period when the early Christians rejoiced when they were deemed worthy to suffer for what they believed. In those days the Church was not merely a thermometer that recorded the ideas and principles of popular opinion; it was a thermostat that transformed the mores of society. Wherever the early Christians entered a town the power structure got disturbed and immediately sought to convict them for being "disturbers of the peace" and "outside agitators." But they went on with the conviction that they were a "colony of heaven" and had to obey God rather than man. They were small in number but big in commitment. They were too God-intoxicated to be "astronomically intimidated." They brought an end to such ancient evils as infanticide and gladiatorial contest.

Things are different now. The contemporary Church is so often a weak, ineffectual voice with an uncertain sound. It is so often the arch-supporter of the status quo. Far from being disturbed by the presence of the Church, the power structure of the average community is consoled by the Church's silent and often vocal sanction of things as they are.

But the judgment of God is upon the Church as never before. If the Church of today does not recapture the sacrificial spirit of the early Church, it will lose its authentic ring, forfeit the loyalty of millions, and be dismissed as an irrelevant social club with no meaning for the twentieth century. I am meeting young people every day whose disappointment with the Church has risen to outright disgust.

Maybe again I have been too optimistic. Is organized religion too inextricably bound to the status quo to save our nation and the world? Maybe I must turn my faith to the inner spiritual Church, the church within the Church, as the true *ecclesia* and the hope of the world. But again I am thankful to God that some noble souls from the ranks of organized religion have broken loose from the paralyzing chains of conformity and joined us as active partners in the struggle for freedom. They have left their secure congregations and walked the streets of Albany, Georgia, with us. They have gone through the highways of the South on torturous rides for freedom. Yes, they have gone to jail with us. Some have been kicked out of their churches and lost the support of their bishops and fellow ministers. But they have gone with the faith that right defeated is stronger than evil triumphant. These men have been the leaven in the lump of the race. Their witness has been the spiritual salt that has preserved the true meaning of the Gospel in these troubled times. They have carved a tunnel of hope through the dark mountain of disappointment.

50 I hope the Church as a whole will meet the challenge of this decisive hour. But even if the Church does not come to the aid of justice, I have no despair about the future. I have no fear about the outcome of our struggle in Birmingham, even if our motives are presently misunderstood. We will reach the goal of freedom in Birmingham and all over the nation, because the goal of America is freedom. Abused and scorned though we may be, our destiny is tied up with the destiny of America. Before the pilgrims landed at Plymouth, we were here. Before the pen of Jefferson etched across the pages of history the majestic words of the Declaration of Independence, we were here. For more than two centuries our foreparents labored in this country without wages; they made cotton "king"; and they built the homes of their masters in the midst of brutal injustice and shameful humiliation—and yet out of a bottomless vitality they continued to thrive and develop. If the inexpressible cruelties of slavery could not stop us, the opposition we now face will surely fail. We will win our freedom because the sacred heritage of our nation and the eternal will of God are embodied in our echoing demands.

I must close now. But before closing I am impelled to mention one other point in your statement that troubled me profoundly. You warmly commended the Birmingham police force for keeping "order" and "preventing violence." I don't believe you would have so warmly commended the police force if you had seen its angry violent dogs literally biting six unarmed, nonviolent Negroes. I don't believe you would so quickly commend the policemen if you would observe their ugly and inhuman treatment of Negroes here in the city jail; if you would watch them push and curse old Negro women and young Negro girls; if you would see them slap and kick old Negro men and young Negro boys; if you will observe them, as they did on two occasions, refuse to give us food because we wanted to sing our grace together. I'm sorry that I can't join you in your praise for the police department.

It is true that they have been rather disciplined in their public handling of the demonstrators. In this sense they have been rather publicly "nonviolent." But for what purpose? To preserve the evil system of segregation. Over the last few years I have consistently preached that nonviolence demands that the means we use must be as pure as the ends we seek. So I have tried to make it clear that it is wrong to use immoral means to attain moral ends. But now I must affirm that it is just as wrong, or even more so, to use moral means to preserve immoral ends. Maybe Mr. Connor and his policemen have been rather publicly nonviolent, as Chief Pritchett was in Albany, Georgia, but they have used the moral means of nonviolence to maintain the immoral end of flagrant racial injustice. T. S. Eliot has said that there is no greater treason than to do the right deed for the wrong reason.

I wish you had commended the Negro sit-inners and demonstrators of Birmingham for their sublime courage, their willingness to suffer, and their amazing discipline in the midst of the most inhuman provocation. One day the South will recognize its real heroes. They will be the James Merediths, courageously and with a majestic sense of purpose, facing jeering and hostile mobs and the agonizing loneliness that characterizes the life of the pioneer. They will be old, oppressed, battered Negro women, symbolized in a seventy-two year old woman of Montgomery, Alabama, who rose up with a sense of dignity and with her people decided not to ride the segregated buses, and responded to one who inquired about her tiredness with ungrammatical profundity: "My feets is tired, but my soul is rested." They will be young high school and college students, young ministers of the gospel and a host of the elders, courageously and nonviolently sitting in at lunch counters and willingly going to jail for conscience sake. One day the South will know that when these disinherited children of God sat down at lunch counters they were in reality standing up for the best in the American dream and the most sacred values in our Judeo-Christian heritage, and thus carrying our whole nation back to great wells of democracy which were dug deep by the founding fathers in the formulation of the Constitution and the Declaration of Independence.

Never before have I written a letter this long (or should I say a book?). I'm afraid that it is much too long to take your precious time.

I can assure you that it would have been much shorter if I had been writing from a comfortable desk, but what else is there to do when you are alone for days in the dull monotony of a narrow jail cell other than write long letters, think strange thoughts, and pray long prayers!

55 　　If I have said anything in this letter that is an overstatement of the 55 truth and is indicative of an unreasonable impatience, I beg you to forgive me. If I have said anything in this letter that is an understatement of the truth and is indicative of my having a patience that makes me patient with anything less than brotherhood, I beg God to forgive me.

I hope this letter finds you strong in the faith. I also hope that circumstances will soon make it possible for me to meet each of you, not as an integrationist or a civil rights leader, but as a fellow clergyman and a Christian brother. Let us all hope that the dark clouds of racial prejudice will soon pass away and the deep fog of misunderstanding will be lifted from our fear-drenched communities and in some not too distant tomorrow the radiant stars of love and brotherhood will shine over our great nation with all of their scintillating beauty.

Yours for the cause of
Peace and Brotherhood
MARTIN LUTHER KING, JR.

Questions on Meaning

1. At the time that this essay was written, King had been active in the civil rights movement for nearly 10 years. How had he usually handled criticisms of his work and ideas? Why?
2. The public statement by the eight clergymen exhibits a distrust for *outsiders*. How does King address that common fear and skepticism? If you had been one of the *local* clergymen, how do you think you would have reacted to King's explanation? Would you have respected his convictions? Embraced his beliefs?
3. Often in this essay, King addresses the issue of the timeliness of nonviolent demonstrations and other political activities. This urgency of action is a common theme of King's. "For years I have heard the word 'Wait!' " he writes. "It rings in the ear of every Negro with a piercing familiarity." What does the word *wait* mean to King?

Questions on Rhetorical Strategy and Style

1. King's dominant rhetorical strategy is clear: persuasion. He is not telling a story; he is not using flowery language or a preacher's oratory. This essay is logos and ethos: a sound argument supported by credibility, integrity, and experience. Analyze how he builds the argument one step at a time through the essay.
2. Repetition helps to drive home an argument. Show two places in this essay where King effectively uses repetition. Rewrite one of the passages without the repeated phrase and compare its effectiveness with the original.
3. Find King's discussion of just and unjust laws and locate the two paragraphs in which he gives examples of these laws ("Let us turn to a more concrete example . . . " and "Let me give another explanation . . . "). What is your reaction to his use of examples here?

Writing Assignments

1. A student of Gandhi, King based his political activities on nonviolent confrontation. In this essay, King outlines four steps of nonviolent activism: collect facts, negotiate, self-purify, and take direct action. Identify an injustice in your lifetime that people are trying or have tried to change through nonviolent activism.

Examples may include a physical barrier to people with physical handicaps, an employment restriction that discriminates against elderly people, or a city ordinance that unfairly restricts the activities of teenagers. Describe the political activity that has occurred, then relate it to King's four steps. Were these steps applied? If not, discuss how the outcome might have been different if these steps had been applied.

2. In this essay, King responds to the charge of being an extremist by admitting that he initially was put off by the label, but then realized that he wore it proudly. What is your reaction to the term? Does "extremist" hold negative or positive connotations for you? Is it used to credit or discredit? Identify some current political figures who are called extremists. Write an essay defining the term and describing how it is commonly applied, using current extremist political figures as examples.

3. King writes that one "has a moral responsibility to disobey unjust laws." Do you agree? Reread his defense of that statement. Does King's stance help overturn unjust laws or create anarchy? Choose a "law" that affects your life that you feel is unjust—perhaps a dormitory rule or campus restriction or a local law. Would you, or do you, intentionally break it? Write an essay describing the "law" and your action, arguing your viewpoint on obeying or disobeying it.

Death of Abraham Lincoln

Walt Whitman

Walt Whitman (1819–1892) was born in a rural part of Long Island, New York, in a Quaker family. After trying various trades, he became a newspaperman but soon turned to writing poetry. In 1955 he published the first edition of Leaves of Grass, *his best-known work, which grew over the years from its original publication of under 100 pages to a volume of over 400 pages. Whitman is one of the most important and influential American poets of the nineteenth century. He is known for his democratic celebration of humanity—from workmen to Abraham Lincoln—and his experiments in free verse to catch the rhythms of life. Written after Whitman was already becoming well known as a writer and speaker, "Death of Abraham Lincoln" was a frequent selection on Whitman's lecture tours. It is characteristic of his style in several ways, its effusive imagery and freewheeling sentences especially, along with its powerful emotions.*

1   I shall not easily forget the first time I ever saw Abraham Lincoln. It must have been about the 18th or 19th of February, 1861. It was rather a pleasant afternoon, in New York City, as he arrived there from the West, to remain a few hours, and then pass on to Washington, to prepare for his inauguration. I saw him in Broadway, near the site of the present Post-office. He came down, I think from Canal street, to stop at the Astor House. The broad spaces, sidewalks, and streets in the neighborhood, and for some distance, were crowded with solid masses of people, many thousands. The omnibuses and other vehicles had all been turn'd off, leaving an unusual hush in that busy part of the city. Presently two or three shabby hack barouches made their way with some difficulty through the crowd, and drew up

at the Astor House entrance. A tall figure stepp'd out of the centre of these barouches, paus'd leisurely on the sidewalk, look'd up at the granite walls and looming architecture of the grand old hotel—then, after a relieving stretch of arms and legs, turn'd round for over a minute to slowly and good-humoredly scan the appearance of the vast and silent crowds. There were no speeches—no compliments—no welcome—as far as I could hear, not a word said. Still much anxiety was conceal'd in the quiet. Cautious persons had fear'd some mark'd insult or indignity to the President-elect—for he possess'd no personal popularity at all in New York City, and very little political. But it was evidently tacitly agreed that if the few political supporters of Mr. Lincoln present would entirely abstain from any demonstration on their side, the immense majority, who were anything but supporters, would abstain on their sides also. The result was a sulky, unbroken silence, such as certainly never before characterized so great a New York crowd.

Almost in the same neighborhood I distinctly remember'd seeing Lafayette on his visit to America in 1825. I had also personally seen and heard, various years afterward, how Andrew Jackson, Clay, Webster, Hungarian Kossuth, Filibuster Walker, the Prince of Wales on his visit, and other *célébres,* native and foreign, had been welcom'd there— all that indescribable human roar and magnetism, unlike any other sound in the universe—the glad exulting thunder-shouts of countless unloos'd throats of men! But on this occasion, not a voice—not a sound. From the top of an omnibus, (driven up one side, close by, and block'd by the curbstone and the crowds), I had, I say, a capital view of it all, and especially of Mr. Lincoln, his look and gait—his perfect composure and coolness—his unusual and uncouth height, his dress of complete black, stovepipe hat push'd back on the head, dark-brown complexion, seam'd and wrinkled yet canny-looking face, black, bushy head of hair, disproportionately long neck, and his hands held behind as he stood observing the people. He look'd with curiosity upon that immense sea of faces, and the sea of faces return'd the look with similar curiosity. In both there was a dash of comedy, almost farce, such as Shakspere puts in his blackest tragedies. The crowd that hemm'd around consisted I should think of thirty to forty thousand men, not a single one his personal friend—while I have no doubt, (so frenzied were the ferments of the time,) many an assassin's knife and pistol lurk'd in hip or breast-pocket there, ready, soon as break and riot came.

But no break or riot came. The tall figure gave another relieving stretch or two of arms and legs; then with moderate pace, and accompanied by a few unknown-looking persons, ascended the portico-steps of the Astor House, disappeared through its broad entrance—and the dumb-show ended.

I saw Abraham Lincoln often the four years following that date. He changed rapidly and much during his Presidency—but this scene, and him in it, are indelibly stamp'd upon my recollection. As I sat on the top of my omnibus, and had a good view of him, the thought, dim and inchoate then, has since come out clear enough, that four sorts of genius, four mighty and primal hands, will be needed to the complete limning of this man's future portrait—the eyes and brains and finger-touch of Plutarch and Eschylus and Michel Angelo, assisted now by Rabelais.

And now—(Mr. Lincoln passing on from this scene to Washington, where he was inaugurated, amid armed cavalry, and sharpshooters at every point—the first instance of the kind in our history—and I hope it will be the last)—now the rapid succession of well-known events, (too well-known—I believe, these days, we almost hate to hear them mention'd)—the national flag fired on at Sumter—the uprising of the North, in paroxysms of astonishment and rage—the chaos of divided councils—the call for troops—the first Bull Run—the stunning cast-down, shock, and dismay of the North—and so in full flood the Secession war. Four years of lurid, bleeding, murky, murderous war. Who paint those years, with all their scenes?—the hard-fought engagements—the defeats, plans, failures—the gloomy hours, days, when our Nationality seem'd hung in pall of doubt, perhaps death—the Mephistophelean sneers of foreign lands and attachés—the dreaded Scylla of European interference, and the Charybdis of the tremendously dangerous latent strata of secession sympathizers throughout the free States, (far more numerous than is supposed)—the long marches in summer—the hot sweat, and many a sunstroke, as on the rush to Gettysburg in '63—the night battles in the woods, as under Hooker at Chancellorsville—the camps in winter—the military prisons—the hospitals—(alas! alas! the hospitals.)

The Secession war? Nay, let me call it the Union war. Though whatever call'd, it is even yet too near us—too vast and too closely overshadowing—its branches uniform'd yet, (but certain,) shooting too far into the future—and the most indicative and mightiest of them yet ungrown. A great literature will yet arise out of the era of those four years, those scenes—era compressing centuries of native passion, first-class pictures, tempests of life and death—an inexhaustible mine for the histories, drama, romance, and even philosophy, of peoples to come—indeed the verteber of poetry and art, (of personal character too,) for all future America—far more grand, in my opinion, to the hands capable of it, than Homer's siege of Troy, or the French wars to Shakspere.

But I must leave these speculations, and come to the theme I have assign'd and limited myself to. Of the actual murder of President Lincoln, though so much has been written, probably the facts are yet very indefinite in most persons' minds. I read from my memoranda, written at the time, and revised frequently and finally since.

The day, April 14, 1865, seems to have been a pleasant one throughout the whole land—the moral atmosphere pleasant too—the long storm, so dark, so fratricidal, full of blood and doubt and gloom, over and ended at last by the sunrise of such an absolute National victory, and utter breakdown of Secessionism—we almost doubted our own senses! Lee had capitulated beneath the apple-tree of Appomattox. The other armies, the flanges of the revolt, swiftly follow'd. And could it really be, then? Out of all the affairs of this world of woe and failure and disorder, was there really come the confirm'd, unerring sign of plan, like a shaft of pure light—of rightful rule—of God? So the day, as I say, was propitious. Early herbage, early flowers, were out. (I remember where I was stopping at the time, the season being advanced, there were many lilacs in full bloom. By one of those caprices that enter and give tinge to events without being at all a part of them, I find myself always reminded of the great tragedy of that day by the sight and odor of these blossoms. It never fails.)

But I must not dwell on accessories. The deed hastens. The popular afternoon paper of Washington, the little *Evening Star,* has spatter'd all over its third page, divided among the advertisements in a sensational manner. In a hundred different places, "*The President and his Lady will be at the Theatre this evening. . . .*" (Lincoln was fond of the theatre. I have myself seen him there several times. I remember thinking how funny it was that he, in some respects the leading actor in the stormiest drama known to real history's stage through centuries, should sit there and be so completely interested and absorb'd in those human jackstraws, moving about with their silly little gestures, foreign spirit, and flatulent text.)

On this occasion the theatre was crowded, many ladies in rich and
gay costumes, officers in their uniforms, many well-known citizens,
young folks, the usual clusters of gas-lights, the usual magnetism of so
many people, cheerful, with perfumes, music of violins and flutes—
(and over all, and saturating all, that vast, vague wonder, *Victory,* the
nation's victory, the triumph of the Union, filling the air, the thought,
the sense, with exhilaration more than all music and perfumes.)

The President came betimes, and, with his wife, witness'd the play
from the large stage-boxes of the second tier, two thrown into one, and
profusely drap'd with the national flag. The acts and scenes of the
piece—one of those singularly written compositions which have at
least the merit of giving entire relief to an audience engaged in mental action or business excitements and cares during the day, as it makes
not the slightest call on either the moral, emotional, esthetic, or spiritual nature—a piece, (*Our American Cousin,*) in which, among other
characters so call'd, a Yankee, certainly such a one as was never seen,
or the least like it ever seen, in North America, is introduced in England, with a varied fol-de-rol of talk, plot, scenery, and such phantas-
magoria as goes to make up a modern popular drama—had progress'd
through perhaps a couple of its acts, when in the midst of this comedy, or non-such, or whatever it is to be call'd, and to offset it, or finish it out, as if in Nature's and the great Muse's mockery of those poor
mimes, came interpolated that scene, not really or exactly to be described at all, (for on the many hundreds who were there it seems to
this hour to have left a passing blur, a dream, a blotch)—and yet partially to be described as I now proceed to give it. There is a scene in
the play representing a modern parlor, in which two unprecedented
English ladies are inform'd by the impossible Yankee that he is not a
man of fortune, and therefore undesirable for marriage-catching
purposes; after which, the comments being finish'd, the dramatic trio
make exit; leaving the stage clear for a moment. At this period came
the murder of Abraham Lincoln. Great as all its manifold train, circling round it, and stretching into the future for many a century, in
the politics, history, art &c., of the New World, in point of fact the
main thing, the actual murder, transpired with the quiet and simplicity of any commonest occurrence—the bursting of a bud or pod in
the growth of vegetation, for instance. Through the general hum following the stage pause, with the change of positions, came the muffled sound of a pistol-shot, which not one-hundredth part of the

audience heard at the time—and yet a moment's hush—somehow, surely, a vague startled thrill—and then, through the ornamented, draperied, starr'd and striped space-way of the President's box, a sudden figure, a man, raises himself with hands and feet, stands a moment on the railing, leaps below to the stage, (a distance of perhaps fourteen or fifteen feet), falls out of position, catching his boot-heel in the copious drapery, (the American flag,) falls on one knee, quickly recovers himself, rises as if nothing had happen'd, (he really sprains his ankle, but unfelt then)—and so the figure, Booth, the murderer, dress'd in plain black broadcloth, bareheaded, with full, glossy, raven hair, and his eyes like some mad animal's flashing with light and resolution, yet with a certain strange calmness, holds aloft in one hand a large knife—walks along not much back from the footlights—turns fully toward the audience his face of statuesque beauty, lit by those basilisk eyes, flashing with desperation, perhaps insanity—launches out in a firm and steady voice the words *Sic semper tyrannis*—and then walks with neither slow nor very rapid pace diagonally across to the back of the stage, and disappears. (Had not all this terrible scene-making the mimic ones preposterous—had it not all been rehears'd, in blank, by Booth, beforehand?)

A moment's hush—a scream—the cry of *"murder"*—Mrs. Lincoln leaning out of the box, with ashy cheeks and lips, with involuntary cry, pointing to the retreating figure, *"He has kill'd the President."* And still a moment's strange, incredulous suspense—and then the deluge! Then that mixture of horror, noises, uncertainty—(the sound, somewhere back, of a horse's hoofs clattering with speed)—the people burst through chairs and railings, and break them up—there is inextricable confusion and terror—women faint—quite feeble persons fall, and are trampl'd on—many cries of agony are heard—the broad stage suddenly fills to suffocation with a dense and motley crowd, like some horrible carnival—the audience rush generally upon it, at least the strong men do—the actors and actresses are all there in their play-costumes and painted faces, with mortal fright showing through the rouge—the screams and calls, confused talk—redoubled, trebled—two or three manage to pass up water from the stage to the President's box—others try to clamber up—&c., &c.

In the midst of all this, the soldiers of the President's guard, with others, suddenly drawn to the scene, burst in—(some two hundred altogether) they storm the house, through all the tiers, especially the

220

upper ones, inflam'd with fury, literally charging the audience with fix'd bayonets, muskets, and pistols, shouting *"Clear out! clear out! you sons of——"*. . . . Such a wild scene, or a suggestion of it rather, inside the play-house that night.

Outside, too, in the atmosphere of shock and craze, crowds of people, fill'd with frenzy, ready to seize any outlet for it, come near committing murder several times on innocent individuals. One such case was especially exciting. The infuriated crowd, through some chance, got started against one man, either for words he utter'd, or perhaps without any cause at all, and were proceeding at once to actually hang him on a neighboring lamp-post, when he was rescued by a few heroic policemen, who placed him in their midst, and fought their way slowly and amid great peril toward the station-house. It was a fitting episode of the whole affair. The crowd rushing and eddying to and fro—the night, the yells, the pale faces, many frighten'd people trying in vain to extricate themselves—the attack'd man, not yet freed from the jaws of death, looking like a corpse—the silent, resolute, half-dozen policemen, with no weapons but their little clubs, yet stern and steady through all those eddying swarms—made a fitting sidescene to the grand tragedy of the murder. They gain'd the station-house with the protected man, whom they placed in security for the night, and discharged him in the morning.

15 And in the midst of that pandemonium, infuriated soldiers, the audience and the crowd, the stage, and all its actors and actresses, its paintpots, spangles, and gas-lights—the life blood from those veins, the best and sweetest of the land, drips slowly down, and death's ooze already begins its little bubbles on the lips.

Thus the visible incidents and surroundings of Abraham Lincoln's murder, as they really occur'd. Thus ended the attempted secession of these States: thus the four years' war. But the main things come subtly and invisibly afterward, perhaps long afterward—neither military, political, nor (great as those are,) historical. I say, certain secondary and indirect results, out of the tragedy of this death, are, in my opinion, greatest. Not the event of the murder itself. Not that Mr. Lincoln strings the principal points and personages of the period, like beads, upon the single string of his career. Not that his idiosyncrasy, in its sudden appearance and disappearance, stamps this Republic with a stamp more mark'd and enduring than any yet given by any one man—(more even than Washington's;)—but, join'd with these, the immeasurable value and meaning of that whole tragedy lies, to me, in senses finally dearest to a nation, (and here all our own)—the imaginative and artistic senses—the literary and dramatic ones. Not in any common or low meaning of those terms, but a meaning precious to the race, and to every age. A long and varied series of contradictory events arrives at last at its highest poetic, single, central, pictorial *dénouement*. The whole involved, baffling, multiform whirl of the secession period comes to a head, and is gather'd in one brief flash of lightning-illumination—one simple, fierce deed. Its sharp culmination, and as it were solution, of so many bloody and angry problems, illustrates those climax-moments on the stage of universal Time, where the historic Muse at one entrance, and the tragic Muse at the other, suddenly ringing down the curtain, close an immense act in the long drama of creative thought, and give it radiation, tableau, stranger than fiction. Fit radiation—fit close! How the imagination—how the student loves these things! America, too, is to have them. For not in all great deaths, not far or near—not Caesar in the Roman senate-house, or Napoleon passing away in the wild night-storm at St. Helena —not Paleologus, falling, desperately fighting, piled over dozens deep with Grecian corpses—not calm old Socrates, drinking the hemlock—out-vies that terminus of the secession war, in one man's life, here in our midst, in our time—that seal of the emancipation of three million slaves—that parturition and delivery of our at last really free Republic, born again, henceforth to commence its career of genuine homogenous Union, compact, consistent with itself.

Nor will ever future American Patriots and Unionists, indifferently over the whole land, or North or South, find a better moral to their lesson. The final use of the greatest men of a Nation is, after all , not with reference to their deeds in themselves, or their direct bearing on their times or lands. The final use of a heroic-eminent life—especially of a heroic-eminent death—is its indirect filtering into the nation and the race, and to give, often at many removes, but unerringly, age after age, color and fibre to the personalism of the youth and maturity of that age, and of mankind. Then, there is a cement to the whole people, subtler, more underlying, than any thing in written constitution, or courts or armies—namely, the cement of a death identified thoroughly with that people, at its head, and for its sake. Strange, (is it not?) that battles, martyrs, agonies, blood, even assassination, should so condense— perhaps only really, lastingly condense—a Nationality.

I repeat it—the grand deaths of the race—the dramatic deaths of every nationality—-are its most important inheritance-value—in some respects beyond its literature and art—(as the hero is beyond his finest portrait, and the battle itself beyond its choicest song or epic.) Is not here indeed the point underlying all tragedy? the famous pieces of the Grecian masters—and all masters? Why, if the old Greeks had had this man, what trilogies of plays—what epics—would have been made out of him! How the rhapsodes would have recited him! How quickly that quaint tall form would have enter'd into the region where men vitalize gods, and gods divinify men! But Lincoln, his times, his death—great as any, any age—belong altogether to our own, and are autochthonic. (Sometimes indeed I think our American days, our own stage—the actors we know and have shaken hands, or talk'd with— more fateful than any thing in Eschylus—more heroic than the fighters around Troy—afford kings of men for our Democracy prouder than Agamemnon—models of character cute and hardy as Ulysses— deaths more pitiful than Priam's.)

When centuries hence, (as it must, in my opinion, be centuries hence before the life of these States, or of Democracy, can be really written and illustrated,) the leading historians and dramatists seek for some personage, some special event, incisive enough to mark with deepest cut, and mnemonize, this turbulent nineteenth century of ours, (not only these States, but all over the political and social world)—something, perhaps, to close that gorgeous procession of European feudalism, with all its pomp and caste-prejudices, (of whose long train we in America are yet so inextricably the heirs)—something to identify with terrible identification, by far the greatest revolutionary step in the history of the United States, (perhaps the greatest of the world, our century)—the absolute extirpation and erasure of slavery from the States—those historians will seek in vain for any point to serve more thoroughly their purpose, than Abraham Lincoln's death.

20 Dear to the Muse—thrice dear to Nationality—to the whole 20 human race—precious to this Union—precious to Democracy— unspeakably and forever precious—their first great Martyr Chief.

Questions on Meaning

1. Why does Whitman start the essay as he does, with a curious non-event that does not reveal much about Lincoln? How does this set the stage for what is coming? How does the Lincoln you see there compare and contrast with the Lincoln Whitman describes later?
2. Why, according to Whitman, is Lincoln such a great man?
3. What does Whitman mean when he writes of Lincoln's death: "the immeasurable value and meaning of that whole tragedy lies, to me, in senses finally dearest to a nation, (and here all our own)—the imaginative and artistic senses—the literary and dramatic ones . . . a long and varied series of contradictory events arrives at last at its highest poetic, single, central, pictorial *denouement*."

Questions on Rhetorical Strategy and Style

1. Make a list of adjectives that describe Whitman's style and use of language, considering his flow, rhythms, sentence structures, use of imagery, and so on.
2. Analyze how Whitman uses detail in his description. Compare the physical descriptions of the two primary figures in the essay, Lincoln and Booth.
3. Explain the overall organization and movement of the essay, from its starting point in physical description to its grand conclusion analyzing Lincoln's place in history.

Writing Assignments

1. Read about Lincoln in a history of the United States. Is his place in history now as significant as Whitman predicted long ago?
2. Think about the idea that history is about *people* more than events, that individual people can personify or symbolize the history of a period. Read a historian's analysis of a period and note how the great figures of the time are described. What do you think really shapes history: people or events? Why?
3. What historical figure or event in your own lifetime holds the greatest interest for you? Write an essay in which you move from a description of the person or event into an analysis of its meaning and place in the larger perspective of history.

In Search of the Enemy of Man
Thich Nhat Hanh

> **Thich Nhat Hanh** (*pronounced* **tick · not · hawn**)
> *(1926–) was born in Vietnam where he became a Bud-*
> *dhist monk at sixteen. During the Vietnam War, Hanh*
> *started the School of Youth Social Service, an organiza-*
> *tion of 10,000 student activists who, in direct opposition*
> *to their government, assisted civilian war victims. As a*
> *result, Hahn was banned from Vietnam while on a peace*
> *mission to the U.S. In exile, Hanh continued to make the*
> *case for peace. (In the following letter, written in 1965,*
> *Hanh encourages Martin Luther King, Jr. to publicly*
> *oppose U.S. military involvement Vietnam.) In 1967,*
> *King nominated Hanh for the Nobel Peace Prize,*
> *describing him as "an apostle of peace and non-violence."*
> *Hahn has published over 85 books of poetry and prose.*
> *He continues to travel, to teach, and to assist those suffer-*
> *ing in developing countries worldwide.*

1   The self-burning of Vietnamese Buddhist monks in 1963 is   1
somehow difficult for the Western Christian conscience to
understand. The Press spoke then of suicide, but in the
essence, it is not. It is not even a protest. What the monks said in
the letters they left before burning themselves aimed only at alarming, at moving the hearts of the oppressors and at calling the attention of the world to the suffering endured then by the Vietnamese.
To burn oneself by fire is to prove that what one is saying is of the
utmost importance. There is nothing more painful than burning
oneself. To say something while experiencing this kind of pain is
to say it with the utmost of courage, frankness, determination and

Reprinted from *Nhat Nanh, Ho Huu Tuong, Tam Ich, Bui Giang, Pham Cong Thien,*
(1965).

sincerity. During the ceremony of ordination, as practiced in the Mahayana tradition, the monk-candidate is required to burn one, or more, small spots on his body in taking the vow to observe the 250 rules of a bhikshu, to live the life of a monk, to attain enlightenment and to devote his life to the salvation of all beings. One can, of course, say these things while sitting in a comfortable armchair; but when the words are uttered while kneeling before the community of sangha and experiencing this kind of pain, they will express all the seriousness of one's heart and mind, and carry much greater weight.

The Vietnamese monk, by burning himself, say with all his strengh [sic] and determination that he can endure the greatest of sufferings to protect his people. But why does he have to burn himself to death? The difference between burning oneself and burning oneself to death is only a difference in degree, not in nature. A man who burns himself too much must die. The importance is not to take one's life, but to burn. What he really aims at is the expression of his will and determination, not death. In the Buddhist belief, life is not confined to a period of 60 or 80 or 100 years: life is eternal. Life is not confined to this body: life is universal. To express will by burning oneself, therefore, is not to commit an act of destruction but to perform an act of construction, i.e., to suffer and to die for the sake of one's people. This is not suicide. Suicide is an act of self-destruction, having as causes the following:

• lack of courage to live and to cope with difficulties
• defeat by life and loss of all hope
• desire for non-existence (abhava)

This self-destruction is considered by Buddhism as one of the most serious crimes. The monk who burns himself has lost neither courage nor hope; nor does he desire non-existence. On the contrary, he is very courageous and hopeful and aspires for something good in the future. He does not think that he is destroying himself; he believes in the good fruition of his act of self-sacrifice for the sake of others. Like the Buddha in one of his former lives—as told in a story of Jataka—who gave himself to a hungry lion which was about to devour her own cubs, the monk believes he is practicing the doctrine of highest compassion by sacrificing himself in order to call the attention of, and to seek help from, the people of the world.

I believe with all my heart that the monks who burned themselves did not aim at the death of the oppressors but only at a change in their policy. Their enemies are not man. They are intolerance, fanaticism, dictatorship, cupidity, hatred and discrimination which lie within the heart of man. I also believe with all my being that the struggle for equality and freedom you lead in Birmingham, Alabama... is not aimed at the whites but only at intolerance, hatred and discrimination. These are real enemies of man–not man himself. In our unfortunate father land we are trying to yield desperately: do not kill man, even in man's name. Please kill the real enemies of man which are present everywhere, in our very hearts and minds.

5 Now in the confrontation of the big powers occurring in our country, hundreds and perhaps thousands of Vietnamese peasants and children lose their lives every day, and our land is unmercifully and tragically torn by a war which is already twenty years old. I am sure that since you have been engaged in one of the hardest struggles for equality and human rights, you are among those who understand fully, and who share with all their hearts, the indescribable suffering of the Vietnamese people. The world's greatest humanists would not remain silent. You yourself can not remain silent. America is said to have a strong religious foundation and spiritual leaders would not allow American political and economic doctrines to be deprived of the spiritual element. You cannot be silent since you have already been in action and you are in action because, in you, God is in action, too–to use Karl Barth's expression. And Albert Schweitzer, with his stress on the reverence for life and Paul Tillich with his courage to be, and thus, to love. And Niebuhr. And Mackay. And Fletcher. And Donald Harrington. All these religious humanists, and many more, are not going to favour the existence of a shame such as the one mankind has to endure in Vietnam. Recently a young Buddhist monk named Thich Giac Thanh burned himself [April 20, 1965, in Saigon] to call the attention of the world to the suffering endured by the Vietnamese, the suffering caused by this unnecessary war—and you know that war is never necessary. Another young Buddhist, a nun named

Hue Thien was about to sacrifice herself in the same way and with the same intent, but her will was not fulfilled because she did not have the time to strike a match before people saw and interfered. Nobody here wants the war. What is the war for, then? And whose is the war?

Yesterday in a class meeting, a student of mine prayed: "Lord Buddha, help us to be alert to realize that we are not victims of each other. We are victims of our own ignorance and the ignorance of others. Help us to avoid engaging ourselves more in mutual slaughter because of the will of others to power and to predominance." In writing to you, as a Buddhist, I profess my faith in Love, in Communion and in the World's Humanists whose thoughts and attitude should be the guide for all human kind in finding who is the real enemy of Man.

June 1, 1965
NHAT HAHN

Questions on Meaning

1. Hanh writes, "To express will by burning oneself, therefore, is not to commit an act of destruction but to perform an act of construction." What does he mean by this? Explain how Hanh distinguishes the two.
2. When Hanh writes about the "real enemies of man," to what is he referring? Where, in Hanh's opinion, are these enemies to be found? Does Hanh reveal how these "real enemies" can be "killed"?
3. Why does Hanh feel that King should be able to "understand fully" the suffering of Vietnamese civilian war victims?

Questions on Rhetorical Strategy and Style

1. Why did Hanh write this letter to King? What's Hanh's thesis? What reasons does he offer for support?
2. Hanh alludes to several religious humanists in his letter to King. Why do you think Hanh chose to make these allusions? Is this an effective strategy?
3. In the letter, Hanh tells the story of Jataka who "gave himself to a hungry lion which was about to devour her own cubs." What role does this story play in Hanh's argument?

Writing Assignments

1. Burning oneself to death as a form of activism is something many westerners find bizarre. At the same time, we treat as heroes those firefighters, police, and military personnel who risk almost certain death to save lives. Is there a fundamental difference between these two behaviors? If so, what is it?

2. Identify a behavior that is normal in your own country, region, or culture but that might be seen as strange by an outsider. Like Hanh, attempt to explain why this behavior makes sense to those who do it.

3. Write a letter to a world leader making a case that he or she commit to a course of action that you feel is important. Like Hanh, consider your audience and utilize allusions and comparisons to connect your reader to this important cause.

From the Margins to Mainstream: The Political Power of Hip-Hop

Katina R. Stapleton

Katina R. Stapleton was born in Baltimore, Maryland in 1973. She was graduated in 1995 from the University of Maryland at College Park with a BA in print journalism and entered Duke University's political science department, where she is currently working on a dissertation that examines the role of the media in the urban education policy process. She writes and teaches on the politics of music. In this 1998 article, she describes the musical phenomenon called hip-hop in relation to African-American and youth culture, demonstrating the relationship between music and political action.

1   'They didn't know what they were playing with, look what   1
they got', spoke Jungle Brothers rapper Mike G from the
floor of a conference on the state of hip-hop in the late
1990s. In the 20-plus years since it emerged in inner-city New York
as an alternative to violence and a way to escape harsh urban realities,
hip-hop has become a worldwide musical and cultural force. But the
widespread popularity of rap music and hip-hop culture among youth
has caught many outside the hip-hop community by surprise. Once
considered 'black noise', hip-hop has claimed for itself the role of cultural and political voice of an entire generation of youth.

When hip-hop emerged in New York City in the 1970s, its primary sphere of influence was the youth in the neighborhoods where

it evolved. In areas like the Bronx, breakdancers, graffiti artists, MCs (rappers), DJs and fans formed the hip-hop community. Hip-hop scholar Tricia Rose argues that 'alternative local identities were forged in fashions and language, street names, and most important, in establishing neighborhood crews or posses' (Rose, 1994: 34). Crews provided an opportunity for youth to form family-like bonds similar to, but not based on, gang affiliation. Instead of always fighting with fists, hip-hop gave youth the option of fighting with words, art, dance or the ability to produce good beats (Fernando, 1994).

Hip-hop emerged at a time of crisis for youth in urban communities. The situation was no less than a 'deindustrialized meltdown where social alienation, prophetic imagination, and yearning intersect' (Rose, 1994: 21). Hip-hop enabled youth to create their own cultural space within the city that countered the poverty and alienation that surrounded them on a day-to-day basis. As a type of genuine street culture, hip-hop evolved for several years before being discovered by the mass media (Shomari, 1995).

As scholars began to research hip-hop, it became clear that while it developed as an alternative youth culture, hip-hop incorporated many elements of the larger African-American and African cultures (DeMott, 1988; Floyd, 1995; Remes, 1991; Stephens, 1991). One such element is 'playing the dozens', a time-honored tradition in the African-American community. Also known as bragging, boasting, toasting or signifying, the process includes 'ritual insults' in which the speakers test their verbal prowess by seeing who can form the best taunt. Dozens-playing was an integral part of the early rap competitions and has remained a significant element of rap music today.

Hip-hop's use of the spoken or sung word to tell stories and teach 'life-lessons' is also part of a tradition among African peoples that goes back to the *griots*, African storytellers who played the important role of oral historians. The griots' role in African communities was to pass down the stories of each generation in song, while imparting knowledge about society. 'Endowed with this much prized oral skill, the griot enjoyed a very respected position within his community, just like many modern-day microphone personalities' (Fernando, 1994: 255). Rappers have become urban griots, using their lyrics to disperse social commentary about what it means to be young and black in the late 20th century (Kuwahara, 1992).

Like more traditional griots, what makes hip-hop artists such successful purveyors of cultural and political information is that they relay messages of importance to youth in a form that they enjoy. Rap music, currently the most visible element of hip-hop, has proven its ability to both capture the ear of those who listen to it for aesthetic reasons and those who look to the genre for deeper meaning. From its rough and tumble forms to the most commercial jams, hip-hop has been able to raise awareness among African-Americans and the general public about the issues that face black youth on a day-to-day basis.

Another strong tradition in African-American music that hip-hop has followed is the use of song to 'tell it like it is' and protest against social injustice (Nelson, 1992; Remes, 1991). In the early 1900s an examination of Negro spirituals as folksongs noted that folksongs were developed out of experience (Krehbiel, 1914). The pathos of what it meant to be a slave was reflected in music of the times. Krehbiel writes, 'as a rule the finest songs are the fruits of suffering undergone and the hope of deliverance from bondage' (Krehbiel, 1914: 26–7). Rochelle Larking (1972) argues that the historic conditions of black Americans will always serve as a basis for protest music. Her 1970s examination of soul music as a form of protest noted that beginning with the blues, black popular music has joined church songs as calls to freedom.

African-Americans, according to the musicologist Jon Spencer, have used secular music such as the blues to reflect the 'hell on earth' which they have been subjected to throughout the ages. These songs, claims Spencer, are no less profound than Old Testament psalms and lamentations. Like these biblical tales of woe, the blues are songs 'that reveal the nitty-gritty details of life as it is lived at the underside of society and the underbelly of history' (Spencer, 1996: xiv). Black music from the blues to funk, soul, jazz and now to hip-hop often shares the hope for deliverance found in Negro folksongs. As noted by Henry Charles (1990), the concept of deliverance is found in many aspects of African-American culture.

The central purpose of this article is to examine how hip-hop culture and music are uniquely situated among youth as a means of political action. While the most obvious means is through lyrical protest, Mark Mattern (1997) provides a larger framework for political action that includes music and the culture in which it develops. In his examination of Cajun music, Mattern suggests three categories of political action that will also form the basis of my analysis: confrontational (protest), deliberative and pragmatic.

Hidden transcripts and confrontational lyrics

> Creating culture is not easy. . . . There is a politically conscious, culturally aware, liberated, Black survival kit side to rap music that is being seriously overlooked. (Jackson, 1994)

One of the greatest contributions of hip-hop artists to the political landscape is one of protest. Mattern (1997) argues that the use of music to provide protest is a clear example of confrontational political action. Protest music is characterized by objections to injustices and oppressions inflicted on certain individuals and groups. Resistance is key and so are clear distinctions between those being subjugated and those perpetrating the injustice. 'Typically, the intent of protest musicians is to oppose the exploitation and oppression exercised by dominant elites and members of dominant groups' (Mattern, 1997: 2). Mattern finds similar elements of resistance in Cajun music that had been previously found in rap music.

In her seminal study of hip-hop, Tricia Rose (1994) provides an examination of rap music and hip-hop culture as a means to resist the dominant social order. Drawing on the work of James Scott (1990), Rose makes the critical distinction between the means by which those in dominant versus marginalized groups are able to get their messages across. Those in power are represented by dominant public transcripts, which are 'maintained through a wide range of social practices', such as setting the terms of public debate (Rose, 1994: 100). Cut out of the public debate, marginalized groups develop their own resistive or hidden transcripts. These communications take place in disguised form and tend to include critiques of the predominant culture. As one of the most marginalized groups in American history, African-Americans have long fought to be included in public debate. Since its inception, one of the areas found to be most problematic for the expression of African-American culture has been television. While there has been more of an influx of television shows and films that feature African-Americans in recent years, critics argue that blacks are mostly portrayed as comedic objects or criminals (Dates and Barlow, 1990; Greenberg and Brand, 1990). Black youths in particular have looked to the media to find representations of their own lives. Rap music and rap music videos gained in popularity among black youth as they recognized rap as their voice. Rap veteran Chuck D of Public Enemy has been widely quoted as calling rap music the 'Black man's CNN'. In the face of under- and/or misrepresentation in traditional media, black youths have turned to hip-hop as a means to define themselves. In terms of resistance, hip-hop provided a forum from which black youth can portray what it means to be young and black in America and protest against it. In its musical form, hip-hop has been able to form what are termed 'hidden transcripts'. While those from dominant cultural groups have public transcripts, those from marginalized groups often must create their own forum from which they can communicate with each other and transmit messages to the dominant culture. The use of resistive transcripts in rap music serves the dual purpose of using symbolism to critique power holders (Rose, 1994) and providing a dialogic arena in which rappers shape the terms of entry (Skeggs, 1993).

The transcripts found in rap music, while often protesting the treatment of all African-Americans, find black youth, not adults, as their primary audience. Dates and Barlow (1990) suggest that this age division among African-Americans over rap is based in part on perceived class consciousness. They argue that this can be seen in radio programming. Many radio formats reflect a class style, with stations wooing urban contemporary listeners with jazz, soul and traditional R&B while other stations woo black youth with hip-hop influenced R&B and rap music (Dates and Barlow, 1990; Jackson, 1994). In terms of political action, this means that black youth and black adults are finding that they have differing ideas of what protest music should sound like. While 'Say it Loud, I'm Black and I'm Proud' by James Brown and 'Respect' by Aretha Franklin were anthems for blacks who came of age in the 1960s, rap is providing new anthems for black youth of the 1990s.

One of the earliest raps credited with going beyond the boast/party elements of rap music to provide a protest anthem was simply called 'The Message'. Released by Grandmaster Flash and the Furious Five in the early 1980s, 'The Message' captured the angst of black youth growing up in the inner city and lent its name to a type of rap music that would follow.

15   Flash's message that society shouldn't push him because he was   15
close to the edge was something that anyone who had grown up in the ghetto could understand. According to Flash, being raised in the impoverished 'second rate' conditions is what often causes young blacks to harbor deep feelings of anger towards society.

While raps like 'The Message' may have started with GrandMaster Flash in 1982, over the years, the group Public Enemy has brought hard-hitting societal critiques to the forefront of hip-hop. Public Enemy has brought hard-hitting societal critiques to the forefront of hip-hop. Public Enemy's founder and lead rapper Chuck D, writes how PE decided to use their music for social purposes:

> The sociopolitical meaning of Public Enemy came after we decided the group would be called that, because the meaning and the connection of what we were about fit right in. The Black man and woman was considered three-fifths of human being in the Constitution of the United States. Since the government and the general public follow the Constitution, then we must be the enemy. (Chuck D, 1997: 86)

Public Enemy credit their strong commitment to protest to the influences of the Black Panther Party and the Nation of Islam. The combination of PE's political background and their ability to create strong musical and video images allowed them to use their songs to provide powerful statements. Two of the most remembered rap commentaries from PE are '911 is a Joke' and 'Fight the Power'. Even before newspaper and television reporters started telling the general public about the problems inner-city residents had with receiving prompt ambulance service, Public Enemy detailed the situation in rhyme. The raps of nationalist groups such as Public Enemy serve as direct examples of confrontational political action. One criterion of this type of political action is the placement of the group, which is perceived as being oppressed in direct opposition to the oppressors (Mattern, 1997). The resistive transcripts of Public Enemy's song 'Hitler Day', locate people of color in direct opposition to white America.

'Hitler Day' is a critique of America's celebration of Columbus Day. According to the rap, a holiday which celebrates the 'discovery' of America at the expense of its native inhabitants is inherently offensive to people of color.

Chuck D explains that asking native and African-American people to celebrate Columbus Day is analogous to asking Jews to celebrate Adolf Hitler Day. 'For me, that's what Christopher Columbus represents to Black, Brown, and Red nations in North America and throughout the world because he opened the gates for five hundred years of mayhem' (Chuck D, 1997: 198). Other more well known confrontational songs by the group include 'Shut 'Em Down', which encouraged the boycotting of businesses that take from the black community without giving back, and the self-explanatory rap 'Fight the Power'.

Other nation-conscious rappers like Brand-Nubian, X-Clan, Poor Righteous Teachers and KRS-One have provided either direct indictments of the dominant social structure or more hidden critiques (Decker, 1993; Eurie and Spady, 1991; Henderson, 1996). But nation-consciousness in rap music also includes messages of empowerment. Next to Public Enemy, Kris Parker is one of the most well known deliverers of political and social messages to the hip-hop community. Ironically, Kris Parker (KRS-One) began his career as part of Boogie Down Productions (BDP) with the late Scott LaRock. Posing on the cover of 'Criminal Minded with Guns', BDP produced some of the earliest music with a gangster ethic, while at the same time promoting messages of black nationalism, safe sex and the rejection of the drug trade. As a solo artist, KRS-One has cemented his role as a teacher among the hip-hop community. From his 1997 album *I Got Next* KRS-One urges the hip-hop nation to shed what he calls ghetto mentality for one of success. Both Public Enemy and KRS-One represent nation-consciousness based in the 1960s black power movement. Jeffery Decker contends that hip-hop nationalists:

> . . . are most effective when they appropriate popular knowledge from within the black community and exploit its most progressive elements in the process of envisioning a new society. At these moments rappers function in a manner resembling what Antonio Gramsci calls 'organic intellectuals'. (Decker, 1993: 59)

Much of the literature on the presence of confrontational political action in music is implicitly or explicitly indebted to Gramscian Marxism. Organic intellectuals are individuals who hold close ties to their class of origin and whose function is to express class identity and goals (Mattern, 1997). The relationship of the hip-hop artist to a class identity has been clear since hip-hop began. Early hip-hop artists came directly from specific inner-city communities and represented a class of youth facing economic deprivation along with social and political marginalization. Even though the hip-hop community has expanded beyond its core to include youth of all classes, races and cultures, hip-hop artists are expected to remain true to their positions as the representative of black youth. 'Hip-hop nationalists are organic cultural intellectuals to the degree that their activities are directly linked to the everyday struggles of black folk and that their music critically engages the popular knowledge of which they have a part' (Decker, 1993: 59). Henderson (1996) and Decker (1993) note that many prominent examples of hip-hop nationalists are not explicitly linked to 1960s nationalism. The Fugees are among rappers whose vision of nationhood is bounded not by geography, but rather one's link to the African or Afro-Hispanic diaspora. Referring to black youth as black diamonds and pearls, Fugees vocalist Lauren Hill raps, 'If I ruled the world, I'd free all my sons'. This type of nationalism is Afrocentric in nature. Rappers like Queen Latifah look to Mother Africa for inspiration in forming their hip-hop identity.

Gangster rap is another prominent source of confrontational nationalist rap (Decker, 1993). Known for their universal distrust of the police, gangster rappers often use their music to provide graphic indictments of the police and the government interspersed with tales of gangster living. Many gangster rappers prefer to be called realists, because they feel their rap describes what is really going on in the 'hood. With black on black violence being the leading source of death for black youth since 1969, it doesn't seem wrong to many rappers to reflect that in their music (Kitwana, 1994: 41). King George, a member of TRU, contends that this type of realism is more than just talk about killing. 'I'm just relating to what's going on and keeping everybody aware at the same time' (Davis, 1996: 63).

Gender and gangsta-rap

Claims to realism aside, however, there has been widespread debate about whether or not songs that call black women 'bitches' and 'hoes' (whores) as well as songs which detail sex acts, drug sales and extreme violence are negative influences of youth. The portrayal of women and whites in hip-hop music have been special sources of concern (Allison, 1994; Hansen, 1995; Johnson et al., 1995). It would seem obvious that no woman would want to be called a female dog on tape, or have their boyfriends 'Treat 'em like a prostitute'. But while female rappers like M.C. Lyte, Queen Latifah, Yo-Yo and Salt 'n' Pepa began to challenge the conception that only males could rap and shape perceptions of women in the urban community, some female rappers responded by becoming hard-core rappers themselves (Rose, 1994; Skeggs, 1993)

In the late 1990s female rappers have emerged as a force equal to male rappers. Skeggs (1993) argues that if rap in general is used to combat racism and oppression, female artists use rap to battle sexism. While many female hip-hop artists rap about female solidarity, others provide images of women being in control of their sexuality. Skeggs theorizes that for black women, 'sexuality is one of the few cultural resources that they can use for the construction of embodied self worth' (Skeggs, 1993: 310). This notion has not gone unchallenged. Female rappers like Lil' Kim and Foxy Brown have been both vilified and held up for praise for their hard-core attitude and blatantly sexy style. The question 'harlots or heroines?' has followed them since they came on the scene. While supporters celebrate the two female rappers' ability to take charge and proclaim their sexuality, critics challenge their claim to feminism. The Lady of Rage, like many other female rappers, holds conflicting views of artists like Kim and Foxy. "I like Little Kim because she sounds so hard. At first I thought what she was saying was not good because we already got problems as far as women getting recognition and being accepted. I felt that might hinder it a little bit.' But, as Rage notes, 'Sex sells and she's good' (Williams, 1997:63).

Many in the hip-hop community contend that while there are valid concerns about the level of sexual and violent content in hip-hop music, the concern from the media and politicians is not genuine. In stead, negative sentiments towards hip-hop are considered to have racial overtones. Hip-hop artists in attendance at the 1997 Life After Death conference contended that the media and politicians are down on hip-hop because it is a black art from that is being consumed by white youth. The consumption of hip-hop by young whites allows them to become 'ghetto chic' without actually having to live in ghetto conditions (Allison, 1994). Though much of the criticism of hip-hop comes from those outside of the black community, there is a large concern about the tone of rap music within African-American discourse. Rose, who applauds rap for its ability to provide resistive transcripts, lambasts rappers for their sexism. 'I am thoroughly frustrated but not surprised by the apparent need for some rappers to craft elaborate and creative stories about the abuse and domination of young black women' (Rose, 1994: 15).

Likewise, trends toward the inclusion of sex, drugs, violence and, most recently, materialism in rap music have not gone unnoticed or unchallenged by member s of the hip-hop community itself (Life After Death, 1997). Hip-hop conferences held in the aftermath of the violent deaths of favorite sons, Tupac Shakur and the Notorious B.I.G. have looked at whether hip-hop has a social responsibility to the youth that listen to the music. Participants at Life After Death (1997) asked serious questions about the role of violence in the genre. The consensus among panel and audience members seemed to be that in many ways hip-hop is out of control. However, they note—and I agree—that rappers who talk about sex and violence should not be expected to take all the blame. Equal shares of blame should lie with record companies and managers who promote violent/sexual rappers, with the youth who buy these records, and with parents who do not take the time to listen to what their children are listening to. Blame also lies with American society itself, which criticizes rappers for talking about ideals that are in fact embedded in the American way of life, as well as the media who often blow up the violence in hip-hop out of context. A sampling of newspaper articles following the shooting death of Biggie Smalls seems to support claims that in a society where black men are killed in record numbers the media still insist on implying that the rap industry, not guns, kills people (Patillo, 1997).

The fact that rappers reflect aspects of American society and the pursuit of the American dream is important in a political context. Rap has many elements in common with country and hard rock music, but receives more critical attention. 'Rap and country lyrics implicate underclass reality, that the alternative symbol systems have a parallel socio-economic provenience' (Armstrong, 1993: 69). Though both genres are based on somewhat different social realities, they both share a rhetoric of violence. Analyses of press coverage of country and rap have found that while the genres share a tendency towards machismo, they are not treated the same way by the press. The difference, as found by Noe, lies not in the song lyrics, but in the racial lenses through which the songs are interpreted.

> When Ice Cube says, 'Let the suburbs see a nigga invasion', many whites interpret that as an incitement to violence. But when Johnny Cash sings, 'Shot a man in Reno/just to watch him die', the public taps its feet and hums. (Noe, 1995: 20)

The irony, says Noe, is that rap is no more amoral than other musical genres, but rappers are being punished for catering to prevalent American themes: sex, violence and materialism.

Setting the boundaries of hip-hop

30 Hip-hop is bigger than any one person's opinion of what it should be, 30 said Chuck D of Public Enemy, now a reporter for the Fox News Channel (Chuck D, 1997: 152). The process of establishing where the boundaries of hip-hop should stand is one of deliberation. Mattern (1997) elaborates on this type of political action. He writes, 'Deliberation is a political process and a form of political action in its own right, as well as a necessary preliminary step in forging agreement on common interests and goals for action in other political arenas to address them' (Mattern, 1997: 7). Mattern uses rap and Cajun music as examples of how differing visions of what a genre should stand for are deliberated within a community. The main point of deliberation within the hip-hop community revolves around the question: 'Has hip-hop gone too far?' Related questions include, but are not limited to: 'Has rap music become too sexual, too violent, and too materialistic?' 'Has hip-hop sold its soul for commercial success?' 'Has hip-hop crossed too far into the territory of other music forms?' 'As a community, has hip-hop become more suburban and white than black and urban?'

The answers to all these questions are not clear-cut. The very nature of hip-hop culture has been one that accommodated many types of people, many types of subject matter, and many types of music. The underlying question, then, is whether or not hip-hop can accommodate varying interests, while still retaining its distinctive urban identity. The presence of intra-group differences and disagreements, and of border zones between different groups, suggests that we consider, at least in some instances, a framework for understanding and action of negotiation, rather than an either-or struggle between opposing forces. Popular music would be viewed in these cases as a site and a medium for disagreement and debate over both intra- and inter-group identity and commitments. This takes shape in a deliberative form of political action (Mattern, 1997:6).

Hip-hop's identity as form of resistance among black youth lies at the heart of deliberation in the hip-hop community. Part of hip-hop's credibility among young blacks lies in its ability to claim that it is an authentic street culture (Powell, 1991). But if hip-hop is 'by the ghetto, for the ghetto', how is the community changed by the fact that it is being played on college campuses across the nation and in the homes of suburban whites? When hip-hop style is being used to sell movies, breath mints, sodas, make-up, fast food, alcohol, clothing, shoes and various other products, one knows that this is a valid concern (Blair, 1993). Similar feelings have been reported from England's hip-hop community. 'Hip-hop's integrity has been prostituted in the pursuit of financial gain', writes a columnist in *Hip-Hop Connection*, one of Britain's hip-hop magazines (Salsa, 1997: 5). Though the author was from England, she accurately summed up concerns that are held across the hip-hop community. Salsa charges that hip-hop is at its best in its resistive mode, but that it has lost its subversiveness due to mainstreaming and commercialization. Bernard-Donais (1994: 133) shares this opinion. 'The very fact that it is covered by an institution like the [*New York*] *Times* suggests that rap has found its way into the canon, and that it has ceased to be the subversive (or in other terms, marginal) form that it had been at one time.'

In the case of hip-hop, the transference from subculture to mainstream has been driven by technological advances. As long as artists performed rap in venues limited to neighborhoods, its marginal status was assured. But as rap music expanded to being mass produced hip-hop spread across the nation (Blair, 1993; Kuwahara, 1992). Hip-hop's influence has not been limited to America. Fans from across the world are able to buy rap music both from traditional record stores and from mail order distribution. The worldwide audience for hip-hop should not be underestimated (Toop, 1991). Hip-hop artists regularly perform to international audiences. Wu Tang Clan and the Fugees are just two examples of what is called global hip-hop. The appeal of hip-hop around the world is based in part on the fact that marginalization, oppression and struggle can be understood by many youth. The love of hip-hop has a universal appeal, agrees Chuck D (1997). He believes that one of the reasons that rap crosses over successfully into mainstream culture is that young whites are able to gain an African-American perspective through the music.

The character of deliberation within the hip-hop community is necessarily shaped by its widespread audience. Stephens (1991) contends that rap provides a 'double-voiced discourse' in which rap crosses racial and geographic boundaries. Hip-hop, writes Stephens, provides a point of intersection where blacks and whites can have a dialogue. Though not always acknowledge in the media, the members of the Hispanic community have also been involved in hip-hop since its inception. In this case, it is urbanity and similar social situations that guide Hispanic contributions to hip-hop (Fernando, 1994; Stephens, 1991). As Rose notes, 'Rap's black cultural address and its focus on marginal identities may appear to be in opposition to its crossover appeal for people from different racial or ethnic groups and social positions', but in reality it suggests 'that rap is a black idiom that prioritizes black culture and that articulates the problems of black urban life in the face of such diverse constituencies' (Rose, 1994: 4).

35 Discussions of hip-hop as a street culture sometimes overlook 35 contributions of college students who have since become hip-hop artists and the strong identification of many black college students with hip-hop culture. Music, if not social class, draws young African-Americans of differing socioeconomic status to hip-hop.

Zillman et al. have looked at the effects of popular rock, non-political rap and radical political rap on African-American and white high-school students. They found that while radical political rap seemed to motivate white students to be more supportive of racial harmony, there was no positive link between political rap and ethnic consciousness or ethnic solidarity among the black students (Zillman et al., 1995). The authors note that this does not imply that message rap does not have an effect on black students. In fact the opposite could be true.

> It can be argued that African-American students, in contrast to white students, are massively exposed to rap and that any effect of rap may have manifested itself already prior to exposure. Several additional exposures thus could have influenced white students, especially those who are relatively unfamiliar with radical rap, but not African-American students—because of the informational saturation and its perceptual and evaluative consequences. (Zillman et al., 1995: 21)

Debate about the relative effects of hip-hop on youth is a major area of discussion within the academic community. Instead of concentrating on consciousness, researchers Johnson et al. looked at the effects of violent rap on youth. They found that there was greater acceptance of dating violence among youth exposed to violent rap videos than those exposed to non-violent rap videos or no video at all. In a slightly different experiment they also found that youth exposed to either type of rap video expressed greater desire to be like the materialistic youth portrayed in a scenario than his college-bound friend (Johnson et al., 1995).

Materialism, sexism and violence are points of deliberation among hip-hop artists and fans. Chuck D (1997) recounts the extremely negative reactions he got from African hip-hop fans to the newest incarnations of hip-hop. But as he also notes, the more negative aspects of rap are the easiest to market. 'If you give a fourteen-year-old a choice between a positive video, and a video with tits and ass, or guns and violence, he's going to choose the tits and ass, guns and violence almost every time' (Chuck D, 1997: 33). Researchers have shown that white youth who listen to rap are particularly attracted to its most violent elements. 'The more rappers are packaged as violent black criminals, the bigger their audiences become', writes Ewan Allison (1994: 449).

40 Is this preoccupation with ghetto culture detrimental to youth, 40 black or white? In some ways it is positive, according to Rose, because the ghetto provides a source of social identity for the millions of youth who call it home. Other positive interpretations include the fact that rap has values both because of its brutal honesty and as a point of deliberation. Freestyle rapper Supernatural feels that gangster rap gives other types of rappers more incentive to present the hip-hop experi-

ence from all points of view. Looking at the situation from a slightly different perspective, KRS-One notes that the existence of more than one type of rap exposes the tendency for the public to choose negative over positive. Among participants at Life After Death (1997), the origins of hip-hop were seen as being positive in contrast to more recent developments. Old-school hip-hop artists stressed that hip-hop has strayed too far from its original intentions of combating gang activity to promoting gangster ethics; from promoting black unity to encouraging east coast-west coast feuds; from MC'ing, DJ'ing, breaking, and painting graffiti to simply rapping; from performing for the love of it to performing for money; and from simple boasting to gross exaggerations of one's sexual prowess (Life After Death, 1997; Nia, 1997). Though each of these issues is important to the future of hip-hop, the charge that there has been a dilution of hip-hop as a distinct, protest-based culture and music form is the most political.

Actions speak louder than words

Though the previous discussion in this article has concentrated on both the resistive and deliberative aspects of hip-hop, Mattern suggests music and its related culture also can be used as a basis for pragmatic political action. This type of action, says Mattern, 'begins from the premise of shared political interests. Pragmatic political action occurs when individuals and groups use music to promote awareness of shared interests and to organize collaborative action to address them' (Mattern, 1997: 7). In the past, hip-hop artists have come together for many causes. One prominent example, though considered ill-fated, was the Stop the Violence movement (STV), an attempt to discourage black-on-black crime. Other movements include HEAL (Human Education Against Lies) and the current Rap the Vote project.

Currently there seems to be a resurgence of hip-hop artists attempting to form groups to further the common interests of African-diasporic peoples and/or members of the hip-hop nation. KRS-One, whose song 'Stop the Violence' typified the spirit of the STV movement, has recently started the Temple of Hip-Hop, a non-profit cultural center with the purpose of preserving hip-hop culture. The Zulu nation remains a long-standing conduit of nationalism within the hip-hop community. Many other rap groups and individual artists have taken on specific service projects in order to give back to the community. Perhaps some of the most interesting projects are coming from the ground up. One such project is the Wiseguys, led by Raymond 'Ray Benzino' Scott, president of Boston-based Surrender Records. Using a similar concept to the one of trading a gang for a team, Scott and three friends encouraged former gang rivals to 'trade their hardware for mics'. The project, called Wiseguys, resulted in former gang members coming together to record an album now distributed nationally. Says Scott, 'It becomes a political platform of hypocrisy when you're scared to actually go in and touch the people who are going through the problems' (Walker, 1997: 30–1).

Whether initiated by artists, producers or fans, it is clear that hip-hop has great potential for becoming a major agent of change. All hip-hop needs, according to Chuck D and others, is organization. 'We have to really tie up some areas in the hip-hop Nation: the Zulu Nation, the Rhyme Syndicate, any organization is good. It's just that we have to drop these badges when we come down to dialogue and figure out how to help our people . . .' (Chuck D, 1997: 181). Robert Jackson, author of the *The Last Black Mecca*, believes that an organized hip-hop nation has the potential to be a powerful social and political base within the African-American community: 'The next revolution should be more than televised—it should be political' (Jackson, 1994: 99). The next level for hip-hop, says Jackson, is to organize around a progressive political agenda which would include housing, education and health reform as well as affirmative action and employment.

Music has always been a major source of cultural identity within the African-American community. Rap music is no exception. As part of the larger hip-hop culture, rap music has served to form a cohesive bond among urban youth. Through the mass distribution of hip-hop records and videos, hip-hop has also been able to at least partially erase lines between young people of different socioeconomic backgrounds and vastly different geographic locations. Equally important, hip-hop culture has established itself as a powerful informational tool and means of resistance. It is not an overstatement to say that despite its faults, hip-hop has provided America with one of its only hard-hitting indictments of the social conditions that continue to be a harsh reality for African-American young people.

45 Hip-hop has shown itself to be both the site of political controversy and a means of more than one type of political action. As Mattern notes, confrontational, deliberative and pragmatic political action 45

can occur 'whenever music is produced and consumed', and thus, '[they] should not be viewed as mutually exclusive of each other' (Mattern, 1997: 8). In the case of hip-hop, this is especially true. Rap music, while a significant source of political action within hip-hop, should not be considered its only source. It is its presence within hip-hop community that lends it the context in which resistance emerges. As the hip-hop community looks towards the 21st century, it will be the challenge of hip-hop to define how hip-hop will continue to evolve as a culture and as genuine political force.

References

Allison, E. (1994) 'It's a Black Thing: Hearing How Whites Can't', *Cultural Studies* 8(3): 438–56.

Armstrong, E.G. (1993) 'The Rhetoric of Violence in Rap and Country Music', *Sociological Inquiry* 63(1): 64–83.

Bernard-Donais, M. (1994) 'Jazz, Rock 'n' Roll, Rap and Politics', *Journal of Popular Culture* 28(2): 127–38.

Blair, M.E. (1993) 'The Commercialization of the Rap Music Youth Subculture', *Journal of Popular Culture* 27(3): 21–32.

Charles, H. (1990) *Culture and African American Politics*. Bloomington: Indiana University Press.

Craddock-Willis, A. (1989) 'Rap Music and the Black Musical Tradition', *Radical America* 23(4): 29–38.

D. Chuck (1997) *Fight the Power: Rap, Race and Reality*. New York: Delacorte Press.

Dates, J.L. and W. Barlow (1990) *Split Image: African Americans in the Mass Media*. Washington, DC: Howard University Press.

Davis, T. (1996) 'King George: Tru Royalty', *4080* 35: 63.

Decker, J. (1993) 'The State of Rap: Time and Place in Hip Hop Nationalism', *Social Text* 34: 53–84.

DeMott, D. (1988) 'The Future is Unwritten: Working-Class Youth Cultures in England and America', *Critical Text* 5(1): 42–56.

Eurie, J.D. and J.G. Spady (eds) (1991) *Nation Conscious Rap*. New York: PC International Press.

Fernando, S.H. (1994) *The New Beats: Exploring the Music, Culture, and Attitudes of Hip-Hop Culture*. New York: Harmony Books.

Floyd, S.A. (1995) *The Power of Black Music: Interpreting its History from Africa to the United States*. New York: Oxford University Press.

Greenberg, B. and J. Brand (1994) 'Minorities and the Mass Media: 1970s to 1990s', pp. 273–314 in J. Bryant and D. Zillman (eds) *Media Effects: Advances in Theory and Research*. Hillsdale, NJ: Lawrence Erlbaum Associates.

Hansen, C.H. (1995) 'Predicting Cognitive and Behavioral Effects of Gangsta Rap,' *Basic and Applied Social Psychology* 16(1–2): 43–52.

Henderson, E.A. (1996) 'Black Nationalism and Rap Music', *Journal of Black Studies* 26(3): 308–39.

Jackson, R. (1994) *The Last Black Mecca: Hip-Hop*. Chicago, IL: Research Associates and Frontline Distribution International Inc.

Johnson, J.D., et al. (1995) 'Violent Attitudes and Deferred Academic Aspirations: Deleterious Effects of Exposure to Rap Music', *Basic and Applied Social Psychology* 16(1–2): 27–41.

Kitwana, B. (1994) *The Rap on Gangsta Rap*. Chicago, IL: Third World Press.

Krehbiel, H.E. (1914) *Afro-American Folksongs: A Study in Racial and National Music*. New York and London: G. Shirmer.

Kuwahara, Y. (1992) 'Power to the People Y'all', *Humanity and Society* 16(1): 54–73.

Larking, R. (1972) 'The Soul Message', pp. 92–104 in R. Serge Denisoff and R. Peterson (eds) *The Sounds of Social Change*. Chicago: Rand McNally.

Life After Death: Rap, Reality and Social Responsibility (1997) Harvard University, Cambridge, MA. 3 May.

Mattern, M. (1997) 'Cajun Music, Cultural Revival: Theorizing Political Action in Popular Music', paper prepared for delivery at the 1997 Annual Meeting of the American Political Science Association, Washington, DC.

Nelson, A. (1992) 'The Persistence of Ethnicity in African American Popular Music', *Explorations in Ethnic Studies* 15(1): 47–57.

Nia, M. (1997) 'From God's to Niggas, From Queens to Bitch's: Do Rappers Have An Identity Crisis?', *Beat Down* 5(5): 20.

Noe, D. (1995) 'Parallel Worlds', *Humanist* 55(4): 20–2.

Patillo, M. (1997) 'The Public Eulogy of a Slain Rapper', *The Source* 92: 83.

Powell, C. (1991) 'Rap Music: An Education with a Beat from the Street', *Journal of Negro Education* 60(3): 245–59.

Remes, P. (1991) 'Rapping: A Sociolinguistic Study of Oral Tradition', *Anthropological Society of Oxford* 22(2): 129–49.

Rose, T. (1994) *Black Noise: Rap and Black Culture in Contemporary America*. Hanover, NH: Wesleyan University Press.

Salsa, M. (1997) 'Hard Lines', *Hip Hop Connection* 104:5.

Scott, J.C. (1990) *Domination and the Arts of Resistance: Hidden Transcripts*. New Haven, CT: Yale University Press.

Shomari, H. (1995) *From the Underground: Hip Hop Culture As An Agent of Social Change*. Fairwood, NJ: X-Factor Publications.

Skeggs, B. (1993) 'Two Minute Brother: Contestation Through Gender, "Race" and Sexuality', *Innovation* 6(3): 299–322.

Spencer, J.M. (1996) *Re-searching Black Music*. Knoxville: University of Tennessee Press.

Stephens, G. (1991) 'Rap Music's Double-Voiced Discourse', *Journal of Communication Inquiry* 15(2): 70–91.

Toop, D. (1991) *Rap Attack 2: African Rap to Global Hip Hop*. London: Serpent's Tail.

Walker, S. (1997) 'Glocks Down', *The Source* 98: 30–1.

Williams, F. (1997) 'Rage against the Machine', *The Source* 94: 63–6.

Zillman, D., et al. (1995) 'Radical Rap: Does it Further Ethnic Division?', *Basic and Applied Social Psychology* 16(1–2): 1–25.

Questions on Meaning

1. Explain the function of the griot in African culture.
2. What are the main goals of the hip-hop culture? How does it accomplish those goals? In what direction is its development taking it, according to Stapleton's sources?
3. Listen to some blues recordings by artists such as Muddy Waters or Aretha Franklin and compare their lyrics to those of hip-hop artists. Do they have common themes? similar language? How do they differ?

Questions on Rhetorical Strategy and Style

1. Stapleton's article is persuasive that mainstream and intellectual cultures should respect hip-hop. Identify passages that would tend to influence an audience that does not already listen to hip-hop.
2. Stapleton describes the sexism and violence in hip-hop in the same context as her description of hip-hop's positive social protest. What is Stapleton's point in creating the comparison? Does she mean to show the shortcomings of hip-hop artists? Is she arguing that the ghetto conditions justify the sexism and violence?

Writing Assignments

1. Find recordings or videos by one of the hip-hop artists Stapleton names. After you have reviewed the materials, write an essay that explains the artist's political position.
2. Social and political protest were an important part of pop music during the 60s in the work of folk artists such as Joan Baez and Pete Seeger, as well as rock groups such as the Beatles, Jefferson Airplane, and Country Joe and the Fish. Listen to some of those recordings and write an essay that identifies the themes of social protest in the pop mainstream then and now.
3. Poets have often spoken out against injustice. Study some of the rap artists that Stapleton cites and then read some of the works of Robert Bly, Robinson Jeffers, Denise Levertov, Allen Ginsberg, or a comparable white poet writing out of the American experience. Does race matter to white protest poets? If not, what does?

Global Politics and Government

Speech on the Signing of the Treaty of Port Elliott, 1855

Chief Seattle

Chief Seattle (c.1788–1866), chief of the Suquamish and Duwamish tribes, was born near the location of Seattle, Washington. A warrior as a youth, he advocated peace with the white man and converted to Christianity in his later years. In 1852, the city of Seattle was named in his honor. In this address, delivered in 1855 (and translated by a white doctor fluent in Indian languages), Chief Seattle pleads for fair treatment of his people and asks that the government respect their cultural differences.

1   Yonder sky that has wept tears of compassion upon my people   1
for centuries untold, and which to us appears changeless and
eternal, may change. Today is fair. Tomorrow may be overcast
with clouds. My words are like the stars that never change. Whatever
Seattle says the great chief at Washington can rely upon with as much
certainty as he can upon the return of the sun or the seasons. The
White Chief says that Big Chief at Washington sends us greetings of
friendship and goodwill. That is kind of him for we know he has little need of our friendship in return. His people are many. They are
like the grass that covers vast prairies. My people are few. They resemble the scattering trees of a storm-swept plain. The great, and—I
presume—good, White Chief sends us word that he wishes to buy our
lands but is willing to allow us enough to live comfortably. This indeed appears just, even generous, for the Red Man no longer has rights
that he need respect, and the offer may be wise also, as we are no
longer in need of an extensive country. . . . I will not dwell on, nor
mourn over, our untimely decay, nor reproach our paleface brothers
with hastening it, as we too may have been somewhat to blame.

Youth is impulsive. When our young men grow angry at some real or imaginary wrong, and disfigure their faces with black paint, it denotes that their hearts are black, and then they are often cruel and relentless, and our old men and old women are unable to restrain them. Thus it has ever been. Thus it was when the white men first began to push our forefathers westward. But let us hope that the hostilities between us may never return. We would have everything to lose and nothing to gain. Revenge by young men is considered gain, even at the cost of their own lives, but old men who stay at home in times of war, and mothers who have sons to lose, know better.

Our good father at Washington—for I presume he is now our father as well as yours, since King George has moved his boundaries further north—our great good father, I say, sends us word that if we do as he desires he will protect us. His brave warriors will be to us a bristling wall of strength, and his wonderful ships of war will fill our harbors so that our ancient enemies far to the northward—the Hydas and Tsimpsians—will cease to frighten our women, children, and old men. Then in reality will he be our father and we his children. But can that ever be? Your God is not our God! Your God loves your people and hates mine. He folds his strong and protecting arms lovingly about the paleface and leads him by the hand as a father leads his infant son—but He has forsaken His red children—if they really are his. Our God, the Great Spirit, seems also to have forsaken us. Your God makes your people wax strong every day. Soon they will fill the land. Our people are ebbing away like a rapidly receding tide that will never return. The white man's God cannot love our people or He would protect them. They seem to be orphans who can look nowhere for help. How then can we be brothers? How can your God become our God and renew our prosperity and awaken in us dreams of returning greatness? If we have a common heavenly father He must be partial—for He came to his paleface children. We never saw Him. He gave you laws but He had no word for His red children whose teeming multitudes once filled this vast continent as stars fill the firmament. No; we are two distinct races with separate origins and separate destinies. There is little in common between us.

To us the ashes of our ancestors are sacred and their resting place is hallowed ground. You wander far from the graves of your ancestors and seemingly without regret. Your religion was written upon tables of stone by the iron finger of your God so that you could not forget.

The Red Man could never comprehend nor remember it. Our religion is the traditions of our ancestors—the dreams of our old men, given them in solemn hours of night by the Great Spirit; and the visions of our sachems; and it is written in the hearts of our people.

5   Your dead cease to love you and the land of their nativity as soon as they pass the portals of the tomb and wander way beyond the stars. They are soon forgotten and never return. Our dead never forget the beautiful world that gave them being.

Day and night cannot dwell together. The Red Man has ever fled the approach of the White Man, as the morning mist flees before the morning sun. However, your proposition seems fair and I think that my people will accept it and will retire to the reservation you offer them. Then we will dwell apart in peace, for the words of the Great White Chief seem to be the words of nature speaking to my people out of dense darkness.

It matters little where we pass the remnant of our days. They will not be many. A few more moons; a few more winters—and not one of the descendants of the mighty hosts that once moved over this broad land or lived in happy homes, protected by the Great Spirit, will remain to mourn over the graves of a people once more powerful and hopeful than yours. But why should I mourn at the untimely fate of my people? Tribe follows tribe, and nation follows nation, like the waves of the sea. It is the order of nature, and regret is useless. Your time of decay may be distant, but it will surely come, for even the White Man whose God walked and talked with him as friend with friend, cannot be exempt from the common destiny. We may be brothers after all. We will see.

We will ponder your proposition, and when we decide we will let you know. But should we accept it, I here and now make this condition that we will not be denied the privilege without molestation of visiting at any time the tombs of our ancestors, friends and children. Every part of this soil is sacred in the estimation of my people. Every hillside, every valley, every plain and grove, has been hallowed by some sad or happy event in days long vanished. . . . The very dust upon which you now stand responds more lovingly to their footsteps than to yours, because it is rich with the blood of our ancestors and our bare feet are conscious of the sympathetic touch. . . . Even the little children who lived here and rejoiced here for a brief season will love these somber solitudes and at eventide they greet shadowy returning spirits. And when the last Red Man shall have perished, and the memory of my tribe shall have become a myth among the White Men, these shores will swarm with the invisible dead of my tribe, and when your children's children think themselves alone in the field, the store, the shop, upon the highway, or in the silence of the pathless woods, they will not be alone. . . . At night when the streets of your cities and villages are silent and you think them deserted, they will throng with the returning hosts that once filled and still love this beautiful land. The White Man will never be alone.

Let him be just and deal kindly with my people, for the dead are not powerless. Dead, did I say? There is no death, only a change of worlds.

Questions on Meaning

1. What is Chief Seattle's primary point? How would you explain it to someone who had not read this 1855 speech?
2. What does Chief Seattle mean by the statement that "day and night cannot dwell together"? How do that statement and his belief about "regret" lead to his acceptance of the white man's offer?
3. Why does he say that the white man will never be alone?

Questions on Rhetorical Strategy and Style

1. How does Chief Seattle use a rhetorical strategy of cause and effect to support his statement that the American Indians and the whites are "two distinct races with separate origins and separate destinies"?
2. Chief Seattle often uses comparison and contrast to reveal differences between Indians and whites. How do Indians and whites differ in their treatment of ancestors and their burial grounds? How do their religions differ?
3. How does Chief Seattle draw an analogy between his words and the stars? What does this say about his character? Given what you know about treaties between Indians and whites, should he have expected the same in return?

Writing Assignments

1. Describe your emotions after you read this speech. How might your reaction differ from that of a white American in the mid 1800s, particularly a white American living in the eastern part of the country. What Indian stereotypes emerge in this translated speech?
2. Research the role that "hallowed burying grounds" play in American Indian culture. How have sacred lands been protected in treaties with the white man? How have they been violated? Write an essay describing the role that sacred Native American lands have played in development, mining, and nuclear/hazardous waste projects in recent years. Use the historical background you have learned to explain why these lands have become central to some of these disputes.

Address to Rally in Cape Town on his Release from Prison

Nelson Mandela

Nelson Mandela was born in 1918 in the Cape Province of South Africa. His father was a Thembu tribal chief and groomed his son to inherit the royal position. Nelson Mandela, however, pursued training as a lawyer instead and helped organize the youth league of the African National Congress (ANC), which opposed the Apartheid policy of racial segregation. In 1961, Mandela became the leader for Umkhonto we Sizwe (Spear of the Nation), the militant wing of the ANC which used sabotage to end Apartheid. This militant defiance resulted in his conviction of treason in 1962 and a 27-year imprisonment. During his imprisonment, Mandela became a worldwide symbol of resistance to white domination in South Africa. After years of ANC and global campaigning, Mandela was released from prison on February 11, 1990, and resumed his own campaign to negotiate a South African democracy. He and President F. W. de Klerk jointly won the Nobel Peace Prize in 1993 for their effort. In 1994, Mandela became the first president of South Africa to be elected in a truly representative democratic election. This address, given upon his release from prison, reflects Mandela's commitment to negotiating a racial peace in South Africa, despite ongoing struggles and tension.

11 February 1990

F riends, comrades and fellow South Africans.

I greet you all in the name of peace, democracy and freedom for all.

I stand here before you not as a prophet but as a humble servant of you, the people. Your tireless and heroic sacrifices have made it possible for me to be here today. I therefore place the remaining years of my life in your hands.

On this day of my release, I extend my sincere and warmest gratitude to the millions of my compatriots and those in every corner of the globe who have campaigned tirelessly for my release.

I send special greetings to the people of Cape Town, this city which has been my home for three decades. Your mass marches and other forms of struggle have served as a constant source of strength to all political prisoners.

I salute the African National Congress. It has fulfilled our every expectation in its role as leader of the great march to freedom.

I salute our President, Comrade Oliver Tambo, for leading the ANC even under the most difficult circumstances.

I salute the rank and file members of the ANC. You have sacrificed life and limb in the pursuit of the noble cause of our struggle.

I salute combatants of Umkhonto we Sizwe, like Solomon Mahlangu and Ashley Kriel, who have paid the ultimate price for the freedom of all South Africans.

I salute the South African Communist Party for its sterling contribution to the struggle for democracy. You have survived 40 years of unrelenting persecution. The memory of great communists like Moses Kotane, Yusuf Dadoo, Bram Fischer and Moses Mabhida will be cherished for generations to come.

I salute General Secretary Joe Slovo, one of our finest patriots. We are heartened by the fact that the alliance between ourselves and the Party remains as strong as it always was.

I salute the United Democratic Front, the National Education Crisis Committee, the South African Youth Congress, the Transvaal and Natal Indian Congresses and COSATU and the many other formations of the Mass Democratic Movement.

I also salute the Black Sash and the National Union of South African Students. We note with pride that you have acted as the conscience of white South Africa. Even during the darkest days in the history of our struggle you held the flag of liberty high. The large-scale mass mobilisation of the past few years is one of the key factors which led to the opening of the final chapter of our struggle.

I extend my greetings to the working class of our country. Your organised strength is the pride of our movement. You remain the most dependable force in the struggle to end exploitation and oppression.

15   I pay tribute to the many religious communities who carried the campaign for justice forward when the organisations for our people were silenced.

I greet the traditional leaders of our country—many of you continue to walk in the footsteps of great heroes like Hintsa and Sekhukune.

I pay tribute to the endless heroism of youth, you, the young lions. You, the young lions, have energised our entire struggle.

I pay tribute to the mothers and wives and sisters of our nation. You are the rock-hard foundation of our struggle. Apartheid has inflicted more pain on you than on anyone else.

On this occasion, we thank the world community for their great contribution to the anti-apartheid struggle. Without your support our struggle would not have reached this advanced stage. The sacrifice of the frontline states will be remembered by South Africans forever.

20   My salutations would be incomplete without expressing my deep appreciation for the strength given to me during my long and lonely years in prison by my beloved wife and family. I am convinced that your pain and suffering was far greater than my own.

Before I go any further I wish to make the point that I intend making only a few preliminary comments at this stage. I will make a more complete statement only after I have had the opportunity to consult with my comrades.

Today the majority of South Africans, black and white, recognise that apartheid has no future. It has to be ended by our own decisive mass action in order to build peace and security. The mass campaign of defiance and other actions of our organisation and people can only culminate in the establishment of democracy. The destruction caused by apartheid on our sub-continent is incalculable. The fabric of family life of millions of my people has been shattered. Millions are homeless and unemployed. Our economy lies in ruins and our people are embroiled in political strife. Our resort to the armed struggle in 1960 with the formation of the military wing of the ANC, Umkhonto we Sizwe, was a purely defensive action against the violence of apartheid. The factors which necessitated the armed struggle still exist today. We have no option but to continue. We express the hope that a climate conducive to a negotiated settlement will be created soon so that there may no longer be the need for the armed struggle.

I am a loyal and disciplined member of the African National Congress. I am therefore in full agreement with all of its objectives, strategies and tactics.

The need to unite the people of our country is as important a task now as it always has been. No individual leader is able to take on this enormous task on his own. It is our task as leaders to place our views before our organisation and to allow the democratic structures to decide. On the question of democratic practice, I feel duty bound to make the point that a leader of the movement is a person who has been democratically elected at a national conference. This is a principle which must be upheld without any exceptions.

25   Today, I wish to report to you that my talks with the government   25
have been aimed at normalising the political situation in the country. We have not as yet begun discussing the basic demands of the struggle. I wish to stress that I myself have at no time entered into negotiations about the future of our country except to insist on a meeting between the ANC and the government.

Mr. De Klerk has gone further than any other Nationalist president in taking real steps to normalise the situation. However, there are further steps as outlined in the Harare Declaration that have to be met before negotiations on the basic demands of our people can begin. I reiterate our call for, inter alia, the immediate ending of the State of Emergency and the freeing of all, and not only some, political prisoners. Only such a normalised situation, which allows for free political activity, can allow us to consult our people in order to obtain a mandate.

The people need to be consulted on who will negotiate and on the content of such negotiations. Negotiations cannot take place above the heads or behind the backs of our people. It is our belief that the future of our country can only be determined by a body which is democratically elected on a non-racial basis. Negotiations on the dismantling of apartheid will have to address the overwhelming demand of our people for a democratic, non-racial and unitary South Africa. There must be an end to white monopoly on political power and a fundamental restructuring of our political and economic systems to ensure that the inequalities of apartheid are addressed and our society thoroughly democratised.

It must be added that Mr. De Klerk himself is a man of integrity who is acutely aware of the dangers of a public figure not honouring his undertakings. But as an organisation we base our policy and strategy on the harsh reality we are faced with. And this reality is that we are still suffering under the policy of the Nationalist government.

Our struggle has reached a decisive moment. We call on our people to seize this moment so that the process towards democracy is rapid and uninterrupted. We have waited too long for our freedom. We can no longer wait. Now is the time to intensify the struggle on all fronts. To relax our efforts now would be a mistake which generations to come will not be able to forgive. The sight of freedom looming on the horizon should encourage us to redouble our efforts.

30   It is only through disciplined mass action that our victory can be   30
assured. We call on our white compatriots to join us in the shaping of a new South Africa. The freedom movement is a political home for you too. We call on the international community to continue the campaign to isolate the apartheid regime. To lift sanctions now would be to run the risk of aborting the process towards the complete eradication of apartheid.

Our march to freedom is irreversible. We must not allow fear to stand in our way. Universal suffrage on a common voters' role in a united democratic and non-racial South Africa is the only way to peace and racial harmony.

In conclusion I wish to quote my own words during my trial in 1964. They are true today as they were then:

'I have fought against white domination and I have fought against black domination. I have cherished the ideal of a democratic and free society in which all persons live together in harmony and with equal opportunities. It is an ideal which I hope to live for and to achieve. But if needs be, it is an ideal for which I am prepared to die.'

Questions on Meaning

1. Why does Mandela say that Apartheid has inflicted more pain on mothers, wives, and sisters of South Africa than anyone else?
2. Mandela ends his speech by saying, "Our march to freedom is irreversible." What does he mean by that?

Questions on Rhetorical Strategy and Style

1. Describe the tone of Mandela's first few paragraphs. What is his strategy? Is it effective?
2. Why does Mandela repeat the phrase "normalise the situation" several times in his address? What are the connotations of the word "normal"?

Writing Assignments

1. Several times in his address, Mandela mentions "youth." He pays tribute to the "endless heroism of youth, you, the young lions." Discuss other examples from history where young people were agents of change in ridding the world of injustice.
2. Read Martin Luther King's "Letter from Birmingham Jail." Discuss the similarities between Mandela's address to the people of Cape Town and Martin Luther King's letter to eight Alabama clergymen. Are their missions the same?

Shooting an Elephant

George Orwell

George Orwell is the pen name used by the British author Eric Blair (1903–1950). Orwell was born in the Indian village of Motihari, near Nepal, where his father was stationed in the Civil Service. India was then part of the British Empire; Orwell's grandfather too had served the Empire in the Indian Army. From 1907 to 1922 Orwell lived in England, returning to India and Burma and a position in the Imperial Police, which he held until 1927. This is the period about which he writes in "Shooting an Elephant." Thereafter he lived in England, Paris, Spain, and elsewhere, writing on a wide range of topics. He fought in the Spanish Civil War and was actively engaged in several political movements, always against totalitarianism of any kind. He is best known today for two novels of political satire: Animal Farm *(1945) and* 1984 *(1949). He was also a prolific journalist and essayist, with his essays collected in five volumes. "Shooting an Elephant" was first published in 1936 and later collected in a book of the same name in 1950. Note that Orwell is writing as an older, wiser man about events that took place when he was in his early twenties some two decades previously. This combined perspective of the young man experiencing the incident and the older man looking back on it is part of the rich reading experience.*

1   In Moulmein, in Lower Burma, I was hated by large numbers of people—the only time in my life that I have been important enough for this to happen to me. I was sub-divisional police officer of the town, and in an aimless, petty, kind of way anti-European feel-

1

From *Shooting an Elephant and Other Essays* by George Orwell. Published by Harcourt Brace and Company. Harcourt Brace and Company and Heath & Co., Ltd.

ing was very bitter. No one had the guts to raise a riot, but if a European woman went through the bazaars alone somebody would probably spit betel juice over her dress. As a police officer I was an obvious target and was baited whenever it seemed safe to do so. When a nimble Burman tripped me up on the football field and the referee (another Burman) looked the other way, the crowd yelled with hideous laughter. This happened more than once. In the end the sneering yellow faces of young men that met me everywhere, the insults hooted after me when I was at a safe distance, got badly on my nerves. The young Buddhist priests were the worst of all. There were several thousand of them in the town and none of them seemed to have anything to do except stand on street corners and jeer at Europeans.

All this was perplexing and upsetting. For at that time I had already made up my mind that imperialism was an evil thing and the sooner I chucked up my job and got out of it the better. Theoretically—and secretly, of course—I was all for the Burmese and all against their oppressors, the British. As for the job I was doing, I hated it more bitterly than I can perhaps make clear. In a job like that you see the dirty work of Empire at close quarters. The wretched prisoners huddling in the stinking cages of the lock-ups, the grey, cowed faces of the long-term convicts, the scarred buttocks of the men who had been flogged with bamboos—all these oppressed me with an intolerable sense of guilt. But I could get nothing into perspective. I was young and ill-educated and I had had to think out my problems in the utter silence that is imposed on every Englishman in the East. I did not even know that the British Empire is dying, still less did I know that it is a great deal better than the younger empires that are going to supplant it. All I knew was that I was stuck between my hatred of the empire I served and my rage against the evil-spirited little beasts who tried to make my job impossible. With one part of my mind I thought of the British Raj as an unbreakable tyranny, as something clamped down, in *saecula saeculorum*, upon the will of prostrate peoples; with another part I thought that the greatest joy in the world would be to drive a bayonet into a Buddhist priest's guts. Feelings like these are the normal by-products of imperialism; ask any Anglo-Indian official, if you can catch him off duty.

One day something happened which in a roundabout way was enlightening. It was a tiny incident in itself, but it gave me a better glimpse than I had had before of the real nature of imperialism—the real motives for which despotic governments act. Early one morning the sub-inspector at a police station the other end of the town rang me up on the 'phone and said that an elephant was ravaging the bazaar. Would I please come and do something about it? I did not know what I could do, but I wanted to see what was happening and I got on to a pony and started out. I took my rifle, an old .44 Winchester and much too small to kill an elephant, but I thought the noise might be useful *in terrorem*. Various Burmans stopped me on the way and told me about the elephant's doings. It was not, of course, a wild elephant, but a tame one which had gone "must." It had been chained up, as tame elephants always are when their attack of "must" is due, but on the previous night it had broken its chain and escaped. Its mahout, the only person who could manage it when it was in that state, had set out in pursuit, but had taken the wrong direction and was now twelve hours' journey away, and in the morning the elephant had suddenly reappeared in the town. The Burmese population had no weapons and were quite helpless against it. It had already destroyed somebody's bamboo hut, killed a cow and raided some fruit-stalls and devoured the stock; also it had met the municipal rubbish van and, when the driver jumped out and took to his heels, had turned the van over and inflicted violence upon it.

The Burmese sub-inspector and some Indian constables were waiting for me in the quarter where the elephant had been seen. It was a very poor quarter, a labyrinth of squalid bamboo huts, thatched with palm-leaf, winding all over a steep hillside. I remember that it was a cloudy, stuffy, morning at the beginning of the rains. We began questioning the people as to where the elephant had gone and, as usual, failed to get any definite information. That is invariably the case in the East; a story always sounds clear enough at a distance, but the nearer you get to the scene of events the vaguer it becomes. Some of the people said that the elephant had gone in one direction, some said that he had gone in another, some professed not even to have heard of any elephant. I had almost made up my mind that the whole story was a pack of lies, when we heard yells a little distance away. There was a loud, scandalized cry of "Go away, child! Go away this instant!" and an old woman with a switch in her hand came round the corner of a hut, violently shooing away a crowd of naked children. Some more women followed, clicking their tongues and exclaiming; evidently there was something that the children ought not to have seen. I rounded the hut and saw a man's dead body sprawling in the mud. He was an Indian, a black Dravidian coolie, almost naked, and he could not have been dead many minutes. The people said that the elephant had come suddenly upon him round the corner of the hut, caught him with its trunk, put its foot on his back and ground him into the earth. This was the rainy season and the ground was soft, and his face had scored a trench a foot deep and a couple of yards long. He was lying on his belly with arms crucified and head sharply twisted to one side. His face was coated with mud, the eyes wide open, the teeth bared and grinning with an expression of unendurable agony. (Never tell me, by the way, that the dead look peaceful. Most of the corpses I have seen looked devilish.) The friction of the great beast's foot had stripped the skin from his back as neatly as one skins a rabbit. As soon as I saw the dead man I sent an orderly to a friend's house nearby to borrow an elephant rifle. I had already sent back the pony, not wanting it to go mad with fright and throw me if it smelt the elephant.

5 The orderly came back in a few minutes with a rifle and five cartridges, and meanwhile some Burmans had arrived and told us that the elephant was in the paddy fields below, only a few hundred yards away. As I started forward practically the whole population of the quarter flocked out of the houses and followed me. They had seen the rifle and were all shouting excitedly that I was going to shoot the elephant. They had not shown much interest in the elephant when he was merely ravaging their homes, but it was different now that he was going to be shot. It was a bit of fun to them, as it would be to an English crowd; besides they wanted the meat. It made me vaguely uneasy. I had no intention of shooting the elephant—I had merely sent for the rifle to defend myself if necessary—and it is always unnerving to have a crowd following you. I marched down the hill, looking and feeling a fool, with the rifle over my shoulder and an evergrowing army of people jostling at my heels. At the bottom, when you got away from the huts, there was a metalled road and beyond that a miry waste of paddy fields a thousand yards across, not yet ploughed but soggy from the first rains and dotted with coarse grass. The elephant was standing eight yards from the road, his left side towards us. He took not the slightest notice of the crowd's approach. He was tearing up bunches of grass, beating them against his knees to clean them and stuffing them into his mouth.

I had halted on the road. As soon as I saw the elephant I knew with perfect certainty that I ought not to shoot him. It is a serious matter to shoot a working elephant—it is comparable to destroying a huge and costly piece of machinery—and obviously one ought not to do it if it can possibly be avoided. And at that distance, peacefully eating, the elephant looked no more dangerous than a cow. I thought then and I think now that his attack of "must" was already passing off; in which case he would merely wander harmlessly about until the mahout came back and caught him. Moreover, I did not in the least want to shoot him. I decided that I would watch him for a little while to make sure that he did not turn savage again, and then go home.

But at that moment I glanced round at the crowd that had followed me. It was an immense crowd, two thousand at the least and growing every minute. It blocked the road for a long distance on either side. I looked at the sea of yellow faces above the garish clothes—faces all happy and excited over this bit of fun, all certain that the elephant was going to be shot. They were watching me as they would watch a conjurer about to perform a trick. They did not like me, but with the magical rifle in my hands I was momentarily worth watching. And suddenly I realized that I should have to shoot the elephant after all. The people expected it of me and I had got to do it; I could feel their two thousand wills pressing me forward, irresistibly. And it was at this moment, as I stood there with the rifle in my hands, that I first grasped the hollowness, the futility of the white man's dominion in the East. Here was I, the white man with his gun, standing in front of the unarmed native crowd—seemingly the leading actor of the piece; but in reality I was only an absurd puppet pushed to and fro by the will of those yellow faces behind. I perceived in this moment that when the white man turns tyrant it is his own freedom that he destroys. He becomes a sort of hollow, posing dummy, the conventionalized figure of a sahib. For it is the condition of his rule that he shall spend his life in trying to impress the "natives," and so in every crisis he has got to do what the "natives" expect of him. He wears a mask, and his face grows to fit it. I had got to shoot the elephant. I had committed myself to doing it when I sent for the rifle. A sahib has got to act like a sahib; he has got to appear resolute, to know his own mind and do definite things. To come all that way, rifle in hand, with a thousand people marching at my heels, and then to trail feebly away, having done nothing—no, that was impossible. The crowd would laugh at me. And my whole life, every white man's life in the East, was one long struggle not to be laughed at.

266

But I did not want to shoot the elephant. I watched him beating his bunch of grass against his knees, with that preoccupied grand-motherly air that elephants have. It seemed to me that it would be murder to shoot him. At that age I was not squeamish about killing animals, but I had never shot an elephant and never wanted to. (Somehow it always seems worse to kill a *large* animal.) Besides, there was the beast's owner to be considered. Alive, the elephant was worth at least a hundred pounds; dead, he would only be worth the value of his tusks, five pounds, possibly. But I had got to act quickly. I turned to some experienced-looking Burmans who had been there when we arrived, and asked them how the elephant had been behaving. They all said the same thing: he took no notice of you if you left him alone, but he might charge if you went too close to him.

It was perfectly clear to me what I ought to do. I ought to walk up to within, say, twenty-five yards of the elephant and test his be-havior. If he charged, I could shoot; if he took no notice of me, it would be safe to leave him until the mahout came back. But also I knew that I was going to do no such thing. I was a poor shot with a rifle and the ground was soft mud into which one would sink at every step. If the elephant charged and I missed him, I should have about as much chance as a toad under a steam-roller. But even then I was not thinking particularly of my own skin, only of the watchful yellow faces behind. For at that moment, with the crowd watching me, I was not afraid in the ordinary sense, as I would have been if I had been alone. A white man mustn't be frightened in front of "natives"; and so, in general, he isn't frightened. The sole thought in my mind was that if anything went wrong those two thousand Burmans would see me pursued, caught, trampled on and reduced to a grinning corpse like that Indian up the hill. And if that happened it was quite probable that some of them would laugh. That would never do. There was only one alternative. I shoved the cartridges into the magazine and lay down on the road to get a better aim.

The crowd grew very still, and a deep, low, happy sigh, as of peo-ple who see the theatre curtain go up at last, breathed from innumer-able throats. They were going to have their bit of fun after all. The rifle was a beautiful German thing with cross-hair sights. I did not then know that in shooting an elephant one would shoot to cut an imaginary bar running from ear-hole to ear-hole. I ought, therefore, as the ele-phant was sideways on, to have aimed straight at his ear-hole; actually

I aimed several inches in front of this, thinking the brain would be further forward.

When I pulled the trigger I did not hear the bang or feel the kick—one never does when a shot goes home—but I heard the devilish roar of glee that went up from the crowd. In that instant, in too short a time, one would have thought, even for the bullet to get there, a mysterious, terrible change had come over the elephant. He neither stirred nor fell, but every line of his body had altered. He looked suddenly stricken, shrunken, immensely old, as though the frightful impact of the bullet had paralysed him without knocking him down. At last, after what seemed a long time—it might have been five seconds, I dare say—he sagged flabbily to his knees. His mouth slobbered. An enormous senility seemed to have settled upon him. One could have imagined him thousands of years old. I fired again into the same spot. At the second shot he did not collapse but climbed with desperate slowness to his feet and stood weakly upright, with legs sagging and head drooping. I fired a third time. That was the shot that did for him. You could see the agony of it jolt his whole body and knock the last remnant of strength from his legs. But in falling he seemed for a moment to rise, for as his hind legs collapsed beneath him he seemed to tower upward like a huge rock toppling, his trunk reaching skywards like a tree. He trumpeted, for the first and only time. And then down he came, his belly towards me, with a crash that seemed to shake the ground even where I lay.

I got up. The Burmans were already racing past me across the mud. It was obvious that the elephant would never rise again, but he was not dead. He was breathing very rhythmically with long rattling gasps, his great mound of a side painfully rising and falling. His mouth was wide open—I could see far down into caverns of pale pink throat. I waited a long time for him to die, but his breathing did not weaken. Finally I fired my two remaining shots into the spot where I thought his heart must be. The thick blood welled out of him like red velvet, but still he did not die. His body did not even jerk when the shots hit him, the tortured breathing continued without a pause. He was dying, very slowly and in great agony, but in some world remote from me where not even a bullet could damage him further. I felt that I had got to put an end to that dreadful noise. It seemed dreadful to see the great beast lying there, powerless to move and yet powerless to die, and not even to be able to finish him. I sent back for my small rifle and poured shot after shot into his heart and down his throat. They seemed to make no impression. The tortured gasps continued as steadily as the ticking of a clock.

In the end I could not stand it any longer and went away. I heard later that it took him half an hour to die. Burmans were bringing dahs and baskets even before I left, and I was told they had stripped his body almost to the bones by the afternoon.

Afterwards, of course, there were endless discussions about the shooting of the elephant. The owner was furious, but he was only an Indian and could do nothing. Besides, legally I had done the right thing, for a mad elephant has to be killed, like a mad dog, if its owner fails to control it. Among the Europeans opinion was divided. The older men said I was right, the younger men said it was a damn shame to shoot an elephant for killing a coolie, because an elephant was worth more than any damn Coringhee coolie. And afterwards I was very glad that the coolie had been killed; it put me legally in the right and it gave me a sufficient pretext for shooting the elephant. I often wondered whether any of the others grasped that I had done it solely to avoid looking a fool.

Questions on Meaning

1. Orwell confesses to many strong emotions about the Burmese people, such as his comment "I thought that the greatest joy in the world would be to drive a bayonet into a Buddhist priest's guts." Does he actually hate these people? Explain your answer with examples from the essay.

2. At the beginning of the third paragraph Orwell introduces the "tiny incident" that will for him reveal the "real motives for which despotic governments act." What are those motives, as revealed by the incident and Orwell's later comments?

3. Even before the incident with the elephant, Orwell tells us he had discovered that "imperialism was an evil thing." How many different kinds of "evil" are shown through the course of the essay?

Questions on Rhetorical Strategy and Style

1. The primary rhetorical strategy used in this essay is narration—telling the story of shooting the elephant. In addition to the story itself, Orwell keeps up a sort of running commentary on the meaning of the story, helping us understand it as he analyzes the events of the story. Reread the essay and chart how Orwell moves back and forth between narration and analysis.

2. Orwell is particularly vivid in his descriptive language, often achieving a larger meaning through descriptive details and figurative language. Reread the section of the essay that describes the elephant's slow death as he seems "thousands of years old" (paragraph 11) What meanings are suggested by the language Orwell uses in this descriptive passage?

Writing Assignments

1. Fear of embarrassment before others can be a powerful motivating force, as the young Orwell discovers in this incident. Search your memory for a time when you yourself took some action simply to avoid embarrassment. How did it feel at the time? Did you feel foolish afterwards? Would you do the same again now in the same circumstances? Try to be as honest in your self-evaluation as Orwell was in his.

2. Have you ever been among a large group of people very different from yourself, either in another country or in a different cultural

group in the United States? Did your concerns lead to fears or negative feelings about these others? Some social scientists have said that people naturally fear things or other people that are very different from themselves, that negative reactions are "normal" even if not healthy or fair to the others. Do you think there is such a natural impulse in people? What are the good and bad effects of this impulse? Present your thoughts in an essay exploring the topic.

3. We all have a "public self" and a "private self." Your public self may be the self you show to others in the academic world or on the job. It may be similar to your private self, what you really are like inside, or it may be very different. The two selves may be harmonious or in conflict, as they were for Orwell. Write an essay defining the difference between these two selves and exploring both the constructive and problematic aspects of this duality.

A Modest Proposal

Jonathan Swift

Born in Dublin, Ireland, Jonathan Swift (1667–1745) entered the clergy after his education at Trinity College and Oxford University. Through his long life he wrote in a wide range of genres, including poetry, religious pamphlets, essays, and satires on various social and political themes. His best-known work is Gulliver's Travels, *a combination of children's story and social satire. Swift was always a supporter of Irish causes, as can be seen in "A Modest Proposal," which was published anonymously in 1729. In this ironic essay, the speaker—the "I"—is not Swift himself but a persona, a fictional voice who gives his proposal to cure the ills of contemporary Ireland. It is true that Ireland at this time had the problems described by this persona: poverty, unemployment, a failing economy, exploitation by the wealthy classes, conflict between the Anglican and Catholic churches, and so on. This is the serious subject Swift addresses through his satire. If you have not read or heard of his "proposal" previously, read slowly and attentively: you might be greatly surprised to learn the nature of his proposition.*

1   It is a melancholy object to those who walk through this great town   1
or travel in the country, when they see the streets, the roads, and
cabin doors, crowded with beggars of the female sex, followed by
three, four, or six children, all in rags and importuning every passenger for an alms. These mothers, instead of being able to work for their
honest livelihood, are forced to employ all their time in strolling to
beg sustenance for their helpless infants, who, as they grow up, either
turn thieves for want of work, or leave their dear native country to
fight for the Pretender in Spain, or sell themselves to the Barbadoes.

     I think it is agreed by all parties that this prodigious number of
children in the arms, or on the backs, or at the heels of their mothers,

and frequently of their fathers, is in the present deplorable state of the kingdom a very great additional grievance; and therefore whoever could find out a fair, cheap, and easy method of making these children sound, useful members of the commonwealth would deserve so well of the public as to have his statue set up for a preserver of the nation.

But my intention is very far from being confined to provide only for the children of professed beggars; it is of a much greater extent, and shall take in the whole number of infants at a certain age who are born of parents in effect as little able to support them as those who demand our charity in the streets.

As to my own part, having turned my thoughts for many years upon this important subject, and maturely weighed the several schemes of other projectors, I have always found them grossly mistaken in their computation. It is true, a child just dropped from its dam may be supported by her milk for a solar year, with little other nourishment; at most not above the value of two shillings, which the mother may certainly get, or the value in scraps, by her lawful occupation of begging; and it is exactly at one year old that I propose to provide for them in such a manner as instead of being a charge upon their parents or the parish, or wanting food and raiment for the rest of their lives, they shall on the contrary contribute to the feeding, and partly to the clothing, of many thousands.

5   There is likewise another great advantage in my scheme, that it will prevent those voluntary abortions, and that horrid practice of women murdering their bastard children, alas, too frequent among us, sacrificing the poor innocent babes, I doubt, more to avoid the expense than the shame, which would move tears and pity in the most savage and inhuman breast.

The number of souls in this kingdom being usually reckoned one million and a half, of these I calculate there may be about two hundred thousand couples whose wives are breeders; from which number I subtract thirty thousand couples who are able to maintain their own children, although I apprehend there cannot be so many under the present distresses of the kingdom; but this being granted, there will remain an hundred and seventy thousand breeders. I again subtract fifty thousand for those women who miscarry, or whose children die by accident or disease within the year. There only remain an hundred and twenty thousand children of poor parents annually born. The question therefore is, how this number shall be reared and provided for, which, as I have already said, under the present situation of affairs, is utterly impossible by all the methods hitherto proposed. For we can neither employ them in handicraft nor agriculture; we neither build houses (I mean in the country) nor cultivate land. They can very seldom pick up livelihood by stealing till they arrive at six years old, except where they are of towardly parts; although I confess they learn the rudiments much earlier, during which time they can however be looked upon only as probationers, as I have been informed by a principal gentleman in the county of Cavan, who protested to me that he never knew above one or two instances under the age of six, even in a part of the kingdom so renowned for the quickest proficiency in that art.

I am assured by our merchants that a boy or a girl before twelve years old is no salable commodity; and even when they come to this age, they will not yield above three pounds, or three pounds and half a crown at most on the Exchange; which cannot turn to account either to the parents or the kingdom, the charge of nutriment and rags having been at least four times that value.

I shall now therefore humbly propose my own thoughts, which I hope will not be liable to the least objection.

I have been assured by a very knowing American of my acquaintance in London, that a young healthy child well nursed is at a year old a most delicious, nourishing, and wholesome food, whether stewed, roasted, baked, or boiled; and I make no doubt that it will equally serve in a fricassee or a ragout.

10   I do therefore humbly offer it to public consideration that of the   10
hundred and twenty thousand children, already computed, twenty thousand may be reserved for breed, whereof only one fourth part to be males, which is more than we allow to sheep, black cattle, or swine; and my reason is that these children are seldom the fruits of marriage, a circumstance not much regarded by our savages, therefore one male will be sufficient to serve four females. That the remaining hundred thousand may at a year old be offered in sale to the persons of quality and fortune through the kingdom, always advising the mother to let them suck plentifully in the last month, so as to render them plump and fat for a good table. A child will make two dishes at an entertainment for friends; and when the family dines alone, the fore or hind quarter will make a reasonable dish, and seasoned with a little pepper or salt will be very good boiled on the fourth day, especially in winter.

I have reckoned upon a medium that a child just born will weigh twelve pounds, and in a solar year if tolerably nursed increaseth to twenty-eight pounds.

I grant this food will be somewhat dear, and therefore very proper for landlords, who, as they have already devoured most of the parents, seem to have the best title to the children.

Infant's flesh will be in season throughout the year, but more plentiful in March, and a little before and after. For we are told by a grave author, an eminent French physician, that fish being a prolific diet, there are more children born in Roman Catholic countries about nine months after Lent, than at any other season; therefore, reckoning a year after Lent, the markets will be more glutted than usual, because the number of popish infants is at least three to one in this kingdom; and therefore it will have one other collateral advantage, by lessening the number of Papists among us.

I have already computed the charge of nursing a beggar's child (in which list I reckon all cottagers, laborers, and four fifths of the farmers) to be about two shillings per annum, rags included; and I believe no gentleman would repine to give ten shillings for the carcass of a good fat child, which, as I have said, will make four dishes of excellent nutritive meat, when he hath only some particular friend or his own family to dine with him. Thus the squire will learn to be a good landlord, and grow popular among the tenants; the mother will have eight shillings net profit, and be fit for work till she produces another child.

15   Those who are more thrifty (as I must confess the times require)   15
may flay the carcass; the skin of which artificially dressed will make admirable gloves for ladies, and summer boots for fine gentlemen.

As to our city of Dublin, shambles may be appointed for this purpose in the most convenient parts of it, and butchers we may be assured will not be wanting; although I rather recommend buying the children alive, and dressing them hot from the knife as we do roasting pigs.

A very worthy person, a true lover of his country, and whose virtues I highly esteem, was lately pleased in discoursing on this matter to offer a refinement upon my scheme. He said that many gentlemen of his kingdom, having of late destroyed their deer, he conceived that the want of venison might be well supplied by the bodies of young lads and maidens, not exceeding fourteen years of age nor under twelve, so great a number of both sexes in every county being now ready to starve for want of work and service; and these to be disposed of by their parents, if alive, or otherwise by their nearest relations. But with due deference to so excellent a friend and so deserving a patriot, I cannot be altogether in his sentiments; for as to the males, my American acquaintance assured me from frequent experience that their flesh was generally tough and lean, like that of our schoolboys, by continual exercise, and their taste disagreeable; and to fatten them would not answer the charge. Then as to the females, it would, I think with humble submission, be a loss to the public, because they soon would become breeders themselves; and besides, it is not improbable that some scrupulous people might be apt to censure such a practice (although indeed very unjustly) as a little bordering upon cruelty; which, I confess, hath always been with me the strongest objection against any project, how well soever intended.

But in order to justify my friend, he confessed that this expedient was put into his head by the famous Psalmanazar, a native of the island Formosa, who came from thence to London above twenty years ago, and in conversation told my friend that in his country when any young person happened to be put to death, the executioner sold the carcass to persons of quality as a prime dainty; and that in his time the body of a plump girl of fifteen, who was crucified for an attempt to poison the emperor, was sold to his Imperial Majesty's prime minister of state, and other great mandarins of the court, in joints from the gibbet, at four hundred crowns. Neither indeed can I deny that if the same use were made of several plump young girls in this town, who without one single groat to their fortunes cannot stir abroad without a chair, and appear at the playhouse and assemblies in foreign fineries which they never will pay for, the kingdom would not be the worse.

Some persons of a desponding spirit are in great concern about that vast number of poor people who are aged, diseased, or maimed, and I have been desired to employ my thoughts what course may be taken to ease the nation of so grievous an encumbrance. But I am not in the least pain upon that matter, because it is very well known that they are every day dying and rotting by cold and famine, and filth and vermin, as fast as can be reasonably expected. And as to the younger laborers, they are now in almost as hopeful a condition. They cannot get work, and consequently pine away for want of nourishment to a degree that if any time they are accidentally hired to common labor,

276

they have not strength to perform it; and thus the country and themselves are happily delivered from the evils to come.

20   I have too long digressed, and therefore shall return to my sub-   20
ject. I think the advantages by the proposal which I have made are obvious and many, as well as of the highest importance.

For first, as I have already observed, it would greatly lessen the number of Papists, with whom we are yearly overrun, being the principal breeders of the nation as well as our most dangerous enemies; and who stay at home on purpose to deliver the kingdom to the Pretender, hoping to take their advantage by the absence of so many good Protestants, who have chosen rather to leave their country than to stay at home and pay tithes against their conscience to an Episcopal curate.

Secondly, the poorer tenants will have something valuable of their own, which by law may be made liable to distress, and help to pay their landlord's rent, their corn and cattle being already seized and money a thing unknown.

Thirdly, whereas the maintenance of an hundred thousand children, from two years old and upwards, cannot be computed at less than ten shillings a piece per annum, the nation's stock will be thereby increased fifty thousand pounds per annum, besides the profit of a new dish introduced to the tables of all gentlemen of fortune in the kingdom who have any refinement in taste. And the money will circulate among ourselves, the goods being entirely of our own growth and manufacture.

Fourthly, the constant breeders, besides the gain of eight shillings sterling per annum by the sale of their children, will be rid of the charge of maintaining them after the first year.

25   Fifthly, this food would likewise bring great custom to taverns,   25
where the vintners will certainly be so prudent as to procure the best receipts for dressing it to perfection, and consequently have their houses frequented by all the fine gentlemen, who justly value themselves upon their knowledge in good eating; and a skillful cook, who understands how to oblige his guests, will contrive to make it as expensive as they please.

Sixthly, this would be a great inducement to marriage, which all wise nations have either encouraged by rewards or enforced by laws and penalties. It would increase the care and tenderness of mothers toward their children, when they were sure of a settlement for life to the poor babes, provided in some sort by the public, to their annual profit instead of expense. We should see an honest emulation among the married women, which of them could bring the fattest child to the market. Men would become as fond of their wives during the time of pregnancy as they are now of their mares in foal, their cows in calf, or sows when they are ready to farrow; nor offer to beat or kick them (as is too frequent a practice) for fear of a miscarriage.

Many other advantages might be enumerated. For instance, the addition of some thousand carcasses in our exportation of barreled beef, the propagation of swine's flesh, and improvement in the art of making good bacon, so much wanted among us by the great destruction of pigs, too frequent at our tables, which are no way comparable in taste or magnificence to a well-grown, fat, yearling child, which roasted whole will make a considerable figure at a lord mayor's feast or any other public entertainment. But this and many others I omit, being studious of brevity.

Supposing that one thousand families in this city would be constant customers for infants' flesh, besides others who might have it at merry meetings, particularly weddings and christenings, I compute that Dublin would take off annually about twenty thousand carcasses, and the rest of the kingdom (where probably they will be sold somewhat cheaper) the remaining eighty thousand.

I can think of no one objection that will possibly be raised against this proposal, unless it should be urged that the number of people will be thereby much lessened in the kingdom. This I freely own, and it was indeed one principal design in offering it to the world. I desire the reader will observe; that I calculate my remedy for this one individual kingdom of Ireland and for no other that ever was, is, or I think ever can be upon earth. Therefore, let no man talk to me of other expedients: of taxing our absentees at five shillings a pound: of using neither clothes nor household furniture except what is of our own growth and manufacture: of utterly rejecting the materials and instruments that promote foreign luxury: of curing the expensiveness of pride, vanity, idleness, and gaming in our women: of introducing a vein of parsimony, prudence, and temperance: of learning to love our country, in the want of which we differ even from Laplanders and the inhabitants of Topinamboo: of quitting our animosities and factions, nor acting any longer like the Jews, who were murdering one another at the very moment their city was taken: of being a little cautious not to sell our country and conscience for nothing: of teaching landlords to have at least one degree of mercy toward their tenants: lastly, of putting a spirit of honesty, industry, and skill into our shopkeepers; who, if a resolution could now be taken to buy only our native goods, would immediately unite to cheat and exact upon us in the price, the measure, and the goodness, nor could ever yet be brought to make one fair proposal of just dealing, though often and earnestly invited to it.

30   Therefore, I repeat, let no man talk to me of these and the like expedients, till he hath at least some glimpse of hope that there will ever be some hearty and sincere attempt to put them in practice.   30

But as to myself, having been wearied out for many years with offering vain, idle, visionary thoughts, and at length utterly despairing of success, I fortunately fell upon this proposal, which, as it is wholly new, so it hath something solid and real, of no expense and little trouble, full in our own power, and whereby we can incur no danger in disobliging England. For this kind of commodity will not bear exportation, the flesh being of too tender a consistence to admit a long continuance in salt, although perhaps I could name a country which would be glad to eat up our whole nation without it.

After all, I am not so violently bent upon my own opinion as to reject any offer proposed by wise men, which shall be found equally innocent, cheap, easy, and effectual. But before something of that kind shall be advanced in contradiction to my scheme, and offering a better, I desire the author or authors will be pleased maturely to consider two points. First, as things now stand, how they will be able to find food and raiment for an hundred thousand useless mouths and backs. And secondly, there being a round million of creatures in human figure throughout this kingdom, whose sole subsistence put into a common stock would leave them in debt two millions of pounds sterling, adding those who are beggars by profession to the bulk of farmers, cottagers, and laborers, with their wives and children who are beggars in effect; I desire those politicians who dislike my overture, and may perhaps be so bold to attempt an answer, that they will first ask the parents of these mortals whether they would not at this day think it a great happiness to have been sold for food at a year old in this manner I prescribe, and thereby have avoided such a perpetual scene of misfortunes as they have since gone through by the oppression of landlords, the impossibility of paying rent without money or trade, the want of common sustenance, with neither house nor clothes to cover them from the inclemencies of the weather, and the most inevitable prospect of entailing the like or greater miseries upon their breed forever.

I profess, in the sincerity of my heart, that I have not the least personal interest in endeavoring to promote this necessary work, having no other motive than the public good of my country, by advancing our trade, providing for infants, relieving the poor, and giving some pleasure to the rich. I have no children by which I can propose to get a single penny; the youngest being nine years old, and my wife past childbearing.

Questions on Meaning

1. Some readers, unfamiliar with satire and perhaps misled by a different use of the English language in another culture almost 300 years ago, read this essay through to the end thinking the author is seriously proposing eating human infants. Indeed, that perfectly serious tone is part of why this essay is so successful and is still read today, as Swift avoids "giving away" the joke by going too far in his exaggeration. Yet even a reader unfamiliar with satire should discern the many ways the essay shows Swift is sympathetic with the plight of the poverty-stricken people of whom he writes. Reread the essay and look for several examples of this sympathy.
2. Given the severity of the social problem Swift is reacting to, one might think he should have taken a more direct approach in addressing it. Why do you think Swift chose irony and what does this method add to the meaning of the essay?

Questions on Rhetorical Strategy and Style

1. At what point did you begin to realize the irony of the essay? Reread the first three paragraphs and underline words and phrases that begin to build the satire from the very beginning. How does Swift continue to build the satire gradually up to the proposal itself in paragraph 10?
2. In this form of irony, things are apt to be the opposite of what is said. In particular, the "fine gentlemen" and landlords mentioned throughout the essay are not actually being praised. Find as many references as you can in the essay to this ruling class, and consider how they, as cannibals, bear the true brunt of Swift's satire.
3. A prominent characteristic of Swift's style in this essay is his use of detail, such as the exact numbers of children and percentages for breeding, specific recipes and seasonings, and exact monetary values versus costs. What effect does this specificity contribute to the essay?
4. Find the paragraph near the end of the essay in which Swift reveals his serious suggestions for solving Ireland's problems. How can you tell these are serious, not ironic, proposals?
5. Swift in this essays uses persuasive rhetorical strategies, even though he turns them upside-down with his satire. A persuasive essay may typically describe a problem, offer a solution, explain the benefits of the solution, and argue the superiority of this solution

over others. Identify these strategies in Swift's essay and explain how he uses them.

Writing Assignments

1. The essay describes some elements of a society in which one class controls resources and exploits another. Have there been any parallels to this in America's history? Explain how some problems such as poverty relate to the presence of different socioeconomic classes.

2. Satire is a particular form of humor in which something can be condemned by praise, for example, or praised by condemnation. What other examples of satire can you identify in today's culture, including works of fiction, movies or television, and newspapers? Has the basic technique of ironic exaggeration changed?

At the Brandenburg Gate

Ronald Reagan

Ronald Reagan (1911–2004), one of twentieth-century America's most popular citizens, was an athlete, sports broadcaster, movie actor, union leader, Governor of California, and fortieth President of the United States of America (1981–1989). He was nicknamed "The Great Communicator" because of his media savvy, campaign success, wit, and charisma. Unlike previous administrations during the Cold War, Reagan publicly denounced communism and called the Soviet Union an "Evil Empire" because Soviet forces dominated and occupied Eastern Europe. Reportedly, he had been advised to tone down his anti-communism rhetoric while he traveled in Europe. Reagan knew his remarks at the Brandenberg Gate could be heard by Germans in East Berlin and other ordinary citizens who lived behind the Iron Curtain. This speech, delivered on June 12, 1987, often is cited as the beginning of the end of the Soviet Union and the Cold War.

West Berlin
June 12, 1987

Standing near the Brandenburg Gate that separates East and West Berlin, President Reagan challenged Soviet leader Mikhail Gorbachev to "tear down" the Berlin Wall.

1   Thank you very much. Chancellor Kohl, Governing Mayor Diepgen, ladies and gentlemen: Twenty four years ago, President John F. Kennedy visited Berlin, speaking to the people

of this city and the world at the city hall. Well, since then two other presidents have come, each in his turn, to Berlin. And today I, myself, make my second visit to your city.

We come to Berlin, we American Presidents, because it's our duty to speak, in this place, of freedom. But I must confess, we're drawn here by other things as well: by the feeling of history in this city, more than 500 years older than our own nation; by the beauty of the Grunewald and the Tiergarten; most of all, by your courage and determination. Perhaps the composer, Paul Lincke, understood something about American Presidents. You see, like so many Presidents before me, I come here today because wherever I go, whatever I do: "Ich hab noch einen koffer in Berlin." [I still have a suitcase in Berlin.]

Our gathering today is being broadcast throughout Western Europe and North America. I understand that it is being seen and heard as well in the East. To those listening throughout Eastern Europe, I extend my warmest greetings and the good will of the American people. To those listening in East Berlin, a special word: Although I cannot be with you, I address my remarks to you just as surely as to those standing here before me. For I join you, as I join your fellow countrymen in the West, in this firm, this unalterable belief: Es gibt nur ein Berlin. [There is only one Berlin.]

Behind me stands a wall that encircles the free sectors of this city, part of a vast system of barriers that divides the entire continent of Europe. From the Baltic, south, those barriers cut across Germany in a gash of barbed wire, concrete, dog runs, and guard-towers. Farther south, there may be no visible, no obvious wall. But there remain armed guards and checkpoints all the same—still a restriction on the right to travel, still an instrument to impose upon ordinary men and women the will of a totalitarian state. Yet it is here in Berlin where the wall emerges most clearly; here, cutting across your city, where the news photo and the television screen have imprinted this brutal division of a continent upon the mind of the world. Standing before the Brandenburg Gate, every man is a German, separated from his fellow men. Every man is a Berliner, forced to look upon a scar.

President von Weizsacker has said: "The German question is open as long as the Brandenburg Gate is closed." Today I say: As long as this gate is closed, as long as this scar of a wall is permitted to stand, it is not the German question alone that remains open, but the question of freedom for all mankind. Yet I do not come here to lament.

For I find in Berlin a message of hope, even in the shadow of this wall, a message of triumph.

In this season of spring in 1945, the people of Berlin emerged from their air-raid shelters to find devastation. Thousands of miles away, the people of the United States reached out to help. And in 1947 Secretary of State—as you've been told—George Marshall announced the creation of what would become known as the Marshall plan. Speaking precisely 40 years ago this month, he said: "Our policy is directed not against any country or doctrine, but against hunger, poverty, desperation, and chaos."

In the Reichstag a few moments ago, I saw a display commemorating this 40th anniversary of the Marshall plan. I was struck by the sign on a burnt-out, gutted structure that was being rebuilt. I understand that Berliners of my own generation can remember seeing signs like it dotted throughout the Western sectors of the city. The sign read simply: "The Marshall plan is helping here to strengthen the free world." A strong, free world in the West, that dream became real. Japan rose from ruin to become an economic giant. Italy, France, Belgium—virtually every nation in Western Europe saw political and economic rebirth; the European Community was founded.

In West Germany and here in Berlin, there took place an economic miracle, the Wirtschaftswunder. Adenauer, Erhard, Reuter, and other leaders understood the practical importance of liberty—that just as truth can flourish only when the journalist is given freedom of speech, so prosperity can come about only when the farmer and businessman enjoy economic freedom. The German leaders reduced tariffs, expanded free trade, lowered taxes. From 1950 to 1960 alone, the standard of living in West Germany and Berlin doubled.

Where four decades ago there was rubble, today in West Berlin there is the greatest industrial output of any city in Germany—busy office blocks, fine homes and apartments, proud avenues, and the spreading lawns of park land. Where a city's culture seemed to have been destroyed, today there are two great universities, orchestras and an opera, countless theaters, and museums. Where there was want, today there's abundance—food, clothing, automobiles—the wonderful goods of the Ku'damm. From devastation, from utter ruin, you Berliners have, in freedom, rebuilt a city that once again ranks as one of the greatest on Earth. The Soviets may have had other plans. But, my friends, there were a few things the Soviets didn't count on—Berliner herz, Berliner humor, ja, und Berliner schnauze. [Berliner heart, Berliner humor, yes, and a Berliner schnauze.] [Laughter]

10   In the 1950's, Khrushchev predicted: "We will bury you." But in 10 the West today, we see a free world that has achieved a level of prosperity and well-being unprecedented in all human history. In the Communist world, we see failure, technological backwardness, declining standards of health, even want of the most basic kind—too little food. Even today, the Soviet Union still cannot feed itself. After these four decades, then, there stands before the entire world one great and inescapable conclusion: Freedom leads to prosperity. Freedom replaces the ancient hatreds among the nations with comity and peace. Freedom is the victor.

And now the Soviets themselves may, in a limited way, be coming to understand the importance of freedom. We hear much from Moscow about a new policy of reform and openness. Some political prisoners have been released. Certain foreign news broadcasts are no longer being jammed. Some economic enterprises have been permitted to operate with greater freedom from state control. Are these the beginnings of profound changes in the Soviet state? Or are they token gestures, intended to raise false hopes in the West, or to strengthen the Soviet system without changing it? We welcome change and openness; for we believe that freedom and security go together, that the advance of human liberty can only strengthen the cause of world peace.

There is one sign the Soviets can make that would be unmistakable, that would advance dramatically the cause of freedom and peace. General Secretary Gorbachev, if you seek peace, if you seek prosperity for the Soviet Union and Eastern Europe, if you seek liberalization: Come here to this gate! Mr. Gorbachev, open this gate! Mr. Gorbachev, tear down this wall!

I understand the fear of war and the pain of division that afflict this continent—and I pledge to you my country's efforts to help overcome these burdens. To be sure, we in the West must resist Soviet expansion. So we must maintain defenses of unassailable strength. Yet we seek peace; so we must strive to reduce arms on both sides. Beginning 10 years ago, the Soviets challenged the Western alliance with a grave new threat, hundreds of new and more deadly SS-20 nuclear missiles, capable of striking every capital in Europe. The Western alliance responded by committing itself to a counterdeployment unless the Soviets agreed to negotiate a better solution; namely, the elimination of such weapons on both sides. For many months, the

Soviets refused to bargain in earnestness. As the alliance, in turn, prepared to go forward with its counterdeployment, there were difficult days—days of protests like those during my 1982 visit to this city—and the Soviets later walked away from the table.

But through it all, the alliance held firm. And I invite those who protested then—I invite those who protest today—to mark this fact: Because we remained strong, the Soviets came back to the table. And because we remained strong, today we have within reach the possibility, not merely of limiting the growth of arms, but of eliminating, for the first time, an entire class of nuclear weapons from the face of the Earth. As I speak, NATO ministers are meeting in Iceland to review the progress of our proposals for eliminating these weapons. At the talks in Geneva, we have also proposed deep cuts in strategic offensive weapons. And the Western allies have likewise made far-reaching proposals to reduce the danger of conventional war and to place a total ban on chemical weapons.

15   While we pursue these arms reductions, I pledge to you that we 15 will maintain the capacity to deter Soviet aggression at any level at which it might occur. And in cooperation with many of our allies, the United States is pursuing the Strategic Defense Initiative—research to base deterrence not on the threat of offensive retaliation, but on defenses that truly defend; on systems, in short, that will not target populations, but shield them. By these means we seek to increase the safety of Europe and all the world. But we must remember a crucial fact: East and West do not mistrust each other because we are armed; we are armed because we mistrust each other. And our differences are not about weapons but about liberty. When President Kennedy spoke at the City Hall those 24 years ago freedom was encircled, Berlin was under siege. And today, despite all the pressures upon this city, Berlin stands secure in its liberty. And freedom itself is transforming the globe.

In the Philippines, in South and Central America, democracy has been given a rebirth. Throughout the Pacific, free markets are working miracle after miracle of economic growth. In the industrialized nations a technological revolution is taking place—a revolution marked by rapid, dramatic advances in computers and telecommunications.

In Europe, only one nation and those it controls refuse to join the community of freedom. Yet in this age of redoubled economic growth, of information and innovation, the Soviet Union faces a choice: It must make fundamental changes, or it will become obsolete. Today thus represents a moment of hope. We in the West stand

REAGAN | AT THE BRANDENBURG GATE

ready to cooperate with the East to promote true openness, to break down barriers that separate people, to create a safer, freer world.

And surely there is no better place than Berlin, the meeting place of East and West, to make a start. Free people of Berlin: Today, as in the past, the United States stands for the strict observance and full implementation of all parts of the Four Power Agreement of 1971. Let us use this occasion, the 750th anniversary of this city, to usher in a new era, to seek a still fuller, richer life for the Berlin of the future. Together, let us maintain and develope the ties between the Federal Republic and the Western sectors of Berlin, which is permitted by the 1971 agreement. And I invite Mr. Gorbachev: Let us work to bring the Eastern and Western parts of the city closer together, so that all the inhabitants of all Berlin can enjoy the benefits that come with life in one of the great cities of the world. To open Berlin still further to all Europe, East and West, let us expand the vital air access to this city, finding ways of making commercial air service to Berlin more convenient, more comfortable, and more economical. We look to the day when West Berlin can become one of the chief aviation hubs in all central Europe.

With our French and British partners, the United States is prepared to help bring international meetings to Berlin. It would be only fitting for Berlin to serve as the site of United Nations meetings, or world conferences on human rights and arms control or other issues that call for international cooperation. There is no better way to establish hope for the future than to enlighten young minds, and we would be honored to sponsor summer youth exchanges, cultural events, and other programs for young Berliners from the East. Our French and British friends, I'm certain, will do the same. And it's my hope that an authority can be found in East Berlin to sponsor visits from young people of the Western sectors.

20 One final proposal, one close to my heart: Sport represents a 20 source of enjoyment and ennoblement, and you many have noted that the Republic of Korea—South Korea—has offered to permit certain events of the 1988 Olympics to take place in the North. International sports competitions of all kinds could take place in both parts of this city. And what better way to demonstrate to the world the openness of this city than to offer in some future year to hold the Olympic games here in Berlin, East and West?

In these four decades, as I have said, you Berliners have built a great city. You've done so in spite of threats—the Soviet attempts to impose the East-mark, the blockade. Today the city thrives in spite of the challenges implicit in the very presence of this wall. What keeps you here? Certainly there's a great deal to be said for your fortitude, for your defiant courage. But I believe there's something deeper, something that involves Berlin's whole look and feel and way of life—not mere sentiment. No one could live long in Berlin without being completely disabused of illusions. Something instead, that has seen the difficulties of life in Berlin but chose to accept them, that continues to build this good and proud city in contrast to a surrounding totalitarian presence that refuses to release human energies or aspirations. Something that speaks with a powerful voice of affirmation, that says yes to this city, yes to the future, yes to freedom. In a word, I would submit that what keeps you in Berlin is love—love both profound and abiding.

Perhaps this gets to the root of the matter, to the most fundamental distinction of all between East and West. The totalitarian world produces backwardness because it does such violence to the spirit, thwarting the human impulse to create, to enjoy, to worship. The totalitarian world finds even symbols of love and of worship an affront. Years ago, before the East Germans began rebuilding their churches, they erected a secular structure: the television tower at Alexander Platz. Virtually ever since, the authorities have been working to correct what they view as the tower's one major flaw, treating the glass sphere at the top with paints and chemicals of every kind. Yet even today when the Sun strikes that sphere—that sphere that towers over all Berlin—the light makes the sign of the cross. There in Berlin, like the city itself, symbols of love, symbols of worship, cannot be suppressed.

As I looked out a moment ago from the Reichstag, that embodiment of German unity, I noticed words crudely spray-painted upon the wall, perhaps by a young Berliner, "This wall will fall. Beliefs become reality." Yes, across Europe, this wall will fall. For it cannot withstand faith; it cannot withstand truth. The wall cannot withstand freedom.

And I would like, before I close, to say one word. I have read, and I have been questioned since I've been here about certain demonstrations against my coming. And I would like to say just one thing, and to those who demonstrate so. I wonder if they have ever asked themselves that if they should have the kind of government they apparently seek, no one would ever be able to do what they're doing again.

Thank you and God bless you all.

25

Questions on Meaning

1. What does Reagan mean when he says, "Wherever I go, whatever I do...I still have a suitcase in Berlin"?
2. Why does Reagan refer to the Berlin Wall as a "scar"? Think of another appropriate metaphor he could have used.

Questions on Rhetorical Strategy and Style

1. While the speech is directed to West Berlin, Reagan also takes the opportunity to launch a verbal attack on communist leaders. What parts of his speech would most anger dictators then and now?
2. Reagan speaks German twice in his speech. Why does he only choose those two sentences?

Writing Assignments

1. Think about an injustice in the world around you. Write a letter to someone who could end the injustice and convince him or her to do so.
2. In his speech, Ronald Reagan insists, "Mr. Gorbachev, tear down this wall." Explain how in 1989 the Berlin Wall finally did come down.

Remarks Concerning the Savages of North America

Benjamin Franklin

Benjamin Franklin (1706–1790) was an inventor, publisher, writer, statesman, and Founding Father of America. As the tenth son and one of fifteen children in an impoverished family in Boston, he was pledged to the church as a future minister by his father and then apprenticed to his printer brother. Franklin ran away from both situations, at ages 12 and 17. Franklin was intelligent, determined, and free-spirited. He understood commercialism and human nature and became a financial, social, and political success. He invented bifocals, the lightning rod, the Franklin stove, the odometer, and swim fins. He wrote Poor Richard's Almanac, *his* Autobiography, *and countless political, economic, philosophical, and scientific essays. He dedicated himself to improving the quality of life for his fellow Americans. His newspaper, the* Pennsylvania Gazette, *was a vital political vehicle for the emerging nation.*

1   SAVAGES we call them, because their manners differ from ours,   1
which we think the perfection of civility; they think the same of
theirs.

Perhaps, if we could examine the manners of different nations with Impartiality, we should find no People so rude, as to be without any Rules of Politeness; nor any so polite, as not to have some remains of Rudeness.

The Indian Men, when young, are Hunters and Warriors; when old, Counselors; for all their Government is by Counsel, or Advice, of the sages; there is no Force, there are no Prisons, no Officers to compel Obedience, or inflict punishment. Hence they generally study Oratory; the best speaker having the most Influence. The Indian Women till the Ground, dress the Food, nurse and bring up the Children, and preserve and hand down to posterity the Memory of Public Transactions. These Employments of Men and Women are accounted natural and honorable. Having few Artificial Wants, they have abundance of Leisure for Improvement by Conversation. Our laborious manner of Life, compared with theirs, they esteem slavish and base; and the Learning, on which we value ourselves, they regard as frivolous and useless. An instance of this occurred at the Treaty of Lancaster, in Pennsylvania, Anno 1744, between the Government of Virginia and the Six Nations. After the principal Business was settled, the commissioners from Virginia acquainted the Indians by a Speech, that there was at Williamsburg a College, with a Fund for Educating Indian Youth; and that, if the Six Nations would send down half a dozen of their sons to that College, the government would take Care that they should be well provided for, and instructed in all the Learning of the white People. It is one of the Indian Rules of Politeness not to answer a public Proposition the same day that it is made; they think it would be treating it as a light Matter; and that they show it Respect by taking time to consider it, as of a Matter important. They therefore deferred their Answer till the day following; when their Speaker began by expressing their deep Sense of the kindness of the Virginia Government, in making them that Offer; for we know, says he, that you highly esteem the kind of Learning taught in those Colleges, and that the Maintenance of our Young men, while with you, would be very expensive to you. We are convinced, therefore, that you mean to do us good by your Proposal, and we thank you heartily. But who are wise, must know that different Nations have different Conceptions of things; and you will therefore not take it amiss, if our Ideas of this Kind of Education happen not to be the same with yours. We have had some Experience of it: Several of our Young People were formerly brought up at the Colleges of the Northern Provinces; they were instructed in all your sciences; but when they came back to us, they were bad runners, ignorant of every means of living in the Woods, unable to bear either Cold or Hunger, knew neither how to build a Cabin, take a Deer, or kill an Enemy, spoke our Language imperfectly; were therefore neither fit for Hunters, Warriors, or Counselors; they were totally good for nothing. We are however not the less obliged by your kind Offer, though we decline accepting it; and to show our grateful Sense of it, if the gentlemen of Virginia will send us a dozen of their Sons, we will take great Care of their Education, instruct them in all we know, and make *Men* of them.

Having frequent occasions to hold public Councils, they have acquired great Order and Decency in conducting them. The old Men sit in the foremost Ranks, the warriors in the next, and the Women and Children in the hindmost. The business of the Women is to take exact notice of what passes, Imprint it in their memories, for they have no Writing, and communicate it to their children. They are the Records of the Council, and they preserve traditions of the Stipulations in Treaties a hundred Years back, which when we compare with our Writings we always find exact. He that would speak, rises. The rest observe a profound Silence. When he has finished and sits down, they leave him five or six Minutes to recollect, that if he has omitted anything he intended to say, or has anything to add, he may rise again and deliver it. To interrupt another, even in common conversation, is reckoned highly indecent. How different this is from the Conduct of a polite British House of Commons, where scarce a Day passes without some Confusion, that makes the speaker hoarse in calling *to order*; and how different from the mode of Conversation in many polite Companies of Europe, where if you do not deliver your Sentence with great rapidity, you are cut off in the middle of it by the impatient Loquacity of those you converse with, and never suffer'd to finish it.

5   The politeness of these savages in conversation is indeed carried   5
to excess, since it does not permit them to contradict or deny the Truth of what is asserted in their Presence. By this means they indeed avoid Disputes, but then it becomes difficult to know their Minds, or what Impression you make upon them. The Missionaries who have attempted to convert them to Christianity, all complain of this as one of the great Difficulties of their Mission. The Indians hear with Patience the Truths of the Gospel explained to them, and give their usual Tokens of assent and Approbation: you would think they were convinced. No such Matter. It is mere Civility.

A Swedish Minister, having assembled the Chiefs of the Susquehanah Indians, made a Sermon to them, acquainting them with the principal historical Facts on which our Religion is founded, such as the Fall of our first Parents by Eating an Apple, the Coming of Christ to repair the Mischief, his Miracles and Suffering, etc. When he had finished, an Indian Orator stood up to thank him. What you have told us, says he, is all very good. It is indeed bad to eat Apples. It is better to make them all into Cyder. We are much obliged by your Kindness in coming so far to tell us those things which you have heard from your Mothers. In Return, I will tell you some of those we have heard from ours.

In the Beginning, our Fathers had only the Flesh of Animals to subsist on, and if their hunting was unsuccessful, they were starving. Two of our young Hunters, having killed a Deer, made a Fire in the Woods to broil some Part of it. When they were about to satisfy their Hunger, they beheld a beautiful young Woman descend from the clouds, and seat herself on that Hill which you see yonder among the blue Mountains. They said to each other, it is a Spirit that perhaps has smelt our broiling Venison and wishes to eat of it: let us offer some to her. They presented her with the Tongue: She was pleased with the taste of it, and said, your Kindness shall be rewarded. Come to this Place after thirteen Moons, and you shall find something that will be of great Benefit in nourishing you and your Children to the latest Generations. They did so, and, to their Surprise, found Plants they had never seen before, but which from that ancient time have been constantly cultivated among us to our great Advantage. Where her right Hand had touch'd the Ground, they found Maize; where her left Hand had touch'd it, they found Kidney-beans; and where her backside had sat on it, they found Tobacco. The good missionary, disgusted with this idle Tale, said, what I delivered to you were sacred truths; but what you tell me is mere Fable, Fiction, and Falsehood. The Indian, offended, repli'd My Brother, it seems your Friends have not done you Justice in your Education; they have not well instructed you in the Rules of common Civility. You saw that we who understand and practice those Rules, believed all your Stories; you refuse to believe ours?

When any of them come into our Towns, our People are apt to crowd round them, gaze upon them, and incommode them where they desire to be private; this they esteem great Rudeness, and the Effect of the want of Instruction in the Rules of Civility and good Manners. We have, say they, as much Curiosity as you, and when you come into our towns we wish for Opportunities of looking at you; but for this purpose we hide ourselves behind Bushes, where you are to pass, and never intrude ourselves into Company.

Their Manner of entering one anothers Village has likewise its Rules. It is reckon'd uncivil in traveling Strangers to enter a Village abruptly, without giving Notice of their Approach. Therefore as soon as they arrive within hearing, they stop and hollow, remaining there till invited to enter. Two old Men usually come out to them, and lead them in. There is in every Village a vacant Dwelling, called the Strangers House. Here they are placed, while the old men go round from Hut to Hut, acquainting the Inhabitants, that Strangers are arrived, who are probably hungry and weary; and every one sends them what he can spare of Victuals and Skins to repose on. When the Strangers are refresh'd, Pipes & Tobacco are brought; and then, but not before, conversation begins, with Enquiries who they are, whither bound, what news, &c. and it usually ends with Offers of service, if the Strangers have Occasion of Guides, or any necessaries for continuing their Journey; and nothing is exacted for the Entertainment.

10 The same Hospitality, esteemed among them as a principal 10 Virtue, is practiced by private Persons; of which *Conrad Weiser*, our Interpreter, gave the following Instances. He had been naturaliz'd among the Six-Nations, and spoke well the Mohawk Language. In going thro' the Indian Country, to carry a message from our Governor to the Council at *Onondaga*, he called at the Habitation of Canassetego, an old Acquaintance, who embraced him, spread Furs for him to sit on, placed before him some boiled Beans and Venison, and mixed some Rum and Water for his drink. When he was well refresh'd, and had lit his Pipe, Canassetego began to converse with him, ask'd how he had fared the many Years since they had seen each other, whence he then came, what occasioned the journey, &c. &c. Conrad answered all his Questions; and when the Discourse began to flag the Indian, to continue it, said, "Conrad, you have lived long among the white People, and know something of their Customs; I have been sometimes at Albany, and have observed, that once in seven Days, they shut up their Shops and assemble all in the great house; tell me, what it is for? what do they do there? They meet there, says Conrad, to hear & learn *good things*. I do not doubt, says the Indian, that they tell you so; they have told me the same; but I doubt the Truth of what they say; & I will tell you my Reasons. I went lately to Albany to sell my Skins, &

buy Blankets, Knives, Powder, Rum, &c. You know I used generally to deal with Hans Hanson; but I was a little inclined this time to try some other Merchants. However, I called first upon Hans, and ask'd him what he would give for Beaver; He said he could not give any more than four Shillings a Pound; but, says he, I cannot talk on Business now; this is the Day when we meet together to learn *good things*, and I am going to the Meeting. So I thought to myself, since we cannot do any Business to day, I may as well go to the Meeting too; and I went with him. There stood up a Man in black, and began to talk to the People very angrily. I did not understand what he said; but, perceiving that he looked much at me, & at Hanson, I imagined he was angry at seeing me there; so I went out, sat down near the House, struck Fire & lit my Pipe; waiting till the Meeting should break up. I thought too, that the Man had mentioned something of Beaver, and I suspected it might be the Subject of their Meeting. So when they came out I accosted any (sic)merchant; well, Hans, says I, I hope you have agreed to give more than four shillings a pound. No, says he, I cannot give so much. I cannot give more than three Shillings and six Pence. I then spoke to several other Dealers, but they all sung the same song, three & six Pence, three & six Pence. This made it clear to me that my Suspicion was right; and that whatever they pretended of Meeting to learn *good things*, the real Purpose was to consult how to cheat Indians in the Price of Beaver. Consider but a little, Conrad, and you must be of my Opinion. If they met so often to learn *good things*, they would certainly have learned some before this time. But they are still ignorant. You know our Practice. If a white man, in traveling thro' our Country, enters one of our Cabins, we all treat him as I treat you; we dry him if he is wet, we warm him if he is cold, and give him Meat & Drink that he may allay his Thirst and Hunger, & we spread soft Furs for him to rest & sleep on: We demand nothing in return * *It is remarkable that in all Ages and Countires, Hospitality has been allowed as the Virtue of those, whom the civiliz'd were pleased to call Barbarians; the Greeks celebrated the Scythians for it. The Saracens possess'd it eminently; and it is to this day the reigning virtue of the wild Arabs. S. Paul too in the Relation of his Voyage & Shipwreck, on the Island of Melita, says,* The Barbarous People shew'd us no little Kindness; for they kindled a Fire, and received us everyone, because of the present Rain & because of the Cold. . But if I go into a White man's House at Albany, and ask for Victuals and Drink, they say, Where is your Money? and if I have none they say, Get out, you Indian Dog. You see they have not yet learnt those little *good things,* that we need no Meetings to be instructed in, because our Mothers taught them to us when we were Children. And therefore it is impossible their Meetings should be as they say for any such Purpose, or have any such Effect; they are only to contrive *the Cheating of Indians in the Price of Beaver.*

Questions on Meaning:

1. What points does Franklin make about cross-cultural judgments? Find specific passages to prove your discussion.
2. Franklin presents an interesting study of cultural courtesy. What points of diplomacy practiced by the Indians would benefit us today?
3. On the basis of information revealed in Franklin's essay, what would the early Native Americans think about our current form of higher education? Explain.

Questions on Rhetorical Strategy and Style

1. Locate specific passages where Franklin uses the rhetorical mode of contrast/comparison to logically refute his contemporaries' opinions of Native Americans as "savages." Why is this technique both compelling and irrefutable?
2. Annotate your text for Franklin's use of the rhetorical mode of exemplification. In each instance, why is this technique particularly convincing?
3. Franklin is a master at using satiric humor to convey serious meaning. In this way, his writing is often ironic. Locate passages that cause you to both think and smile. Explain how this stylistic portrayal of these incidents often provides his strongest and most appealing proof.

Writing Assignments

1. Franklin offers his readers a cultural catalogue of beliefs and practices of Native Americans in 1784. Summarize these beliefs and practices and then explain how application of these practices could improve the quality of life in particular aspects of our current society.

2. In the second paragraph of his essay, Franklin suggests that no group of people is completely rude or totally polite. Is this the thesis of his essay? Or is Franklin actually proving a different point? State in your own words what you believe to be his thesis and then quote particular passages from the essay to prove your point.

3. Consider brief narratives embedded within the essay where Franklin makes particular points about organized religion and hypocrisy. Summarize these narratives and explain why Franklin includes them in this writing. Whose point of view does he defend in these mini-stories? Why? What do these passages reveal about Franklin's own belief system?

Poetry and Fiction

Poetry

Praise Song for the Day

Elizabeth Alexander

Elizabeth Alexander is the Chair of the African American Studies Department at Yale University. She is a teacher, a scholar, a poet, a play write, an essayist, an activist, a wife, and a mother. Over the course of her career, she has published five books of poems and won numerous awards and fellowships. As many poets do, Alexander prompts her readers to become more conscious of the power of language. As she puts it: "Words matter. Language matters. We live in and express ourselves with language, and that is how we communicate and move through the world in community." Alexander, only the fourth poet to be invited to write and read an inaugural poem, delivered the following poem on January 20, 2009, at the inauguration of President Barack Obama. To learn more about her and her work, visit her website at www.elizabethalexander.net.

Each day we go about our business,
walking past each other, catching each other's
eyes or not, about to speak or speaking.

All about us is noise. All about us is
noise and bramble, thorn and din, each
one of our ancestors on our tongues.

Someone is stitching up a hem, darning
a hole in a uniform, patching a tire,
repairing the things in need of repair.

Someone is trying to make music somewhere,
with a pair of wooden spoons on an oil drum,
with cello, boom box, harmonica, voice.

A woman and her son wait for the bus.
A farmer considers the changing sky.
A teacher says, Take out your pencils. Begin.

We encounter each other in words, words
spiny or smooth, whispered or declaimed,
words to consider, reconsider.

We cross dirt roads and highways that mark
the will of some one and then others, who said
I need to see what's on the other side.

I know there's something better down the road.
We need to find a place where we are safe.
We walk into that which we cannot yet see.

Say it plain: that many have died for this day.
Sing the names of the dead who brought us here,
who laid the train tracks, raised the bridges,

picked the cotton and the lettuce, built
brick by brick the glittering edifices
they would then keep clean and work inside of.

Praise song for struggle, praise song for the day.
Praise song for every hand-lettered sign,
the figuring-it-out at kitchen tables.

Some live by love thy neighbor as thyself,
others by first do no harm or take no more
than you need. What if the mightiest word is love?

Love beyond marital, filial, national,
love that casts a widening pool of light,
love with no need to pre-empt grievance.

In today's sharp sparkle, this winter air,
any thing can be made, any sentence begun.
On the brink, on the brim, on the cusp,
praise song for walking forward in that light.

Questions on Meaning:

1. Define the word "praise" in your own words, and then explain what the speaker means when she calls this poem a "Praise song for struggle; praise song for the day." Why would we praise struggle on Inauguration Day?
2. This poem begins with the declarative statement, "Each day we go about our own business." The speaker then gives examples of what that "business" might entail. What statement, or argument, is she making here about the way we live?
3. Where do you notice references to American history in this poem? What do those references say about our past, and why does the speaker remind us of these particular historical experiences?

Questions on Rhetorical Strategy and Style:

1. How would you describe the tone, or mood, at the beginning of the poem? At what point does the tone shift? What feeling does this poem leave us with?
2. This poem is narrated from multiple perspectives: first, second, and third person points of view. What do these shifts in perspective tell us about the speaker(s) of the poem? Who, or what, is the speaker of the poem?
3. Repetition is used throughout the poem, possibly to emphasize certain ideas and to develop a specific type of rhythm. Choose a

stanza that uses repetition as a rhetorical device, and describe the purpose behind that repetition.

4. Who is the intended audience of this poem? Explain how the speaker attempts to directly connect with that audience.

Writing Assignments

1. Write your own "Praise Poem" or "Praise Essay" celebrating a moment in history where our hope (as a community, nation, culture, gender, race, or world) was restored.

2. Write an essay exploring what it means to be "walking forward in that light." Write an essay exploring three things you'd like to see happen in that "light" or future.

3. On a daily basis, we engage in many forms of communication. In addition to talking face-to-face with friends, co-workers or family members, we are relying more and more on the use of cell phones and computers as mediums for communication. Consider the different ways you communicate with others on a daily basis. Write an essay explaining the different forms of communication that you depend on daily, and discuss the pros and cons of each.

Because I Could Not Stop For Death—

Emily Dickinson

Emily Dickinson (1830-1886) was born in Amherst, Massachusetts, where she lived an almost hidden life. She attended Mount Holyoke Female Seminary (1847-1848); in 1854 she met the Reverend Charles Wadsworth, who some say became her imaginary lover. Whatever the facts, he soon left for California and reclusiveness became Dickinson's permanent way of life. She wrote many poems, some of which she showed to her sister-in-law Susan, but most of her work remained hidden until after her death. The poems first began to be published in 1890, but the definitive edition, The Poems of Emily Dickinson, *edited by Thomas H. Johnson, did not appear until 1955.*

1 Because I could not stop for Death—   1
 He kindly stopped for me—
 The Carriage held but just Ourselves—
 And Immortality.

5 We slowly drove—He knew no haste   5
 And I had put away
 My labor and my leisure too,
 For His Civility—

We passed the School, where Children strove
10   At Recess—in the Ring—   10
We passed the Fields of Gazing Grain—
We passed the Setting Sun—

Or rather—He passed Us—
The Dews drew quivering and chill—
15   For only Gossamer, my Gown—   15
My Tippet—only Tulle—

We paused before a House that seemed
A Swelling of the Ground—
The Roof was scarcely visible—
20   The Cornice—in the Ground—   20

Since then—'tis Centuries—and yet
Feels shorter than the Day
I first surmised the Horses' Heads
Were toward Eternity—

Questions on Meaning

1. Dickinson may have had an unhappy love affair, after which she seems to have withdrawn from all social life. How does the death imagery in the poem reflect feelings of lost love?
2. The speaker says that she has put away her "labor and leisure" and that she has done so for death's "civility." What kind of values about death does the word "civility" imply? Is death always a bad thing?
3. How does Dickinson leave the reader with more questions about death than answers? Do these kinds of questions still trouble people? Find a current news event or news report that brings up these same questions and write about the meaning of the story.

Questions on Rhetorical Strategy and Style

1. Death is compared to a kindly coachman who stops his horse and carriage for the poem's speaker. What effect does the comparison have on the reader? Is death at all like a coachman? How?
2. What does the use of the words gossamer (like a spider web) and tulle (fine net) to describe the speaker's clothing suggest about the state of the speaker? Is she a ghost or a corpse? How do we know?
3. What is the "house"? Why is it a "swelling"? Does comparing the grave to a house make the poem more or less disturbing? How does the comparison make the reader respond to both graves and houses?

Writing Assignments

1. Critics have noted that all Dickinson's poems can be sung to hymn tunes. Find a popular song that deals with the kinds of issues that Dickinson takes up in this poem and compare both the meaning and the rhythms of the two works.
2. Dickinson lived to be only fifty-six years old and lived most of her life by herself. Did she appear to have an unhappy life? Find other stories about people, especially women, who have lived private lives alone, either as scholars or as religious people. How do such lives contrast with society's expectations about happiness? Write about your beliefs or values on this subject.
3. Dickinson did not publish her poems but appears to have written them for her personal pleasure. What do you write for pleasure? If you do not write for pleasure, try keeping a journal or log book for a week. Read back over your entries at the end of the week, and write about what you discovered from them.

Mending Wall

Robert Frost

Robert Frost (1874–1963), the American poet everyone knows, was born in San Fransisco, studied at Dartmouth and Harvard, worked in a mill, taught school, and farmed in New Hampshire before his first volume of poems was published. Having achieved prominence in the United States by 1915, he taught at many colleges and universities as well as at the famous Bread Loaf Writer's Conference. He won the Pulitzer four times, had a mountain in Vermont named after him, and read at John F. Kennedy's inaguration. He aspired to write a few poems it would be hard to get rid of, an ambition he achieved in "Stopping by Woods on a Snowy Evening," "The Death of the Hired Man," and "Birches," among others. This 1914 poem recounts the annual spring ritual of neighbors repairing a stone wall, prompting the poet to wonder why people believe that good fences make good neighbors.

1   Something there is that doesn't love a wall,
That sends the frozen-ground-swell under it,
And spills the upper boulders in the sun;
And makes gaps even two can pass abreast.
5   The work of hunters is another thing:
I have come after them and made repair
Where they have left not one stone on a stone,
But they would have the rabbit out of hiding,
To please the yelping dogs. The gaps I mean,
10   No one has seen them made or heard them made,
But at spring mending-time we find them there.
I let my neighbor know beyond the hill;

And on a day we meet to walk the line
And set the wall between us once again.
15 We keep the wall between us as we go.
To each the boulders that have fallen to each.
And some are loaves and some so nearly balls
We have to use a spell to make them balance:
"Stay where you are until our backs are turned!"
20 We wear our fingers rough with handling them.
Oh, just another kind of outdoor game,
One on a side. It comes to little more:
There where it is we do not need the wall:
He is all pine and I am apple orchard.
25 My apple trees will never get across
And eat the cones under his pines, I tell him.
He only says, "Good fences make good neighbors."
Spring is the mischief in me, and I wonder
If I could put a notion in his head:
30 "*Why* do they make good neighbors? Isn't it
Where there are cows? But here there are no cows.
Before I built a wall I'd ask to know
What I was walling in or walling out,
And to whom I was like to give offense.
35 Something there is that doesn't love a wall,
That wants it down." I could say "Elves" to him,
But it's not elves exactly, and I'd rather
He said it for himself. I see him there
Bringing a stone grasped firmly by the top
40 In each hand, like an old-stone savage armed.
He moves in darkness as it seems to me,
Not of woods only and the shade of trees.
He will not go behind his father's saying,
And he likes having thought of it so well
45 He says again, "Good fences make good neighbors."

Questions on Meaning

1. What forces conspire to break up the wall in this poem? What is the difference in motivation between the forces?
2. To what does the narrator refer when he says, "Spring is the mischief in me" (l. 28)? Why does he choose not to play that mischief on his neighbor?
3. The narrator believes that his neighbor "moves in darkness . . . /Not of woods only" (ll. 41–42). What other darkness envelops the neighbor? How does this darkness keep him from communicating with the narrator?

Questions on Rhetorical Strategy and Style

1. How does the narrator's analysis of the process of wall mending emphasize the separation between the neighbors? How deep does the division run?
2. In lines 38–40, the narrator describes his neighbor approaching the wall. What does this description say about the purpose of the wall, and of walls in general? How does the narrator respond to the knowledge of this purpose?
3. The poem begins and ends with contrasting interpretations of the value of the wall. How does this contrast create tension in the poem? As you read the poem, which interpretation predominates, and why?

Writing Assignments

1. Think of a yearly ritual of nature that you perform (e.g., raking leaves, planting flowers). Write a description of that ritual, exploring the various levels of meaning it holds in your life.
2. The poet questions the old axiom, "Good fences make good neighbors." Think of another axiom that we live by, and write an essay questioning the reasoning behind it.

Do Not Go Gentle into That Good Night

Dylan Thomas

Dylan Thomas was born on October 27, 1914, in Swansea, Glamorgan, Wales. The son of an English teacher, he became an excellent student of English and a failure at almost everything else. He dropped out of school when he was sixteen, and he went to work as a reporter. When he was twenty, his first book, Eighteen Poems, *was published. Suddenly he was famous. Subsequent research has suggested that most of his best work was begun before he turned twenty-one. Depressive, incapable of handling money, and inclined to alcoholism, Thomas struggled for the next fifteen years to make a living in England while his eloquent books of poetry continued to appear:* Twenty-Five Poems, *1936;* The World I Breath, *1939;* The Map of Love, *1939;* New Poems, *1942;* New Poems, *1943; and* Deaths and Entrances, *1946. In 1950, at the age of thirty-five, Thomas visited America where he delivered a series of passionate poetry readings that made him famous on this side of the Atlantic. The books published during this period—*In Country Sleep, and Other Poems, *1952; and* Collected Poems, *1952—further contributed to his legendary status as a romantic hero. Unfortunately, he also became famous for roaring bouts of drunkenness, one of which killed him at the age of thirty-nine. He died in New York City on November 9, 1953, of an alcohol overdose, leaving behind him a wife, two sons, a daughter, and an exquisite body of poetic work. The elegant villanelle, "Do not go gentle into that good night," a meditation on death*

"Do Not Go Gentle Into That Good Night," by Dylan Thomas, reprinted from *Poems of Dylan Thomas*, 1952, New Directions Publishing Corporation.

and dying, is among the most memorable poems that he wrote. As you read the poem, try to puzzle out the complex rules by which he composed the lines—a villanelle is a great test of a poet's skill—and note that, despite the complex form, his lines sound easy and natural. You may wonder, as others have done, how a man who could not discipline himself at all could discipline language so beautifully.

1   Do not go gentle into that good night,
Old age should burn and rave at the close of day;
Rage, rage against the dying of the light.

Though wise men at their end know dark is right,
5   Because their words had forked no lightning they
Do not go gentle into that good night.

Good men, the last wave by, crying how bright
Their frail deeds might have danced in a green bay,
Rage, rage against the dying of the light.

10   Wild men who caught and sang the sun in flight,
And learn, too late, they grieved it on its way,
Do not go gentle into that good night.

Grave men, near death, who see with blinding sight
Blind eyes could blaze like meteors and be gay,
15   Rage, rage against the dying of the light.

And you, my father, there on the sad height,
Curse, bless, me now with your fierce tears, I pray.
Do not go gentle into that good night.
Rage, rage against the dying of the light.

Questions on Meaning

1. Read the poem aloud and then paraphrase it in writing.
2. A villanelle is an extremely challenging and complex poetic form. Here are the rules: it must contain nineteen lines divided into six stanzas. The first five must be three-line stanzas (called tercets), and the sixth must be a four-line stanza (called a quatrain). The first and third lines of the first tercet must be repeated alternately as a refrain in tercets two through five and repeated as the last two lines of the quatrain. What is gained and lost when a writer commits to a complex organizational scheme like this one? Cite specific instances from the poem to illustrate your answer.

Questions on Rhetorical Strategy and Style

1. The poem works with an extended analogy in which night and day become death and life. Explain the meaning and appropriateness of the analogy.
2. Two of the lines—"Do not go gentle into that good night" and "Rage, rage against the dying of the light"—are repeated. They seem to restate the same idea. Why do you think the poet chose to restate the same idea? What advantages does he gain in making his message clear? What advantages does he gain in satisfying the requirements of writing a villanelle?

Writing Assignments

1. Write an essay about someone you have known who did not go gentle into that good night.
2. The poem's plea—do not go gentle into that good night—may be more a young person's than an older person's view of death. Ask some older people, perhaps grandparents or people in a nursing home, their views about death and report what you learn.

We Real Cool

Gwendolyn Brooks

Gwendolyn Brooks (1917-) was born in Topeka, Kansas, but has lived her life in Chicago and has become one of the most beloved of Illinois poets. She attended Wilson Junior College in Chicago and was graduated in 1938. Her first poem, "Eventide," appeared in the magazine American Childhood *when she was yet in her early teens. She published many poems in the* Chicago Defender, *a local paper. Her first book of poems,* A Street in Bronzeville *was published in 1945.* Annie Allen *(1949) won Brooks a Pulitzer Prize. Other collections of her poetry include* Bronzeville Boy and Girls *(1956),* The Bean Eaters *(1960),* Selected Poems *(1963),* In the Mecca *(1968),* Riot *(1969),* Blacks *(1987), and* Children Coming Home *(1991). She also has written an autobiographical novel,* Maud Martha *(1953) and a book of memoirs,* Report from Part One *(1972). "We Real Cool" expresses the quality of life in the city for young African-American men in the early 1960s.*

The Pool Players.
Seven at the Golden Shovel.

1   We real cool. We   1
     Left school. We

     Lurk late. We
     Strike straight. We

     Sing sin. We
     Thin gin. We

     Jazz June. We
     Die soon.

Questions on Meaning

1. The subtitle of "We Real Cool" is "The Pool Players. Seven at the Golden Shovel." What associations does the poem make with pool playing and the life of young men?
2. Does Brooks' poem have a political edge? What persuasive intention might she have for the speakers in the poem and for her readers?
3. The speakers in "We Real Cool" may become an example to other young people. Does Brooks seem to be giving a reason for picking these particular young men for her example of the dangerous life? Why?

Questions on Rhetorical Strategy and Style

1. What kind of language is Brooks approximating in the poem? What kinds of reactions might readers have to that language?
2. Who is speaking in the poem, and what is the reader supposed to think and feel about the speakers?
3. The life of the youngsters in the poem will clearly lead to a bad end, or so says the poem. What chain of causation does the poem imply? Do young people believe that their actions will lead to bad effects?

Writing Assignments

1. Find current rap lyrics that use the same types of rhythm and style as Brooks' poem. Write about your reaction to the effects of these rhythms.
2. Does the social commentary in the poem have as strong an effect in the beginning of the twenty-first century as it did in the middle of the twentieth century? What does your answer to this question say about human progress?
3. "We Real Cool" appears to be about not growing up, but what does it say about the need to grow up? Write an essay or poem that give examples of behaviors that imply acceptance of adult responsibilities.

Mid-term Break

Seamus Heaney

Seamus Heaney (1939–) was born in Londonderry in Northern Ireland, studied in Belfast at St. Joseph's College, and moved to Dublin in 1976. He has won many honors as a poet, most significantly the Nobel Prize for Literature in 1995 "for works of lyrical beauty and ethical depth, which exalt everyday miracles and the living past." He has taught at Oxford, Berkeley, and Harvard. Noteworthy collections include Haw Lantern *(1987),* Seeing Things *(1991),* Selected Poems: 1966-1987 *(1990),* The Spirit Level *(1996),* Electric Light *(2001), and* District and Circle *(2006). Heaney has also written plays and essays. "Mid-term Break" was first published in 1980.*

1   I sat all morning in the college sick bay
    Counting bells knelling classes to a close.
    At two o'clock our neighbors drove me home.

    In the porch I met my father crying—
5   He had always taken funerals in his stride —
    And Big Jim Evans saying it was a hard blow.

    The baby cooed and laughed and rocked the pram
    When I came in, and I was embarrassed
    By old men standing up to shake my hand

10 And tell me they were "sorry for my trouble,"
    Whispers informed strangers I was the eldest,
    Away at school, as my mother held my hand

In hers and coughed out angry tearless sighs.
At ten o'clock the ambulance arrived
15 With the corpse, stanched and bandaged by the nurses.

Next morning 1 went up into the room. Snowdrops
And candles soothed the bedside; I saw him
For the first time in six weeks. Paler now,

Wearing a poppy bruise on his left temple,
20 He lay in the four foot box as in his cot.
No gaudy scars, the bumper knocked him clear.

A four foot box, a foot for every year.

Questions on Meaning

1. What event does Heaney recount in this poem? What is the significance of the title?
2. Why does the poet mention that his father "had always taken funerals in his stride"?

Questions on Rhetorical Strategy and Style

1. We can discover much about a poem's meaning by examining its tone. How would you describe Heaney's tone here? What is his attitude toward the event?
2. You might notice that the poet never mentions the child's name. Why?
3. Each stanza in the poem, except for the last, is three lines in length. How does this form serve its overall meaning?

Writing Assignments

1. Write an essay about a sad event in your life. Try to capture your state of mind at the time by describing in detail things you remember seeing and hearing. As you recount these details, consider what dominant impression you want to create.
2. Write an essay in which you recount your memories of returning home for the first time. Was it on the occasion of a significant family event? How did you feel at the time? In what way were things different?

Theme for English B

Langston Hughes

Langston Hughes (1902–1967) was born in Joplin, Missouri, and grew up in Kansas and Ohio. A poet from childhood, he attended Columbia University to study engineering but dropped out. In 1923, Hughes shipped out on a freighter to Africa, and later to Italy and France, Russia and Spain. He eventually returned to college at Lincoln University, from which he was graduated in 1929. In his long career as a writer, Hughes published sixteen books of poetry.

1 The instructor said,

Go home and write
a page tonight.
And let that page come out of you—
5 Then, it will be true.

I wonder if it's that simple?
I am twenty-two, colored, born in Winston-Salem.
I went to school there, then Durham, then here
to this college on the hill above Harlem.
10 I am the only colored student in my class.

The steps from the hill lead down into Harlem,
through a park, then I cross St. Nicholas,
Eighth Avenue, Seventh, and I come to the Y,
the Harlem Branch Y, where I take the elevator
15 up to my room, sit down, and write this page:

It's not easy to know what is true for you or me
at twenty-two, my age. But I guess I'm what

"Theme for English B," by Langston Hughes, reprinted from *The Collected Poems of Langston Hughes,* edited by Arnold Rampersad and David Roessel, 1951, Alfred A. Knopf.

I feel and see and hear. Harlem, I hear you:
hear you, hear me—we too—you, me, talk on this page,
(I hear New York, too.) Me—who?

Well, I like to eat, sleep, drink, and be in love.
I like to work, read, learn, and understand life.
I like a pipe for a Christmas present,
or records—Bessie, bop, or Bach.
I guess being colored doesn't make me *not* like
the same things other folks like who are other races.
So will my page be colored that I write?
Being me, it will not be white.
But it will be
a part of you, instructor.
You are white—
yet a part of me, as I am a part of you.
That's American.
Sometimes perhaps you don't want to be a part of me
Nor do I often want to be a part of you.
But we are, that's true,
I guess you learn from me—
although you're older—and white—
and sometimes more free.

This is my page for English B.

Questions on Meaning

1. This poem ironically comments on a teacher's assignment. What clues do you get that the poet wants you to understand that the teacher doesn't know what he or she is asking for with the instructions to let a page "come out of you" in order to be true?

2. Ask your teacher what he or she would hope or expect to see from students who write in response to an assignment like the one that begins this poem.

Questions on Rhetorical Strategy and Style

1. Why does the poet divide the verse paragraphs where he does? (Hint: "for no good reason" is the wrong answer.) Explain.

2. Rewrite this poem, substituting your own places and names for those that Hughes supplies. Then comment on the differences between you and the poet. Are they a factor of race, gender, age, social class, region, or something else?

Writing Assignments

1. Describe a writing assignment that worked well for you or a writing experience that was postive. Explain what about the assignment helped you most. Describe your writing processes including such features as planning, researching, drafting, consulting with others, or anything else that seems relevant.

2. The poem gives extremely condensed descriptions of important preferences and experiences. Choose one of the poem's statements (e.g., "I wonder if it's that simple," "I am twenty-two," "It's not easy to know what is true"), and write an essay exploring the meaning of the statement in your life.

Indian Boarding School:
The Runaways

Louise Erdrich

Karen Lousie Erdrich (1954–) was born in Little Falls, Minnesota and grew up in Wahpeton, North Dakota, where her parents worked at the Bureau of Indian Affairs School. She attended Dartmouth and Johns Hopkins universities. She claims a French Ojibwe heritage from her mother and is a member of the Turtle Mountain Band of Chippewa. A prize-winning fiction writer, Erdrich is probably best known for her novels, which include Love Medicine *(1984),* The Beet Queen *(1986),* Tracks *(1988),* The Bingo Palace *(1994),* The Antelope Wife *(1998),* The Last Report on the Miracles at Little No Horse *(2001), and* The Master Butcher's Singing Club *(2003). Erdrich and her husband, Michael Dorris, separated in 1995; Dorris committed suicide in 1997. Erdrich now lives in Minneapolis, Minnesota with their children. In this poem, she writes from the point of view of the Native American child struggling in the environment of the government school.*

1   Home's the place we head for in our sleep.
    Boxcars stumbling north in dreams
    don't wait for us. We catch them on the run.
    The rails, old lacerations that we love,
5   shoot parallel across the face and break
    just under Turtle Mountains. Riding scars
    you can't get lost. Home is the place they cross.

    The lame guard strikes a match and makes the dark
    less tolerant. We watch through cracks in boards

10 as the land starts rolling, rolling till it hurts
    to be here, cold in regulation clothes.
    We know the sheriff's waiting at midrun
    to take us back. His car is dumb and warm.
    The highway doesn't rock, it only hums
15 like a wing of long insults. The worn-down welts
    of ancient punishments lead back and forth.
    All runaways wear dresses, long green ones,
    the color you would think shame was. We scrub
    the sidewalks down because it's shameful work.
20 Our brushes cut the stone in watered arcs
    and in the soak frail outlines shiver clear
    a moment, things us kids pressed on the dark
    face before it hardened, pale, remembering
    delicate old injuries, the spines of names and leaves.

Questions on Meaning

1. Erdrich uses the conflict between Native Americans and the white culture to set the background of the poem's similes and metaphors. Consider the lines, "The highway doesn't rock, it only hums / like a wing of long insults. The worn-down welts / of ancient punishments lead back and forth." Explain the literal and figurative meanings implied in these lines.
2. The punishment given runaways is to clean sidewalks, yet another in the series of references to hard surfaces that are the signs of white civilization. What is Erdrich's point?

Questions on Rhetorical Strategy and Style

1. In the first verse paragraph of the poem, the train's rails are "lacerations" or "scars." Explain the implied comparison between railroads and highways.
2. Erdrich uses language in complex ways. For example, she refers to the car as "dumb and warm." The words' sounds are similar, but their meanings seem odd together. She probably means you to understand *dumb* in the sense of "silent," but the other meanings of *dumb* provide interesting alternate possibilities for meaning. Define the words and explain how you would interpret the line.

Writing Assignments

1. Investigate the history of the boarding schools for Native American children administered by the United States government. Write an essay that explains the historical background of this poem.
2. The runaways in this poem have boarded a freight train to try to return to their homes on a reservation, fleeing from one form of imprisonment to another. Does their situation resemble any that you have experienced? Write a narrative essay that describes a time when you were in flight.

Fiction

Girl

Jamaica Kincaid

Born Elaine Potter Richardson in St. John's, Antigua, in the West Indies, Jamaica Kincaid (1949-) left Antigua for New York when she was seventeen, took classes at a community college, studied photography at the New School for Social Research, and attended Franconia College. She has been a staff writer for The New Yorker *and has published her work in* Rolling Stone, The Village Voice, *and* The Paris Review. *Her first book,* At the Bottom of the River *(1983) won an award from the American Academy and Institute of Arts and Letters. Her more recent works include* The Autobiography of My Mother *(1996) and* My Brother *(1997). The following selection originally appeared in* The New Yorker *and was included in* At the Bottom of the River. *It vividly narrates a relationship between a powerful mother and her young daughter and confronts us with the advice the daughter must listen to.*

1   Wash the white clothes on Monday and put them on the stone heap; wash the color clothes on Tuesday and put them on the clothesline to dry; don't walk barehead in the hot sun; cook pumpkin fritters in very hot sweet oil; soak your little clothes right after you take them off; when buying cotton to make yourself a nice blouse, be sure that it doesn't have gum on it, because that way it won't hold up well after a wash; soak salt fish overnight before you cook it; is it true that you sing benna in Sunday school?; always eat your food in such a way that it won't turn someone else's stomach; on Sundays try to walk like a lady and not like the slut you are so bent on becoming; don't sing benna in Sunday school; you

mustn't speak to wharf-rat boys, not even to give directions; don't eat fruits on the street—flies will follow you; *but I don't sing benna on Sundays at all and never in Sunday school*; this is how to sew on a button; this is how to make a buttonhole for the button you have just sewed on; this is how to hem a dress when you see the hem coming down and so to prevent yourself from looking like the slut I know you are so bent on becoming; this is how you iron your father's khaki shirt so that it doesn't have a crease; this is how you iron your father's khaki pants so that they don't have a crease; this is how you grow okra—far from the house, because okra tree harbors red ants; when you are growing dasheen, make sure it gets plenty of water or else it makes your throat itch when you are eating it; this is how you sweep a corner; this is how you sweep a whole house; this is how you sweep a yard; this is how you smile to someone you don't like too much; this how you smile to someone you don't like at all; this is how you smile to someone you like completely; this is how you set a table for tea; this is how you set a table for dinner; this is how you set a table for dinner with an important guest; this is how you set a table for lunch; this is how you set a table for breakfast; this is how to behave in the presence of men who don't know you very well, and this way they won't recognize immediately the slut I have warned you against becoming; be sure to wash every day, even if it is with your own spit; don't squat down to play marbles—you are not a boy, you know; don't pick people's flowers—you might catch something; don't throw stones at blackbirds, because it might not be a blackbird at all; this is how to make a bread pudding; this is how to make doukona; this is how to make pepper pot; this is how to make a good medicine for a cold; this is how to make a good medicine to throw away a child before it even becomes a child; this is how to catch a fish; this is how to throw back a fish you don't like, and that way something bad won't fall on you; this is how to bully a man; this is how a man bullies you; this is how to love a man, and if this doesn't work there are other ways, and if they don't work don't feel too bad about giving up; this is how to spit up in the air if you feel like it and this is how to move quick so that it doesn't fall on you; this is how to make ends meet; always squeeze bread to make sure it's fresh; *but what if the baker won't let me feel the bread?*; you mean to say that after all you are really going to be the kind of woman who the baker won't let near the bread?

Questions on Meaning

1. In this short piece, Kincaid gives us a glimpse into the relationship between a mother and daughter. How would you describe that relationship?
2. How would you characterize the advice offered by the mother in this story? What information about her community and its assumptions regarding gender roles can you infer from it?

Questions on Rhetorical Strategy and Style

1. What is this story's texture? How does it make you feel? Why do you think Kincaid chose to present it as a brief monologue?
2. Kincaid doesn't describe the physical setting of "Girl" directly, but provides clues in the content of the mother's advice. Go through the story and find as many details about place as you can, then write a description of the characters' home and neighborhood.
3. "Girl" makes an interesting use of example: Kincaid strings together a barrage of examples to tell her reader something about the characters, but doesn't explain precisely what they're meant to illustrate. What point do you think she is trying to make with them?

Writing Assignments

1. Write a short narrative piece about a time when someone with authority over you gave you advice. What kind of advice was it? How did you feel about receiving it? What was your response? In your narrative, try to convey a sense of the mood surrounding the exchange by the way you describe the things around you.
2. Write an essay about your relationship with one of your parents. Recount in detail significant moments you spent together. Your purpose is to convey something about the understandings you share.

The Lottery

Shirley Jackson

Shirley Hardie Jackson (1919-1965) was born in San Francisco. She received her B.A. from Syracuse University in 1940, then married literary critic Stanley Edgar Hyman, settling in North Bennington, Vermont, where they raised four children. Both parents continued vigorous literary careers. Jackson published the light and charming works Life among the Savages *(1953) and* Raising Demons *(1957) out of her experiences as a parent. At the same time, she was writing more disturbing works of horror and moral criticism,* The Lottery and Other Stories *(1949) and* The Haunting of Hill House *(1959). She said of "The Lottery" that she was hoping to force readers to see that their own lives contained inhumanity and cruelty.*

1   The morning of June 27th was clear and sunny, with the fresh warmth of a full-summer day; the flowers were blossoming profusely and the grass was richly green. The people of the village began to gather in the square, between the post office and the bank, around ten o'clock; in some towns there were so many people that the lottery took two days and had to be started on June 26th, but in this village, where there were only about three hundred people, the whole lottery took less than two hours, so it could begin at ten o'clock in the morning and still be through in time to allow the villagers to get home for noon dinner.

The children assembled first, of course. School was recently over for the summer, and the feeling of liberty sat uneasily on most of them; they tended to gather together quietly for a while before they broke into boisterous play, and their talk was still of the classroom and the teacher, of books and reprimands. Bobby Martin had already stuffed his pockets full of stones, and the other boys soon followed his example, selecting the smoothest and roundest stones; Bobby and Harry Jones and Dickie Delacroix—the villagers pronounced this name "Dellacroy"—eventually made a great pile of stones in one corner of the square and guarded it against the raids of the other boys. The girls stood aside, talking among themselves, looking over their shoulders at the boys, and the very small children rolled in the dust or clung to the hands of their older brothers or sisters.

Soon the men began to gather, surveying their own children, speaking of planting and rain, tractors and taxes. They stood together, away from the pile of stones in the corner, and their jokes were quiet and they smiled rather than laughed. The women, wearing faded house dresses and sweaters, came shortly after their menfolk. They greeted one another and exchanged bits of gossip as they went to join their husbands. Soon the women, standing by their husbands, began to call to their children, and the children came reluctantly, having to be called four or five times. Bobby Martin ducked under his mother's grasping hand and ran, laughing, back to the pile of stones. His father spoke up sharply, and Bobby came quickly and took his place between his father and his oldest brother.

The lottery was conducted—as were the square dances, the teenage club, the Halloween program—by Mr. Summers, who had time and energy to devote to civic activities. He was a round-faced, jovial man and he ran the coal business, and people were sorry for him, because he had no children and his wife was a scold. When he arrived in the square, carrying the black wooden box, there was a murmur of conversation among the villagers, and he waved and called, "Little late today, folks." The postmaster, Mr. Graves, followed him, carrying a three-legged stool, and the stool was put in the center of the square and Mr. Summers set the black box down on it. The villagers kept their distance, leaving a space between themselves and the stool, and when Mr. Summers said, "Some of you fellows want to give me a hand?" there was a hesitation before two men, Mr. Martin and his oldest son, Baxter, came forward to hold the box steady on the stool while Mr. Summers stirred up the papers inside it.

The original paraphernalia for the lottery had been lost long ago, and the black box now resting on the stool had been put into use even before Old Man Warner, the oldest man in town, was born. Mr. Summers spoke frequently to the villagers about making a new box, but no one liked to upset even as much tradition as was represented by the black box. There was a story that the present box had been made with some pieces of the box that had preceded it, the one that had been constructed when the first people settled down to make a village here. Every year, after the lottery, Mr. Summers began talking again about a new box, but every year the subject was allowed to fade off without anything's being done. The black box grew shabbier each year; by now it was no longer completely black but splintered badly along one side to show the original wood color, and in some places faded or stained.

Mr. Martin and his oldest son, Baxter, held the black box securely on the stool until Mr. Summers had stirred the papers thoroughly with his hand. Because so much of the ritual had been forgotten or discarded, Mr. Summers had been successful in having slips of paper substituted for the chips of wood that had been used for generations. Chips of wood, Mr. Summers had argued, had been all very well when the village was tiny, but now that the population was more than three hundred and likely to keep on growing, it was necessary to use something that would fit more easily into the black box. The night before the lottery, Mr. Summers and Mr. Graves made up the slips of paper and put them in the box, and it was then taken to the safe of Mr. Summers' coal company and locked up until Mr. Summers was ready to take it to the square next morning. The rest of the year, the box was put away, sometimes one place, sometimes another; it had spent one year in Mr. Graves's barn and another year underfoot in the post office, and sometimes it was set on a shelf in the Martin grocery and left there.

There was a great deal of fussing to be done before Mr. Summers declared the lottery open. There were the lists to make up—of heads of families, heads of households in each family, members of each household in each family. There was the proper swearing-in of Mr. Summers by the postmaster, as the official of the lottery; at one time, some people remembered, there had been a recital of some sort, performed by the official of the lottery, a perfunctory, tuneless chant that had been rattled off duly each year; some people believed that the official of the lottery used to stand just so when he said or sang it, others believed that he was supposed to walk among the people, but years and years ago this part of the ritual had been allowed to lapse. There had been, also, a ritual salute, which the official of the lottery had had to use in addressing each person who came up to draw from the box, but this also had changed with time, until now it was felt necessary only for the official to speak to each person approaching. Mr. Summers was very good at all this; in his clean white shirt and blue jeans, with one hand resting carelessly on the black box, he seemed very proper and important as he talked interminably to Mr. Graves and the Martins.

Just as Mr. Summers finally left off talking and turned to the assembled villagers, Mrs. Hutchinson came hurriedly along the path to the square, her sweater thrown over her shoulders, and slid into place in the back of the crowd. "Clean forgot what day it was," she said to Mrs. Delacroix, who stood next to her, and they both laughed softly. "Thought my old man was out back stacking wood," Mrs. Hutchinson went on, "and then I looked out the window and the kids were gone, and then I remembered it was the twentyseventh and came a-running." She dried her hands on her apron, and Mrs. Delacroix said, "You're in time, though. They're still talking away up there."

Mrs. Hutchinson craned her neck to see through the crowd and found her husband and children standing near the front. She tapped Mrs. Delacroix on the arm as a farewell and began to make her way through the crowd. The people separated good-humoredly to let her through; two or three people said, in voices just loud enough to be heard across the crowd, "Here comes your Missus, Hutchinson," and "Bill, she made it after all." Mrs. Hutchinson reached her husband, and Mr. Summers, who had been waiting, said cheerfully, "Thought we were going to have to get on without you, Tessie." Mrs. Hutchinson said, grinning, "Wouldn't have me leave m'dishes in the sink, now, would you, Joe?" and soft laughter ran through the crowd as the people stirred back into position after Mrs. Hutchinson's arrival.

10 "Well, now," Mr. Summers said soberly, "guess we better get 10 started, get this over with, so's we can go back to work. Anybody ain't here?"

"Dunbar," several people said. "Dunbar, Dunbar."

Mr. Summers consulted his list. "Clyde Dunbar," he said. "That's right. He's broke his leg, hasn't he? Who's drawing for him?"

"Me, I guess," a woman said, and Mr. Summers turned to look at her. "Wife draws for her husband," Mr. Summers said. "Don't you have a grown boy to do it for you, Janey?" Although Mr. Summers and everyone else in the village knew the answer perfectly well, it was the business of the official of the lottery to ask such questions formally. Mr. Summers waited with an expression of polite interest while Mrs. Dunbar answered.

"Horace's not but sixteen yet," Mrs. Dunbar said regretfully. "Guess I gotta fill in for the old man this year."

15 "Right," Mr. Summers said. He made a note on the list he was 15 holding. Then he asked, "Watson boy drawing this year?"

A tall boy in the crowd raised his hand. "Here," he said. "I'm drawing for m'mother and me." He blinked his eyes nervously and ducked his head as several voices in the crowd said things like "Good fellow, Jack," and "Glad to see your mother's got a man to do it."

"Well," Mr. Summers said, "guess that's everyone. Old Man Warner make it?"

"Here," a voice said, and Mr. Summers nodded.

A sudden hush fell on the crowd as Mr. Summers cleared his throat and looked at the list. "All ready?" he called. "Now, I'll read the names—heads of families first—and the men come up and take a paper out of the box. Keep the paper folded in your hand without looking at it until everyone has had a turn. Everything clear?"

20 The people had done it so many times that they only half listened 20 to the directions; most of them were quiet, wetting their lips, not looking around. Then Mr. Summers raised one hand high and said, "Adams." A man disengaged himself from the crowd and came forward. "Hi, Steve," Mr. Summers said, and Mr. Adams said, "Hi, Joe." They grinned at one another humorlessly and nervously. Then Mr. Adams reached into the black box and took out a folded paper. He held it firmly by one corner as he turned and went hastily back to his place in the crowd, where he stood a little apart from his family, not looking down at his hand.

"Allen," Mr. Summers said. "Anderson . . . Bentham."

"Seems like there's no time at all between lotteries any more," Mrs. Delacroix said to Mrs. Graves in the back row. "Seems like we got through with the last one only last week."

"Time sure goes fast," Mrs. Graves said.

"Clark . . . Delacroix."

25   "There goes my old man," Mrs. Delacroix said. She held her breath while her husband went forward.

"Dunbar," Mr. Summers said, and Mrs. Dunbar went steadily to the box while one of the women said, "Go on, Janey," and another said, "There she goes."

"We're next," Mrs. Graves said. She watched while Mr. Graves came around from the side of the box, greeted Mr. Summers gravely, and selected a slip of paper from the box. By now, all through the crowd there were men holding the small folded papers in their large hands, turning them over and over nervously. Mrs. Dunbar and her two sons stood together, Mrs. Dunbar holding the slip of paper.

"Harburt . . . Hutchinson."

"Get up there, Bill," Mrs. Hutchinson said, and the people near her laughed.

30   "Jones."

"They do say," Mr. Adams said to Old Man Warner, who stood next to him, "that over in the north village they're talking of giving up the lottery."

Old Man Warner snorted. "Pack of crazy fools," he said. "Listening to the young folks, nothing's good enough for *them*. Next thing you know, they'll be wanting to go back to living in caves, nobody work any more, live *that* way for a while. Used to be a saying about 'Lottery in June, corn be heavy soon.' First thing you know, we'd all be eating stewed chickweed and acorns. There's *always* been a lottery," he added petulantly. "Bad enough to see young Joe Summers up there joking with everybody."

"Some places have already quit lotteries," Mrs. Adams said.

"Nothing but trouble in *that*," Old Man Warner said stoutly. "Pack of young fools."

35   "Martin." And Bobby Martin watched his father go forward. "Overdyke . . . Percy."

"I wish they'd hurry," Mrs. Dunbar said to her older son. "I wish they'd hurry."

"They're almost through," her son said.

"You get ready to run tell Dad," Mrs. Dunbar said.

Mr. Summers called his own name and then stepped forward precisely and selected a slip from the box. Then he called, "Warner."

40   "Seventy-seventh year I been in the lottery," Old Man Warner said as he went through the crowd. "Seventy-seventh time."

"Watson." The tall boy came awkwardly through the crowd. Someone said, "Don't be nervous, Jack," and Mr. Summers said, "Take your time, son."

"Zanini."

After that, there was a long pause, a breathless pause, until Mr. Summers, holding his slip of paper in the air, said, "All right, fellows." For a minute, no one moved, and then all the slips of paper were opened. Suddenly, all the women began to speak at once, saying, "Who is it?" "Who's got it?" "Is it the Dunbars?" "Is it the Watsons?" Then the voices began to say, "It's Hutchinson. It's Bill," "Bill Hutchinson's got it."

"Go tell your father," Mrs. Dunbar said to her older son.

45 People began to look around to see the Hutchinsons. Bill 45 Hutchinson was standing quiet, staring down at the paper in his hand. Suddenly, Tessie Hutchinson shouted to Mr. Summers, "You didn't give him time enough to take any paper he wanted. I saw you. It wasn't fair."

"Be a good sport, Tessie," Mrs. Delacroix called, and Mrs. Graves said, "All of us took the same chance."

"Shut up, Tessie," Bill Hutchinson said.

"Well, everyone," Mr. Summers said, "that was done pretty fast, and now we've got to be hurrying a little more to get done in time." He consulted his next list. "Bill," he said, "you draw for the Hutchinson family. You got any other households in the Hutchinsons?"

"There's Don and Eva," Mrs. Hutchinson yelled. "Make them take their chance!"

50 "Daughters draw with their husbands' families, Tessie," Mr. Sum- 50 mers said gently. "You know that as well as anyone else."

"It wasn't *fair*," Tessie said.

"I guess not, Joe," Bill Hutchinson said regretfully. "My daughter draws with her husband's family, that's only fair. And I've got no other family except the kids."

"Then, as far as drawing for families is concerned, it's you." Mr. Summers said in explanation, "and as far as drawing for households is concerned, that's you, too. Right?"

"Right," Bill Hutchinson said.

55 "How many kids, Bill?" Mr. Summers asked formally. 55

"Three," Bill Hutchinson said. "There's Bill, Jr., and Nancy, and little Dave. And Tessie and me."

"All right, then," Mr. Summers said. "Harry, you got their tickets back?"

Mr. Graves nodded and held up the slips of paper. "Put them in the box, then," Mr. Summers directed. "Take Bill's and put it in."

"I think we ought to start over," Mrs. Hutchinson said, as quietly as she could. "I tell you it wasn't *fair*. You didn't give him time enough to choose. *Every*body saw that."

60 Mr. Graves had selected the five slips and put them in the box, 60 and he dropped all the papers but those onto the ground, where the breeze caught them and lifted them off.

"Listen, everybody," Mrs. Hutchinson was saying to the people around her.

"Ready, Bill?" Mr. Summers asked, and Bill Hutchinson, with one quick glance around at his wife and children, nodded.

"Remember," Mr. Summers said, "take the slips and keep them folded until each person has taken one. Harry, you help little Dave." Mr. Graves took the hand of the little boy, who came willingly with him up to the box. "Take a paper out of the box, Davy," Mr. Summers said. Davy put his hand into the box and laughed. "Take just *one* paper," Mr. Summers said. "Harry, you hold it for him." Mr. Graves took the child's hand and removed the folded paper from the tight fist and held it while little Dave stood next to him and looked up at him wonderingly.

"Nancy next," Mr. Summers said. Nancy was twelve, and her school friends breathed heavily as she went forward, switching her skirt, and took a slip daintily from the box. "Bill, Jr.," Mr. Summers said, and Billy, his face red and his feet over-large, nearly knocked the box over as he got a paper out. "Tessie," Mr. Summers said. She hesitated for a minute, looking around defiantly, and then set her lips and went up to the box. She snatched a paper out and held it behind her.

65 "Bill," Mr. Summers said, and Bill Hutchinson reached into the 65 box and felt around, bringing his hand out at last with the slip of paper in it.

The crowd was quiet. A girl whispered, "I hope it's not Nancy," and the sound of the whisper reached the edges of the crowd.

"It's not the way it used to be," Old Man Warner said clearly. "People ain't the way they used to be."

"All right," Mr. Summers said. "Open the papers. Harry, you open little Dave's."

Mr. Graves opened the slip of paper and there was a general sigh through the crowd as he held it up and everyone could see that it was blank. Nancy and Bill, Jr., opened theirs at the same time, and both beamed and laughed, turning around to the crowd and holding their slips of paper above their heads.

70 "Tessie," Mr. Summers said. There was a pause, and then Mr. 70 Summers looked at Bill Hutchinson, and Bill unfolded his paper and showed it. It was blank.

"It's Tessie," Mr. Summers said, and his voice was hushed. "Show us her paper, Bill."

Bill Hutchinson went over to his wife and forced the slip of paper out of her hand. It had a black spot on it, the black spot Mr. Summers had made the night before with the heavy pencil in the coal-company office. Bill Hutchinson held it up, and there was a stir in the crowd.

"All right, folks," Mr. Summers said. "Let's finish quickly."

Although the villagers had forgotten the ritual and lost the original black box, they still remembered to use stones. The pile of stones the boys had made earlier was ready; there were stones on the ground with the blowing scraps of paper that had come out of the box. Mrs. Delacroix selected a stone so large she had to pick it up with both hands and turned, to Mrs. Dunbar. "Come on," she said. "Hurry up."

Mrs. Dunbar had small stones in both hands, and she said, gasping for breath, "I can't run at all. You'll have to go ahead and I'll catch up with you."

75 The children had stones already, and someone gave little Davy 75 Hutchinson a few pebbles.

Tessie Hutchinson was in the center of a cleared space by now, and she held her hands out desperately as the villagers moved in on her. "It isn't fair," she said. A stone hit her on the side of the head.

Old Man Warner was saying, "Come on, come on, everyone." Steve Adams was in the front of the crowd of villagers, with Mrs. Graves beside him.

"It isn't fair, it isn't right," Mrs. Hutchinson screamed, and then they were upon her.

Questions on Meaning

1. Why does the story begin with the children, and why does it end with the little boy being given a few stones?
2. Tessie Hutchinson becomes a scapegoat for the community. Look up the word "scapegoat" to see exactly what it means and where it originated.
3. Is this story possible? Could people act so casually about such a horrifying prospect as killing a friend or neighbor? Discuss the possibilities of such behavior.

Questions on Rhetorical Strategy and Style

1. At what point in the story does the reader know that something horrible is about to happen? How does the mood of the whole story lead to that moment? Or does it?
2. The families are divided into prescribed groupings, daughters with husbands' families, children with parents until a certain age. Why do we classify and divide groups of people in these ways? What is to be gained from family groupings? What is lost?
3. A news reporter recently described villagers he had met in Rwanda, where the Tutsi massacres took place. He said that the people told him that they must conform to everyone else's behavior, or they too would be killed. Discuss this kind of argument for military and civil violence. Do you believe it to be a sound argument for any occasion?

Writing Assignments

1. A famous German minister, Diedrich Bonhoeffer, said of the Nazis, "When they came for the Jews, I said nothing; when they came for the Communists, I said nothing; when they came for the Catholics, I said nothing; so when they came for me, there was no one to speak." What does such a statement show about our responsibility for others?
2. Traditions can be good for a society or culture, but they can also cause great damage. Choose a holiday or event and discuss the pros and cons of the traditional approaches to the occasion.
3. The story revolves around an election. Why are elections surrounded with so much ceremony? We have election judges, election officials, and election rules and regulations. Does the right to vote deserve so much time and ceremony? Why or why not?

This Way for the Gas, Ladies and Gentlemen

Tadeusz Borowski

Tadeusz Borowski (1922–1951) was no stranger to political turmoil even during his childhood. Born in a Soviet-ruled Polish city to dissident parents, he lived with an aunt after his parents were deported in early Soviet purges. After privately publishing a book of poetry in 1942, Borowski was arrested as a dissident by the Nazis and imprisoned in Auschwitz and Dachau for two years. While in Auschwitz, Borowski worked in the camp hospital that became notorious for its sadistic human medical experiments. His experiences in the concentration camp formed the basis of his collection of stories, Farewell to Maria, *in which "This Way to the Gas, Ladies and Gentlemen" first appeared. Although Borowski joined the Communist party and committed himself to revolutionary politics after the World War II, he remained haunted by the role of ordinary people like himself in the horrors that the Nazis perpetrated. In 1951, he killed himself by asphyxiation from a gas stove. In this story, Borowski suggests that concentration-camp life dehumanized Nazis, and prisoners alike.*

1   All of us walk around naked. The delousing is finally over, and our striped suits are back from the tanks of Cyclone B solution, an efficient killer of lice in clothing and of men in gas chambers. Only the inmates in the blocks cut off from ours by the "Spanish goats"[1] still have nothing to wear. But all the same, all of us walk around naked: the heat is unbearable. The camp has been sealed

---

"This Way for the Gas, Ladies and Gentleman" by Tadeusz Borowski, Translated by Barbara Vedder. Penguin Classics, Penguin Books, Ltd.

off tight. Not a single prisoner, not one solitary louse, can sneak through the gate. The labour Kommandos have stopped working. All day, thousands of naked men shuffle up and down the roads, cluster around the squares, or lie against the walls and on top of the roofs. We have been sleeping on plain boards, since our mattresses and blankets are still being disinfected. From the rear blockhouses we have a view of the F.K.L.—*Frauen Konzentration Lager*;[2] there too the delousing is in full swing. Twenty-eight thousand women have been stripped naked and driven out of the barracks. Now they swarm around the large yard between the blockhouses.

The heat rises, the hours are endless. We are without even our usual diversion: the wide roads leading to the crematoria are empty. For several days now, no new transports have come in. Part of "Canada"[3] has been liquidated and detailed to a labour Kommando— one of the very toughest—at Harmenz. For there exists in the camp a special brand of justice based on envy: when the rich and mighty fall, their friends see to it that they fall to the very bottom. And Canada, our Canada, which smells not of maple forests but of French perfume, has amassed great fortunes and currency from all over Europe.

Several of us sit on the top bunk, our legs dangling over the edge. We slice the neat loaves of crisp, crunchy bread, It is a bit coarse to the taste, the kind that stays fresh for days. Sent all the way from Warsaw—only a week ago my mother held this white loaf in her hands . . . dear Lord . . .

We unwrap the bacon, the onion, we open a can of evaporate milk. Henri, the fat Frenchman, dreams aloud of the French wine brought by the transports from Strasbourg, Paris, Marseille . . . Sweat streams down his body.

"Listen, *mon ami*,[4] next time we go up on the loading ramp, I'll bring you real champagne. You haven't tried it before, eh?"

"No. But you'll never be able to smuggle it through the gate, so stop teasing. Why not try and 'organize' some shoes for me instead— you know, the perforated kind, with a double sole, and what about that shirt you promised me long ago?"

"*Patience, patience.* When the new transports come, I'll bring all you want. We'll be going on the ramp again!"

"And what if there aren't any more 'cremo' transports?" I say spitefully. "Can't you see how much easier life is becoming around here: no limit on packages, no more beatings? You even write letters home. . . One hears all kind of talk, and, dammit, they'll run out of people!"

"Stop talking nonsense." Henri's serious fat face moves rhythmically, his mouth is full of sardines. We have been friends for a long time, but I do not even know his last name. "Stop talking nonsense," he repeats, swallowing with effort. "They can't run out of people, or we'll starve to death in this blasted camp. All of us live on what they bring."

10   "All? We have our packages. . ."   10

"Sure, you and your friend, and ten other friends of yours. Some of you Poles get packages. But what about us, and the Jews, and the Russkis? And what if we had no food, no 'organization' from the transports, do you think you'd be eating those packages of yours in peace? We wouldn't let you!"

"You would, you'd starve to death like the Greeks. Around here, whoever has grub, has power."

"Anyway, you have enough, we have enough, so why argue?"

Right, why argue? They have enough, I have enough, we eat together and we sleep on the same bunks. Henri slices the bread, he makes a tomato salad. It tastes good with the commissary mustard.

Below us, naked sweat-drenched men crowd the narrow barracks aisles or lie packed in eights and tens in the lower bunks. Their nude, withered bodies stink of sweat and excrement; their cheeks are hollow. Directly beneath me, in the bottom bunk, lies a rabbi. He has covered head with a piece of rag torn off a blanket and reads from a Hebrew prayer book (there is no shortage of this type of literature at the camp), wailing loudly, monotonously.

15   "Can't somebody shut him up? He's been raving as if he'd caught   15
God himself by the feet."

"I don't feel like moving. Let him rave. They'll take him to the oven that much sooner."

"Religion is the opium of the people," Henri, who is a Communist and a *rentier*, says sententiously. "If they didn't believe in God and eternal life, they'd have smashed the crematoria long ago."

"Why haven't you done it then?"

The question is rhetorical; the Frenchman ignores it.

20   "Idiot," he says simply, and stuffs a tomato in his mouth.   20

Just as we finish our snack, there is a sudden commotion at the door. The Muslims[5] scurry in fright to the safety of their bunks, a messenger runs into the Block Elder's shack. The Elder, his face solemn, steps out at once.

"Canada! *Antreten*![6] But fast! There's a transport coming!"

"Great God!" yells Henri, jumping off the bunk. He swallows the rest of his tomato, snatches his coat, screams "*Raus*"[7] at the men below, and in a flash is at the door. We can hear a scramble in the other bunks. Canada is leaving for the ramp.

"Henri, the shoes!" I call after him.

"*Keine Angst!*"[8] he shouts back, already outside.

I proceed to put away the food. I tie a piece of rope around the suitcase where the onions and the tomatoes from my father's garden in Warsaw mingle with Portuguese sardines, bacon from Lublin (that's from my brother), and authentic sweetmeats from Salonica. I tie it all up, pull on my trousers, an slide off the bunk.

"*Platz!*"[9] I yell, pushing my way through the Greeks. They step aside. At the door I bump into Henri.

"*Was ist los?*[10]

"Want to come with us on the ramp?"

"Sure, why not?"

"Come along then, grab your coat! We're short a few men. I've ahead told the Kapo," and he shoves me out of the barracks door.

We line up. Someone has marked down our numbers, someone up ahead yells, "March, march," and now we are running towards the gate accompanied by the shouts of a multilingual throng that is already being pushed back to the barracks. Not everybody is lucky enough to be going on the ramp. . . We have almost reached the gate. *Links, zwei, drei, vier! Mützen ab!*[11] Erect, arms stretched stiffly along our hips, we march past the gate briskly, smartly, almost gracefully. A sleepy S.S. man with a large pad in his hand checks us off, waving us ahead in groups of five.

"*Hundert!*" he calls after we have all passed.

"*Stimmt!*"[12] comes a hoarse answer from out front.

We march fast, almost at a run. There are guards all around, young men with automatics. We pass camp II B, then some deserted barracks and a clump of unfamiliar green—apple and pear trees. We cross the circle of watchtowers and, running, burst on to the highway. We have arrived. Just a few more yards There surrounded by trees, is the ramp.

A cheerful little station, very much like any other provincial railway stop: a small square framed by tall chestnuts and paved with yellow gravel. Not far off, beside the road, squats a tiny wooden shed, uglier and more flimsy than the ugliest and flimsiest railway shack; farther along lie stacks of old rails, heaps of wooden beams, barracks parts, bricks, paving stones. This is where they load freight for Birkenau: supplies for the construction of the camp, and people for the gas chambers. Trucks drive around, load up lumber, cement, people—a regular daily routine.

And now the guards are being posted along the rails, across the beams, in the green shade of the Silesian chestnuts, to form a tight circle around the ramp. They wipe the sweat from their faces and sip out of their canteens. It is unbearably hot; the sun stands motionless at its zenith.

"Fall out!"

We sit down in the narrow streaks of shade along the stacked rails. The hungry Greeks (several of them managed to come along, God only knows how) rummage underneath the rails. One of them finds some pieces of mildewed bread, another a few half-rotten sardines. They eat.

40   "*Schweinedreck*,"[13] spits a young, tall guard with corn-coloured 40 hair and dreamy blue eyes. "For God's sake, any minute you'll have so much food to stuff down your guts, you'll bust!" He adjusts his gun, wipes his face with a handkerchief.

"Hey you, fatso!" His boot lightly touches Henri's shoulder. "*Pass mal auf*,[14] want a drink?"

"Sure, but I haven't got any marks," replies the Frenchman with a professional air.

"*Schade*, too bad."

"Come, come, Herr Posten, isn't my word good enough any more? Haven't we done business before? How much?"

45   "One hundred. *Gemacht*?"[15]   45

"*Gemacht*."

We drink the water, lukewarm and tasteless. It will be paid for by the people who have not yet arrived.

"Now you be careful," says Henri, turning to me. He tosses away the empty bottle. It strikes the rails and bursts into tiny fragments. "Don't take any money, they might be checking. Anyway, who the hell needs money? You've got enough to eat. Don't take suits, either, or they'll think you're planning to escape. Just get a shirt, silk only, with a collar. And a vest. And if you find something to drink, don't bother calling me. I know how to shift for myself, but you watch your step or they'll let you have it."

"Do they beat you up here?"

"Naturally. You've got to have eyes in your ass. *Arschaugen.*"[16]

Around us sit the Greeks, their jaws working greedily, like huge human insects. They munch on stale lumps of bread. They are restless, wondering what will happen next. The sight of the large beams and the stacks of rails has them worried. They dislike carrying heavy loads.

"*Was wir arbeiten?*"[17] they ask.

"*Niks. Transport kommen, alles Krematorium, compris?*"[18]

"*Alles verstehen,*"[19] they answer in crematorium Esperanto. All is well—they will not have to move the heavy rails or carry the beams.

In the meantime, the ramp has become increasingly alive with activity, increasingly noisy. The crews are being divided into those who will open and unload the arriving cattle cars and those who will be posted by the wooden steps. They receive instructions on how to proceed most efficiently. Motor cycles drive up, delivering S.S. officers, bemedalled, glittering brass, beefy men with highly polished boots and shiny brutal faces. Some have brought their briefcases, others hold thin, flexible whips. This gives them an air of military readiness and agility. They walk in and out of the commissary—for the miserable little shack by the road serves as their commissary, where in the summertime they drink mineral water, *Studentenquelle,* and where in winter they can warm up with a glass of hot wine. They greet each other in the state-approved way, raising an arm Roman fashion, then shake hands cordially, exchange warm smiles, discuss mail from home their children, their families. Some stroll majestically on the ramp. The silver squares on their collars glitter, the gravel crunches under their boots, their bamboo, whips snap impatiently.

We lie against the rails in the narrow streaks of shade, breathe unevenly, occasionally exchange a few words in our various tongues, and gaze listlessly at the majestic men in green uniforms, at the green trees, and at the church steeple of a distant village.

"The transport is coming," somebody says. We spring to our feet, all eyes turn in one direction. Around the bend, one after another, the cattle cars begin rolling in. The train backs into the station, a conductor leans out, waves his hand, blows a whistle. The locomotive whistles back with a shrieking noise, puffs, the train rolls slowly alongside the ramp. In the tiny barred windows appear pale wilted exhausted human faces, terror-stricken women with tangled hair, unshaven men. They gaze at the station in silence. And then, suddenly, there is a stir inside the cars and a pounding against the wooden boards.

"Water! Air!"—weary, desperate cries.

Heads push through the windows, mouths gasp frantically for air. They draw a few breaths, then disappear; others come in their place, then also disappear. The cries and moans grow louder.

60 A man in a green uniform covered with more glitter than any of 60 the others jerks his head impatiently, his lips twist in annoyance. He inhales deeply, then with a rapid gesture throws his cigarette away and signals to the guard. The guard removes the automatic from his shoulder, aims, sends a series of shots along the train. All is quiet now. Meanwhile, the trucks have arrived, steps are being drawn up, and the Canada men stand ready at their posts by the train doors. The S.S. officer with the briefcase raises his hand.

"Whoever takes gold, or anything at all besides food, will be shot for stealing Reich property. Understand? *Verstanden?*"

"*Jawohl!*"[20] we answer eagerly.

"*Also los!* Begin!"

The bolts crack, the doors fall open. A wave of fresh air rushes inside the train. People. . . inhumanly crammed, buried under incredible heaps of luggage, suitcases, trunks, packages, crates, bundles of every description (everything that had been their past and was to start their future). Monstrously squeezed together, they have fainted from heat, suffocated, crushed one another. Now they push towards the opened doors, breathing like fish cast out on the sand.

65 "Attention! Out, and take your luggage with you! Take out 65 everything. Pile all your stuff near the exits. Yes, your coats too. It is summer. March to the left. Understand?"

"Sir, what's going to happen to us?" They jump from the train on to the gravel, anxious, worn-out.

"Where are you people from?"

"Sosnowiec-Bedzin. Sir, what's going to happen to us?" They repeat the question stubbornly, gazing into our tired eyes.

"I don't know. I don't understand Polish."

70   It is the camp law: people going to their death must be deceived   70
to the very end. This is the only permissible form of charity. The heat
is treamendous. The sun hangs directly over our heads, the white, hot
sky quivers, the air vibrates, an occasional breeze feels like a sizzling
blast from a furnace. Our lips are parched, the mouth fills with the
salty taste of blood, the body is weak and heavy from lying in the sun.
Water!

A huge, multicoloured wave of people loaded down with luggage
pours from the train like a blind, mad river trying to find a new bed.
But before they have a chance to recover, before they can draw a
breath of fresh air and look at the sky, bundles are snatched from their
hands, coats ripped off their backs, their purses and umbrellas taken
away.

"But please, sir, it's for the sun, I cannot. . ."

"*Verboten!*"[21] one of us barks through clenched teeth. There is an
S.S. man standing behind your back, calm, efficient, watchful.

"*Meine Herrschaften,*[22] this way, ladies and gentlemen, try not to
throw your things around, please. Show some goodwill," he says
courteously, his restless hands playing with the slender whip.

75   "Of course, of course," they answer as they pass, and now they   75
walk alongside the train somewhat more cheerfully. A woman reaches
down quickly to pick up her handbag. The whip flies, the woman
screams, stumbles, and falls under the feet of the surging crowd.
Behind her, a child cries in a thin little voice "Mamele!"—a very small
girl with tangled black curls.

The heaps grow. Suitcases, bundles, blankets, coats, handbags
that open as they fall, spilling coins, gold, watches; mountains of
bread pile up at the exits, heaps of marmalade, jams, masses of meat,
sausages; sugar spills on the gravel. Trucks, loaded with people, start
up with a deafening roar and drive off amidst the wailing and
screaming of the women separated from their children, and the
stupefied silence of the men left behind. They are the ones who had
been ordered to step to the right—the healthy and the young who will
go to the camp. In the end, they too will not escape death, but first
they must work.

Trucks leave and return, without interruption, as on a monstrous
conveyor belt. A Red Cross van drives back and forth, incessantly: it
transports the gas that will kill these people. The enormous cross on
the hood, red as blood, seems to dissolve in the sun.

The Canada men at the trucks cannot stop for a single moment, even to catch their breath. They shove the people up the steps, pack them in tightly, sixty per truck, more or less. Near by stands a young, cleanshaven "gentleman," an S.S. officer with a notebook in his hand. For each departing truck he enters a mark; sixteen gone means one thousand people, more or less. The gentleman is calm, precise. No truck can leave without a signal from him, or a mark in his notebook: *Ordnung muss sein.*[23] The marks swell into thousands, the thousands into whole transports, which afterwards we shall simply call "from Salonica," "from Strasbourg," "from Rotterdam." This one will be called "Sosnowiec-Bedzin." The new prisoners from Sosnowiec-Bedzin will receive serial numbers 131–2—thousand, of course, though afterwards we shall simply say 131–2, for short.

The transports swell into weeks, months, years. When the war is over, they will count up the marks in their notebooks—all four and a half million of them. The bloodiest battle of the war, the greatest victory of the strong, united Germany. *Ein Reich, ein Volk, ein Führer*[24]—and four crematoria.

80   The train has been emptied. A thin, pock-marked S.S. man peers   80
inside, shakes his head in disgust, and motions to our group, pointing his finger at the door.

"*Rein.* Clean it up!"

We climb inside. In the corners amid human excrement and abandoned wrist-watches he squashed, trampled infants, naked little monsters with enormous heads and bloated bellies. We carry them out like chickens, holding several in each hand.

"Don't take them to the trucks, pass them on to the women," says the S.S. man, lighting a cigarette. His cigarette lighter is not working properly; he examines it carefully.

"Take them, for God's sake!" I explode as the women run from me in horror, covering their eyes.

85   The name of God sounds strangely pointless, since the women   85
and the infants will go on the trucks, every one of them, without exception. We all know what this means, and we look at each other with hate and horror.

"What, you don't want to take them?" asks the pock-marked S.S. man with a note of surprise and reproach in his voice, and reaches for his revolver.

"You mustn't shoot, I'll carry them." A tall grey-haired woman takes the little corpses out of my hands and for an instant gazes straight into my eyes.

"My poor boy," she whispers and smiles at me. Then she walks away, staggering along the path. I lean against the side of the train. I am terribly tired. Someone pulls at my sleeve.

"*En avant*, to the rails, come on!"

90   I look up, but the face swims before my eyes, dissolves, huge and   90 transparent, melts into the motionless trees and the sea of people. . . I blink rapidly: Henri.

"Listen, Henri, are we good people?"

"That's stupid. Why do you ask?"

"You see, my friend, you see, I don't know why, but I am furious, simply furious with these people—furious because I must be here because of them. I feel no pity. I am not sorry they're going to the gas chamber. Damn them all! I could throw myself at them, beat them with my fists. It must be pathological, I just can't understand. . ."

"Ah, on the contrary, it is natural, predictable, calculated. The ramp exhausts you, you rebel—and the easiest way to relieve your hate is to turn against someone weaker. Why, I'd even call it healthy, It's simple logic, *compris?*" He props himself up comfortably against the heap of rails. "Look at the Greeks, they know how to make the best of it! They stuff their bellies with anything they find. One of them has just devoured a full jar of marmalade."

95   "Pigs!" Tomorrow half of them will die of the shits."   95

"Pigs? You've been hungry."

"Pigs!" I repeat furiously. I close my eyes. The air is filled with ghastly cries, the earth trembles beneath me. I can feel sticky moisture on my eyelids. My throat is completely dry.

The morbid procession streams on and on—trucks growl like mad dogs. I shut my eyes tight, but I can still see corpses dragged from the train, trampled infants, cripples piled on top of the dead, wave after wave. . . freight cars roll in, the heaps of clothing, suitcases, and bundles grow, people climb out, look at the sun, take a few breaths, beg for water, get into the trucks, drive away. And again freight cars roll in, again people. . . The scenes become confused in my mind—I am not sure if all of this is actually happening, or if I am dreaming. There is a humming inside my head; I feel that I must vomit.

Henri tugs at my arm.

345

"Don't sleep, we're off to load up the loot."

All the people are gone. In the distance, the last few trucks roll along the road in clouds of dust, the train has left, several S.S. officers promenade up and down the ramp. The silver glitters on their collars. Their boots shine, the red, beefy faces shine. Among them there is a woman—only now I realize she has been here all along—withered, flat-chested, bony, her thin, colourless hair pulled back and tied in a "Nordic" knot; her hands are in the pockets in her wide skirt. With a rat-like, resolute smile glued on her thin lips she sniffs around the corners of the ramp. She detests feminine beauty with the hatred of a woman who is herself repulsive, and knows it. Yes, I have seen her many times before and I know her well: she is the commandant of the F.K.L. She has come to look over the new crop of women, for some of them, instead of going on the trucks, will go on foot—to the concentration camp. There our boys, the barbers from Zauna, will shave their heads and will have a good laugh at their "outside world" modesty.

We proceed to load the loot. We lift huge trunks, heave them on to the trucks. There they are arranged in stacks, packed tightly. Occasionally somebody slashes one open with a knife, for pleasure or in search of vodka and perfume. One of the crates falls open; suits, shirts, books drop out on ground. . . I pick up a small, heavy package. I unwrap it—gold, about two handfuls, bracelets, rings, brooches, diamonds. . .

"*Gib hier,*"[25] an S.S. man says calmly, holding up his briefcase already full of gold and colourful foreign currency. He locks the case, hands it to an officer, takes another, an empty one, and stands by the next truck, waiting. The gold will go to the Reich.

It is hot, terribly hot. Our throats are dry, each word hurts. Anything for a sip of water! Faster, faster, so that it is over, so that we may rest. At last we are done, all the trucks have gone. Now we swiftly clean up the remaining dirt: there must be "no trace left of the *Schweinerei.*"[26] But just as the last truck disappears behind the trees and we walk, finally, to rest in the shade, a shrill whistle sounds around the bend. Slowly, terribly slowly, a train rolls in, the engine whistles back with a deafening shriek. Again weary, pale faces at the windows, flat as though cut out of paper, with huge, feverishly burning eyes. Already trucks are pulling up, already the composed gentleman with his notebook is at his post, and the S.S. men emerge from the commissary carrying briefcases for the gold and money. We unseal the train doors.

105   It is impossible to control oneself any longer. Brutally we tear suitcases from their hands, impatiently pull off their coats. Go on, go on, vanish! They go, they vanish. Men, women, children. Some of them know.

Here is a woman—she walks quickly, but tries to appear calm. A small child with a pink cherub's face runs after her and, unable to keep up, stretches out his little arms and cries: "Mama! Mama!"

"Pick up your child, woman!"

"It's not mine, sir, not mine!" she shouts hysterically and runs on, covering her face with her hands. She wants to hide, she wants to reach those who will not ride the trucks, those who will go on foot, those who will stay alive. She is young, healthy, good-looking, she wants to live.

But the child runs after her, wailing loudly: "Mama, mama, don't leave me!"

110   "It's not mine, not mine, no!"

Andrei, a sailor from Sevastopol, grabs hold of her. His eyes are glassy from vodka and the heat. With one powerful blow he knocks her off her feet, then, as she falls, takes her by the hair and pulls her up again. His face twitches with rage.

"Ah, you bloody Jewess! So you're running from your own child! I'll show you, you whore!" His huge hand chokes her, he lifts her in the air and heaves her on to the truck like a heavy sack of grain.

"Here! And take this with you, bitch!" and he throws the child at her feet.

"*Gut gemacht*, good work. That's the way to deal with degenerate mothers," says the S.S. man standing at the foot of the truck. "*Gut, gut, Russki.*"

"Shut your mouth," growls Andrei through clenched teeth, and walks away. From under a pile of rags he pulls out a canteen, unscrews the cork, takes a few deep swallows, passes it to me. The strong vodka burns the throat. My head swims, my legs are shaky, again I feel like throwing up.

115   And suddenly, above the teeming crowd pushing forward like a river driven by an unseen power, a girl appears. She descends lightly from the train, hops on to the gravel, looks around inquiringly, as if somewhat surprised. Her soft, blonde hair has fallen on her shoulders

in a torrent, she throws it back impatiently. With a natural gesture she runs her hands down her blouse, casually straightens her skirt. She stands like this for an instant, gazing at the crowd then turns and with a gliding look examines our faces, as though searching for someone. Unknowingly, I continue to stare at her, until our eyes meet.

"Listen, tell me, where are they taking us?"

I look at her without saying a word. Here, standing before me, is a girl, a girl with enchanting blonde hair, with beautiful breasts, wearing a little cotton blouse, a girl with a wise, mature look in her eyes. Here she stands, gazing straight into my face, waiting. And over there is the gas chamber: communal death, disgusting and ugly. And over in the other direction is the concentration camp: the shaved head, the heavy Soviet trousers in sweltering heat, the sickening, stale odour of dirty, damp female bodies, the animal hunger, the inhuman labour, and later the same gas chamber, only an even more hideous, more terrible death . . .

Why did she bring it? I think to myself, noticing a lovely gold watch on her delicate wrist They'll take it away from her anyway.

"Listen, tell me," she repeats.

I remain silent. Her lips tighten.

"I know," she says with a shade of proud contempt in her voice, tossing her head. She walks off resolutely in the direction of the trucks. Someone tries to stop her; she boldly pushes him aside and runs up the steps. In the distance I can only catch a glimpse of her blonde hair flying in the breeze.

I go back inside the train; I carry out dead infants; I unload luggage. I touch corpses, but I cannot overcome the mounting, uncontrollable terror. I try to escape from the corpses, but they are everywhere: lined up on gravel, on the cement edge of the ramp, inside the cattle cars. Babies, hideous naked women, men twisted by convulsions. I run off as far as I can go, but immediately a whip slashes across my back. Out of the corner of my eye I see an S.S. man, swearing profusely. I stagger forward and run, lose myself in the Canada group. Now, at last, I can once more rest against the stack of rails. The sun has leaned low over the horizon and illuminates the ramp with a reddish glow; the shadows of the trees have become elongated, ghostlike. In the silence that settles over nature at this time of day, the human cries seem to rise all the way to the sky.

Only from this distance does one have a full view of the inferno on the teeming ramp. I see a pair of human beings who have fallen to the ground locked in a last desperate embrace. The man has dug his fingers into I woman's flesh and has caught her clothing with his teeth. She screams hysterically, swears, cries, until at last a large boot comes down over her throat and she is silent. They are pulled apart and dragged like cattle to the truck. I see four Canada men lugging a corpse: a huge, swollen female corpse. Cursing, dripping wet from the strain, they kick out of their way some stray children who have been running all over the ramp, howling like dogs. The men pick them up by the collars, heads, arms, and toss them inside the trucks on top of the heaps. The four men have trouble lifting the fat corpse on to the car, they call others for help, and all together they hoist up the mound of meat. Big, swollen, puffed-up corpses are being collected from all over the ramp; on top of them are piled the invalids, the smothered, the sick, the unconscious. The heap seethes, howls, groans. The driver starts the motor, the truck begins rolling.

"Halt! Halt!" an S.S. man yells after them. "Stop, damn you!"

125 They are dragging to the truck an old man wearing tails and a 125 band around his arm. His head knocks against the gravel and pavement; he moans and wails in an uninterrupted monotone: "*Ich will mit dem Herrn Kommandanten sprechen*—I wish to speak with the commandant. . ." With senile stubbornness he keeps repeating these words all the way. Thrown on the truck, trampled by others, choked, he still wails: "*Ich will mit dem. . .*"

"Look here, old man!" a young S.S. man calls, laughing jovially. "In half an hour you'll be talking with the top commandant! Only don't forget to greet him with a *Heil Hitler*!"

Several other men are carrying a small girl with only one leg, They hold her by the arms and the one leg. Tears are running down her face and she whispers faintly: "Sir, it hurts, it hurts. . ." They throw her on the truck of the corpses. She will burn alive along with them.

The evening has come, cool and clear. The stars are out. We lie against the rails. It is incredibly quiet. Anaemic bulbs hang from the top of the high lamp-posts; beyond the circle of light stretches an impenetrable darkness. Just one step, and a man could vanish for ever. But the guards are watching, their automatics ready.

"Did you get the shoes?" asks Henri.

130 "No." 130

349

"Why?"

"My God, man, I am finished, absolutely finished!"

"So soon? After only two transports? Just look at me, I. . . since Christmas, at least a million people have passed through my hands. The worst of all are the transports from around Paris—one is always bumping into friends."

"And what do you say to them?"

135 "That first they will have a bath, and later we'll meet at the camp. 135 What would you say?"

I do not answer. We drink coffee with vodka; somebody opens a tin of cocoa and mixes it with sugar. We scoop it up by the handful, the cocoa sticks to the lips. Again coffee, again vodka.

"Henri, what are we waiting for?"

"There'll be another transport."

"I'm not going to unload it! I can't take any more."

140 "So, it's got you down? Canada is nice, eh?" Henri grins 140 indulgently and disappears into the darkness. In a moment he is back again.

"All right. Just sit here quietly and don't let an S.S. man see you. I'll try to find you your shoes."

"Just leave me alone. Never mind the shoes." I want to sleep. It is very late.

Another whistle, another transport. Freight cars emerge out of the darkness, pass under the lamp-posts, and again vanish in the night. The ramp is small, but the circle of lights is smaller. The unloading will have to be done gradually. Somewhere the trucks are growling. They back up against the steps, black, ghostlike, their searchlights flash across the trees. *Wasser! Luft!* The same all over again, like a late showing of the same film: a volley of shots, the train falls silent. Only this time a little girl pushes herself halfway through the small window and, losing her balance, falls out on to the gravel. Stunned, she lies still for a moment, then stands up and begins walking around in a circle, faster and faster, waving her rigid arms in the air, breathing loudly and spasmodically, whining in a faint voice. Her mind has given way in the inferno inside the train. The whining is hard on the nerves: an S.S. man approaches calmly, his heavy boot strikes between her shoulders. She falls. Holding her down with his foot, he draws his revolver, fires once, then again. She remains face down, kicking the gravel with her feet, until she stiffens. They proceed to unseal the train.

I am back on the ramp, standing by the doors. A warm, sickening smell gushes from inside. The mountain of people filling the car almost halfway up to the ceiling is motionless, horribly tangled, but still steaming.

145   "*Ausladen!*"27 comes the command. An S.S. man steps out from   145 the darkness. Across his chest hangs a portable searchlight He throws a stream of light inside.

"Why are you standing about like sheep? Start unloading!" His whip flies and falls across our backs. I seize a corpse by the hand; the fingers close tightly around mine. I pull back with a shriek and stagger away. My heart pounds, jumps up to my throat. I can no longer control the nausea. Hunched under the train I begin to vomit. Then, like a drunk, I weave over to the stack of rails.

I lie against the cool, kind metal and dream about returning to the camp, about my bunk, on which there is no mattress, about sleep among comrades who are not going to the gas tonight. Suddenly I see the camp as a haven of peace. It is true, others may be dying, but one is somehow still alive, one has enough food, enough strength to work. . .

The lights flicker with a spectral glow, the wave of people—feverish, agitated, stupefied people—flows on and on, endlessly. They think that now they will have to face a new life in the camp, and they prepare themselves emotionally for the hard struggle ahead. They do not know that in just a few moments they will die, that the gold, money, and diamonds which they have so prudently hidden in their clothing and on their bodies are now be useless to them. Experienced professionals will probe into every recess of their flesh, will pull the gold from under the tongue and the diamonds from the uterus and the colon. They will rip out gold teeth. In tightly sealed crates they will ship them to Berlin.

The S.S. men's black figures move about, dignified, businesslike. The gentleman with the notebook puts down his final marks, rounds out the figures: fifteen thousand.

150   Many, very many, trucks have been driven to the crematoria   150 today.

It is almost over. The dead are being cleared off the ramp and piled into the last truck. The Canada men, weighed down under a load of bread, marmalade, and sugar, and smelling of perfume and fresh linen, line up to go. For several days the entire camp will live off this transport For several days the entire camp will talk about "Sosnowiec-Bedzin." "Sosnowiec-Bedzin" was a good, rich transport.

The stars are already beginning to pale as we walk back to the camp. The sky grows translucent and opens high above our heads—it is getting light.

Great columns of smoke rise from the crematoria and merge up above into a huge black river which very slowly floats across the sky over Birkenau and disappears beyond the forests in the direction of Trzebinia. the "Sosnowiec-Bedzin" transport is already burning.

We pass a heavily armed S.S. detachment on its way to change guard. The men march briskly, in step, shoulder to shoulder, one mass, one will.

155   "*Und morgen die ganze Welt. . .*"[28] they sing at the top of their   155 lungs.

"*Rechts ran!* To the right march!" snaps a command from up front. We move out of their way.

Endnotes

1.   Crossed wooden beams wrapped in barbed wire.
2.   Women's concentration camp (Unless otherwise indicated all foreign phrases are in German)
3.   A designation of wealth and well-being in the camp. More specifically, the members of the labor gang, or Kommando who helped to unload the incoming transports of people destined for the gas chambers.
4.   My friend (French).
5.   The camp name for a prisoner who had been destroyed physically and spiritually, and who had neither the strength nor the will to go on living—a man ripe for the gas chamber.
6.   "Get going."
7.   "Get out."
8.   "Don't worry."
9.   "Place!" (In the sense of "Take your place!")
10.   "What's the matter?"
11.   "Left, two, three, four! Hats off!"
12.   "One hundred! . . . "OK!"
13.   "Filthy pigs."
14.   "Pay attention."
15.   "Done."

16.   "Ass eyes."
17.   "What will we be working on?"
18.   "Nothing. Transport coming, all Crematorium, understand?"
19.   "We understand."
20.   "Yes, indeed!"
21.   "Forbidden!"
22.   "Distinguished ladies and gentlemen."
23.   There must be order.
24.   One Empire, one People, one Leader.
25.   "Give it here."
26.   "Obscenity."
27.   "Unload."
28.   "And tomorrow the whole world. . ."

Questions on Meaning

1. Early in the story, the narrator and Henri speak disdainfully of "Muslims," prisoners who have lost the will to survive. What does this attitude tell you about the narrator? How does this passage prepare you for what is to come?

2. Explaining why the new prisoners are kept ignorant of their fate, the narrator says, "People going to their death must be deceived to the very end. This is the only permissible form of charity." What does this statement reveal about life in the camp? How is it charitable to deny people the opportunity to prepare for death?

3. The story ends with the coming dawn, as the returning prisoners encounter a troop of S.S. guards. What is the significance of ending the story with the beginning of a new day? How does the encounter with the guards reinforce the theme of the story?

Questions on Rhetorical Strategy and Style

1. The impact of any narrative depends heavily on the reader's perception of the narrator. How would you characterize the narrator of this story? For example, is he sympathetic? Reliable? Objective? How does your perception of him affect your reading of the story?

2. The narrator describes the scene at the railway station in great detail. Choose one passage from this section of the story and explain how the use of sensory images (sight, smell, sound) enhances your appreciation of the story.

3. Amid the mass of humanity exiting the trains, several specific prisoners are described in some detail. What is the purpose of these examples? What do these prisoners mean to the narrator? What do they mean to you?

Writing Assignments

1. When the narrator, momentarily realizing what he is doing, asks Henri, "Are we good people?" Henri responds, "That's stupid." Write an essay analyzing this story as a statement about the dehumanizing effects of Nazi concentration camps. Focus on the ways in which life in the camp blurred the lines between good and evil.

2. An appreciation of point of view is crucial to readers' understanding of a story. Choose one of the incidents involving individual prisoners from the transport train, and rewrite the passage from the point of view of the prisoner. Then write a brief analysis of the differences between the narrator's account and the prisoner's.

3. Borowski's story makes clear that the camps housed, not only Jews but also many people imprisoned for other reasons. Find information on the Nazi concentration camps and write a report explaining the various "crimes" for which people were sent to the camps. Explain the relative severity of each crime.

Battle Royal

Ralph Ellison

*Ralph Waldo Ellison was born in Oklahoma City in 1914
and died of cancer in 1994. He developed a youthful interest in music and accepted a scholarship to Tuskegee Institute in Alabama to pursue it. There he developed an
interest in writing, and after moving to New York City in
1936, joined the Federal Writers' Project. His first novel,*
Invisible Man *(1952), was an international success and
won him won the National Book Award. This excerpt from*
Invisible Man *illustrates Ellison's elegant prose style and
the disciplined storytelling style that enables his reader to
experience firsthand the naiveté and suffering of a young
man who is being tortured by white racists.*

1   It goes a long way back, some twenty years. All my life I had been
looking for something, and everywhere I turned someone tried to
tell me what it was. I accepted their answers too, though they were
often in contradiction and even self-contradictory. I was naive. I was
looking for myself and asking everyone except myself questions which
I, and only I, could answer. It took me a long time and much painful
boomeranging of my expectations to achieve a realization everyone
else appears to have been born with: That I am nobody but myself.
But first I had to discover that I am an invisible man!

   And yet I am no freak of nature, nor of history. I was in the cards,
other things having been equal (or unequal) eighty-five years ago. I am
not ashamed of my grandparents for having been slaves. I am only
ashamed of myself for having at one time been ashamed. About
eighty-five years ago they were told that they were free, united with
others of our country in everything pertaining to the common good,
and, in everything social, separate like the fingers of the hand. And

they believed it. They exulted in it. They stayed in their place, worked hard, and brought up my father to do the same. But my grandfather is the one. He was an odd old guy, my grandfather, and I am told I take after him. It was he who caused the trouble. On his deathbed he called my father to him and said, "Son, after I'm gone I want you to keep up the good fight. I never told you, but our life is a war and I have been a traitor all my born days, a spy in the enemy's country ever since I give up my gun back in the Reconstruction. Live with your head in the lion's mouth. I want you to overcome 'em with yeses, undermine 'em with grins, agree 'em to death and destruction, let 'em swoller you till they vomit or bust wide open." They thought the old man had gone out of his mind. He had been the meekest of men. The younger children were rushed from the room, the shades drawn and the flame of the lamp turned so low that it sputtered on the wick like the old man's breathing. "Learn it to the younguns," he whispered fiercely; then he died.

But my folks were more alarmed over his last words than over his dying. It was as though he had not died at all, his words caused so much anxiety. I was warned emphatically to forget what he had said and, indeed, this is the first time it has been mentioned outside the family circle. It had a tremendous effect upon me, however, I could never be sure of what he meant. Grandfather had been a quiet old man who never made any trouble, yet on his deathbed he had called himself a traitor and a spy, and he had spoken of his meekness as a dangerous activity. It became a constant puzzle which lay unanswered in the back of my mind. And whenever things went well for me I remembered my grandfather and felt guilty and uncomfortable. It was as though I was carrying out his advice in spite of myself. And to make it worse, everyone loved me for it. I was praised by the most lily-white men of the town. I was considered an example of desirable conduct— just as my grandfather had been. And what puzzled me was that the old man had defined it as *treachery*. When I was praised for my conduct I felt a guilt that in some way I was doing something that was really against the wishes of the white folks, that if they had understood they would have desired me to act just the opposite, that I should have been sulky and mean, and that that really would have been what they wanted, even though they were fooled and thought they wanted me to act as I did. It made me afraid that some day they would look upon me as a traitor and I would be lost. Still I was more afraid to act any other way because they didn't like that at all. The old man's words were like a curse. On my graduation day I delivered an oration in which I showed that humility was the secret, indeed, the very essence of progress. (Not that I believed this—how could I, remembering my grandfather?—I only believed that it worked.) It was a great success. Everyone praised me and I was invited to give the speech at a gathering of the town's leading white citizens. It was a triumph for our whole community.

It was in the main ballroom of the leading hotel. When I got there I discovered that it was on the occasion of a smoker, and I was told that since I was to be there anyway I might as well take part in the battle royal to be fought by some of my schoolmates as part of the entertainment. The battle royal came first.

5   All of the town's big shots were there in their tuxedoes, wolfing   5 down the buffet foods, drinking beer and whiskey and smoking black cigars. It was a large room with a high ceiling. Chairs were arranged in neat rows around three sides of a portable boxing ring. The fourth side was clear, revealing a gleaming space of polished floor. I had some misgivings over the battle royal, by the way. Not from a distaste for fighting, but because I didn't care too much for the other fellows who were to take part. They were tough guys who seemed to have no grandfather's curse worrying their minds. No one could mistake their toughness. And besides, I suspected that fighting a battle royal might detract from the dignity of my speech. In those pre-invisible days I visualized myself as a potential Booker T. Washington. But the other fellows didn't care too much for me either, and there were nine of them. I felt superior to them in my way, and I didn't like the manner in which we were all crowded together into the servants' elevator. Nor did they like my being there. In fact, as the warmly lighted floors flashed past the elevator we had words over the fact that I, by taking part in the fight, had knocked one of their friends out of a night's work.

We were led out of the elevator through a rococo hall into an anteroom and told to get into our fighting togs. Each of us was issued a pair of boxing gloves and ushered out into the big mirrored hall, which we entered looking cautiously about us and whispering, lest we might accidentally be heard above the noise of the room. It was foggy with cigar smoke. And already the whiskey was taking effect. I was shocked to see some of the most important men of the town quite tipsy. They were all there—bankers, lawyers, judges, doctors, fire chiefs, teachers, merchants. Even one of the more fashionable pastors. Something we could not see was going on up front. A clarinet was vibrating sensuously and the men were standing up and moving eagerly forward. We were a small tight group, clustered together, our bare upper bodies touching and shining with anticipatory sweat; while up front the big shots were becoming increasingly excited over something we still could not see. Suddenly I heard the school superintendent, who had told me to come, yell, "Bring up the shines, gentlemen! Bring up the little shines!"

We were rushed up to the front of the ballroom, where it smelled even more strongly of tobacco and whiskey. Then we were pushed into place. I almost wet my pants. A sea of faces, some hostile, some amused, ringed around us, and in the center, facing us, stood a magnificent blonde—stark naked. There was dead silence. I felt a blast of cold air chill me. I tried to back away, but they were behind me and around me. Some of the boys stood with lowered heads, trembling. I felt a wave of irrational guilt and fear. My teeth chattered, my skin turned to goose flesh, my knees knocked. Yet I was strongly attracted and looked in spite of myself. Had the price of looking been blindness, I would have looked. The hair was yellow like that of a circus kewpie doll, the face heavily powdered and rouged, as though to form an abstract mask, the eyes hollow and smeared a cool blue, the color of a baboon's butt. I felt a desire to spit upon her as my eyes brushed slowly over her body. Her breasts were firm and round as the domes of East Indian temples, and I stood so close as to see the fine skin texture and beads of pearly perspiration glistening like dew around the pink and erected buds of her nipples. I wanted at one and the same time to run from the room, to sink through the floor, or go to her and cover her from my eyes and the eyes of the others with my body; to feel the soft thighs, to caress her and destroy her, to love her and murder her, to hide from her, and yet to stroke where below the small American flag tattooed upon her belly her thighs formed a capital V. I had a notion that of all in the room she saw only me with her impersonal eyes.

And then she began to dance, a slow sensuous movement; the smoke of a hundred cigars clinging to her like the thinnest of veils. She seemed like a fair bird-girl girdled in veils calling to me from the angry surface of some gray and threatening sea. I was transported.

Then I became aware of the clarinet playing and the big shots yelling at us. Some threatened us if we looked and others if we did not. On my right I saw one boy faint. And now a man grabbed a silver pitcher from a table and stepped close as he dashed ice water upon him and stood him up and forced two of us to support him as his head hung and moans issued from his thick bluish lips. Another boy began to plead to go home. He was the largest of the group, wearing dark red fighting trunks much too small to conceal the erection which projected from him as though in answer to the insinuating low-registered moaning of the clarinet. He tried to hide himself with his boxing gloves.

And all the while the blonde continued dancing, smiling faintly at the big shots who watched her with fascination, and faintly smiling at our fear. I noticed a certain merchant who followed her hungrily, his lips loose and drooling. He was a large man who wore diamond studs in a shirtfront which swelled with the ample paunch underneath, and each time the blonde swayed her undulating hips he ran his hand through the thin hair of his bald head and, with his arms upheld, his posture clumsy like that of an intoxicated panda, wound his belly in a slow and obscene grind. This creature was completely hypnotized. The music had quickened. As the dancer flung herself about with a detached expression on her face, the men began reaching out to touch her. I could see their beefy fingers sink into the soft flesh. Some of the others tried to stop them and she began to move around the floor in graceful circles, as they gave chase, slipping and sliding over the polished floor. It was mad. Chairs went crashing, drinks were spilt, as they ran laughing and howling after her. They caught her just as she reached a door, raised her from the floor, and tossed her as college boys are tossed at a hazing, and above her red, fixed-smiling lips I saw the terror and disgust in her eyes, almost like my own terror and that which I saw in some of the other boys. As I watched, they tossed her twice and her soft breasts seemed to flatten against the air and her legs flung wildly as she spun. Some of the sober ones helped her to escape. And I started off the floor, heading for the anteroom with the rest of the boys.

10 Some were still crying and in hysteria. But as we tried to leave we were stopped and ordered to get into the ring. There was nothing to do but what we were told. All ten of us climbed under the ropes and allowed ourselves to be blindfolded with broad bands of white cloth.

One of the men seemed to feel a bit sympathetic and tried to cheer us up as we stood with our backs against the ropes. Some of us tried to grin. "See that boy over there?" one of the men said. "I want you to run across at the bell and give it to him right in the belly. If you don't get him, I'm going to get you. I don't like his looks." Each of us was told the same. The blindfolds were put on. Yet even then I had been going over my speech. In my mind each word was as bright as flame. I felt the cloth pressed into place, and frowned so that it would be loosened when I relaxed.

But now I felt a sudden fit of blind terror. I was unused to darkness. It was as though I had suddenly found myself in a dark room filled with poisonous cottonmouths. I could hear the bleary voices yelling insistently for the battle royal to begin.

"Get going in there!"

15 "Let me at that big nigger!" 15

I strained to pick up the school superintendent's voice, as though to squeeze some security out of that slightly more familiar sound.

"Let me at those black sonsabitches!" someone yelled.

"No, Jackson, no!" another voice yelled. "Here, somebody, help me hold Jack."

"I want to get at that ginger-colored nigger. Tear him limb from limb," the first voice yelled.

I stood against the ropes trembling. For in those days I was what they called ginger-colored, and he sounded as though he might crunch me between his teeth like a crisp ginger cookie.

Quite a struggle was going on. Chairs were being kicked about and I could hear voices grunting as with a terrific effort. I wanted to see, to see more desperately than ever before. But the blindfold was tight as a thick skin-puckering scab and when I raised my gloved hands to push the layers of white aside a voice yelled, "Oh, no you don't, black bastard! Leave that alone!"

20 "Ring the bell before Jackson kills him a coon!" someone boomed 20 in the sudden silence. And I heard the bell clang and the sound of the feet scuffling forward.

A glove smacked against my head. I pivoted, striking out stiffly as someone went past, and felt the jar ripple along the length of my arm to my shoulder. Then it seemed as though all nine boys had turned upon me at once. Blows pounded me from all sides while I struck out as best I could. So many blows landed upon me that I wondered if I were not the only blindfolded fighter in the ring, or if the man called Jackson hadn't succeeded in getting me after all.

Blindfolded, I could no longer control my motions. I had no dignity. I stumbled about like a baby or a drunken man. The smoke had become thicker and with each new blow it seemed to sear and further restrict my lungs. My saliva became like hot bitter glue. A glove connected with my head, filling my mouth with warm blood. It was everywhere. I could not tell if the moisture I felt upon my body was sweat or blood. A blow landed hard against the nape of my neck. I felt myself going over, my head hitting the floor. Streaks of blue light filled the black world behind the blindfold. I lay prone, pretending that I was knocked out, but felt myself seized by hands and yanked to my feet. "Get going, black boy! Mix it up!" My arms were like lead, my head smarting from blows. I managed to feel my way to the ropes and held on, trying to catch my breath. A glove landed in my mid-section and I went over again, feeling as though the smoke had become a knife jabbed into my guts. Pushed this way and that by the legs milling around me, I finally pulled erect and discovered that I could see the black, sweat-washed forms weaving in the smoky-blue atmosphere like drunken dancers weaving to the rapid drum-like thuds of blows.

Everyone fought hysterically. It was complete anarchy. Everybody fought everybody else. No group fought together for long. Two, three, four, fought one, then turned to fight each other, were themselves attacked. Blows landed below the belt and in the kidney, with the gloves open as well as closed, and with my eye partly opened now there was not so much terror. I moved carefully, avoiding blows, although not too many to attract attention, fighting from group to group. The boys groped about like blind, cautious crabs crouching to protect their mid-sections, their heads pulled in short against their shoulders, their arms stretched nervously before them, with their fists testing the smoke-filled air like the knobbed feelers of hypersensitive snails. In one corner I glimpsed a boy violently punching the air and heard him scream in pain as he smashed his hand against a ring post. For a second I saw him bent over holding his hand, then going down as a blow caught his unprotected head. I played one group against the other, slipping in and throwing a punch then stepping out of range while pushing the others into the melee to take the blows blindly aimed at me. The smoke was agonizing and there were no rounds, no bells at three minute intervals to relieve our exhaustion. The room spun round me, a swirl of lights, smoke, sweating bodies sourrounded by tense white faces. I bled from both nose and mouth, the blood spattering upon my chest.

The men kept yelling, "Slug him, black boy! Knock his guts out!" "Uppercut him! Kill him! Kill that big boy!"

Taking a fake fall, I saw a boy going down heavily beside me as though we were felled by a single blow, saw a sneaker-clad foot shot into his groin as the two who had knocked him down stumbled upon him. I rolled out of range, feeling a twinge of nausea.

The harder we fought the more threatening the men became. And yet, I had begun to worry about my speech again. How would it go? Would they recognize my ability? What would they give me?

I was fighting automatically when suddenly I noticed that one after another of the boys was leaving the ring. I was surprised, filled with panic, as though I had been left alone with an unknown danger. Then I understood. The boys had arranged it among themselves. It was the custom for the two men left in the ring to slug it out for the winner's prize. I discovered this too late. When the bell sounded two men in tuxedoes leaped into the ring and removed the blindfold. I found myself facing Tatlock, the biggest of the gang. I felt sick at my stomach. Hardly had the bell stopped ringing in my ears than it clanged again and I saw him moving swiftly toward me. Thinking of nothing else to do I hit him smash on the nose. He kept coming, bringing the rank sharp violence of stale sweat. His face was a black blank of a face, only his eyes alive—with hate of me and aglow with a feverish terror from what had happened to us all. I became anxious. I wanted to deliver my speech and he came at me as though he meant to beat it out of me. I smashed him again and again, taking his blows as they came. Then on a sudden impulse I struck him lightly and as we clinched, I whispered, "Fake like I knocked you out, you can have the prize."

"I'll break your behind," he whispered hoarsely.

"For *them*?"

"For *me*, sonofabitch!"

They were yelling for us to break it up and Tatlock spun me half around with a blow, and as a joggled camera sweeps in a reefing scene, I saw the howling red faces crouching tense beneath the cloud of blue-gray smoke. For a moment the world wavered, unraveled, flowed, then my head cleared and Tatlock bounced before me. The fluttering shadow before my eyes was his jabbing left hand. Then falling forward, my head against his damp shoulder, I whispered, "I'll make it five dollars more."

"Go to hell!"

35   But his muscles relaxed a trifle beneath my pressure and I breathed, "Seven?"

"Give it to your ma," he said, ripping me beneath the heart.

And while I still held him I butted him and moved away. I felt myself bombarded with punches. I fought back with hopeless desperation. I wanted to deliver my speech more than anything else in the world, because I felt that only these men could judge truly my ability, and now this stupid clown was ruining my chances. I began fighting carefully now, moving in to punch him and out again with my greater speed. A lucky blow to his chin and I had him going too—until I heard a loud voice yell, "I got my money on the big boy."

Hearing this, I almost dropped my guard. I was confused: Should I try to win against the voice out there? Would not this go against my speech, and was not this a moment for humility, for nonresistance? A blow to my head as I danced about sent my right eye popping like a jack-in-the-box and settled my dilemma. The room went red as I fell. It was a dream fall, my body languid and fastidious as to where to land, until the floor became impatient and smashed up to meet me. A moment later I came to. An hypnotic vice said FIVE emphatically. And I lay there, hazily watching a dark red spot of my own blood shaping itself into a butterfly, glistening and soaking into the soiled gray world of the canvas.

When the voice drawled TEN I was lifted up and dragged to a chair. I sat dazed. My eye pained and swelled with each throb of my pounding heart and I wondered if now I would be allowed to speak. I was wringing wet, my mouth still bleeding. We were grouped along the wall now. The other boys ignored me as they congratulated Tatlock and speculated as to how much they would be paid. One boy whimpered over his smashed hand. Looking up front, I saw attendants in white jackets rolling the portable ring away and placing a small square rug in the vacant space surrounded by chairs. Perhaps, I thought, I will stand on the rug to deliver my speech.

40   Then the M. C. called to us, "Come on up here boys and get your money."

We ran forward to where the men laughed and talked in their chairs, waiting. Everyone seemed friendly now.

"There it is on the rug," the man said. I saw the rug covered with coins of all dimensions and a few crumpled bills. But what excited me, scattered here and there, were the gold pieces.

"Boys, it's all yours," the man said. "You get all you grab."

"That's right, Sambo," a blond man said, winking at me confidentially.

45   I trembled with excitement, forgetting my pain. I would get the gold and the bills, I thought. I would use both hands. I would throw my body against the boys nearest me to block them from the gold.

"Get down on the rug now," the man commanded, "and don't anyone touch it until I give the signal."

"This ought to be good," I heard.

As told, we got around the square rug on our knees. Slowly the man raised his freckled hand as we followed it upward with our eyes.

I heard, "These niggers look like they're about to pray!"

50   Then, "Ready," the man said, "Go!"

I lunged for a yellow coin lying on the blue design of the carpet, touching it and sending a surprised shriek to join those rising around me. I tried frantically to remove my hand but could not let go. A hot, violent force tore through my body, shaking me like a wet rage. The rug was electrified. The hair bristled up on my head as I shook myself free. My muscles jumped, my nerves jangled, writhed. But I saw that this was not stopping the other boys. Laughing in fear and embarrassment, some were holding back and scooping up the coins knocked off by the painful contortions of the others. The men roared above us as we struggled.

"Pick it up, goddamnit, pick it up!" someone called like a bass-voiced parrot. "Go on, get it!"

I crawled rapidly around the floor, picking up the coins, trying to avoid the coppers and to get greenbacks and the gold. Ignoring the shock by laughing, as I brushed the coins off quickly, I discovered that I could contain the electricity—a contradiction, but it works. Then the men began to push us onto the rug. Laughing embarrassedly, we struggled out of their hands and kept after the coins. We were all wet and slippery and hard to hold. Suddenly I saw a boy lifted into the air, glistening with sweat like a circus seal, and dropped, his wet back landing flush upon the charged rug, heard him yell and saw him literally dance upon his back, his elbows beating a frenzied tattoo upon the floor, his muscles twitching like the flesh of a horse stung by many flies. When he finally rolled off, his face was gray and no one stopped him when he ran from the floor amid booming laughter.

"Get the money," the M. C. called. "That's good hard American cash!"

And we snatched and grabbed, snatched and grabbed. I was careful not to come too close to the rug now, and when I felt the hot whiskey breath descend upon me like a cloud of foul air I reached out and grabbed the leg of a chair. It was occupied and I held on desperately.

"Leggo, nigger! Leggo!"

The huge face wavered down to mine as he tried to push me free. But my body was slippery and he was too drunk. It was Mr. Colcord, who owned a chain of movie houses and "entertainment palaces." Each time he grabbed me I slipped out of his hands. It became a real struggle. I feared the rug more than I did the drunk, so I held on, surprising myself for a moment by trying to topple *him* upon the rug. It was such an enormous idea that I found myself actually carrying it out. I tried not to be obvious, yet when I grabbed his leg, trying to tumble him out of the chair, he raised up roaring with laughter, and, looking at me with soberness dead in the eye, kicked me viciously in the chest. The chair leg flew out of my hand and I felt myself going and rolled. It was as though I had rolled through a bed of hot coals. It seemed a whole century would pass before I would roll free, a century in which I was seared through the deepest levels of my body to the fearful breath within me and the breath seared and heated to the point of explosion. It'll all be over in a flash, I thought as I rolled clear. It'll all be over in a flash.

But not yet, the men on the other side were waiting, red faces swollen as though from apoplexy as they bent forward in their chairs. Seeing their fingers coming toward me, I rolled away as a fumbled football rolls off the receiver's fingertips, back into the coals. That time I luckily sent the rug sliding out of place and heard the coins ringing against the floor and the boys scuffling to pick them up and the M.C. calling, "All right, boys that's all. Go get dressed and get your money."

I was limp as a dish rag. My back felt as though it had been beaten with wires.

60   When we had dressed the M.C. came in and gave us each five dol-   60
lars, except Tatlock, who got ten for being last in the ring. Then he
told us to leave. I was not to get a chance to deliver my speech, I
thought. I was going out into the dim alley in despair when I was
stopped and told to go back. I returned to the ballroom, where the
men were pushing back their chairs and gathering in groups to talk.

    The M.C. knocked on a table for quiet. "Gentlemen," he said,
"we almost forgot about an important part of the program. A most serious part, gentlemen. This boy was brought here to deliver a speech
which he made at his graduation yesterday . . ."

    "Bravo! "

    "I'm told that he is the smartest boy we've got out there in Green-
wood. I'm told that he knows more big words than a pocket-sized dictionary."

    Much applause and laughter.

    "So now, gentlemen, I want you to give him your attention."

65   There was still laughter as I faced them, my mouth dry, my eye   65
throbbing. I began slowly, but evidently my throat was tense, because
they began shouting, "Louder! Louder!"

    "We of the younger generation extol the wisdom of that great
leader and educator," I shouted, "who first spoke these flaming words
of wisdom: 'A ship lost at sea for many days suddenly sighted a
friendly vessel. From the mast of the unfortunate vessel was seen a signal: "Water, water; we die of thirst!" The answer from the friendly vessel came back: "Cast down your bucket where you are." The captain
of the distressed vessel, at last heeding the injunction, cast down his
bucket, and it came up fill of fresh sparkling water from the mouth of
the Amazon River.' And like him I say, and in his words, 'To those of
my race who depend upon bettering their condition in a foreign land,
or who underestimate the importance of cultivating friendly relations
with the Southern white man, who is his next-door neighbor, I would
say: "Cast down your bucket where you are"—cast it down in making
friends in every manly way of the people of all races by whom we are
surrounded . . ."

    I spoke automatically and with such fervor that I did not realize
that the men were still talking and laughing until my dry mouth, filling up with blood from the cut, almost strangled me. I coughed,
wanting to stop and go to one of the tall brass, sand-filled spittoons
to relieve myself, but a few of the men, especially the superintendent,

were listening and I was afraid. So I gulped it down, blood, saliva and all, and continued. (What powers of endurance I had during those days! What enthusiasm! What a belief in the rightness of things!) I spoke even louder in spite of the pain. But still they talked and still they laughed, as though deaf with cotton in dirty ears. So I spoke with greater emotional emphasis. I closed my ears and swallowed blood until I was nauseated. The speech seemed a hundred times as long as before, but I could not leave out a single word. All had to be said, each memorized nuance considered, rendered. Nor was that all. Whenever I uttered a word of three syllables a group of voices would yell for me to repeat it. I used the phrase "social responsibility" and they yelled:

"What's that word you say, boy?"

"Social responsibility," I said.

70 "What?"

"Social. . . ."

"Louder."

". . . responsibility."

"More!"

75 "Respon—"

"Repeat!"

"—sibility."

The room filled with the uproar of laughter until, no doubt, distracted by having to gulp down my blood, I made a mistake and yelled a phrase I had often seen denounced in newspaper editorials, heard debated in private.

"Social . . ."

"Louder."

80 "What?" they yelled.

". . . equality—"

The laughter hung smokelike in the sudden stillness. I opened my eyes, puzzled. Sounds of displeasure filled the room. The M.C. rushed forward. They shouted hostile phrases at me. But I did not understand.

A small dry mustached man in the front row blared out, "Say that slowly, son!"

"What, sir?"

85 "What you just said!"

"Social responsibility, sir," I said.

"You weren't being smart, were you, boy?" he said, not unkindly.

"No, sir!"

"You sure that about 'equality' was a mistake?"

90 "Oh, yes sir," I said. "I was swallowing blood." 90

"Well, you had better speak more slowly so we can understand. We mean to do right by you, but you've got to know your place at all times. All right, now, go on with your speech."

I was afraid. I wanted to leave but I wanted also to speak and I was afraid they'd snatch me down.

"Thank you, sir," I said, beginning where I had left off, and having them ignore me as before.

Yet when I finished there was a thunderous applause. I was surprised to see the superintendent come forth with a package wrapped in white tissue paper, and, gesturing for quiet, address the men.

95 "Gentlemen, you see that I did not overpraise this boy. He makes 95 a good speech and some day he'll lead his people in the proper paths. And I don't have to tell you that that is important in these days and times. This is a good, smart boy, and so to encourage him in the right direction, in the name of the Board of Education I wish to present him a prize in the form of this . . ."

He paused, removing the tissue paper and revealing a gleaming calfskin brief case.

". . . in the form of this first-class article from Shad Whitmore's shop."

"Boy," he said, addressing me, "take this prize and keep it well. Consider it a badge of office. Prize it. Keep developing as you are and some day it will be filled with important papers that will help shape the destiny of your people."

I was so moved that I could hardly express my thanks. A rope of bloody saliva forming a shape like an undiscovered continent drooled upon the leather and I wiped it quickly away. I felt an importance that I had never dreamed.

100 "Open it and see what's inside," I was told. 100

My fingers a-tremble, I complied, smelling the fresh leather and finding an official-looking document inside. It was a scholarship to the state college for Negroes. My eyes filled with tears and I ran awkwardly off the floor.

I was overjoyed; I did not even mind when I discovered that the gold pieces I had scrambled for were brass pocket tokens advertising a certain make of automobile.

When I reached home everyone was excited. Next day the neighbors came to congratulate me. I even felt safe from grandfather, whose deathbed curse usually spoiled my triumphs. I stood beneath his photograph with my brief case in hand and smiled triumphantly into his stolid black peasant's face. It was a face that fascinated me. The eyes seemed to follow everywhere I went.

That night I dreamed I was at a circus with him and that he refused to laugh at the clowns no matter what they did. Then later he told me to open my brief case and read what was inside and I did, finding an official envelope stamped with the state seal; and inside the envelope, I found another and another, endlessly, and I thought I would fall of weariness. "Them's years," he said. "Now open that one." And I did and in it I found an engraved document containing a short message in letters of gold. "Read it," my grandfather said. "Out loud!"

105 "To Whom It May Concern," I intoned. "Keep This Nigger-Boy 105 Running."

I awoke with the old man's laughter ringing in my ears.

(It was a dream I was to remember and dream again for many years after. But at that time I had no insight into its meaning. First I had to attend college.)

Questions on Meaning

1. "Battle Royal" deals with the injustices and injuries that African-American citizens have endured at the hands of the white majority. What thesis is Ellison arguing about the theme of injustice?
2. As you probably gathered, a "smoker" is a kind of party with entertainment involving various kinds of excess—drinking, fighting, strip-tease dancers, and so forth—often assumed to be characteristic of men. What contemporary events resemble the smoker of the 1930s? Explain.
3. What did the boy's grandfather mean when he called himself a traitor?

Questions on Rhetorical Strategy and Style

1. Most evils in the world have many causes. Name some of the causes of the events in "Battle Royal."
2. Why is it ironic that the boy's speech was on the theme of humility?

Writing Assignments

1. How many contemporary laws in your community were violated by the men at the smoker? Find the applicable federal, state, and community statutes, and write an essay describing the legal limits of racism in your town. Note as well the forms of racism that are not covered by law.
2. Interview some members of minority groups of which you are not a member to gain insight into the kinds of injustices they have experienced. Many injustices—such as poor schools—are less violent but no less far-reaching than the battle royal, so be sure to ask your interviewees to mention everything that comes to mind. Write an essay that reports the results of your research.
3. We may wonder how we would react to the kind of oppression that the protagonist in "Battle Royal" experienced. Tell the story of your response to a dangerous, potentially humiliating situation.

There Will Come Soft Rains

Ray Bradbury

Ray Douglas Bradbury (1920–) was born in Waukegan, Illinois. A storywriter and novelist, a playwright, a screenwriter, and a poet, Bradbury is one of the most distinguished and beloved science fiction writers. In 1934, Bradbury moved to Los Angeles, California where he met such famous people as the great comedian, George Burns, who paid Bradbury for his very first work—a joke for Burns's comedy show. In 1947 Bradbury published his first collection of short stories, Dark Carnival. The Martian Chronicles (1950), in which he imagined humans colonizing Mars, made him famous. In 1953 Fahrenheit 451 struck a darker note as it imagined a world where books were burned and ideas suppressed. Bradbury has won the O. Henry Memorial Award; the Benjamin Franklin Award (1954); the Aviation-Space Writer's Association Award for Best Space Article in an American Magazine (1967); and the World Fantasy Award for Lifetime Achievement. His work was included in the Best American Short Stories collections for 1946, 1948, and 1952. Bradbury's most unusual honor came when an Apollo astronaut named Dandelion Crater on the moon after Bradbury's novel, Dandelion Wine.

"There Will Come Soft Rains" was first published in Colliers magazine on May 6, 1950. The story revolves around a house that was built to withstand nuclear blasts and to run itself for human convenience. In the story the

Reprinted from The Martian Chronicles by permission of Don Congdon Associates. Copyright © 1977 by Ray Bradbury.

house stands, but the family is burned into the outer wall by a blast. The tale ends with the house reading Sara Teasedale's poem about the world without humans.

1   In the living room the voice-clock sang, *Tick-tock, seven o'clock, time to get up, time to get up, seven o'clock!* as if it were afraid that nobody would. The morning house lay empty. The clock ticked on, repeating and repeating its sounds into the emptiness. *Seven-nine, breakfast time, seven-nine!*

In the kitchen the breakfast stove gave a hissing sigh and ejected from its warm interior eight pieces of perfectly browned toast, eight eggs sunnyside up, sixteen slices of bacon, two coffees, and two cool glasses of milk.

"Today is August 4, 2026," said a second voice from the kitchen ceiling, "in the city of Allendale, California." It repeated the date three times for memory's sake. "Today is Mr. Featherstone's birthday. Today is the anniversary of Tilita's marriage. Insurance is payable, as are the water, gas, and light bills."

Somewhere in the walls, relays clicked, memory tapes glided under electric eyes.

5   *Eight-one, tick-tock, eight-one o'clock, off to school, off to work, run, run, eight-one!* But no doors slammed, no carpets took the soft tread of rubber heels. It was raining outside. The weather box on the front door sang quietly: "Rain, rain, go away; rubbers, raincoats for today . . ." And the rain tapped on the empty house, echoing.

Outside, the garage chimed and lifted its door to reveal the waiting car. After a long wait the door swung down again.

At eight-thirty the eggs were shriveled and the toast was like stone. An aluminum wedge scraped them into the sink, where hot water whirled them down a metal throat which digested and flushed them away to the distant sea. The dirty dishes were dropped into a hot washer and emerged twinkling dry.

Nine-fifteen, sang the clock, *time to clean.*

Out of warrens in the wall, tiny robot mice darted. The rooms were acrawl with the small cleaning animals, all rubber and metal. They thudded against chairs, whirling their mustached runners, kneading the rug nap, sucking gently at hidden dust. Then, like mysterious invaders, they popped into their burrows. Their pink electric eyes faded. The house was clean.

10   *Ten o'clock.* The sun came out from behind the rain. The house   10 stood alone in a city of rubble and ashes. This was the one house left standing. At night the ruined city gave off a radioactive glow which could be seen for miles.

    Ten-fifteen. The garden sprinklers whirled up in golden founts, filling the soft morning air with scatterings of brightness. The water pelted windowpanes, running down the charred west side where the house had been burned evenly free of its white paint. The entire west face of the house was black, save for five places. Here the silhouette in paint of a man mowing a lawn. Here, as in a photograph, a woman bent to pick flowers. Still farther over, their images burned on wood in one titanic instant, a small boy, hands flung into the air; higher up, the image of a thrown ball, and opposite him a girl, hands raised to catch a ball which never came down.

    The five spots of paint—the man, the woman, the children, the ball—remained. The rest was a thin charcoaled layer.

    The gentle sprinkler rain filled the garden with falling light.

    Until this day, how well the house had kept its peace. How carefully it had inquired, "Who goes there? What's the password?" and, getting no answer from lonely foxes and whining cats, it had shut up its windows and drawn shades in an old- maidenly preoccupation with self-protection which bordered on a mechanical paranoia.

15   It quivered at each sound, the house did. If a sparrow brushed a   15 window, the shade shapped up. The bird, startled, flew off! No, not even a bird must touch the house!

    The house was an altar with ten thousand attendants, big, small, servicing, attending, in choirs. But the gods had gone away, and the ritual of the religion continued senselessly, uselessly.

    Twelve noon.

    A dog whined, shivering, on the front porch.

    The front door recognized the dog voice and opened. The dog, once huge and fleshy, but now gone to bone and covered with sores, moved in and through the house, tracking mud. Behind it whirred angry mice, angry at having to pick up mud, angry at inconvenience.

20   For not a leaf fragment blew under the door but what the wall   20 panels flipped open and the copper scrap rats flashed swiftly out. The

offending dust, hair, or paper, seized in miniature steel jaws, was raced back to the burrows. There, down tubes which fed into the cellar, it was dropped into the sighing vent of an incinerator which sat like evil Baal in a dark corner.

The dog ran upstairs, hysterically yelping to each door, at last realizing, as the house realized, that only silence was here.

It sniffed the air and scratched the kitchen door. Behind the door, the stove was making pancakes which filled the house with a rich baked odor and the scent of maple syrup.

The dog frothed at the mouth, lying at the door, sniffing, its eyes turned to fire. It ran wildly in circles, biting at its tail, spun in a frenzy, and died. It lay in the parlor for an hour.

Two o'clock, sang a voice.

25   Delicately sensing decay at last, the regiments of mice hummed   25
out as softly as blown gray leaves in an electrical wind.

Two-fifteen.

The dog was gone.

In the cellar, the incinerator glowed suddenly and a whirl of sparks leaped up the chimney.

Two thirty-five.

30   Bridge tables sprouted from patio walls. Playing cards fluttered   30
onto pads in a shower of pips. Martinis manifested on an oaken bench with egg-salad sandwiches. Music played.

But the tables were silent and the cards untouched.

At four o'clock the tables folded like great butterflies back through the paneled walls.

Four-thirty.

The nursery walls glowed.

35   Animals took shape: yellow giraffes, blue lions, pink antelopes,   35
lilac panthers cavorting in crystal substance. The walls were glass. They looked out upon color and fantasy. Hidden films clocked through well-oiled sprockets, and the walls lived. The nursery floor was woven to resemble a crisp, cereal meadow. Over this ran aluminum roaches and iron crickets, and in the hot still air butterflies of delicate red tissue wavered among the sharp aroma of animal spoors! There was the sound like a great matted yellow hive of bees within a dark bellows, the lazy bumble of a purring lion. And there was the patter of okapi feet and the murmur of a fresh jungle rain, like other

hoofs, falling upon the summer-starched grass. Now the walls dissolved into distances of parched weed, mile on mile, and warm endless sky. The animals drew away into thorn brakes and water holes.

It was the children's hour.

Five o'clock. The bath filled with clear hot water.

Six, seven, eight o'clock. The dinner dishes manipulated like magic tricks, and in the study a *click.* In the metal stand opposite the hearth where a fire now blazed up warmly, a cigar popped out, half an inch of soft gray ash on it, smoking, waiting.

Nine o'clock. The beds warmed their hidden circuits, for nights were cool here.

Nine-five. A voice spoke from the study ceiling:

"Mrs. McClellan, which poem would you like this evening?"

The house was silent.

The voice said at last, "Since you express no preference, I shall select a poem at random." Quiet music rose to back the voice. "Sara Teasdale. As I recall, your favorite. . . .

"There will come soft rains and the smell of the ground,
And swallows circling with their shimmering sound;

And frogs in the pools singing at night,
And wild plum trees in tremulous white;

Robins will wear their feathery fire,
Whistling their whims on a low fence-wire;

And not one will know of the war, not one
Will care at last when it is done.

Not one would mind, neither bird nor tree,
If mankind perished utterly;

And Spring herself, when she woke at dawn
Would scarcely know that we were gone."

The fire burned on the stone hearth and the cigar fell away into a mound of quiet ash on its tray. The empty chairs faced each other between the silent walls, and the music played.

45   At ten o'clock the house began to die.   45

The wind blew. A falling tree bough crashed through the kitchen window. Cleaning solvent, bottled, shattered over the stove. The room was ablaze in an instant!

"Fire!" screamed a voice. The house lights flashed, water pumps shot water from the ceilings. But the solvent spread on the linoleum, licking, eating, under the kitchen door, while the voices took it up in chorus: "Fire, fire, fire!"

The house tried to save itself. Doors sprang tightly shut, but the windows were broken by the heat and the wind blew and sucked upon the fire.

The house gave ground as the fire in ten billion angry sparks moved with flaming ease from room to room and then up the stairs. While scurrying water rats squeaked from the walls, pistoled their water, and ran for more. And the wall sprays let down showers of mechanical rain.

50   But too late. Somewhere, sighing, a pump shrugged to a stop. 50
The quenching rain ceased. The reserve water supply which had filled baths and washed dishes for many quiet days was gone.

The fire crackled up the stairs. It fed upon Picassos and Matisses in the upper halls, like delicacies, baking off the oily flesh, tenderly crisping the canvases into black shavings.

Now the fire lay in beds, stood in windows, changed the colors of drapes!

And then, reinforcements.

From attic trapdoors, blind robot faces peered down with faucet mouths gushing green chemical.

55   The fire backed off, as even an elephant must at the sight of a 55
dead snake. Now there were twenty snakes whipping over the floor, killing the fire with a clear cold venom of green froth.

But the fire was clever. It had sent flames outside the house, up through the attic to the pumps there. An explosion! The attic brain which directed the pumps was shattered into bronze shrapnel on the beams.

The fire rushed back into every closet and felt of the clothes hung there.

The house shuddered, oak bone on bone, its bared skeleton cringing from the heat, its wire, its nerves revealed as if a surgeon had torn the skin off to let the red veins and capillaries quiver in the scalded air. Help, help! Fire! Run, run! Heat snapped mirrors like the brittle winter ice. And the voices wailed Fire, fire, run, run, like a tragic nursery rhyme, a dozen voices, high, low, like children dying in a forest, alone, alone. And the voices fading as the wires popped their sheathings like hot chestnuts. One, two, three, four, five voices died.

In the nursery the jungle burned. Blue lions roared, purple giraffes bounded off. The panthers ran in circles, changing color, and ten million animals, running before the fire, vanished off toward a distant steaming river. . . .

60 Ten more voices died. In the last instant under the fire avalanche, 60 other choruses, oblivious, could be heard announcing the time, playing music, cutting the lawn by remote-control mower, or setting an umbrella frantically out and in the slamming and opening front door, a thousand things happening, like a clock shop when each clock strikes the hour insanely before or after the other, a scene of maniac confusion, yet unity; singing, screaming, a few last cleaning mice darting bravely out to carry the horrid ashes away! And one voice, with sublime disregard for the situation, read poetry aloud in the fiery study, until all the film spools burned, until all the wires withered and the circuits cracked.

The fire burst the house and let it slam flat down, puffing out skirts of spark and smoke.

In the kitchen, an instant before the rain of fire and timber, the stove could be seen making breakfasts at a psychopathic rate, ten dozen eggs, six loaves of toast, twenty dozen bacon strips, which, eaten by fire, started the stove working again, hysterically hissing!

The crash. The attic smashing into kitchen and parlor. The parlor into cellar, cellar into sub-cellar. Deep freeze, armchair, film tapes, circuits, beds, and all like skeletons thrown in a cluttered mound deep under.

Smoke and silence. A great quantity of smoke.

65 Dawn showed faintly in the east. Among the ruins, one wall 65 stood alone. Within the wall, a last voice said, over and over again and again, even as the sun rose to shine upon the heaped rubble and steam:

"Today is August 5, 2026, today is August 5, 2026, today is . . ."

Questions on Meaning

1. What is the significance of a house that can withstand destruction and humans who cannot? Why does the house survive? What does the death of the dog mean?
2. What kind of people lived in a house that did all the housework and even planned the days? What is the story saying about our tendency to rely on technology? Are we able to take care of ourselves without that technology?
3. Why is the poem so poignant? What does it say about the ability of nature to come back even if all the brilliant humans have disappeared? Is the poem hopeful or negative or both? Why?

Questions on Rhetorical Strategy and Style

1. The story plays on human fears by introducing the worst of those fears being fulfilled at the beginning of the tale. Why does the image of the dying dog seem to end all human hope?
2. The house reads the poem as the center of the story. Why does the poem work as the centerpiece of the tale? How does it work as the turning point for both humanity and for the house?
3. At the end of the story the house begins to self-destruct, just as the human race has done. What are the stages of the destruction? How do these stages show the breakdown of society?

Writing Assignments

1. Bradbury wrote this story just after the first atomic bombs were dropped on Japan. Find images of the destruction of the Japanese cities, and write about the images of them.
2. Many people think that terrorism is the worst that the human race has faced. Read about the Cuban missile crisis. How close did the world come to atomic destruction? Write about the Cold War and its fear factors, and compare those factors to the world today.
3. Consider the images in the poem that centers the story. Write about the world of nature and the human effects on nature. Would nature be better off without the destructive species that humans have proved to be? What could we do better?

A Worn Path

Eudora Welty

Born in Jackson, Mississippi, Eudora Welty (1909-) attended Mississippi State College for Women and was graduated from the University of Wisconsin in 1929. She lived briefly in New York, where she worked in an advertising firm, but returned to her native Mississippi during the Great Depression to help her family and to write. Welty has published three novels and many stories and articles; she won the O. Henry short fiction award, the Pulitzer Prize for her novel The Optimist's Daughter *(1972), the National Medal for Literature, and the Presidential Medal of Freedom, thus becoming one of the most honored and admired writers of the century. Welty captures the life of the South and the lives of the people she knew and loved. That tenderness is clearly demonstrated in "A Worn Path."*

1   It was December—a bright frozen day in the early morning. Far   1
out in the country there was an old Negro woman with her head
tied in a red rag, coming along a path through the pinewoods. Her
name was Phoenix Jackson. She was very old and small and she
walked, slowly in the dark pine shadows, moving a little from side to
side in her steps, with the balanced heaviness and lightness of a pen-
dulum in a grandfather clock. She carried a thin, small cane made
from an umbrella, and with this she kept tapping the frozen earth in
front of her. This made a grave and persistent noise in the still air, that
seemed meditative, like the chirping of a solitary little bird.

She wore a dark striped dress reaching down to her shoetops, and
an equally long apron of bleached sugar sacks, with a full pocket; all,
neat and tidy, but every time she took a step she might have fallen over

her shoelaces, which dragged from her unlaced shoes. She looked straight ahead. Her eyes were blue with age. Her skin had a pattern all its own of numberless branching wrinkles and as though a whole little tree stood in the middle of her forehead, but a golden color ran underneath, and the two knobs of her cheeks were illuminated by a yellow burning under the dark. Under the red rag her hair came down on her neck in the frailest of ringlets, still black, and with an odor like copper.

Now and then there was a quivering in the thicket. Old Phoenix said, "Out of my way, all you foxes, owls, beetles, jack rabbits, coons, and wild animals! . . . Keep out from under these feet, little bobwhites. . . . Keep the big wild hogs out of my path. Don't let none of those come running in my direction. I got a long way." Under her small black-freckled hand her cane, limber as a buggy whip, would switch at the brush as if to rouse up any hiding things.

On she went. The woods were deep and still. The sun made the pine needles almost too bright to look at, up where the wind rocked. The cones dropped as light as feathers. Down in the hollow was the mourning dove—it was not too late for him.

5   The path ran up a hill. "Seem like there is chains about my feet,   5
time I get this far," she said, in the voice of argument old people keep to use with themselves. "Something always take a hold on this hill—pleads I should stay."

After she got to the top she turned and gave a full, severe look behind her where she had come. "Up through pines," she said at length. "Now down through oaks."

Her eyes opened their widest and she started down gently. But before she got to the bottom of the hill a bush caught her dress.

Her fingers were busy and intent, but her skirts were full and long, so that before she could pull them free in one place they were caught in another. It was not possible to allow the dress to tear. "I in the thorny bush," she said. "Thorns, you doing your appointed work. Never want to let folks past—no sir. Old eyes thought you was a pretty little *green* bush."

Finally, trembling all over, she stood free, and after a moment dared to stoop for her cane.

10   "Sun so high!" she cried, leaning back and looking, while the   10
thick tears went over her eyes. "The time getting all gone here."

At the foot of this hill was a place where a log was laid across the creek.

"Now comes the trial," said Phoenix.

Putting her right foot out, she mounted the log and shut her eyes. Lifting her skirt, leveling her cane fiercely before her, like a festival figure in some parade, she began to march across. Then she opened her eyes and she was safe on the other side.

"I wasn't as old as I thought," she said.

15 But she sat down to rest. She spread her skirts on the bank around 15 her and folded her hands over her knees. Up above her was a tree in a pearly cloud of mistletoe. She did not dare to close her eyes, and when a little boy brought her a little plate with a slice of marble-cake on it she spoke to him. "That would be acceptable," she said. But when she went to take it there was just her own hand in the air.

So she left that tree, and had to go through a barbed-wire fence. There she had to creep and crawl, spreading her knees and stretching her fingers like a baby trying to climb the steps. But she talked loudly to herself: she could not let her dress be torn now, so late in the day, and she could not pay for having her arm or leg sawed off if she got caught fast where she was.

At last she was safe through the fence and risen up out in the clearing. Big dead trees, like black men with one arm, were standing in the purple stalks of the withered cotton field. There sat a buzzard.

"Who you watching?"

In the furrow she made her way along

20 "Glad this not the season for bulls," she said, looking sideways, 20 "and the good Lord made his snakes to curl up and sleep in the winter. A pleasure I don't see no two-headed snake coming around that tree, where it come once. It took a while to get by him, back in the summer."

She passed through the old cotton and went into a field of dead corn. It whispered and shook, and was taller than her head. "Through the maze now," she said, for there was no path.

Then there was something tall, black, and skinny there, moving before her.

At first she took it for a man. It could have been a man dancing in the field. But she stood still and listened, and it did not make a sound. It was as silent as a ghost.

"Ghost," she said sharply, "who be you the ghost of? For I have heard of nary death close by."

But there was no answer, only the ragged dancing in the wind.

She shut her eyes, reached out her hand, and touched a sleeve. She found a coat and inside that an emptiness, cold as ice.

"You scarecrow," she said. Her face lighted. "I ought to be shut up for good," she said with laughter. "My senses is gone. I too old. I the oldest people I ever know. Dance, old scarecrow," she said, "while I dancing with you."

She kicked her foot over the furrow, and with mouth drawn down shook her head once or twice in a little strutting way. Some husks blew down and whirled in streamers about her skirts.

Then she went on, parting her way from side to side with the cane, through the whispering field. At last she came to the end, to a wagon track, where the silver grass blew between the red ruts. The quail were walking around like pullets, seeming all dainty and unseen.

"Walk pretty," she said. "This the easy place. This the easy going."

She followed the track, swaying through the quiet bare fields, through the little strings of trees silver in their dead leaves, past cabins silver from weather, with the doors and windows boarded shut, all like old women under a spell sitting there. "I walking in their sleep," she said, nodding her head vigorously.

In a ravine she went where a spring was silently flowing through a hollow log. Old Phoenix bent and drank. "Sweetgum makes the water sweet," she said, and drank more. "Nobody knows who made this well, for it was here when I was born."

The track crossed a swampy part where the moss hung as white as lace from every limb. "Sleep on, alligators, and blow your bubbles." Then the track went into the road.

Deep, deep the road went down between the high green-colored banks. Overhead the live-oaks met, and it was as dark as a cave.

A black dog with a lolling tongue came up out of the weeds by the ditch. She was meditating, and not ready, and when he came at her she only hit him a little with her cane. Over she went in the ditch, like a little puff of milk-weed.

Down there, her senses drifted away. A dream visited her, and she reached her hand up, but nothing reached down and gave her a pull. So she lay there and presently went to talking. "Old woman," she said to herself, "that black dog come up out of the weeds to stall you off, and now there he sitting on his fine tail, smiling at you."

A white man finally came along and found her—a hunter, a young man, with his dog on a chain.

"Well, Granny!" he laughed. "What are you doing there?"

"Lying on my back like a June-bug waiting to be turned over, mister," she said, reaching up her hand.

40 He lifted her up, gave her a swing in the air, and set her down. 40 "Anything broken, Granny?"

"No, sir, them old dead weeds is springy enough," said Phoenix, when she had got her breath. "I thank you for your trouble."

"Where do you live, Granny?" he asked, while the two dogs were growling at each other.

"Away back yonder, sir, behind that ridge. You can't even see it from here."

"On your way home?"

45 "No, sir, I going to town." 45

"Why that's too far! That's as far as I walk when I come out myself, and I get something for my trouble." He patted the stuffed bag he carried, and there hung down a little closed claw. It was one of the bobwhites, with its beak hooked bitterly to show it was dead. "Now you go on home, Granny!"

"I bound to go to town, mister," said Phoenix. "The time come around."

He gave another laugh, filling the whole landscape. "I know you colored people! Wouldn't miss going to town to see Santa Claus!"

But something held Old Phoenix very still. The deep lines in her face went into a fierce and different radiation. Without warning she had seen with her own eyes a flashing nickel fall out of the man's pocket on to the ground.

50 "How old are you, Granny?" he was saying. 50

"There is no telling, mister," she said, "no telling."

Then she gave a little cry and clapped her hands, and said, "Git on away from here, dog! Look! Look at that dog!" She laughed as if in admiration. "He ain't scared of nobody. He a big black dog." She whispered, "Sick him!"

"Watch me get rid of that cur," said the man. "Sick him, Pete! Sick him!"

Phoenix heard the dogs fighting and heard the man running and throwing sticks. She even heard a gunshot. But she was slowly bending forward by that time, further and further forward, the lids stretched down over her eyes, as if she were doing this in her sleep. Her chin was lowered almost to her knees. The yellow palm of her hand came out from the fold of her apron. Her fingers slid down and along the ground under the piece of money with the grace and care they would have in lifting an egg from under a sitting hen. Then she slowly straightened up, she stood erect, and the nickel was in her apron pocket. A bird flew by. Her lips moved. "God watching me the whole time. I come to stealing."

55 The man came back, and his own dog panted about them. "Well, 55 I scared him off that time," he said, and then he laughed and lifted his gun and pointed it at Phoenix.

She stood straight and faced him.

"Doesn't the gun scare you?" he said, still pointing it.

"No, sir, I seen plenty go off closer by, in my day, and for less what I done," she said, holding utterly still.

He smiled, and shouldered the gun. "Well, Granny," he said, "you must be a hundred years old, and scared of nothing. I'd give you a dime if I had any money with me. But you take my advice and stay home, and nothing will happen to you."

60 "I bound to go on my way, mister," said Phoenix. She inclined her 60 head in the red rag. Then they went in different directions, but she could hear the gun shooting again and again over the hill.

She walked on. The shadows hung from the oak trees to the road like curtains. Then she smelled wood-smoke, and smelled the river, and she saw a steeple and the cabins on their steep steps. Dozens of little black children whirled around her. There ahead was Natchez shining. Bells were ringing. She walked on.

In the paved city it was Christmas time. There were red and green electric lights strung and crisscrossed everywhere, and all turned on in the daytime. Old Phoenix would have been lost if she had not distrusted her eyesight and depended on her feet to know where to take her.

She paused quietly on the sidewalk, where people were passing by. A lady came along in the crowd, carrying an armful of red-, green-, and silver-wrapped presents; she gave off perfume like the red roses in hot summer, and Phoenix stopped her.

"Please, missy, will you lace up my shoe?" She held up her foot.

65 "What do you want, Grandma?"

"See my shoe," said Phoenix. "Do all right for out in the country, but wouldn't look right to go in a big building."

"Stand still then, Grandma," said the lady. She put her packages down carefully on the sidewalk beside her and laced and tied both shoes tightly.

"Can't lace 'em with a cane," said Phoenix. "Thank you, missy. I doesn't mind asking a nice lady to tie up my shoe when I gets out on the street."

Moving slowly and from side to side, she went into the stone building and into a tower of steps, where she walked up and around and around until her feet knew to stop.

70 She entered a door, and there she saw nailed up on the wall the document that had been stamped with the gold seal and framed in the gold frame which matched the dream that was hung up in her head.

"Here I be," she said. There was a fixed and ceremonial stiffness over her body.

"A charity case, I suppose," said an attendant who sat at the desk before her.

But Phoenix only looked above her head. There was sweat on her face; the wrinkles shone like a bright net.

"Speak up, Grandma" the woman said. "What's your name? We must have your history, you know. Have you been here before? What seems to be the trouble with you?"

75 Old Phoenix only gave a twitch to her face as if a fly were bothering her.

"Are you deaf?" cried the attendant.

But then the nurse came in.

"Oh, that's just old Aunt Phoenix," she said. "She doesn't come for herself—she has a little grandson. She makes these trips just as regular as clockwork. She lives away back off the Old Natchez Trace." She bent down. "Well, Aunt Phoenix, why don't you just take a seat? We won't keep you standing after your long trip." She pointed.

The old woman sat down, bolt upright in the chair.

"Now, how is the boy?" asked the nurse.

80 Old Phoenix did not speak.

"I said, how is the boy?"

But Phoenix only waited and stared straight ahead, her face very solemn and withdrawn into rigidity.

"Is his throat any better?" asked the nurse. "Aunt Phoenix, don't you hear me? Is your grandson's throat any better since the last time you came for the medicine?"

85   With her hand on her knees, the old woman waited, silent, erect, and motionless, just as if she were in armor.

"You mustn't take up our time this way, Aunt Phoenix," the nurse said. "Tell us quickly about your grandson, and get it over. He isn't dead, is he?"

At last there came a flicker and then a flame of comprehension across her face, and she spoke.

"My grandson. It was my memory had left me. There I sat and forgot why I made my long trip."

"Forgot?" The nurse frowned. "After you came so far?"

90   Then Phoenix was like an old woman begging a dignified forgiveness for waking up frightened in the night. "I never did go to school—I was too old at the Surrender," she said in a soft voice. "I'm an old woman without an education. It was my memory fail me. My little grandson, he is just the same, and I forgot it in the coming."

"Throat never heals, does it?" said the nurse, speaking in a loud, sure voice to Old Phoenix. By now she had a card with something written on it, a little list. "Yes, Swallowed lye. When was it—January—two—three years ago—"

Phoenix spoke unasked now. "No, missy, he not dead, he just the same. Every little while his throat begin to close up again, and he not able to swallow. He not get his breath. He not able to help himself. So the time come around, and I go on another trip for soothing medicine."

"All right. The doctor said as long as you came to get it you could have it," said the nurse. "But it's an obstinate case."

"My little grandson, he sit up there in the house all wrapped up, waiting by himself," Phoenix went on. "We is the only two left in the world. He suffer and it don't seem to put him back at all. He got a sweet look. He going to last. He wear a little patch quilt and peep out, holding his mouth open like a little bird. I remembers so plain now. I not going to forget him again, no, the whole enduring time. I could tell him from all the others in creation."

95   "All right." The nurse was trying to hush her now. She brought 95
her a bottle of medicine. "Charity," she said, making a check mark in
a book.

Old Phoenix held the bottle close to her eyes and then carefully
put it into her pocket.

"I thank you," she said.

"It's Christmas time, Grandma," said the attendant. "Could I give
you a few pennies out of my purse?"

"Five pennies is a nickel," said Phoenix stiffly.

100   "Here's a nickel," said the attendant.   100

Phoenix rose carefully and held out her hand. She received the
nickel and then fished the other nickel out of her pocket and laid it
beside the new one. She stared at her palm closely, with her head on
one side.

Then she gave a tap with her cane on the floor.

"This is what come to me to do," she said. "I going to the store
and buy my child a little windmill they sells, make out of paper. He
going to find it hard to believe there such a thing in the world. I'll
march myself back where he waiting, holding it straight up in this
hand."

She lifted her free hand, gave a little nod, turned round, and
walked out of the doctor's office. Then her slow step began on the
stairs, going down.

Questions on Meaning

1. Phoenix Jackson is contrasted to the hunter who talks to her in the wood. What does Welty achieve by contrasting her to this bold young man with a gun?
2. Phoenix says that she was "too old at the Surrender" to have learned to read. She is a woman who knew slavery. What kind of education did she gain from her experience, and how does that learning differ from schooling?
3. The ailing grandson for whom Phoenix walks so far almost seems to be a dream of the old woman's imagination. He is her only family, and in the end she goes to buy him a toy with her two nickels. Why doesn't she buy food or more medicine for the next month? What does the windmill represent in her relationship with the child?

Questions on Rhetorical Strategy and Style

1. Welty said that she wrote this tale after having seen an old woman walk along a path on a winter day. How does her description of Phoenix Jackson bring to mind that experience?
2. Why does Phoenix put on her shoes when she gets to town? What does that act do to the narrative line of the story?
3. The reader is taken into the mind of the old woman, Phoenix, and brought to see and feel through her eyes and skin. What is the effect of that perspective? What do we learn about multiculturalism and diversity by being in her consciousness?

Writing Assignments

1. Consider a time when you have spent your money on something pretty or foolish rather than on something practical. Why did you do so, and what was the result?
2. Welty uses her stories to show rather than to tell. Write a description of something or some place that gives the kind of vivid detail that Welty presents. What is the difference between showing and telling?
3. What knowledge can be gained from very elderly members of your community? Interview at least one elderly person. Ask about that person's life experiences, and then write a paper bringing those experiences into some kind of connection with your own.

The Monkey Garden

Sandra Cisneros

Sandra Cisneros (1954–) was born into a Mexican-American family in Chicago. She spent much of her childhood moving from place to place in both the United States and Mexico. The only girl among seven brothers, Cisneros soon learned that she had to fight for her rights as a female in a male world. She attended primarily Catholic schools through college, graduating from Loyola University in 1976. At the prestigious University of Iowa Writers' Workshop, Cisneros discovered the power of writing from the perspective of a Latina woman. Five years after earning her M.F.A. from Iowa, she published her first book, The House on Mango Street. *Other collections of fiction and poetry followed, notably* My Wicked, Wicked Ways *(poetry) (1987),* Woman Hollering Creek and Other Stories *(1991), and* Carmelo *(2002). She also published a children's book,* Pelitos *(1994) as well as a collection of essays,* Vintage Cisneros *(2004). She has taught at both the high school and the university level, and has done community work in the arts in San Antonio, where she has lived for a number of years. In this story from* The House on Mango Street, *Cisneros explores the painful passage of a young girl from childhood to adolescence.*

1 The monkey doesn't live there anymore. The monkey moved—to Kentucky—and took his people with him. And I was glad because I couldn't listen anymore to his wild screaming at night, the twangy yakkety-yak of the people who owned him. The green metal cage, the porcelain table top, the family that spoke like guitars. Monkey, family, table. All gone.

"The Monkey Garden" published in *The House on Mango Street* by Sandra Cisneros, Arte Publico, 1996, Susan Bergholtz Literary Services.

And it was then we took over the garden we had been afraid to go into when the monkey screamed and showed its yellow teeth.

There were sunflowers big as flowers on Mars and thick cockscombs bleeding the deep red fringe of theater curtains. There were dizzy bees and bow-tied fruit flies turning somersaults and humming in the air. Sweet sweet peach trees. Thorn roses and thistle and pears. Weeds like so many squinty-eyed stars and brush that made your ankles itch and itch until you washed with soap and water. There were big green apples hard as knees. And everywhere the sleepy smell of rotting wood, damp earth and dusty hollyhocks thick and perfumy like the blue-blond hair of the dead.

Yellow spiders ran when we turned rocks over and pale worms blind and afraid of light rolled over in their sleep. Poke a stick in the sandy soil and a few blue-skinned beetles would appear, an avenue of ants, so many crusty lady bugs. This was a garden, a wonderful thing to look at in the spring. But bit by bit, after the monkey left, the garden began to take over itself. Flowers stopped obeying the little bricks that kept them from growing beyond their paths. Weeds mixed in. Dead cars appeared overnight like mushrooms. First one and then another and then a pale blue pickup with the front windshield missing. Before you knew it, the monkey garden became filled with sleepy cars.

Things had a way of disappearing in the garden, as if the garden itself ate them, or, as if with its old-man memory, it put them away and forgot them. Nenny found a dollar and a dead mouse between two rocks in the stone wall where the morning glories climbed, and once when we were playing hide-and-seek, Eddie Vargas laid his head beneath a hibiscus tree and fell asleep there like a Rip Van Winkle until somebody remembered he was in the game and went back to look for him.

This, I suppose, was the reason why we went there. Far away from where our mothers could find us. We and a few old dogs who lived inside the empty cars. We made a clubhouse once on the back of that old blue pickup. And besides, we liked to jump from the roof of one car to another and pretend they were giant mushrooms.

Somebody started the lie that the monkey garden had been there before anything. We liked to think the garden could hide things for a thousand years. There beneath the roots of soggy flowers were the bones of murdered pirates and dinosaurs, the eye of a unicorn turned to coal.

This is where I wanted to die and where I tried one day but not even the monkey garden would have me. It was the last day I would go there.

Who was it that said I was getting too old to play the games? Who was it I didn't listen to? I only remember that when the others ran, I wanted to run too, up and down and through the monkey garden, fast as the boys, not like Sally who screamed if she got her stockings muddy.

10   I said, Sally, come on, but she wouldn't. She stayed by the curb   10 talking to Tito and his friends. Play with the kids if you want, she said, I'm staying here. She could be stuck-up like that if she wanted to, so I just left.

It was her own fault too. When I got back Sally was pretending to be mad . . . something about the boys having stolen her keys. Please give them back to me, she said punching the nearest one with a soft fist. They were laughing. She was too. It was a joke I didn't get.

I wanted to go back with the other kids who were still jumping on cars, still chasing each other through the garden, but Sally had her own game.

One of the boys invented the rules. One of Tito's friends said you can't get the keys back unless you kiss us and Sally pretended to be mad at first but she said yes. It was that simple.

I don't know why, but something inside me wanted to throw a stick. Something wanted to say no when I watched Sally going into the garden with Tito's buddies all grinning. It was just a kiss, that's all. A kiss for each one. So what, she said.

15   Only how come I felt angry inside. Like something wasn't right.   15 Sally went behind that old blue pickup to kiss the boys and get her keys back, and I ran up three flights of stairs to where Tito lived. His mother was ironing shirts. She was sprinkling water on them from an empty pop bottle and smoking a cigarette.

Your son and his friends stole Sally's keys and now they won't give them back unles she kisses them and right now they're making her kiss them, I said all out of breath from the three flights of stairs.

Those kids, she said, not looking up from her ironing.

That's all?

What do you want me to do, she said, call the cops? And kept on ironing.

I looked at her a long time, but couldn't think of anything to say,
and ran back down the three flights to the garden where Sally needed
to be saved. I took three big sticks and a brick and figured this was
enough.

But when I got there Sally said go home. Those boys said leave us
alone. I felt stupid with my brick. They all looked at me as if *I* was the
one that was crazy and made me feel ashamed.

And then I don't know why but I had to run away. I had to hide
myself at the other end of the garden, in the jungle part, under a tree
that wouldn't mind if I lay down and cried a long time. I closed my
eyes like tight stars so that I wouldn't, but I did. My face felt hot.
Everything inside hiccupped.

I read somewhere in India there are priests who can will their
heart to stop beating. I wanted to will my blood to stop, my heart to
quit its pumping. I wanted to be dead, to turn into the rain, my eyes
melt into the ground like two black snails. I wished and wished. I
closed my eyes and willed it, but when I got up my dress was green
and I had a headache.

I looked at my feet in their white socks and ugly round shoes.
They seemed far away. They didn't seem to be my feet anymore. And
the garden that had been such a good place to play didn't seem mine
either.

Questions on Meaning

1. Why does the monkey garden appeal to the children? What do the weeds, the overgrown flowers, the cars, and the junk mean to them?
2. What kind of game is Sally playing with Tito and the boys? Why is it significant to Esperanza that the boys make up the rules?
3. Why does the garden no longer seem to belong to Esperanza after the incident with Sally and the boys? What is the significance of her looking at her feet?

Questions on Rhetorical Strategy and Style

1. The point of view from which a story is told has significant impact on the narrative itself. Identify several passages in the story that reflect Esperanza's childlike point of view. Explain the significance of these passages to the story.
2. Esperanza describes the garden in rather vivid and creative detail. How do these details help her make the garden come alive for you, the reader? How would a more literal description of the garden have affected the story?
3. At the heart of this narrative lies the contrast between childhood innocence and adult experience. Identify the points at which Esperanza confronts these two perspectives, and explain her response to the contrast.

Writing Assignments

1. Write an essay describing the character of Esperanza. Focus on the conflict between childhood and innocence, the appeal of the garden, and the significance of Sally's behavior.
2. Sally obviously loses interest in the childhood games that Esperanza clings to. Write a response to Esperanza in Sally's voice. Explain why Sally now wants to play games with the boys and why the garden holds no more appeal for her.
3. Think back to an experience in which you found yourself on the brink of adulthood. How did you feel? Excited? Frightened? Melancholy? Hopeful? In retrospect, how important was that ex-

perience to your maturation process? (If you cannot think of an experience of your own, interview friends and ask the same questions of them.) Write an essay exploring the significance of such experiences to children as they grow up.

The Things They Carried
Tim O'Brien

Born in 1946 into a typical middle-class family in Minnesota, Tim O'Brien was the son of an elementary school teacher and an insurance salesman who fought in the Pacific in World War II. A political science major at Macalester College in the 1960s, he participated in antiwar protests and toyed with the idea of fleeing to Canada after being drafted in 1969. Instead, he became an infantry soldier in Vietnam, earning a Purple Heart for a shrapnel wound. Upon his return, O'Brien tried graduate school and journalism, eventually devoting himself to writing. The central focus of all of O'Brien's work is his Vietnam experience. His first work, the memoir If I Die in a Combat Zone, Box Me Up and Send Me Home, *was published in 1973, and his novel* Going After Cacciato *won the National Book Award in 1978. A later collection of interrelated short stories,* The Things They Carried, *was a finalist for the National Book Critics Circle Award and the Pulitzer Prize in 1990. In this, the title story of that collection, O'Brien writes vividly about how young soldiers endured their tour of duty in Vietnam, reciting a seemingly endless litany of the burdens borne by his infantry comrades.*

1 First Lieutenant Jimmy Cross carried letters from a girl named Martha, a junior at Mount Sebastian College in New Jersey. They were not love letters, but Lieutenant Cross was hoping, so he kept them folded in plastic at the bottom of his rucksack. In the late afternoon, after a day's march, he would dig his foxhole, wash his

"The Things They Carried" by Tim O'Brien, reprinted from *The Things They Carried,* 1990, Houghton Mifflin Co.

hands under a canteen, unwrap the letters, hold them with the tips of his fingers, and spend the last hour of light pretending. He would imagine romantic camping trips into the White Mountains in New Hampshire. He would sometimes taste the envelope flaps, knowing her tongue had been there. More than anything, he wanted Martha to love him as he loved her, but the letters were mostly chatty, elusive on the matter of love. She was a virgin, he was almost sure. She was an English major at Mount Sebastian, and she wrote beautifully about her professors and roommates and midterm exams, about her respect for Chaucer and her great affection for Virginia Woolf. She often quoted lines of poetry; she never mentioned the war, except to say, Jimmy, take care of yourself. The letters weighed ten ounces. They were signed "Love, Martha," but Lieutenant Cross understood that "Love" was only a way of signing and did not mean what he sometimes pretended it meant. At dusk, he would carefully return the letters to his rucksack. Slowly, a bit distracted, he would get up and move among his men, checking the perimeter, then at full dark he would return to his hole and watch the night and wonder if Martha was a virgin.

The things they carried were largely determined by necessity. Among the necessities or near-necessities were P-38 can openers, pocket knives, heat tabs, wristwatches, dog tags, mosquito repellent, chewing gum, candy, cigarettes, salt tablets, packets of Kool-Aid, lighters, matches, sewing kits, Military Payment Certificates, C rations, and two or three canteens of water. Together, these items weighed between fifteen and twenty pounds, depending upon a man's habits or rate of metabolism. Henry Dobbins, who was a big man, carried extra rations; he was especially fond of canned peaches in heavy syrup over pound cake. Dave Jensen, who practiced field hygiene, carried a toothbrush, dental floss, and several hotel-size bars of soap he'd stolen on R&R in Sydney, Australia. Ted Lavender, who was scared, carried tranquilizers until he was shot in the head outside the village of Than Khe in mid-April. By necessity, and because it was SOP, they all carried steel helmets that weighed five pounds including the liner and camouflage cover. They carried the standard fatigue jackets and trousers. Very few carried underwear. On their feet they carried jungle boots—2.1 pounds—and Dave Jensen carried three pairs of socks and a can of Dr. Scholl's foot powder as a precaution against trench foot. Until he was shot, Ted Lavender carried 6 or 7 ounces of premium dope, which for him was a necessity. Mitchell Sanders, the RTO, carried condoms. Norman Bowker carried a diary. Rat Kiley carried comic books. Kiowa, a devout Baptist, carried an illustrated New Testament that had been presented to him by his father, who taught Sunday school in Oklahoma City, Oklahoma. As a hedge against bad times, however, Kiowa also carried his grandmother's distrust of the white man, his grandfather's old hunting hatchet. Necessity dictated. Because the land was mined and booby-trapped, it was SOP for each man to carry a steel-centered, nylon-covered flak jacket, which weighed 6.7 pounds, but which on hot days seemed much heavier. Because you could die so quickly, each man carried at least one large compress bandage, usually in the helmet band for easy access. Because the nights were cold, and because the monsoons were wet, each carried a green plastic poncho that could be used as a raincoat or groundsheet or makeshift tent. With its quilted liner, the poncho weighed almost 2 pounds, but it was worth every ounce. In April, for instance, when Ted Lavender was shot, they used his poncho to wrap him up, then to carry him across the paddy, then to lift him into the chopper that took him away.

They were called legs or grunts.

To carry something was to hump it, as when Lieutenant Jimmy Cross humped his love for Martha up the hills and through the swamps. In its intransitive form, to hump meant to walk, or to march, but it implied burdens far beyond the intransitive.

Almost everyone humped photographs. In his wallet, Lieutenant Cross carried two photographs of Martha. The first was a Kodacolor snapshot signed Love, though he knew better. She stood against a brick wall. Her eyes were gray and neutral, her lips slightly open as she stared straight-on at the camera. At night, sometimes, Lieutenant Cross wondered who had taken the picture, because he knew she had boyfriends, because he loved her so much, and because he could see the shadow of the picture-taker spreading out against the brick wall. The second photograph had been clipped from the 1968 Mount Sebastian yearbook. It was an action shot—women's volleyball—and Martha was bent horizontal to the floor, reaching, the palms of her hands in sharp focus, the tongue taut, the expression frank and competitive. There was no visible sweat. She wore white gym shorts. Her legs, he thought, were almost certainly the legs of a virgin, dry and without hair, the left knee cocked and carrying her entire weight, which was just over 100 pounds. Lieutenant Cross remembered touching that left knee. A dark theater, he remembered, and the movie was *Bonnie and Clyde,* and Martha wore a tweed skirt, and during the final scene, when he touched her knee, she turned and looked at him in a sad, sober way that made him pull his hand back, but he would always remember the feel of the tweed skirt and the knee beneath it and the sound of the gunfire that killed Bonnie and Clyde, how embarrassing it was, how slow and oppressive. He remembered kissing her good night at the dorm door. Right then, he thought, he should've done something brave. He should've carried her up the stairs to her room and tied her to the bed and touched that left knee all night long. He should've risked it. Whenever he looked at the photographs, he thought of new things he should've done.

What they carried was partly a function of rank, partly of field specialty.

As a first lieutenant and platoon leader, Jimmy Cross carried a compass, maps, code books, binoculars, and a .45-caliber pistol that weighed 2.9 pounds fully loaded. He carried a strobe light and the responsibility for the lives of his men.

As an RTO, Mitchell Sanders carried the PRC-25 radio, a killer, 26 pounds with its battery.

As a medic, Rat Kiley carried a canvas satchel filled with morphine and plasma and malaria tablets and surgical tape and comic books and all the things a medic must carry, including M&M's for especially bad wounds, for a total weight of nearly 20 pounds.

As a big man, therefore a machine gunner, Henry Dobbins carried the M-60, which weighed 23 pounds unloaded, but which was almost always loaded. In addition, Dobbins carried between 10 and 15 pounds of ammunition draped in belts across his chest and shoulders.

As PFCs or Spec 4s, most of them were common grunts and carried the standard M-16 gas-operated assault rifle. The weapon weighed 7.5 pounds unloaded, 8.2 pounds with its full 20-round magazine. Depending on numerous factors, such as topography and psychology, the riflemen carried anywhere from 12 to 20 magazines, usually in cloth bandoliers, adding on another 8.4 pounds at minimum, 14 pounds at maximum. When it was available, they also carried M-16 maintenance gear—rods and steel brushes and swabs and tubes of LSA oil—all of which weighed about a pound. Among the grunts, some carried the M-79 grenade launcher, 5.9 pounds unloaded, a reasonably light weapon except for the ammunition, which was heavy. A single round weighed 10 ounces. The typical load was 25 rounds. But Ted Lavender, who was scared, carried 34 rounds when he was shot and killed outside Than Khe, and he went down under an exceptional burden, more than 20 pounds of ammunition, plus the flak jacket and helmet and rations and water and toilet paper and tranquilizers and all the rest, plus the unweighed fear. He was dead weight. There was no twitching or flopping. Kiowa, who saw it happen, said it was like watching a rock fall, or a big sandbag or something—just boom, then down—not like the movies where the dead guy rolls around and does fancy spins and goes ass over teakettle—not like that, Kiowa said, the poor bastard just flat-fuck fell. Boom. Down. Nothing else. It was a bright morning in mid-April. Lieutenant Cross felt the pain. He blamed himself. They stripped off Lavender's canteens and ammo, all the heavy things, and Rat Kiley said the obvious, the guy's dead, and Mitchell Sanders used his radio to report one U.S. KIA and to request a chopper. Then they wrapped Lavender in his poncho. They carried him out to a dry paddy, established security, and sat smoking the dead man's dope until the chopper came. Lieutenant Cross kept to himself. He pictured Martha's smooth young face, thinking he loved her more than anything, more than his men, and now Ted Lavender was dead because he loved her so much and could not stop thinking about her. When the dustoff arrived, they carried Lavender aboard. Afterward they burned Than Khe. They marched until dusk, then dug their holes, and that night Kiowa kept explaining how you had to be there, how fast it was, how the poor guy just dropped like so much concrete. Boom-down, he said. Like cement.

In addition to the three standard weapons—the M-60, M-16, and M-79-they carried whatever presented itself, or whatever seemed appropriate as a means of killing or staying alive. They carried catch-as-catch-can. At various times, in various situations, they carried M-14s and CAR-15s and Swedish Ks and grease guns and captured AK-47s and Chi-Coms and RPGs and Simonov carbines and black market Uzis and .38-caliber Smith & Wesson handguns and 66 mm LAWs and shotguns and silencers and blackjacks and bayonets and C-4 plastic explosives. Lee Strunk carried a slingshot; a weapon of last resort, he called it. Mitchell Sanders carried brass knuckles. Kiowa carried his grandfather's feathered hatchet. Every third or fourth man carried a Claymore antipersonnel mine—3.5 pounds with its firing device. They all carried framentation grenades—14 ounces each. They all carried at least one M-18 colored smoke grenade—24 ounces. Some carried CS or teargas grenades. Some carried white phosphorus grenades. They carried all they could bear, and then some, including a silent awe for the terrible power of the things they carried.

In the first week of April, before Lavender died, Lieutenant Jimmy Cross received a good-luck charm from Martha. It was a simple pebble, an ounce at most. Smooth to the touch, it was a milky-white color with flecks of orange and violet, oval-shaped, like a miniature egg. In the accompanying letter, Martha wrote that she had found the pebble on the Jersey shoreline, precisely where the land touched water at high tide, where things came together but also separated. It was this separate-but-together quality, she wrote, that had inspired her to pick up the pebble and to carry it in her breast pocket for several days, where it seemed weightless, and then to send it through the mail, by air, as a token of her truest feelings for him. Lieutenant Cross found this romantic. But he wondered what her truest feelings were, exactly, and what she meant by separate-but-together. He wondered how the tides and waves had come into play on that afternoon along the Jersey shoreline when Martha saw the pebble and bent down to rescue it from geology. He imagined bare feet. Martha was a poet, with the poet's sensibilities, and her feet would be brown and bare, the toenails unpainted, the eyes chilly and somber like the ocean in March, and though it was painful, he wondered who had been with her that afternoon. He imagined a pair of shadows moving along the strip of sand where things came together but also separated. It was phantom jealousy, he knew, but he couldn't help himself. He loved her so much. On the march, through the hot days of early April, he carried the pebble in his mouth, turning it with his tongue, tasting sea salt and moisture. His mind wandered. He had difficulty keeping his attention on the war. On occasion he would yell at his men to spread out the column, to keep their eyes open, but then he would slip away into daydreams, just pretending, walking barefoot along the

Jersey shore, with Martha, carrying nothing. He would feel himself rising. Sun and waves and gentle winds, all love and lightness.

What they carried varied by mission.

When a mission took them to the mountains, they carried mosquito netting, machetes, canvas tarps, and extra bug juice.

If a mission seemed especially hazardous, or if it involved a place they knew to be bad, they carried everything they could. In certain heavily mined AOs, where the land was dense with Toe Poppers and Bouncing Betties, they took turns humping a 28-pound mine detector. With its headphones and big sensing plate, the equipment was stress on the lower back and shoulders, awkward to handle, often useless because of the shrapnel in the earth, but they carried it anyway, partly for safety, partly for the illuson of safety.

On ambush, or other night missions, they carried peculiar little odds and ends. Kiowa always took along his new Testament and a pair of moccasins for silence. Dave Jensen carried night-sight vitamins high in carotene. Lee Strunk carried his slingshot; ammo, he claimed, would never be a problem. Rat Kiley carried brandy and M&M's candy. Until he was shot, Ted Lavender carried the starlight scope, which weighed 6.3 pounds with its aluminum carrying case. Henry Dobbins carried his girlfriend's pantyhose wrapped around his neck as a comfort. They all carried ghosts. When dark came, they would move out single file across the meadows and paddies to their ambush coordinates, where they would quietly set up the Claymores and lie down and spend the night waiting.

Other missions were more complicated and required special equipment. In mid-April, it was their missison to search out and destroy the elaborate tunnel complexes in the Than Khe area south of Chu Lai. To blow the tunnels they carried one-pound blocks of pentrite high explosives, four blocks to a man, 68 pounds in all. They carried wiring, detonators, and battery-powered clackers. Dave Jensen carried earplugs. Most often, before blowing the tunnels, they were ordered by higher command to search them, which was considered bad news, but by and large they just shrugged and carried out orders. Because he was a big man, Henry Dobbins was excused from tunnel duty. The others would draw numbers. Before Lavender died there were 17 men in the platoon, and whoever drew the number 17 would strip off his gear and crawl in headfirst with a flashlight and

Lieutenant Cross's .45-caliber pistol. The rest of them would fan out as security. They would sit down or kneel, not facing the hole, listening to the ground beneath them, imagining cobwebs and ghosts, whatever was down there—the tunnel walls squeezing in—how the flashlight seemed impossibly heavy in the hand and how it was tunnel vision in the very strictest sense, compression in all ways, even time, and how you had to wiggle in—ass and elbows—a swallowed-up feeling—and how you found yourself worrying about odd things: will your flashlight go dead? Do rats carry rabies? If you screamed, how far would the sound carry? Would your buddies hear it? Would they have the courage to drag you out? In some respects, though not many, the waiting was worse than the tunnel itself. Imagination was a killer.

On April 16, when Lee Strunk drew the number 17, he laughed and muttered something and went down quickly. The morning was hot and very still. Not good, Kiowa said. He looked at the tunnel opening, then out across a dry paddy toward the village of Than Khe. Nothing moved. No clouds or birds or people. As they waited, the men smoked and drank Kool-Aid, not talking much, feeling sympathy for Lee Strunk but also feeling the luck of the draw. You win some, you lose some, said Mitchell Sanders, and sometimes you settle for a rain check. It was a tired line and no one laughed.

20   Henry Dobbins ate a tropical chocolate bar. Ted Lavender popped 20 a tranquilizer and went off to pee.

After five minutes, Lieutenant Jimmy Cross moved to the tunnel, leaned down, and examined the darkness. Trouble, he thought—cave-in maybe. And then suddenly, without willing it, he was thinking about Martha. The stresses and fractures, the quick collapse, the two of them buried alive under all that weight. Dense, crushing love. Kneeling, watching the hole, he tried to concentrate on Lee Strunk and the war, all the dangers, but his love was too much for him, he felt paralyzed, he wanted to sleep inside her lungs and breathe her blood and be smothered. He wanted her to be a virgin and not a virgin, all at once. He wanted to know her. Intimate secrets—why poetry? Why so sad? Why that grayness in her eyes? Why so alone? Not lonely, just alone—riding her bike across campus or sitting off by herself in the cafeteria. Even dancing, she danced alone—and it was the aloneness that filled him with love. He remembered telling her that one evening. How she nodded and looked away. And how, later, when he kissed her, she received the kiss without returning it, her eyes wide open, not afraid, not a virgin's eyes, just flat and uninvolved.

Lieutenant Cross gazed at the tunnel. But he was not there. He was buried with Martha under the white sand at the Jersey shore. They were pressed together, and the pebble in his mouth was her tongue. He was smiling. Vaguely, he was aware of how quiet the day was, the sullen paddies, yet he could not bring himself to worry about matters of security. He was beyond that. He was just a kid at war, in love. He was twenty-two years old. He couldn't help it.

A few moments later Lee Strunk crawled out of the tunnel. He came up grinning, filthy but alive. Lieutenant Cross nodded and closed his eyes while the others clapped Strunk on the back and made jokes about rising from the dead.

Worms, Rat Kiley said. Right out of the grave. Fuckin' zombie.

The men laughed. They all felt great relief.

Spook City, said Mitchell Sanders.

Lee Strunk made a funny ghost sound, a kind of moaning, yet very happy, and right then, when Strunk made that high happy moaning sound, when he went Ahhooooo, right then Ted Lavender was shot in the head on his way back from peeing. He lay with his mouth open. The teeth were broken. There was a swollen black bruise under his left eye. The cheekbone was gone. Oh shit, Rat Kiley said, the guy's dead. The guy's dead, he kept saying, which seemed profound—the guy's dead. I mean really.

The things they carried were determined to some extent by superstition. Lieutenant Cross carried his good-luck pebble. Dave Jensen carried a rabbit's foot. Norman Bowker, otherwise a very gentle person, carried a thumb that had been presented to him as a gift by Mitchell Sanders. The thumb was dark brown, rubbery to the touch, and weighed four ounces at most. It had been cut from a VC corpse, a boy of fifteen or sixteen. They'd found him at the bottom of an irrigation ditch, badly burned, flies in his mouth and eyes. The boy wore black shorts and sandals. At the time of his death he had been carrying a pouch of rice, a rifle, and three magazines of ammunition.

You want my opinion, Mitchell Sanders said, there's a definite moral here.

30 He put his hand on the dead boy's wrist. He was quiet for a time, 30
as if counting a pulse, then he patted the stomach, almost affection-
ately, and used Kiowa's hunting hatchet to remove the thumb.

Henry Dobbins asked what the moral was.

Moral?

You know. *Moral.*

Sanders wrapped the thumb in toilet paper and handed it across
to Norman Bowker. There was no blood. Smiling, he kicked the boy's
head, watched the flies scatter, and said, It's like with that old TV
show—Paladin. Have gun, will travel.

35 Henry Dobbins thought about it.   35

Yeah, well, he finally said. I don't see no moral.

There it *is*, man.

Fuck off.

They carried USO stationery and pencils and pens. They carried
Sterno, safety pins, trip flares, signal flares, spools of wire, razor blades,
chewing tobacco, liberated joss sticks and statuettes of the smiling
Buddha, candles, grease pencils, *The Stars and Stripes,* fingernail clip-
pers, Psy Ops leaflets, bush hats, bolos, and much more. Twice a week,
when the resupply choppers came in, they carried hot chow in green
mermite cans and large canvas bags filled with iced beer and soda pop.
They carried plastic water containers, each with a 2-gallon capacity.
Mitchell Sanders carried a set of starched tiger fatigues for special occasions. Henry Dobbins carried Black Flag insecticide. Dave Jensen
carried empty sandbags that could be filled at night for added protection. Lee Strunk carried tanning lotion. Some things they carried in
common. Taking turns, they carried the big PRC-77 scrambler radio,
which weighed 30 pounds with its battery. They shared the weight of
memory. They took up what others could no longer bear. Often, they
carried each other, the wounded or weak. They carried infections.
They carried chess sets, basketballs, Vietnamese-English dictionaries,
insignia of rank, Bronze Stars and Purple Hearts, plastic cards imprinted with the Code of Conduct. They carried diseases, among
them malaria and dysentery. They carried lice and ringworm and
leeches and paddy algae and various rots and molds. They carried the
land itself—Vietnam, the place, the soil—a powdery orange-red dust
that covered their boots and fatigues and faces. They carried the sky.
The whole atmosphere, they carried it, the humidity, the monsoons,

the stink of fungus and decay, all of it, they carried gravity. They moved like mules. By daylight they took sniper fire, at night they were mortared, but it was not battle, it was just the endless march, village to village, without purpose, nothing won or lost. They marched for the sake of the march. They plodded along slowly, dumbly, leaning forward against the heat, unthinking, all blood and bone, simple grunts, soldiering with their legs, toiling up the hills and down into the paddies and across the rivers and up again and down, just humping, one step and then the next and then another, but no volition, no will, because it was automatic, it was anatomy, and the war was entirely a matter of posture and carriage, the hump was everything, a kind of inertia, a kind of emptiness, a dullness of desire and intellect and conscience and hope and human sensibility. Their principles were in their feet. Their calculations were biological. They had no sense of strategy or mission. They searched the villages without knowing what to look for, not caring, kicking over jars of rice, frisking children and old men, blowing tunnels, sometimes setting fires and sometimes not, then forming up and moving on to the next village, then other villages, where it would always be the same. They carried their own lives. The pressures were enormous. In the heat of early afternoon, they would remove their helmets and flak jackets, walking bare, which was dangerous but which helped ease the strain. They would often discard things along the route of march. Purely for comfort, they would throw away rations, blow their Claymores and grenades, no matter, because by nightfall the resupply choppers would arrive with more of the same, then a day or two later still more, fresh watermelons and crates of ammunition and sunglasses and woolen sweaters—the resources were stunning—sparklers for the Fourth of July, colored eggs for Easter. It was the great American war chest—the fruits of science, the smokestacks, the canneries, the arsenals at Hartford, the Minnesota forests, the machine shops, the vast fields of corn and wheat—they carried like freight trains; they carried it on their backs and shoulders—and for all the ambiguities of Vietnam, all the mysteries and unknowns, there was at least the single abiding certainty that they would never be at a loss for things to carry.

40   After the chopper took Lavender away, Lieutenant Jimmy Cross   40
led his men into the village of Than Khe. They burned everything. They shot chickens and dogs, they trashed the village well, they called

in artillery and watched the wreckage, then they marched for several hours through the hot afternoon, and then at dusk, while Kiowa explained how Lavender died, Lieutenant Cross found himself trembling.

He tried not to cry. With his entrenching tool, which weighed five pounds, he began digging a hole in the earth.

He felt shame. He hated himself. He had loved Martha more than his men, and as a consequence Lavender was now dead, and this was something he would have to carry like a stone in his stomach for the rest of the war.

All he could do was dig. He used his entrenching tool like an ax, slashing, feeling both love and hate, and then later, when it was full dark, he sat at the bottom of his foxhole and wept. It went on for a long while. In part, he was grieving for Ted Lavender, but mostly it was for Martha, and for himself, because she belonged to another world, which was not quite real, and because she was a junior at Mount Sebastian college in New Jersey, a poet and a virgin and uninvolved, and because he realized she did not love him and never would.

Like cement, Kiowa whispered in the dark. I swear to God— boom, down. Not a word.

45   I've heard this, said Norman Bowker.   45

A pisser, you know? Still zipping himself up. Zapped while zipping.

All right, fine. That's enough.

Yeah, but you had to see it, the guy just—

I *heard,* man. Cement. So why not shut the fuck *up?*

50   Kiowa shook his head sadly and glanced over at the hole where   50
Lieutenant Jimmy Cross sat watching the night. The air was thick and wet. A warm, dense fog had settled over the paddies and there was the stillness that precedes rain.

After a time Kiowa sighed.

One thing for sure, he said. The lieutenant's in some deep hurt. I mean that crying jag—the way he was carrying on—it wasn't fake or anything, it was real heavy-duty hurt. The man cares.

Sure, Norman Bowker said.

Say what you want, the man does care.

55   We all got problems.   55

Not Lavender.

No, I guess not. Bowker said. Do me a favor, though.

Shut up?

That's a smart Indian. Shut up.

60   Shrugging, Kiowa pulled off his boots. He wanted to say more,   60
just to lighten up his sleep, but instead he opened his New Testament
and arranged it beneath his head as a pillow. The fog made things seem
hollow and unattached. He tried not to think about Ted Lavender, but
then he was thinking how fast it was, no drama, down and dead, and
how it was hard to feel anything except surprise. It seemed unchrist-
ian. He wished he could find some great sadness, or even anger, but
the emotion wasn't there and he couldn't make it happen. Mostly he
felt pleased to be alive. He liked the smell of the New Testament under
his cheek, the leather and ink and paper and glue, whatever the chemicals were. He liked hearing the sounds of night. Even his fatigue, it
felt fine, the stiff muscles and the prickly awareness of his own body,
a floating feeling. He enjoyed not being dead. Lying there, Kiowa admired Lieutenant Jimmy Cross's capacity for grief. He wanted to share
the man's pain, he wanted to care as Jimmy Cross cared. And yet when
he closed his eyes, all he could think was Boom-down, and all he could
feel was the pleasure of having his boots off and the fog curling in
around him and the damp soil and the Bible smells and the plush
comfort of night.

After a moment Norman Bowker sat up in the dark.

What the hell, he said. You want to talk, *talk*. Tell it to me.

Forget it.

No, man, go on. One thing I hate, it's a silent Indian.

65   For the most part they carried themselves with poise, a kind of   65
dignity. Now and then, however, there were times of panic, when they
squealed or wanted to squeal but couldn't, when they twitched and
made moaning sounds and covered their heads and said Dear Jesus
and flopped around on the earth and fired their weapons blindly and
cringed and sobbed and begged for the noise to stop and went wild
and made stupid promises to themselves and to God and to their
mothers and fathers, hoping not to die. In different ways, it happened
to all of them. Afterward, when the firing ended, they would blink
and peek up. They would touch their bodies, feeling shame, then
quickly hiding it. They would force themselves to stand. As if in slow
motion, frame by frame, the world would take on the old logic—

absolute silence, then the wind, then sunlight, then voices. It was the burden of being alive. Awkwardly, the men would reassemble themselves, first in private, then in groups, becoming soldiers again. They would repair the leaks in their eyes. They would check for casualties, call in dustoffs, light cigarettes, try to smile, clear their throats and spit and begin cleaning their weapons. After a time someone would shake his head and say, No lie, I almost shit my pants, and someone else would laugh, which meant it was bad, yes, but the guy had obviously not shit his pants, it wasn't that bad, and in any case nobody would ever do such a thing and then go ahead and talk about it. They would squint into the dense, oppressive sunlight. For a few moments, perhaps, they would fall silent, lighting a joint and tracking its passage from man to man, inhaling, holding in the humiliation. Scary stuff, one of them might say. But then someone else would grin or flick his eyebrows and say, Roger-dodger, almost cut me a new asshole, *almost.*

There were numerous such poses. Some carried themselves with a sort of wistful resignation, others with pride or stiff soldierly discipline or good humor or macho zeal. They were afraid of dying but they were even more afraid to show it.

They found jokes to tell.

They used a hard vocabulary to contain the terrible softness. *Greased,* they'd say. *Offed, lit up, zapped while zipping.* It wasn't cruelty, just stage presence. They were actors. When someone died, it wasn't quite dying, because in a curious way it seemed scripted, and because they had their lines mostly memorized, irony mixed with tragedy, and because they called it by other names, as if to encyst and destroy the reality of death itself. They kicked corpses. They cut off thumbs. They talked grunt lingo. They told stories about Ted Lavender's supply of tranquilizers, how the poor guy didn't feel a thing, how incredibly tranquil he was.

There's a moral here, said Mitchell Sanders.

70 They were waiting for Lavender's chopper, smoking the dead 70 man's dope.

The moral's pretty obvious, Sanders said, and winked. Stay away from drugs. No joke, they'll ruin your day every time.

Cute, said Henry Dobbins.

Mind blower, get it? Talk about wiggy. Nothing left, just blood and brains.

They made themselves laugh.

There it is, they'd say. Over and over—there it is, my friend, there it is—as if the repetition itself were an act of poise, a balance between crazy and almost crazy, knowing without going, there it is, which meant be cool, let it ride, because Oh yeah, man, you can't change what can't be changed, there it is, there it absolutely and positively and fucking well *is*.

They were tough.

They carried all the emotional baggage of men who might die. Grief, terror, love, longing—these were intangibles, but the intangibles had their own mass and specific gravity, they had tangible weight. They carried shameful memories. They carried the common secret of cowardice barely restrained, the instinct to run or freeze or hide, and in many respects this was the heaviest burden of all, for it could never be put down, it required perfect balance and perfect posture. They carried their reputations. They carried the soldier's greatest fear, which was the fear of blushing. Men killed, and died, because they were embarrassed not to. It was what had brought them to the war in the first place, nothing positive, no dreams of glory or honor, just to avoid the blush of dishonor. They died so as not to die of embarrassment. They crawled into tunnels and walked point and advanced under fire. Each morning, despite the unknowns, they made their legs move. They endured. They kept humping. They did not submit to the obvious alternative, which was simply to close the eyes and fall. So easy, really. Go limp and tumble to the ground and let the muscles unwind and not speak and not budge until your buddies picked you up and lifted you into the chopper that would roar and dip its nose and carry you off to the world. A mere matter of falling, yet no one ever fell. It was not courage, exactly; the object was not valor. Rather, they were too frightened to be cowards.

By and large they carried these things inside, maintaining the masks of composure. They sneered at sick call. They spoke bitterly about guys who had found release by shooting off their own toes or fingers. Pussies, they'd say. Candy-asses. It was fierce, mocking talk, with only a trace of envy or awe, but even so the image played itself out behind their eyes.

They imagined the muzzle against flesh. So easy: squeeze the trigger and blow away a toe. They imagined it. They imagined the quick, sweet pain, then the evacuation to Japan, then a hospital with warm beds and cute geisha nurses.

80 And they dreamed of freedom birds.

At night, on guard, staring into the dark, they were carried away by jumbo jets. They felt the rush of takeoff. *Gone!* they yelled. And then velocity—wings and engines—a smiling stewardess—but it was more than a plane, it was a real bird, a big sleek silver bird with feathers and talons and high screeching. They were flying. The weights fell off; there was nothing to bear. They laughed and held on tight, feeling the cold slap of wind and altitude, soaring, thinking *It's over, I'm gone!*—they were naked, they were light and free—it was all lightness, bright and fast and buoyant, light as light, a helium buzz in the brain, a giddy bubbling in the lungs as they were taken up over the clouds and the war, beyond duty, beyond gravity and mortification and global entanglements—*Sin loi!* they yelled. *I'm sorry, motherfuckers, but I'm out of it, I'm goofed, I'm on a space cruise, I'm gone!*— and it was a restful, unencumbered sensation, just riding the light waves, sailing that big silver freedom bird over the mountains and oceans, over America, over the farms and great sleeping cities and cemeteries and highways and the golden arches of McDonald's, it was flight, a kind of fleeing, a kind of falling, falling higher and higher, spinning off the edge of the earth and beyond the sun and through the vast, silent vacuum where there were no burdens and where everything weighed exactly nothing—*Gone!* they screamed. *I'm sorry but I'm gone!*—and so at night, not quite dreaming, they gave themselves over to lightness, they were carried, they were purely borne.

On the morning after Ted Lavender died, First Lieutenant Jimmy Cross crouched at the bottom of his foxhole and burned Martha's letters. Then he burned the two photographs. There was a steady rain falling, which made it difficult, but he used heat tabs and Sterno to build a small fire, screening it with his body, holding the photographs over the tight blue flame with the tips of his fingers.

He realized it was only a gesture. Stupid, he thought. Sentimental, too, but mostly just stupid.

Lavender was dead. You couldn't burn the blame.

85 Besides, the letters were in his head. And even now, without photographs, Lieutenant Cross could see Martha playing volleyball in her white gym shorts and yellow T-shirt. He could see her moving in the rain.

When the fire died out, Lieutenant Cross pulled his poncho over his shoulders and ate breakfast from a can.

There was no great mystery, he decided.

In those burned letters Martha had never mentioned the war, except to say, Jimmy, take care of yourself. She wasn't involved. She signed the letters "Love," but it wasn't love, and all the fine lines and technicalities did not matter. Virginity was no longer an issue. He hated her. Yes, he did. He hated her. Love, too, but it was a hard, hating kind of love.

The morning came up wet and blurry. Everything seemed part of everything else, the fog and Martha and the deepening rain.

90 He was a soldier, after all. 90

Half smiling, Lieutenant Jimmy Cross took out his maps. He shook his head hard, as if to clear it, then bent forward and began planning the day's march. In ten minutes, or maybe twenty, he would rouse the men and they would pack up and head west, where the maps showed the country to be green and inviting. They would do what they had always done. The rain might add some weight, but otherwise it would be one more day layered upon all the other days.

He was realistic about it. There was that new hardness in his stomach. He loved her but he hated her.

No more fantasies, he told himself.

Henceforth, when he thought about Martha, it would be only to think that she belonged elsewhere. He would shut down the daydreams. This was not Mount Sebastian, it was another world, where there were no pretty poems or midterm exams, a place where men died because of carelessness and gross stupidity. Kiowa was right. Boom-down, and you were dead, never partly dead.

95 Briefly, in the rain, Lieutenant Cross saw Martha's gray eyes gaz- 95 ing back at him.

He understood.

It was very sad, he thought. The things men carried inside. The things men did or felt they had to do.

He almost nodded at her, but didn't.

Instead he went back to his maps. He was now determined to perform his duties firmly and without negligence. It wouldn't help Lavender, he knew that, but from this point on he would comport himself as a soldier. He would dispose of his good-luck pebble. Swallow it, maybe, or use Lee Strunk's slingshot, or just drop it along the trail. On

412

the march he would impose strict field discipline. He would be careful to send out flank security, to prevent straggling or bunching up, to keep his troops moving at the proper pace and at the proper interval. He would insist on clean weapons. He would confiscate the remainder of Lavender's dope. Later in the day, perhaps, he would call the men together and speak to them plainly. He would accept the blame for what had happened to Ted Lavender. He would be a man about it. He would look them in the eyes, keeping his chin level, and he would issue the new SOPs in a calm, impersonal tone of voice, a lieutenant's voice, leaving no room for argument or discussion. Commencing immediately, he'd tell them, they would no longer abandon equipment along the route of march. They would police up their acts. They would get their shit together, and keep it together, and maintain it neatly and in good working order.

100   He would not tolerate laxity. He would show strength, distancing 100 himself.

Among the men there would be grumbling, of course, and maybe worse, because their days would seem longer and their loads heavier, but Lieutenant Jimmy Cross reminded himself that his obligation was not to be loved but to lead. He would dispense with love; it was not now a factor. And if anyone quarreled or complained, he would simply tighten his lips and arrange his shoulders in the correct command posture. He might give a curt little nod. Or he might not. He might just shrug and say, Carry on, then they would saddle up and form into a column and move out toward the villages west of Than Khe.

Questions on Meaning

1. What is the nature of the things that the soldiers carry? How do those things weigh them down? How do those things sustain them?
2. What is the real nature of the relationship between Lieutenant Cross and Martha? How does he characterize the relationship? What purpose do his daydreams about Martha serve?
3. What or who is primarily responsible for Lavender's death—Cross, Lavender himself, the war? To what extent will Lieutenant Cross's new plans for discipline prevent further casualties? Explain your response.

Questions on Rhetorical Strategy and Style

1. The most common form of narrative involves a straight chronological progression, but O'Brien moves back and forth between the story of Lavender's death and the lists of things carried by the soldiers, with occasional commentary on Cross's fantasies. What is the effect of this arrangement? How does the additional material contribute to the impact of the story?
2. O'Brien provides vivid descriptions of the climate in which the soldiers march, fight, and sleep. How does the climate of Vietnam affect the soldiers? How do his descriptions of that climate contribute to the impact of the story?
3. The things carried by the soldiers can be divided into several categories. What are some of these categories, and what items fall into them? What is the significance of these lists to the story?

Writing Assignments

1. It is clear that Lavender's death constitutes a turning point in Lieutenant Cross's life. Write an essay analyzing Cross's response to the death, focusing on such issues as the lieutenant's responsibility to Lavender and his men, the value of his fantasy relationship with Martha, and his role in fighting this war.
2. Write a character analysis of Martha. Consider not only Cross's characterization of her, but also what her letters, her actions, and

her photographs tell us about her. Focus on the question why she writes to Cross as she does despite the fact that she does not share his feelings.

3. Research the attitudes of soldiers and the American public to the Vietnam war. Using material from that research, write an essay analyzing "The Things They Carried" as a protest against the war.

The Man to Send Rain Clouds

Leslie Marmon Silko

Leslie Marmon Silko (1948–), who has Pueblo and Laguna Indian, Mexican, and white ancestors, was born in Albuquerque, N.M. She grew up on the Laguna Pueblo reservation and attended both Indian schools and public schools in Albuquerque. She graduated from the University of New Mexico (1969) and attended law school for a short time before turning to writing and teaching. In 1981 she received a MacArthur Foundation grant. Silko's books include Laguna Woman's Poems *(1974),* Ceremony *(1977),* Storyteller *(1986),* Delicacy and the Strength of Love: Letters *(1986),* Almanac of the Dead *(1991),* Sacred White Narratives and Pictures *(1993),* Yellow Woman *(1993), and* Yellow Woman and a Beauty of the Spirit *(1996). In this short story, two men on a Pueblo Indian reservation happen upon the body of an old man who has died under a cottonwood tree.*

One

1   They found him under a big cottonwood tree. His Levi jacket and pants were faded light-blue so that he had been easy to find. The big cottonwood tree stood apart from a small grove of winterbare cottonwoods which grew in the wide, sandy *arroyo*.[1] He had been dead for a day or more, and the sheep had wandered and scattered up and down the arroyo. Leon and his brother-in-law, Ken, gathered the sheep and left them in the pen at the sheep camp before they returned to the cottonwood tree. Leon waited under the tree while Ken

drove the truck through the deep sand to the edge of the arroyo. He squinted up at the sun and unzipped his jacket—it sure was hot for this time of year. But high and northwest the blue mountains were still deep in snow. Ken came sliding down the low, crumbling bank about fifty yards down, and he was bringing the red blanket.

Before they wrapped the old man, Leon took a piece of string out of his pocket and tied a small gray feather in the old man's long white hair. Ken gave him the paint. Across the brown wrinkled forehead he drew a streak of white and along the high cheekbones he drew a strip of blue paint. He paused and watched Ken throw pinches of corn meal and pollen into the wind that fluttered the small gray feather. Then Leon painted with yellow under the old man's broad nose, and finally, when he had painted green across the chin, he smiled.

"Send us rain clouds, Grandfather." They laid the bundle in the back of the pickup and covered it with a heavy tarp before they started back to the pueblo.

They turned off the highway onto the sandy pueblo road. Not long after they passed the store and post office they saw Father Paul's car coming toward them. When he recognized their faces he slowed his car and waved for them to stop. The young priest rolled down the car window.

5 "Did you find old Teofilo?" he asked loudly.

Leon stopped the truck. "Good morning, Father. We were just out to the sheep camp. Everything is O.K. now."

"Thank God for that. Teofilo is a very old man. You really shouldn't allow him to stay at the sheep camp alone."

"No, he won't do that anymore now."

"Well, I'm glad you understand. I hope I'll be seeing you at Mass[2] this week—we missed you last Sunday. See if you can get old Teofilo to come with you." The priest smiled and waved at them as they drove away.

Two

10 Louise and Teresa were waiting. The table was set for lunch, and the coffee was boiling on the black iron stove. Leon looked at Louise and then at Teresa.

"We found him under a cottonwood tree in the big arroyo near sheep camp. I guess he sat down to rest in the shade and never got up again." Leon walked toward the old man's bed. The red plaid shawl had been shaken and spread carefully over the bed, and a new brown flannel shirt and pair of stiff new Levis were arranged neatly beside the pillow. Louise held the screen door open while Leon and Ken carried in the red blanket. He looked small and shriveled, and after they dressed him in the new shirt and pants he seemed more shrunken.

It was noontime now because the church bells rang the Angelus.[3] They ate the beans with hot bread, and nobody said anything until after Teresa poured the coffee.

Ken stood up and put on his jacket. "I'll see about the grave-diggers. Only the top layer of soil is frozen. I think it can be ready before dark."

Leon nodded his head and finished his coffee. After Ken had been gone for a while, the neighbors and clanspeople came quietly to embrace Teofilo's family and to leave food on the table because the gravediggers would come to eat when they were finished.

Three

15 The sky in the west was full of pale-yellow light. Louise stood outside with her hands in the pockets of Leon's green army jacket that was too big for her. The funeral was over, and the old men had taken their candles and medicine bags and were gone. She waited until the body was laid into the pickup before she said anything to Leon. She touched his arm, and he noticed that her hands were still dusty from the corn meal that she had sprinkled around the old man. When she spoke, Leon could not hear her.

"What did you say? I didn't hear you."

"I said that I had been thinking about something."

"About what?"

"About the priest sprinkling holy water for Grandpa. So he won't be thirsty." Leon stared at the new moccasins that Teofilo had made for the ceremonial dances in the summer. They were nearly hidden by the red blanket. It was getting colder, and the wind pushed gray dust down the narrow pueblo road. The sun was approaching the long mesa[4] where it disappeared during the winter. Louise stood there shivering and watching his face. Then he zipped up his jacket and opened the truck door. "I'll see if he's there."

Four

20 Ken stopped the pickup at the church, and Leon got out. And then 20
Ken drove down the hill to the graveyard where people were waiting.
Leon knocked at the old carved door with its symbols of the Lamb.[5]
While he waited he looked up at the twin bells from the king of Spain
with the last sunlight pouring around them in their tower.

The priest opened the door and smiled when he saw who it was.
"Come in! What brings you here this evening?"

The priest walked toward the kitchen, and Leon stood with his
cap in his hand, playing with the earflaps and examining the living
room—the brown sofa, the green armchair, and the brass lamp that
hung down from the ceiling by links of chain. The priest dragged a
chair out of the kitchen and offered it to Leon.

"No thank you, Father. I only came to ask you if you would bring
your holy water to the graveyard."

The priest turned away from Leon and looked out the window at
the patio full of shadows and the dining-room windows of the nuns'
cloister across the patio. The curtains were heavy, and the light from
within faintly penetrated: it was impossible to see the nuns inside eating supper. "Why didn't you tell me he was dead? I could have brought
the Last Rites[6] anyway."

25 Leon smiled. "It wasn't necessary, Father." 25

The priest stared down at his scuffed brown loafers and the worn
hem of his cassock.[7] For a Christian burial it was necessary."

His voice was distant, and Leon thought that his blue eyes looked
tired.

"It's O.K. Father, we just want him to have plenty of water."

The priest sank down into the green chair and picked up a glossy
missionary magazine. He turned the colored pages full of lepers and
pagans without looking at them.

30 "You know I can't do that, Leon. There should have been the Last 30
Rites and a funeral Mass at the very least."

Leon put on his green cap and pulled the flaps down over his
ears. "It's getting late, Father. I've got to go."

When Leon opened the door Father Paul stood up and said,
"Wait." He left the room and came back wearing a long brown over-
coat. He followed Leon out the door and across the dim churchyard
to the adobe steps in front of the church. They both stooped to fit

through the low adobe entrance. And when they started down the hill to the graveyard only half of the sun was visible above the mesa.

The priest approached the grave slowly, wondering how they had managed to dig into the frozen ground; and then he remembered that this was New Mexico, and saw the pile of cold loose sand beside the hole. The people stood close to each other with little clouds of steam puffing from their faces. The priest looked at them and saw a pile of jackets, gloves, and scarves in the yellow, dry tumbleweeds that grew in the graveyard. He looked at the red blanket, not sure that Teofilo was so small, wondering if it wasn't some perverse Indian trick—something they did in March to ensure a good harvest—wondering if maybe old Teofilo was actually at sheep camp corralling the sheep for the night. But there he was, facing into a cold dry wind and squinting at the last sunlight, ready to bury a red wool blanket while the faces of his parishioners were in shadow with the last warmth of the sun on their backs.

His fingers were stiff, and it took him a long time to twist the lid off the holy water. Drops of water fell on the red blanket and soaked into dark icy spots. He sprinkled the grave and the water disappeared almost before it touched the dim, cold sand; it reminded him of something—he tried to remember what it was, because he thought if he could remember he might understand this. He sprinkled more water; he shook the container until it was empty, and the water fell through the light from sundown like August rain that fell while the sun was still shining, almost evaporating before it touched the wilted squash flowers.

35 The wind pulled at the priest's brown Franciscan[8] robe and 35 swirled away the corn meal and pollen that had been sprinkled on the blanket. They lowered the bundle into the ground, and they didn't bother to untie the stiff pieces of new rope that were tied around the ends of the blanket. The sun was gone, and over on the highway the eastbound lane was full of headlights. The priest walked away slowly. Leon watched him climb the hill, and when he had disappeared within the tall, thick walls, Leon turned to look up at the high blue mountains in the deep snow that reflected a faint red light from the west. He felt good because it was finished, and he was happy about the sprinkling of the holy water; now the old man could send them big thunderclouds for sure.

End Notes

1. Spanish: a small river; the word here suggests a sandy creek bed.
2. A Catholic religious service.
3. Afternoon call to prayer.
4. Spanish: table; it here denotes a flat-topped hill with steep sides.
5. In the King James Bible, Christ is described as "the Lamb of God, which taketh away the sin of the world" (John 1:29).
6. Also known as "extreme unction," the Last Rites is a Catholic sacrament or ritual in which a priest anoints a dying person with oil and prays for their salvation.
7. A long robe worn by Catholic priests.
8. Founded in 1209 by St. Francis of Assisi, the Franciscans are an order of Catholic monks who established missions in the American Southwest in 1539.

Questions on Meaning

1. What is Leon's relationship to the old man, Teofilo? What rituals does Leon engage to prepare the old man's body? Why does he smile as he paints Teofilo's face?
2. Were you surprised by the men's reaction to finding the old man's body? Why didn't they seem more emotional?
3. When the men encounter the priest, Leon does not reveal to him that the old man has died. Why not? What was the priest's reaction to not being informed of Teofilo's death?
4. Why does Leon, seemingly as an afterthought, want the priest to sprinkle holy water over the grave?

Questions on Rhetorical Strategy and Style

1. The story is organized in four sections. How does this structure reflect one of the story's themes? How would you describe the author's point of view and her narrative technique? Explain why Silko has approached the narrative in this fashion and describe the tone it achieves.
2. The burial ritual described follows the Pueblo tradition. However, Silko also incorporates Catholic imagery into the story. Locate the passages that reflect a Christian viewpoint. What does the contrast between Native American and Christian imagery and references suggest about Leon's perspective?
3. What does the author's narrative style convey about her attitude toward Pueblo culture and ritual? Why does she include the priest in the story and what is his presence meant to suggest?

Writing Assignments

1. To some extent, one is better able to appreciate this story with an enhanced understanding of Pueblo burial rituals and attitudes toward death in general. Consult a few sources on this subject and write an essay on the concept of spirituality as reflected in this story.
2. Write an analysis of the characters in the story. What function does each of them serve? Why and how is Leon the protagonist and what does his character suggest about conditions on Indian reservations today?

Appendix I: Ways of Writing

Ways of Writing

Robert A. Schwegler

1 Confident writers know that the path to an effective essay calls for more than stringing loosely related ideas and information together. Their confidence comes in part from their understanding of the importance of each of the stages of the composing process: discovering, drafting, revising, editing, and proofreading.

They also know there is no single formula for all writing tasks, so they try to develop a variety of techniques. Making choices among strategies means paying attention to the needs of potential readers and the demands of a particular writing task, as well as the subject matter and purposes for writing.

Viewed from a distance, the stages of the writing process look regular and orderly: Discovering, Planning, Drafting, Revising, Editing, and Proofreading. Viewed from inside, however, the lines between these activities often blur: writers often discover worthwhile new ideas as they draft and revise or amend an essay's plan in response to further insight or reader's responses.

In your own writing you need to maintain an awareness of the stages of the writing process while remaining flexible in response to the demands of your writing task, audience, and purpose.

Getting Started

5 Most writing begins with an assignment or invitation: an essay for a college course, a report at work, or a call for submissions to a local newspaper, for example. Your success as a writer depends to a great extent on your ability to analyze and respond. At the same time, good writing is frequently self-sponsored, growing from a writer's experiences and feelings and taking initial shape in the writer's journal or personal writing. Some of the best writers are those able to blend an understanding of task and audience with the impulse toward personal expression.

Reprinted from *Patterns of Exposition* (2006), by permission of Pearson Education.

Look for the Assignment's Focus and Purpose—Nouns

When your writing begins with an assignment, make sure you have the exact wording—along with any explanatory comments from the person making the assignment.

Sometimes an assignment will announce a topic clearly. Often, however, assignments use nouns and noun phrases to introduce the various elements of the topic. Consider underlining any direct statements and associated nouns and noun phrases in your assignment. Then, draw on them as you write out the topic focus of the assignment. Rachel Baez underlined terms in the following assignment, then summarized it for herself.

> Many of the <u>studies</u> we have read about <u>violent behavior among teens</u> point to the influence of <u>violent scenes on television and in movies.</u> In the <u>interviews</u> we read, however, teenagers themselves point to <u>different causes</u>: social pressures, the personalities of individuals, drug and alcohol use, or a "desire for excitement and adventure." Analyze the differences among these explanations, tell which you find most convincing, and support your conclusions.

What do I see as the focus of this assignment? Two sets of explanations, one set in the studies and one set in the interviews.

Look for Purposes and Patterns in an Assignment—Verbs

The verbs and verb phrases in an assignment set goals (purposes) for your writing and may even suggest patterns for organizing and developing an essay. Verbs like *inform, explain, analyze, discuss,* and *show* suggest that your purpose will be *expository:* helping readers understand ideas, events, and information and offering carefully reasoned and supported conclusions about a subject. Words like *argue, persuade,* and *evaluate* suggest that your purpose will be argumentative: presenting reasoned arguments and supporting evidence designed to convince readers to share your opinion on an issue.

10   Underline such words in your assignment and write a purpose 10
statement for your task, including information about the topic. When she went back to her assignment, here are the action words Rachel Baez underlined and the purpose statement she prepared.

> Many of the studies we have read about violent behavior among teens point to the influence of violent scenes on television and in movies. In the interviews we read, however,

teenagers themselves point to different causes: social pressures, the personalities of individuals, drug and alcohol use, or a "desire for excitement and adventure." <u>Analyze</u> the differences among these explanations, <u>tell</u> which you find most convincing, and <u>support</u> your conclusions.

What are my purposes for this assignment? To give specific information about the differences, to offer my conclusion about the causes, and to give reasons and information that will help readers understand why my conclusions are reasonable.

Verbs and other words in the assignment may suggest (or require) patterns of exposition (or argument) for you to employ in all or part of an essay, alone or in combination with other patterns. Look for words like the following (or their synonyms) and consult the appropriate chapters in this book for ideas on using these patterns.

illustrate or provide *examples*
classify or *classification*
compare and *contrast*
create an *analogy*
analyze or explain a *process* or *process analysis*
analyze *cause* and *effect*
define or provide a *definition*
describe or create a *description*
narrate or use *narration*
reason *inductively* and *deductively* or use *induction* and *deduction*
argue or present an *argument*

Use these words, combined with information about your topic and purpose, to create a *design statement* for your writing, as did Rachel Baez.

I plan to begin with a section contrasting the sets of explanations for violent behavior among teens and indicating the specific differences. Then I will state clearly those I find convincing: media influence, social pressures, and the personalities of individuals. Finally, I will present examples and reasons why I think these are probably the most important causes for violent behavior.

Keep a Writing Journal

15 A *writing journal* (or *academic journal*) is a place (often a notebook or 15 a computer file) in which you jot down ideas and discoveries, try out

425

different perspectives on a topic, prepare rough drafts of paragraphs or essays, and note responses to readings or observations. Journals are not diaries: journals are starting places for public writing while diaries are places to record and keep your private observations.

This passage from Scott Giglio's journal, made in response to an article in his local newspaper, illustrates some of the ways journals can provide an imaginative start for the essay-writing process while at the same time be hard for anyone but the author to read.

> Article in PrJo 6/10/05 "Hispanics losing ground in strong economy" hadn't thought about this. Why? I figured unemployment was down etc. and that most people were either doing well or things getting better for them so what abt. Hispanics? Article claims—uh, where is it—Census Bureau claims Hispanic families income down 5.1% rest up 2.7 (can get rest of stats from article if impt. cut it out of paper) Ok Ok why happening and why important is this something to argue about or can I use it as part of paper on how people just seem to be same but lead diff. lives?? A campaign issue or do people vote on personality rather than how things are going?

Ask Questions to Develop a Topic

Once you have a topic in mind, you can begin envisioning how to develop it into an essay. Many writers use groups of questions to identify aspects of a subject likely to interest readers, to develop perspectives and insights worth sharing, or to clarify their purposes for writing. Questions can also suggest possible designs for an essay.

Focusing questions help you identify goals or main ideas for your writing and may suggest general ways to divide a topic into parts and organize an essay around key points. They may even point toward a thesis around which you can build an essay.

Here are some focusing questions that ask you to consider both your perspective on a topic and your readers' likely responses.

- What parts of this subject or ways of looking at it interest me the most? Is the subject as a whole interesting or does some part of it or specific way of looking at it seem more intriguing?
- What aspect of the subject is most likely to interest readers?
- What would I most like to learn about this subject? Would readers like to learn the same thing?

- What feelings about the subject do I want to share with readers? What knowledge, opinions, or insights do I want to share?
- How is my perspective different from the ones readers will likely bring with them?
- What are two (three? four?) fresh, unusual, unsettling, or controversial insights I have to share? Why may some readers have trouble understanding or accepting them?

Planning

20 Planning before you draft an essay does not mean deciding ahead of time the exact order in which you will present each detail or idea. It does not mean determining at the start the precise conclusions you will offer and support in each paragraph. 20

For most writers, writing is itself a form of discovery. The very act of putting sentences and paragraphs together brings ideas and information into often unanticipated relationships that create fresh perspectives worth sharing with readers.

But a lack of planning can be harmful to the quality of an essay or report and frustrating to you as the writer. If you begin writing without any plan, you are probably dooming yourself to false starts and long periods of inactivity when you try to decide what to say next—or whether to scrap the whole draft and start over.

How can you know when to begin planning? Sometimes your exploration of a topic suggests a clear pattern and direction for your writing. Sometimes your **discovering** activities suggest a point or **thesis** as a focus. And still other times, you have gathered so many ideas, opinions, and details that you need to move ahead before you are overwhelmed. All these are good times to begin planning.

Cluster and Diagram

Both clustering and diagramming (creating tree diagrams) lead to conceptual maps that group ideas to help you see relationships and develop focal points for your writing.

25 In **clustering** you develop ideas related to a central topic and link the ideas with lines to display how they are associated. Clustering encourages the interconnection of ideas. You may begin by developing a single idea into several seemingly unconnected nodes, but on further reflection recognize some connections you hadn't yet considered. 25

427

Begin by writing a concept, idea, or topic in the center of a page, and circle it. Then randomly jot down associations with the central idea, circling them and connecting them with lines to the center, like the spokes of a wheel. As you continue to generate ideas around the central focus, think about the interconnections among subsidiary ideas, and draw lines to show those.

You can also create clusters in cycles, each subsidiary idea becoming the central focus on a new page. You'll soon find that some clusters begin petering out once you've exhausted your fund of knowledge. Stand back and assess what you have. Is there enough to go on, without further consideration? If so, you may be ready to start some harder, more critical consideration of your paper's direction. If not, perhaps further strategies will open up additional ideas.

Tree diagrams resemble clusters, but their branches tend to be a little more linear, with few interconnections. Tree diagrams rely on the notion of subordination: each larger branch can lead to smaller and smaller branches. For this reason, tree diagramming can provide a useful way to visualize the components of your paper. You can even revise a tree diagram into a sort of preliminary outline to use when deciding what to place in each paragraph of your paper.

Use Patterns of Exposition and Argument

As you become familiar with the patterns of exposition (and argument) discussed in the text, you can use them to develop a plan for an essay, using them either alone or in combination. One way to do this is to treat the patterns like questions.

- Can I develop my essay through examples that illustrate a generality or by examining the categories into which the ideas and information fall?
- Can I look at similarities and differences or at the surprising similarities between seemingly very different subjects?
- Should I write about how my subject works or can be done, or about how it happened and what is likely to occur in the future?
- Should I define my subject, or describe it in detail?
- Should I talk about what happened, or should I reason from facts a conclusion and use the conclusion to arrive at further interpretations?
- Should I argue for a proposition and provide evidence to convince readers?

Develop a Thesis

30 Perhaps the most important and useful planning technique involves 30 focusing on what you want to say and do. In a finished essay, a **thesis statement** creates focus by announcing your main idea(s) to readers and helping organize supporting ideas, evidence, and discussions. An effective thesis statement is specific and limited; it announces and highlights the main idea without getting bogged down in details.

Specific: A good community exercise program makes provisions for four kinds of exercisers: people dedicated to fitness, people wanting to become fit, people struggling with health problems, and children building a base for a healthy lifestyle.

Vague: A community exercise program is good when it has room for people who want to exercise for all sorts of different reasons.

Limited: Extensive use of fossil fuels and widespread changes in agriculture have had significant effects on our climate in the last 75 years.

Too Broad: The last several centuries have seen massive changes in industrial production, in the use of fossil fuels, in transportation, in the development of cities, in agriculture, and in many other areas that have had an impact on our climate.

Direct: Despite all their protests to the contrary, people tend to value appearance, likelihood of success, and similarity of background in choosing a mate.

Bogged: People may say they look for spiritual qualities rather than looks in choosing a mate, yet research points out that they are more likely to be influenced by some traditional factors, and these are likely to include how a person looks, whether or not a person is likely to succeed financially or in social terms, and the extent to which the people's families, experiences, and social class are similar.

But effective thesis statements seldom start out specific, limited, and direct. They begin as **tentative thesis statements** that provide a focus for planning. As you draft and revise, they become clearer and more sharply focused, eventually taking final form in a finished essay.

Here are some techniques for developing a tentative thesis statement as part of your planning.

List Your Conclusions and Evidence

Create a list of possible conclusions and evidence you wish to offer in an essay. Then sum them up in **generalization**, which highlights the main idea linking them all.

> **Support:** Fashions in children's toys change quickly—sometimes several times a year.
>
> **Support:** Toy manufacturers must make product decisions a year before the toys appear in stores, so they need to predict trends a year ahead.
>
> **Support:** Bringing a new toy to market can cost millions of dollars.
>
> **Support:** Most new toys are not successes; many make very little money.
>
> **Support:** There are many well-managed and imaginative companies competing for business in the toy market.
>
> **Generalization (Tentative Thesis):** Manufacturing children's toys is a risky business.

Create a Tentative Purpose Statement

Try writing yourself a note stating your potential topic along with your conclusions and possible goals for writing. To remain flexible and open to new ideas, you might begin your statement with a phrase like "I'd like to. . . ." or "I'm planning to. . . ."

> I'm planning to explain the reasons why many college students lose their motivation to work hard at their studies.
>
> —Bippin Kumar

> I'd like to tell what it felt like to be forced to leave my homeland, Haiti, so that my readers can understand why to leave something you love is to die a little.
>
> —Fredza Léger

Create a Rough Purpose/Thesis Outline

35 When you have in mind the various ideas and details you wish to 35 present in an essay, create a **purpose/thesis outline** arranging the

ideas and details in groups by clustering the details and summing up your conclusions and purpose for each section of an essay.

Here is Bippin Kumar's purpose outline for a paper exploring the reasons why college students may lose the motivation necessary to succeed at their studies.

1. Get readers' attention by mentioning the *bad habits* most of us have and that we may be able to correct on our own. (minor causes of the problem)

   lack of sleep

   disorganization

   distractions (television, etc.)

2. Show how we are often responsible because of the choices we make and explain that we need to make wiser choices. (more serious causes)

   sports and other extracurricular activities

   friends and socializing

   Greek life

   letting ourselves get frustrated and angry over daily hassles (bookstores, commuting)

3. Conclude with problems that we can't avoid and that may require special planning or counseling to overcome. (more serious causes)

   work

   financial stresses

   family demands or problems

   lack of necessary skills

Drafting

Drafting involves a good deal more than setting pen to paper or fingers to keyboard and letting the words flow according to your plan. It means paying attention to the way each section of an essay relates to the other sections and to the central theme. It means making sure you begin and end the essay in ways that are clear, helpful, and interesting to readers. And it means making sure each section and each paragraph present sufficient, detailed information so that readers can understand your subject and have reasons to agree with your explanations and conclusions.

Drafting does not mean getting everything right the first time. Such a goal is likely to prove both exhausting and impossible to achieve. A much better goal is to draft with the most important features of an essay in mind and to work quickly enough so that you have sufficient time to revise later and then pay attention to details.

Keep Your Plan in Mind

As you draft, therefore, make sure that you introduce readers to your topic, indicate its importance, generate interest in it, and suggest the direction your essay will take. The essays in this collection can provide you with models of successful strategies for the beginnings of essays.

40   Keep in mind the various sections you have planned for your   40 essay, or keep at hand a copy of any planning strategies you have used, especially those that identify the planned parts of your essay, their general content, and their purposes.

Keep Your Focus in Mind

Most likely, you will also alter, revise, or change the main point (theme or thesis) of your essay as you write, and such changes often make for a better essay. By the time your essay is complete, moreover, you will also have to decide whether to announce your main point directly to readers in a concise **thesis statement** (see below), to present it less directly in a series of statements in the body of the essay, or to imply it through the details and arrangement of the paper. No matter which strategy you choose, you should have a relatively clear idea of your thesis before you begin drafting. Try stating your thesis to yourself in a tentative form. You can do this in several ways:

- Start with a phrase like "I want my readers to understand...." or "The point of the whole essay is...."
- Make up a title that embodies your main idea.
- Send an imaginary note to your readers: "By the time you are finished with this essay, I hope you will see (or agree with me) that...."

If you want to share your knowledge of bicycling as a sport, for instance, you might try one or more of these thesis-building strategies, as in the following examples.

1. The point of the whole essay is that people can choose what kind of bicycle riders they want to be—recreational, competitive, or cross-country.

2. What Kind of Bicycle Rider Do You Want to Be?

3. By the time you finish this essay, I hope you will be able to choose the kind of bicycle riding—recreational, competitive, or cross-country—that is best for you.

A tentative thesis statement can guide your drafting by reminding you of your essay's main point. You can create a **tentative thesis statement** by summing up in a sentence or two your main point, the conclusion you plan to draw from the information and ideas you will present, or the proposition for which you plan to argue. You may eventually use a revised form of the tentative thesis statement in your completed essay as a way of announcing clearly to readers the main idea behind your writing.

For example, when Ken Chin was preparing a paper on different meanings of the phrase "recent immigrant," he used the following tentative thesis statement: "For some people, *recent immigrant* means a threat to their jobs or more strain on the resources of schools and social service agencies. For others it means fresh ideas and a broadening of our culture and outlook." In his final paper he used this thesis statement: "For some, *recent immigrant* means *cheap labor* or *higher taxes;* for others, it means *fresh ideas* and *a richer, more diverse culture.*"

Pay Attention to Sections

45 As you write, include statements that alert readers to the various sections, along with transitions marking the movement from one section to the next (or from paragraph to paragraph). Make sure, too, that in making shifts in time, place, ideas, and content you do not confuse readers, but instead give them adequate indication of the shifts. Remember to provide readers with concrete, specific details and evidence that will give them the information they need about your topic, or the support necessary to make your explanations or arguments convincing.

Pay attention to the arrangement of your essay, especially to the patterns of exposition or argument you are employing. In any essay that classifies, for example, don't provide a detailed treatment of one category in the classification but skimpy treatment of the others—unless you have a special reason for doing so. Let your readers know, directly or indirectly, whatever pattern(s) you are employing. This will make them aware of your essay's design and will help to guide their attention to the key points you cover. Make every effort to stick to your main idea (perhaps using your tentative thesis statement as a guide), and check to see that the parts of the essay are clearly related to and support the main idea. If you have trouble developing a section because you need more information, or because you can't express ideas as clearly as you want, make a note of the things that need to be done and then move on.

Revising

When you shift your focus to revising, you pay special attention to the success with which your draft essay embodies your intentions and meets your readers' likely expectations. You examine the draft to see if it does a good job presenting insights, reasoning, and details. You look at the draft from a reader's perspective to see if the discussions are clear and informative, the reasoning is logical, and the examples and supporting details are related to the central theme.

Read for Revision

Revision starts with rereading—looking over your draft with a dual perspective: as an author and as a member of your potential audience. As you read for revision, keep track of the places that need more work and make note of the directions your rewriting might take. Most writers find it hard to read for revision directly from a computer screen, and they print a hard copy of their drafts for this purpose.

Whether you are working with a handwritten text, a typed copy, or a print from a word processor, you may find reading for revision most effective if you do it with a pencil or pen in hand to record your reactions and plans for revision.

50   Reading for revision can be even more effective when another writer   50 does it for you (and you return the favor). Remember, collaborative readings of this sort are best done in a cooperative, rather than harshly critical, atmosphere. Your job and that of your reader(s) is to identify strengths as well as weaknesses and to suggest (if possible) ways to turn weaknesses into strong points. (For more about collaborative revising and editing, see the *Peer Response* section.)

Whether you are reading your own work or someone else's, you may find these symbols useful shortcuts for making marginal comments to guide revision.

Reader Response Symbols

?	*Could you explain this a bit more? I can't really understand this.*
Add?	*I would like to know more about this. I think you could use more detail here.*
Leave out?	*This information or this passage may not be necessary. You have already said this.*
Missing?	*Did you leave something out? I think there is a gap in the information, explanation, or argument here.*
Confusing?	*I have trouble following this explanation/argument. The information here is presented in a confusing manner.*
Reorganize?	*I think this section (or paper) would be more effective if you presented it in a different order.*
Interesting, Good, Effective, etc.	*Your writing really works here. I like it.*

You may be tempted to revise as you read, and for sentences or paragraphs that need a quick fix, this approach is often adequate. In most cases, however, your revisions need to go beyond tinkering with words and sentences if they are to lead to real improvement. You will need to pay attention to the overall focus, to the need for additional paragraphs presenting detailed evidence, and to the arrangement of the steps in an explanation or argument. To see the need for such large-scale changes, you need to read the draft paying attention to the essay as a whole, something you cannot do if you stop frequently to rework the parts. In addition, it makes little sense to correct the flaws in a sentence if you realize later on that the entire paragraph ought to be dropped.

Read with Questions

One good way to read for revision is to prepare questions that will focus your attention as you read—questions appropriate for your topic, your purposes, your pattern(s) of exposition or argument, and your intended readers. You may wish to direct attention to those features you worked on while drafting (introductions or transitions, for example). You may wish to use questions that reflect the specific topic or purposes of your essay or that reflect the probable outlook of your intended readers. Make notes in the margins of your draft or on a separate sheet of paper (or computer file). Don't keep too many questions in mind as you read; instead, reread as many times as necessary, each time with a different set of questions. Following are some possible questions to help you evaluate your draft.

Questions for Revision

General

> Does my essay have a clear topic and focus?
> Does it stick to the topic and focus throughout?
> How have I signaled the topic and focus to readers?
> Is the essay divided into parts? What are they?
> Are the parts clearly identified for readers?

Thesis and theme

> Does the essay have a thesis statement? Is it clearly stated?
> Is the thesis statement in the best possible location?
> Should the thesis statement be more (or less) specific?
> Are all the different parts of the essay clearly related to the thesis statement or the central theme?
> In what ways have I reminded readers of the thesis or theme in the course of the essay? Do I need to remind them more often or in other ways?

Introductions and conclusions

> Does my introduction make the topic clear? Does it interest readers in what I will have to say?
> Does my introduction give readers some indication of the arrangement of the essay and its purpose(s)?
> Does the conclusion help tie together the main points of the essay or remind readers of the significance of the information and ideas I have presented?
> Does my conclusion have a clear purpose or have I ended the essay without any clear strategy?

Information and ideas

> Have I presented enough information and enough details so that readers will feel they have learned something worthwhile about the topic?

436

At what specific places would the essay be improved if I added more information?

What information can be cut because it is repetitive, uninteresting, or unrelated to the topic or theme of the essay?

Is my information fresh and worth sharing? Do I need to do more thinking or research so that the content of my essay is worth sharing?

Do the examples and details I present support my conclusions in a convincing way? Do I need to explain them more fully?

Would more research or thinking enable me to offer better support? What kinds of support would readers find helpful?

Have I learned something new or worthwhile about my topic and communicated it to readers?

Sentences and paragraphs

Have I divided the essay into paragraphs that help readers identify shifts in topic, stages in an explanation, steps in a line of reasoning, key ideas, or important segments of information?

Does each paragraph make its topic or purpose clear to readers?

Which short paragraphs need greater development through the addition of details or explanations?

Which long paragraphs could be trimmed or divided?

Do the sentences reflect what I want to say? Which sentences could be clearer?

Are the sentences varied in length? Do they provide appropriate emphasis to key ideas?

Can I word the explanations or arguments more clearly?

Can I use more vivid and concrete language?

Would the paper benefit from more complicated or imaginative language? From simpler, more direct wording?

Readers' perspective

In what ways are my readers likely to view this topic or argument? Have I taken their perspectives into account?

What do I want my readers to learn from this essay? What opinion do I want them to share? What do I want them to do?

Have I considered what my readers are likely to know or believe and how this will shape their response to my purpose(s) for writing?

Sample Student Essay

Here is the draft of an essay Sarah Lake produced in response to an assignment asking her to write about a community of some sort, taking the perspective of an outsider trying to understand how the community works and what kinds of relationships people in the community form. The marginal comments on the paper are notes she has addressed to the classmates (peer readers) who will be responding to her paper with revision suggestions.

Welcome to the Gym!

As I stepped up to the door to the field house I saw myself in the reflection from the door. I had chosen mesh shorts, a white v-neck T-shirt, and tattered old sneakers in hope to "fit in" with the crowd. Luckily, I still possess the Ram sticker on the back of my I.D. I was all set. I was in. A cheery eyed student asked for my I.D., and pointed me towards the training room. So far, so good, I thought. My only hopes were that the gym was going to be a great place.

The smell was rather distinct; one part sweat, one part machine oil, and one part cleaner, or maybe it was the chlorine coming from the pool. Surprisingly, it was a rather welcoming smell. The kind of smell that says "Come on in, have fun, workout, sweat, be hot and sticky and smelly, it's O.K." I liked what it had to say, so I continued on, farther into the training room. As I stepped inside to the training room, heavy breathing and strenuous shouts of "One!, Two!, Three!" could be heard. The shouting seemed common, and went unnoticed by regulars. Weightlifters, mostly men, would grunt, scream, moan, and sometimes yell in agony as they tried to lift weights two, three times the weight they could handle. Their heads turned a tomato red and looked as if they were about to explode. Their veins, like thick rope, popped through the skin on their necks, arms, and legs. Due to the fact that I'm not a weightlifter or a man, I surely don't understand the meaning behind this behavior. It looked rather painful

I've tried to make this interesting. Is it?

This is the community I studied. Is my purpose clear?

I added a lot of detail. Does it work?

and it wasn't very flattering to them, but it was entertaining.

I squirmed my way through the machines, and people, and found myself a spot on one of the stair masters. I curiously stared at the screen in front of me. Blinking letters zoomed across the screen reading enter your weight and then press enter. Enter my weight? That's a lot to ask of a girl. I thought about it, and even considered lying to the machine, but reality set in, I realized it was just a machine. Why lie to a machine? I punched in my weight, and continued to answer the questions the screen produced.

As I started my workout, I began to gaze around and inspect everyone's interaction with each other. "Rules of the Gym" were listed on the wall and were followed by everyone. Everyone respected everyone and everything. On the other hand rules for socializing weren't posted, but underlying rules seemed to be understood. Socializing while working out or better yet, while in motion was not encouraged. Talking only took place while one was motionless or waiting for a machine. It seemed as if it took so much concentration to work out that no one could even talk while doing so. I, on the other hand, couldn't wait to talk when I got finished. I felt like I had gone through withdrawal. I needed some sort of outlet to make the time go by and my workout faster so I turned from people behavior watching to people's attire watching.

Gym attire was rather diverse. Some wore the typical workout uniform, which consisted of tight spandex. It included tops, tops over tops, bottoms, bottoms over bottoms, etc., etc. Others wore outfits very similar to my own which was very comforting. My favorite outfit (I'm being sarcastic) was on a young woman, about 21, who turned more heads in twenty minutes than Cindy Crawford has in her whole career. It consisted of, from top to bottom: a bright pink scrunchie (one of those cloth elastics), a black headband, a bright pink jog bra, black lycra

> **I think my punctuation and grammar got a bit out of control at times in this draft. Help!**

65

65

439

*spandex, covered by a workout g-string, also
bright pink in color. As I worked my eyes down
to her legs and then to her feet I noticed she had
boxing sneakers on. The ones NIKE made in the
eighties with the high laces. Smashing, was the
only word to describe her ensemble.*

**Is this too
much detail?**

Peer Response

Before you revise (or in between successive drafts), getting a look at your work through another's eyes can help you spot strengths and weaknesses and identify steps you can take to improve your essay. To do this, ask a person or a group of people to read and comment on the strengths and weaknesses of your draft essay. Ask them, too, to suggest ways the writing might be improved. Their comments are most likely to be useful if you ask them to respond to specific questions and to make concrete suggestions for improvement.

Here are some comments Tonya Williams and Dave Cisneros made on Sarah Lake's essay.

Does this essay have a clear and interesting thesis statement or generalization?

TONYA: I don't see any thesis statement. The assignment asked us to make a generalization about the community. What is yours?

DAVE: In the planning materials you shared with us, you talked about the reasons people were exercising. Could you add a generalization about the motivations of people in this community?

Does this essay provide detailed examples that support or explain the essay's thesis statement or generalization?

TONYA: I like some of the pictures of gym life that you provide, but I don't see how they fit with any kind of generalization. The last example probably talks too much about clothes.

DAVE: I suggest cutting the last paragraph. It doesn't fit with the rest of the paper.

Are the sentences clear and effective? How might they be improved?

TONYA: A lot of the sentences begin with "I," so the paper seems to focus on you rather than the community you are exploring.

DAVE: I like the way you write. I think your sentences are easy to read in general. At times, though, the paper seems a bit informal. I'm not sure whether the writing is too informal in style or whether you are focusing more on your personal feelings than on the kinds of observations and conclusions you are trying to explain.

Are there any places the grammar and spelling might be improved?

TONYA: I think you have some grammar problems, especially fragments and run-ons. I put a question mark next to these on the paper.

DAVE: I noticed a few spelling problems and other small errors. I tried to mark them, but I may have missed a few.

Editing and Final Revision

After you have carefully rewritten your essay at least one time and perhaps several, you can focus on editing and on the final revision. In creating your finished paper, pay special attention to matters such as the style and clarity of sentences and paragraphs as well as correctness in grammar and usage. Before you hand in your final draft, carefully correct any typographical errors along with any mistakes in spelling or expression that remain.

70   Here is the final version of Sarah Lake's paper, including 70 some revision that she made during a last reading and some editing before she typed the final copy. In revising, Sarah took into account the comments of her classmates and those her instructor wrote on a copy of her draft. In addition, she went back to her planning document for ideas she left out of the draft, and she developed these ideas at some length in the revised version of the paper. The comments in the margin of the paper below have been added to highlight features of the essay.

Welcome to the Gym:

A Community of Worriers

As I stepped up to the door of the field house, I saw my reflection in the glass, and I started worrying. I had chosen mesh shorts, a white V-necked T-shirt, and tattered old sneakers in hopes of fitting in with the community I planned to observe: people exercising for fitness inside the gym. I was worrying about how well I would fit in. After my visit, I realized I fit in quite well. Not only had I dressed appropriately, but I was also worried, and worrying about appearance seemed to be one trait everybody at the gym shared. <u>*It seems to be the attribute that defines this community and ties its members together.*</u>

As I stepped inside the training room I heard heavy breathing and strenuous shouts of "One! Two! Three!" Weightlifters, mostly men, were grunting, screaming, moaning, and yelling in agony as they tried to lift weights two, three times more than they could handle. Their heads turned tomato red, and they looked as if they were about to explode. I'm neither a man nor a weightlifter, and I had no idea why they were trying to overexert themselves, or so it seemed to me.

When I spoke with several of the weightlifters, they admitted that for many people who spend time lifting weights, appearance is a primary concern. They claimed that many male weightlifters begin exercising because they feel inferior about their physical appearance or because they want to get that "He-man" or "Caveman" look that they consider an ideal for men. Though the men I talked to said that they, personally, weren't that anxious about the way they looked, they also admitted that they felt that potential dates pay more attention to a man who has "bulked up."

I asked why they felt it was important to have a muscular and masculine appearance in today's society, especially when a lot of people (women especially) talk about the need for men to be

Moves from personal experience to the conclusion that will be explored in the essay

Thesis statement

Paragraph presents observations

Evidence supports overall thesis

Observations likely to surprise and intrigue reader

"sensitive." I was surprised by the answers because they seemed to reveal worry and insecurity—which was surprising coming from a group of very well-muscled college men. The weightlifters said they thought sensitivity was a good thing, and they claimed to work toward it in their relationships. They also said that sensitivity grows out of self-confidence, and that for men self-confidence often comes through physical fitness and athletic ability.

Though the weightlifters seemed sincere, as a woman I felt rather awed by their appearance and kept waiting for one of them to knock one of the female exercisers over the head and drag her back to his cave. This thought made me shift my attention to the women, most of whom were working on machines like Stair Masters, stationary bicycles, or Nautilus. To enter into the women's part of this community, I squirmed my way through the machines and people, and I found a spot on one of the Stair Masters. I stared curiously at the screen in front of me. Blinking letters zoomed across the screen asking me to enter my weight. "Enter my weight," I thought. "That's a lot to ask of a girl." I even thought about lying, but then I got embarrassed about lying to a machine. Later, when I shared this worry with some of the women at the gym, I realized they shared my apprehension and a lot of my other worries.

Like the men, the women shared many concerns about their appearance, especially about their attractiveness and about the relationship of appearance to self-confidence. They spoke of how the Baywatch girls are the ideals of appearance for women in our society, and of how they felt a need to compete with the "Barbies" of this world, even though such an appearance is unrealistic for the average woman. They also talked about having a kind of balance scale in their heads. As their weight increases, they feel less attractive, and as their weight decreases, they feel more attractive. They pointed out how magazines, TV programs, and movies seem to equate thinness with attractiveness

Transition to second set of observations

Personal experience supports thesis

Observations act as evidence for thesis

Summarizes Interviews

75

75

443

and link attractiveness to self-confidence. Though they admitted that working women with responsibilities as wives and mothers might not have time or energy to work out in a gym, they worried about how their self-confidence might suffer if they didn't have the opportunity to exercise to control their weight.

After my time on the Stair Master came to an end and I had finished talking to the members of the gym community, I left, feeling as though I fit in. I was a worrier and I had dressed like many of the women. On my way out, however, I passed a woman dressed in a daring pink and black outfit who began turning heads as soon as she walked in the door. I started worrying again, and I knew the people in the gym were now worrying even more about their looks.

Conclusion echoes main point

Appendix II:
Rhetorical Modes

Rhetorical Modes

Robert A. Schwegler

Illustrating Ideas by Use of *Example*

1 The use of examples to illustrate an idea under discussion is the most common, and frequently the most efficient, pattern of exposition. It is a method we use almost instinctively; for instance, instead of talking in generalities about the qualities of a good city manager, we cite Angela Lopes as an example. We may go further and illustrate her virtues as a manager by a specific account of her handling a crucial situation during the last power shortage or hurricane. In this way, we put our abstract ideas into concrete form—making them clearer and more convincing. As readers, we look for examples as well, often responding to general statements with a silently voiced question, "For instance?" and expecting the writer to provide us with appropriate specifics.

Examples can be short or long: a brief illustration within a sentence or a fully developed instance filling a paragraph or more. They can appear singly, or they can work together in clusters, as in the following paragraph where brief examples serve to make a generalization vivid and convincing.

> *There were many superstitions regarding food.* Dropping a fork meant that company would be coming. If we were to take a second helping of potatoes while we still had some left on our plate, someone always predicted that a person more hungry than we were would drop in during the day. Every housewife believed that food from a tin can had to be removed immediately after opening, or it would become deadly poison within a few seconds. My mother always ran across the room to dump the contents immediately.
>
> —Lewis Hill, "Black Cats and Horse Hairs"

Reprinted from *Patterns of Exposition* (2006), by permission of Pearson Education.

Generality

> Example 1
> Example 2
> Example 3
> Example 4

Whether making an explanation clear, a generality more convincing, or an argument more persuasive, examples work in the same way. They make the general more specific, the abstract more concrete, and in so doing they illustrate a sound principle of writing.

Why Use Examples?

5 Examples clarify by showing readers what a general statement means in terms of individual events, people, or ideas. By pointing out students who use "lucky" pens to take a test, lawyers who wear "special" ties or shoes to a big day in court, and engineers who begin a new project with a special breakfast, a writer can aid understanding of the statement, "Even educated people often make superstition part of their everyday lives."

On the other hand, lack of clear illustrations may leave readers with only a hazy conception of the points the writer has tried to make. Even worse, readers may try to supply examples from their own knowledge or experience, leading them to an impression different from that intended by the author. Since writers are the ones trying to communicate, clarity is primarily their responsibility.

Not only do good examples put into clear form what otherwise might remain vague and abstract, but they also serve to make generalizations and conclusions convincing. Not every generality requires supporting examples, of course. An audience with even a passing familiarity with films probably does not need extended examples to understand and accept the statement, "Action films are characterized by physical violence, explosions, chase scenes, and broadly drawn characters." Conclusions about unfamiliar or complicated subjects, technical discussions, and perspectives that may be difficult for readers to share initially usually call for examples. College instructors, for instance, will usually look for examples to render an interpretation convincing; business and public audiences will search reports and memorandums for examples that make the writer's judgments plausible.

With something specific for readers to visualize, a statement becomes more convincing—but convincing within certain limitations. If

446

you use the Volvo as an example of Swedish manufacturing, the reader is probably aware that this car may not be entirely typical. For ordinary purposes of explanation, the Volvo example could make its point convincingly enough. In supporting an argument, however, you need either to choose an example that is clearly typical or to present several examples to show that you have represented the situation fairly.

Choosing a Strategy

As a writer, you need to recognize not only places where individual examples can aid your writing but also occasions when your ideas might be most effectively presented through the use of examples as the primary strategy for an essay. If you have a fresh, unusual, or surprising conclusion to offer readers, consider using examples in a **thesis-and-support strategy.** Announce your thesis (perspective, interpretation) to readers, then offer evidence of its reasonableness in the form of varied, carefully developed examples, as illustrated in the following plan for an essay.

Tentative Thesis	Modern technology offers many new creative outlets for writers, musicians, and artists.
Supporting Point	Cable television has multiplied the opportunities for creative work by increasing greatly the number of television programs.
	Example: It provides more work for scriptwriters of all kinds: dramatic, documentary, news, sports, and comedy.
	Example: It creates more opportunities for actors, cinematographers, and directors.
	Example: It produces more programs calling for original music, art, and graphics.
Supporting Point	Software development calls for creative artists as well as software engineers.
	Example: Games require scriptwriters, artistic designers, graphic artists, and composers (for music to accompany the action).
	Example: Office programs require graphic design; home and landscape design programs involve artistic and graphic design;

447

educational software calls for writers and designers (sometimes even music).

Supporting Point Personal computers and the Internet provide the means to create and distribute works of art without significant financial resources.

> **Example:** Composers and performers can create musical works without hiring performers or renting a studio and distribute their work on the World Wide Web.

> **Example:** Desktop publishing allows writers to create printed copies of their novels, essays, and other writing without the expense or difficulty of working with publishers and printers.

> **Example:** Design programs and drawing/painting programs let visual artists create without having to maintain a studio or buy expensive materials, and the World Wide Web gives them a way to advertise and distribute their work.

10   If an extended, especially detailed example covers all aspects of 10 your topic that need explaining or provides a particularly appropriate instance of your main idea, consider using a **representative example strategy.** A representative example needs to be interesting in itself because it will serve as the main focus of the writing, preceded or followed (or both) by the main idea it illustrates.

In this chapter, Andy Rooney's "In and of Ourselves We Trust" provides a particularly successful instance of a representative example (stopping at a red light when no one is around) followed by the writer's conclusion that "the whole structure of our society depends on mutual trust, not distrust."

Choosing Examples

Successful writers select and use example cautiously, keeping in mind their readers and their own specific purposes for communicating. To be effective, an example must be pertinent to the chief qualities of the generality it illustrates. In writing about horror films, for instance, you might offer this interpretation: "The films generally have contemporary settings, yet most reinforce traditional, even old-fashioned, roles for both men and women." To be pertinent, examples would need to address the various elements of this thesis, including the contrast between the contemporary setting and the old-fashioned values, the roles of both men and women, and exceptions to the conclusion (the interpretation applies to "most" horror films, but not all).

Examples should be representative as well, presenting in a fair manner the range of situations, people, or ideas to which a generality applies. In discussing a new approach to education, you should be ready to consider it in terms of urban and rural as well as suburban communities. Your interpretation of a play, film, novel, or recording should take into account the work as a whole, not simply those parts corresponding most directly to your thesis. If you wish readers to adopt your perspective, you should choose examples that represent any important differences among their outlooks, often the product of differences in background, gender, ethnicity, or education.

It is possible to provide too many examples and make them too long, but for most writers, the opposite is usually the problem. We frequently underestimate the number of examples needed because we pay attention only to those that come to mind most readily. Almost any part of a subject can provide potential examples, however. With your generality or thesis in mind, look for representative events, situations, quotations, or people; typical attitudes, opinions, or ideas; and characteristic physical and emotional details. Make a conscious effort to draw examples from a variety of sources.

- *Your Experiences:* Draw on your involvement with the topic. For an essay on work, draw on jobs you have held. For an essay on sports, think of your experiences (pleasant and unpleasant) as an athlete or spectator. For a report on health care, begin with your own broken bones, doctor's appointments, sessions in the dentist's chair, and trips to the hospital either as patient or visitor.
- *Your Reading:* Add to your knowledge of a topic by searching a library catalog or using an Internet search engine. Choose articles and reports that expand your understanding and suggest the ways others may respond to your conclusions. Draw examples (including statistics) from your reading, being careful to acknowledge your sources.

- *Other People:* Think about other people whose experiences are consistent with your conclusions: the neighbor whose job history reflects a changing view of loyalty to an employer or your cousin whose reliance on the Internet for shopping illustrates changing patterns of consumption.
- *One from a Group:* When your thesis or generalization applies to a wide variety of people, situations, organizations, or experiences, you may be tempted to provide numerous examples as a way of representing the group as a whole but instead end up with a cluster of indistinct, ineffective illustrations. Instead, consider focusing on one or two members of the group and presenting them in extended detail that explains and supports your conclusions. To illustrate the features of science fiction movies, for example, turn to one or two films likely to be familiar to your readers.

15   There is no set length for effective examples. They can be as short   15
as a few words or as long as several paragraphs in length, depending
on the purpose they serve. For a thesis-and-support essay, however, a
paragraph of four to six sentences provides a good measure.

Each paragraph supporting your main idea should provide several
brief examples or several sentences presenting the example and discussing it in detail. Writers often overestimate how much their readers
know about a subject and offer examples lacking in important ideas
and information, as in the following student example from a paper
for a course on public health policy.

> Nonprescription drugs are still drugs and can be dangerous if
> misused. Many people make themselves ill by doubling or
> tripling the dosage of nonprescription drugs in order to get a
> greater effect.

When her instructor and fellow students pointed out the lack of
information in this paragraph, the writer realized that she could have
included examples of the toxic effects of high dosages of aspirin and
other painkillers, of allergic reactions to excessive intake of vitamin
and mineral supplements, and of physical damage that can result
from overuse of digestive remedies—examples her readers would have
found informative and useful.

Remember, a good example must be either instantly obvious to
readers or fully developed so that they learn exactly what it illustrates,

and how. Sometimes, however, illustration may be provided best by something other than a real-life example—a fictional anecdote, an analogy, or perhaps a parable that demonstrates the general idea. Here even greater care is needed to be sure these examples are both precise and clear.

Analyzing a Subject by *Classification*

People naturally like to sort and classify things. A young child, moving into a new dresser of her own, will put handkerchiefs together, socks and underwear in separate stacks, and hair clips in a pretty holder for the dresser top. Another young child may classify animals as those with legs, those with wings, and those with neither. As they get older, they may find schoolteachers have ways of classifying them, not only into reading or math groups, but periodically on the basis of "A," "B," or "C" papers. On errands to the grocery store, they discover macaroni in the same department as spaghetti, pork chops somewhere near the ham, and apples just down from the miniature carrots (themselves part of larger groups like "carrots" and "root vegetables"). In reading the local newspaper, they observe that its staff has done some classifying for them, putting most of the comics together and seldom mixing sports stories with news of social affairs and marriage announcements (classifications based in turn on traditional categories of behavior). Eventually, they find courses neatly classified in college catalogs, and they know enough not to look for biology courses under "Social Science" or "Arts and Letters."

20 Classification also helps writers and readers sort through and 20
understand detailed information or ideas. It groups people, ideas, objects, experiences, or concepts according to shared qualities and helps point out patterns of relationships among them. For example, if you were writing an article to help people understand their personal characteristics, you might draw on the ancient Indian concept of "ayurveda," as does the author of the following paragraph.

> The three ayurvedic types (or doshas) are vata, pitta, and kapha. Vatas (space and air) are creative, thin people with light bones and dark hair and eyes who are light sleepers, dislike routine, and tend toward fear and anxiety when they're under stress. Pittas (fire and water) are medium built, light-eyed,

oily-skinned people who enjoy routine, make good leaders and initiators, are opinionated, and tend toward anger and frustration when they're under stress. Kaphas (water and earth) are amply built, thick-skinned and thick-haired people who are good at running projects, love leisure, sleep soundly, and tend to avoid difficult situations.

—Lynette Lamb, "Living the Ayurvedic Way"

Why Use Classification?

A classification creates groups on the basis of shared characteristics. It is a useful strategy when you are dealing with facts, events, or ideas whose differences are worth detailed examination. Many subjects that you may need to write and think about will remain a hodgepodge of facts and opinions unless you can find some system of analyzing the material, dividing the subject into categories, and classifying individual elements into those categories. The two patterns, **division** and **classification**, or *dividing* and *grouping*, move in different directions, at least to begin with. But when put in use for analysis and understanding, the two processes become inevitable companions that lead to a system of classification you can employ in your writing.

Expository writing both explains and informs, and classification is a pattern that enables writers to bring clarity to discussions of complicated subjects. Exercise programs, undergraduate majors, investment strategies, personal computers, ways to prepare for tests, even used cars—all these come in various types that are worth understanding. So, too, do other possible subjects for writing: behavior patterns; literary or anthropological theories; careers in engineering, business, or communications; management techniques; or environmental policies.

When readers encounter a classification, however, they expect more than a simple identification of categories. They look for an explanation of the qualities that distinguish each category and an explanation of the overall arrangement of the categories. In short, they expect the writer to provide a conclusion—a thesis—about the categories themselves, perhaps an explanation of why the subject falls into a particular set of categories or what implications the pattern of sorting has. A conclusion helps readers decide what to do with the information being presented; it helps them choose among alternatives, understand the specific uses of each set of policies or products; or grasp the implications of different psychological perspectives and social groupings.

Choosing a Strategy

If you choose to employ classification as a strategy for sharing information and ideas, your readers will expect you to take them into account from the beginning. They will want to know what information you are going to present and why it is important to them. They will expect you to make clear the purpose for your classification and the main idea or thesis tying it together.

25 From the start, therefore, you need to focus clearly on a **principle** 25 **of classification,** that is, the quality that members of each group share and what distinguishes them from the members of other groups. The simplest classifications form two groups, those with a particular quality and those without it: vegetarians and meat-eaters, closed-end mutual funds and open-ended funds, introverts and extroverts, environmentally sensitive policies and environmentally destructive policies. But such simple classifications often break down, usually because the differences among groups are matters of degree or level (varying levels of environmental sensitivity; different degrees of strictness in adhering to a vegetarian diet) and not absolute.

In creating a classification, then, you should choose a strategy that reflects your purpose for writing while allowing you to maintain clear and logical distinctions among the categories. If your purpose is to help people understand the dietary options available to them—vegan, ovo-lacto-vegetarian, avoidance of all meat except fish, and meat eating, for example—then your categories should be built around the kinds of food that people choose to include or avoid in their diet. In addition, the principle of classification should be consistent throughout the categories and complete with respect to the subject being investigated.

It would not be logical to divide movies into categories such as action films, science fiction films, romantic films, political films, serious films, and entertaining films because the principles of classification are not consistent and the categories therefore overlap: romantic films can be serious, entertaining, or both, for example. Likewise, it would not make sense to limit discussion of religious practices in North America to those of Christians, Jews, and Moslems because to do so would exclude, for example, the many people who identify themselves as Buddhists and Hindus. A more limited system might be appropriate, however, when discussing the religious backgrounds of residents in a particular region (southwest Louisiana, rural Mexico) or from a particular cultural or ethnic group (Hungarians, Native Americans in Alaska or northern Canada). Although your classification system need not be exhaustive, it should at the same time not omit significant numbers of whatever behaviors, people, or ideas you are planning to discuss.

In many cases, the pattern of classification you choose will also serve to organize your writing, as the following tentative plan for an essay illustrates.

Tentative Thesis

> People who love sports but have only limited athletic talent need not give up their dreams of a career in professional sports because being a player is only one of many career paths.

Category

> Name: administrators. Definition: people involved in management of sports teams. Members: managers, coaches, public relations specialists, personnel managers.

Category

> Name: medical staff. Definition: people concerned with physical and mental health of athletes. Members: trainers, team doctors, sports psychologists.

Category

> Name: facilities staff. Definition: people who create and maintain sports facilities. Members: sports architects and designers, engineers, groundskeepers, facilities managers.

Category

> Name: equipment specialists. Definition: people who design, manufacture, and sell sports equipment. Members: designers, testers, advertisers, manufacturing engineers, sales representatives.

A plan like this could logically include players' agents and legal representatives, people who work in financing sports, and people who arrange travel for sports teams. But although this would be a logical classification, it would be far too detailed for most readers. You should therefore limit the number of categories you present in an essay to avoid overwhelming and confusing your readers, but make sure you do not leave out any that are essential to the subject. Four categories of sports-related jobs should be enough to support and explain the writer's thesis (though some mention of sports broadcasting might be appropriate because most readers will expect discussion of the category). A brief mention of the other kinds of jobs, perhaps near the essay's conclusion, would help complete the classification without overburdening readers with detail.

Any plan like this seems almost absurdly obvious, of course—*after* the planning is done. It appears less obvious, however, to inexperienced writers who are dealing with a jumble of information they must explain to someone else. This is when writers should be aware of the patterns at their disposal, and one of the most useful of these, alone or combined with others, is classification.

Developing Categories

At the center of any essay employing classification are the paragraphs that present, explain, and illustrate categories. There is no single strategy for presenting categories, and the way you approach the task should vary according to your subject and purpose for writing. Nonetheless, many writers find the following techniques useful for alerting readers to the structure of an essay, structuring the presentation of categories, and making sure they present each category with enough explanatory detail.

- *Use Transitions:* You can make effective use of transitional terms to signal the beginning of a new category.

type	sort	trait	segment
category	kind	species	characteristic
class	aspect	element	component
part	subcategory	subset	group

- *Name the Categories:* To help identify categories and also help readers remember them, try giving each a name when you explain it. The names can be purely descriptive ("supporters/opponents/compromisers of the policy") or they can be somewhat imaginative ("lookers/browsers/testers/buyers").

- *Provide Detailed Examples:* To help readers visualize and understand each category, consider providing at least one extended example or a cluster of shorter ones. By making the examples detailed and specific, you help explain the categories while making them more memorable.

- *Explain:* Remind readers of the principle of classification, of the qualities that characterize a category, and of the ways it differs from other categories. Let them know, too, how the categories are related: Do they represent differing or contradictory approaches to a problem? Are they different products with similar functions? Will readers be faced with sharply differing options or a gradual range of choices?

Here is how one student, Hung Bui, put these techniques to work in a paragraph.

> Cigarettes play an even larger role in the lives of the next group, habitual smokers. They cannot quit as readily as the casual smoker can because of one key factor: habit. When the phone rings, they quickly grab an ashtray and cigarettes and chat. When having a cup of coffee in the morning, they simply must have a cigarette because "the coffee won't taste as good without it." And always, without fail, a good meal is followed by a good cigarette. Habitual smokers also smoke on a regular basis—a pack or two a day, never more, never less. They become irritated when they discover they are down to their last cigarette and rush to buy another pack. They also play games by buying only packs instead of cartons, rationalizing that because cigarettes aren't always on hand, they can't be smoking too much. They are constantly trying to cut down and tell everyone so, but never actually do, because in reality, smoking is an essential part of their lives.

Explaining by Means of *Comparison* and *Contrast*

One of the first expository methods we used as children was **comparison**, noticing similarities of objects, qualities, and actions, or **contrast**, noticing their differences. We compared the color of the new puppies with that of their mother, contrasted a parent's height with our own. Then the process became more complicated. Now we employ it frequently in college essay examinations or term papers when we compare or contrast forms of government, reproductive systems of animals, or ethical philosophies of humans. In the business or professional world, we prepare important reports based on comparison and contrast—between kinds of equipment for purchase, the personnel policies of different departments, or precedents in legal matters. Nearly all people use the process of comparison (meaning both *comparing* and *contrasting*) many times a day—in choosing a head of lettuce, in deciding what to wear to school, in selecting a house, or a friend, or a religion.

In expository writing, brief comparisons—a sentence or two—may serve to alert readers to similarities or highlight differences. Longer comparisons need to do more; they need to explore the subject and convey the writer's perspective. For a longer comparison or contrast that explains or explores ideas, you need an ordered plan to avoid having a mere list of characteristics or a frustrating jumble of similarities and differences. You also need to give attention to all the important points of similarity (or difference). The following paragraph accomplishes all these things.

> We really are terribly confused about our relationship with nature. On the one hand, we like to live in houses that are tidy and clean, and if nature should be rude enough to enter—in the form of a bat in the attic, or a mouse in the kitchen, or a cockroach crawling along the skirting boards— we stalk it with the blood-lust of a tabby cat; we resort to chemical warfare. In fact, we judge people harshly if their house is full of dust and dirt. And yet, on the other hand, we just as obsessively bring nature indoors. We touch a switch and light floods the room. We turn a dial and suddenly it feels like summer or winter. We live in a perpetual breeze or bake of our devising. We buy posters and calendars with photographs of nature. We hang paintings of landscapes on our walls. We scent everything that touches our lives. We fill our houses with flowers and pets. We try hard to remove ourselves from all the dramas and sensations of nature, and yet without them we feel lost and disconnected. So, subconsciously, we bring them right back indoors again. Then we obsessively visit nature—we go swimming, jogging, or cross-country skiing, we take strolls in a park. Confusing, isn't it?
>
> —Diane Ackerman, *Deep Play*

Why Use Comparison?

Highlighting similarities and differences is the most obvious use for comparison, but merely a starting point for effective writing. Whenever you employ the pattern, therefore, make sure you give it a worthwhile

457

purpose. You can contrast llamas with potbellied pigs, for example, but your efforts will likely seem silly or trivial unless tied to some larger goal, as in the case of Judith Stone's essay, "Personal Beast," in which she contrasts their relatively suitability as pets.

The question of purpose is especially important in a formal, full-scale analysis by comparison and contrast where the pattern lends shape to an entire essay. Sometimes the purpose may be merely to reveal *surprising or frequently overlooked likenesses and differences,* with the goal of adding to readers' knowledge, satisfying their curiosity, or developing their self-awareness. For example, an essay on generational differences over responsibility for housework might explain that younger people are more likely to share the work of cooking and cleaning, but that all generations seem to be maintaining traditional gender differences in the responsibility of home maintenance. Mark Twain, in the selection "Two Ways of Seeing a River," contrasts his view of the Mississippi as a young man with his perspective as an experienced river pilot. In doing so, he helps readers understand how radically experience and changes in attitude can affect our perceptions of the external world—even making the same stretch of scenery appear a different place.

The aim may be to show *the superiority* of one thing over another. Or it may be to *explain* and *evaluate,* as in a discussion of alternatives or of differing points of view on an issue. For instance, you might examine competing proposals for an antismoking campaign, one designed by teenagers and the other by advertising professionals, evaluating the strengths and limitations of each.

Choosing a Strategy

To take a comparison beyond the obvious and develop knowledge and insight worth sharing with readers, you need to begin by identify-ing **points of comparison** (or **points of contrast**), both major and minor. Some important points of comparison will be apparent to you (and your readers) from the outset, and therefore should be part of your analysis. Others will be less apparent, though not necessarily less important. Including them will enable you to provide a fresh or more thorough perspective, adding to your reader's understanding. Con-sider using the following questions to identify and explore points of comparison, adapted, of course, to the particular demands of your subjects.

What are the similar (or different) **physical aspects** (shape, color, size, texture, movement) of the subjects you are analyzing?

Parts and Processes (elements and their relationships, methods of operation, instructions)?
Benefits (individual, social, political, environmental)?
Problems (dangers, difficulties, limitations)?
Costs (financial, emotional, political)?
Uses (personal, social, environmental; to provide benefits, to create relationships, to accomplish a particular goal)?

As you develop responses to questions like these, keep in mind that you are trying to develop fresh insights both for yourself and your readers. Consider using questions like these to help you develop such a perspective.

What similarities (or differences) are readers likely to consider....

Intriguing or surprising?
Useful or worth learning about?
Quite different from what they expected before they began reading?
Significant enough to make them more likely to consider different opinions on an issue or approaches to a problem?
Important enough to guide their choice among alternative policies, products, or conclusions?

The points of comparison you choose, along with your tentative thesis, your purpose for writing, and the complexity of your materials, will usually suggest an arrangement for your writing. The number of subjects making up any comparison (two or more) and the likelihood that you will be exploring multiple points of comparison along with their supporting details mean that you should plan the organization of an essay carefully and remember to make this arrangement clear to readers.

One of the two basic methods of comparison is to present all the information on the two (or more) subjects, one at a time, and to summarize by combining their most important similarities and differences. Here is a subject-by-subject plan for an essay.

Subject-by-Subject Pattern
Introduction
Subjects: Bella Costa Medical Center (curing illness) and Foothills Regional Health Complex (creating wellness)

Tentative Thesis: Today's health care dilemmas have gone beyond choices among insurance plans to choices between two very different kinds of medical treatment: one focused on curing illness (represented by Bella Costa M.C.), the other focused on creating wellness (represented by Foothills R.H.C.).

Subject 1: Bella Costa Medical Center

    Feature 1: Traditional medicine—curing illness

    Feature 2: Large hospital, newest equipment

    Feature 3: Large staff of physicians

    Feature 4: Emphasis on drugs, surgery, physical therapy

Subject 2: Foothills Regional Health Complex

    Feature 1: Preventive medicine—creating wellness

    Feature 2: Small hospital, limited facilities, local clinics

    Feature 3: Some physicians, other staff including nutritionists, exercise specialists, and alternative therapists

    Feature 4: Emphasis on diet, exercise, alternative therapies (acupuncture, holistic medicine), healthy lifestyle

Conclusion (summary): Summarize reasons for choosing either one and suggest that personal preferences may play an important role.

45   This method may be desirable if there are few points to compare, 45 or if the individual points are less important than the overall picture they present.

However, if there are several points of comparison to be considered, or if the points are of individual importance, alternation of the material would be a better arrangement.

Point-by-Point Pattern

Subjects: *The Mummy* (1932) starring Boris Karloff

    The Mummy (1999) starring Brendan Fraser

Tentative Thesis: The original version of *The Mummy* (1932) takes itself and the horror movie form seriously and provides an often scary portrait of evil. The remake (1999) takes itself only half-seriously and gently pokes fun at the conventions of the horror movie, so it is only occasionally scary and conveys no sense of evil.

Subject 1: Original version of *The Mummy*

    Feature 1 (acting): Boris Karloff, serious acting style, dramatic scenes and speeches

Feature 2 (script): Provides motivation for characters, emphasizes force of evil desires

Feature 3 (special effects): Support story line, emphasize unnatural desires and presence of evil

Subject 2: Remake of *The Mummy*

Feature 1 (acting): Brendan Fraser, comic or ironic acting style, action scenes and physical comedy

Feature 2 (script): Little motivation for characters, highlights stereotypes and conventions of horror movies

Feature 3 (special effects): Call attention to themselves, emphasize unreal and exaggerated elements of horror stories

Conclusion (summary):

Original and remake show changing attitudes toward the horror movie as a portrait of evil.

Often the subject matter or the purpose itself will suggest a more casual treatment, or some combination or variation of the two basic methods. We might present the complete information on the first subject, then summarize it point by point within the complete information on the second. And although expository comparisons and contrasts are frequently handled together, it is sometimes best to present all similarities first, then all differences—or vice versa, depending on the emphasis desired. In any basic use of comparison, the important thing is to have a plan that suits the purpose and material, thoughtfully worked out in advance.

Developing Comparisons

In writing an essay using comparison as a primary pattern of exposition, keep these two important tasks in mind: 1) take care that your comparisons are logical and arranged in a manner that will be clear to your readers, and 2) provide detailed explanations of the similarities and differences in order to support your conclusions.

Above all, your comparison needs to be *logical*. A logical comparison or contrast can be made only between subjects of the same general type. (Analogy, a special form of comparison used for another purpose, is discussed in the next section.) For example, contrasting modern medicine (prescription drugs, surgery) and traditional medicine (herbal remedies, acupuncture) could be useful or meaningful, but little would be gained by contrasting surgery and carpentry.

50

50

Transition words and phrases are a big help with both logic and the arrangement of an essay, reminding you of an essay's plan as you write and signaling the arrangement to readers. Some transition words identify the elements of a subject, some indicate logical relationships or highlight the place of a paragraph in the overall organization, and some identify conclusions and supporting detail.

Elements of a Subject: trait, characteristic, element, part, segment, unit, feature

Logical Relationships and Arrangement: in comparison, in contrast, on the other side, on the other hand, likewise, moreover, similarly, in the same (or different) manner, in addition, then, further, yet, but, however, nonetheless, first, second, third, although, still

Conclusions and Supporting Detail: in conclusion, to sum up, finally, for example, for instance

Paragraphs are especially important in writing that compares or contrasts. Typically, they are devoted to one of the major steps in the exposition, often to one of the main points of comparison. In focusing on points of similarity or dissimilarity, be thorough. Provide facts, concrete details, and examples. Consider those that support your conclusions or recommendations as well as those that provide contrary evidence. Remember, too, that effective comparisons serve a purpose, so include details that support your overall thesis and further the purpose for which you are writing.

Explaining Through *Process Analysis*

Process analysis focuses on *how* something happens. As an expository pattern, it appears most frequently in *instructions* that tell us how to do something or in *explanations* that explain how something is or was done. Instructions can range from the simple and everyday to the complex and challenging: from the directions for using a new appliance or piece of electronic equipment to a detailed plan showing how to make the United Nations more effective. Effective instructions do more than simply list the steps to be taken. They generally provide detailed justification for individual steps or for the plan as a whole, and they take into account readers' background knowledge and abilities.

Explanations, on the other hand, might explain the stages of a wide variety of operations or actions, of mental or evolutionary process—how stress affects judgment and health, how volcanoes cause earthquakes and mudslides, or how digital telephones work. Effective explanations take into account the things readers want or need to know about, but they can also appeal to curiosity and imagination. You can speculate how space exploration might work or how societies might be better organized.

55   The following process analysis by L. Rust Hills shows how   55 process analysis can be used in imaginative ways to talk about everyday matters. It takes the form of a set of directions, and though it is short, it is a whole essay in miniature. The second example is an explanation that helps readers understand some of the reasons hurricanes can be so dangerous.

What to Do About Soap Ends

This is admittedly not a problem qualitative on the order of what to do about the proliferation of nuclear weaponry, but quantitatively it disturbs a great deal of Mankind—all those millions, in fact, who've ever used a bar of soap—except, of course, me. I've solved the problem of what to do about those troublesome, wasteful, messy little soap ends, and I'm ready now to deliver my solution to a grateful world.

The solution depends on a fact not commonly known, which I discovered in the shower. Archimedes made his great discovery about displacement ("Eureka!" and all that) in the bathtub, but I made mine in the shower. It is not commonly known that if, when you soap yourself, you hold *the same side* of the bar of soap cupped in the palm of your hand, that side will, after a few days, become curved and rounded, while the side of the bar you're soaping yourself *with* will become flat. (In between showers or baths, leave the bar curved side down so it won't stick to whatever it's resting on.) When the bar diminishes sufficiently, the flat side can be pressed onto a new bar of soap and will adhere sufficiently overnight to become, with the next day's use, a just slightly oversized new bar, ready to be treated in the same way as the one that came before it, in perpetuity, one bar after another, down through the length of your days on earth, with never a nasty soap end to trouble you ever again. Eureka, and now on to those nuclear weapons. Man is at his best, I feel, when in his problem-solving mode.

—L. Rust Hills

It's not the wind, though, that's the most dangerous part of a hurricane. It's the water, especially when something called the "storm surge" occurs. As the low-pressure eye of the hurricane sits over the ocean, the sea level literally rises into a dome of water. For every inch drop in barometric pressure, the ocean rises a foot higher. Now, out at sea, that means nothing. The rise is not even noticeable. But when that mound of water starts moving toward land, the situation becomes crucial. As the water approaches a shallow beach, the dome of water rises. It may rise ten to fifteen feet in an hour and span fifty miles. Like a marine bulldozer, the surge may rise up twenty feet high, crash onto land, and wash everything away. Then with six- to eight-foot waves riding atop this mound of water, the storm surge destroys buildings, trees, cars, and anything else in its path. It's this storm surge that accounts for 90 percent of the deaths during a hurricane.

—Ira Flatow, "Storm Surge"

Why Use Process Analysis?

In almost every part of our lives, we rely on **instructions**. They help us cook a meal, repair a car, get to a vacation spot, perform an experiment, and calculate income tax. Essays offering instruction appear in newspapers, magazines, and books on topics from fashion, fitness, and sports to technology, pets, and personal relationships.

We turn to **explanations** not when we want to do things but when we want to understand how things work. Explanations can focus on mechanical or technical subjects (how computer operating systems work), on social matters (how societies create groups of insiders and outsiders), on psychological topics (how stress builds up), or on natural subjects (how cancer cells take over from normal cells).

Process analysis can have imaginative uses as well, helping us speculate about building floating cities, changing our diets for better

464

health, or considering steps that might close the ozone hole over the South Pole. Writers sometimes explain a process in order to amuse or criticize—analyzing with a critical eye some aspects of behavior (as do Kilbourne and Mitford in this chapter) or looking at some surprising natural phenomenon. And process analysis often appears in combination with other expository patterns. You might use it to help readers understand the steps by which a cause (such as meditating) leads to an effect (reduced physical and mental stress), for example. Or you might explain differences in the processes of forming social relationships as part of an essay contrasting the behaviors of men and women.

Expository writing built around process analysis generally responds to a need for information and understanding. The need may be immediate (how to prepare for an upcoming sales meeting or an exam). It may be practical or helpful (understanding the ways our bodies respond to stress; strategies for incorporating a healthy diet and exercise into a busy schedule). Or it may be a matter of curiosity or a desire for understanding (discovering how puppeteers in Indonesia create hours-long shows that appeal to both children and adults; investigating the ways our brains process information).

Choosing a Strategy

Having encountered instructions and explanations many times before, your readers will probably expect you to employ some basic strategies. For example, they will expect the opening of a set of instructions to announce its purpose, establish the need for a step-by-step explanation of the process, and indicate any materials needed to accomplish it. The way you choose to accomplish these things should vary from situation to situation and topic to topic, however. If you are addressing a need your readers can readily recognize, such as finding effective ways to take a test, make a speech, or apply for a student loan, you might begin with a brief example of how important such knowledge is. Or you might even state the need directly: "Would you like to know how to give a speech without getting so flustered that you forget half of what you planned to say?" or "Wouldn't you like to know how to get a student loan without all the hassle and paperwork most people encounter?"

In many instances, however, you will have to convince readers that they ought to be interested in the instructions you are offering. This is the situation Heather Kaye faced when she decided to tell readers how to play the game "Bones." In response, she created an opening paragraph reminding her readers how often they get bored and telling them of the simple equipment they will need to pass the time with an amusing game.

> When boredom strikes, what can you do if you are tired of computer games, don't like chess, and don't have the money or time to go to a movie? Just collect a pad of paper, a pen, six dice, and a friend, and you are ready to play a game called "Bones." Bones provides fun and excitement, and you don't have to be Einstein to learn how to play. It is a game of chance and luck, laughter and friendship.

65   For an explanation, however, you may need to appeal to readers' curiosity or their desire for understanding (practical or otherwise). Emphasizing the mystery, adventure, or even oddity of a process will engage most readers' curiosity: What bodily processes allow pearl divers to stay underwater for several minutes when most of us can hold our breath for only ten or twenty seconds? How do bats produce a kind of "radar" that enables them to fly in the dark and catch minute insects? When you appeal to readers' desire for understanding, you will be most likely to succeed when you suggest a practical dimension for the knowledge. For instance, some readers interested in the natural world may be interested in the complex stages of the honey-making process. Yet to attract the majority of readers you may need to suggest that such knowledge can help them understand honey's virtues as a sweetener or choose among different kinds of honey as they shop.

Most process analyses are organized into simple, chronological units, either the *steps* involved in accomplishing the task or the *stages* of operation. In planning a set of instructions, begin by breaking it down into steps, approaching the activity as if you were doing it for the first time so that you do not leave out any necessary elements that have become so routine you might easily overlook them. Then create an organization that will help readers keep track of the many steps, perhaps dividing the task into several units, each containing smaller steps. Consider building your plan around a framework like the following.

Introduction: Need for the information, materials, statement of purpose
Step 1: Explanations, details
    Substeps 1, 2, 3…. (if any)

Step 2: Explanations, details
    Substeps 1, 2, 3....
Step 3: Explanations, details
    Substeps 1, 2, 3....
Summary (if necessary)

In planning an explanation, identify the various stages or components, including any that overlap, and create an organization that presents them in an easy-to-follow, logical order. If the process is complex, divide it into major components and subdivide each in turn, just as the following rough plan does.

Introduction (tentative thesis identifying need for the information): Because most people do not understand the amount of energy, natural resources, and human effort needed to create paper, they use it wastefully; understanding the process and the resources it requires is an important first step for all of us concerned with preserving our environment.
Stage 1: Bringing together natural resources
    a. Wood—logging
    b. Water—drawing from rivers or lakes
    c. Fuel for heat and power (oil, gas, or electric)
Stage 2: Turning logs into pulp
    a. Grinding up logs (uses water and power) *or*
    b. Breaking wood into pulp using chemicals
Stage 3: Turning pulp into paper
    a. Paper machine
        1. Feeding pulp into machine
        2. Using heated screen to congeal pulp into a mushy sheet of paper
    b. Dryer
        1. Using heat to further congeal pulp
        2. Using rollers to stretch and thin the sheet (consumes energy)
Stage 4: Turning paper into paper products (energy and labor intensive)
    a. Creating giant rolls of paper
    b. Cutting and folding rolls of paper into tissues, newsprint, pads, paper towels, and other everyday products

Maintaining the exact order of a process is sometimes of greatest importance, as in a recipe. But occasionally the organization of an analysis may present problems. You may need to interrupt the step-by-step format to give descriptions, definitions, and other explanatory asides. Some processes may even defy a strict chronological treatment because several things occur simultaneously. In explaining the operating process of a gasoline engine, for example, you would be unable to convey at once everything that happens at the same time. Instead, you would need to present the material in *general* stages, each with subdivisions, so your readers could see each stage by itself yet also become aware of interacting relationships.

Developing a Process Analysis

In developing the paragraphs and sentences that make up an explanation of a process, you also need to pay attention to your readers' expectations. When you are presenting instructions, your readers will expect you to tell them of any necessary materials and will look for frequent summaries to allow them to check if they have followed the steps correctly. They will benefit from warnings of special difficulties they may encounter or any dangers the procedure entails. In addition, they will appreciate words of encouragement ("The procedure may seem strange, but it *will* work") or reminders of the goal of the process ("No pain, no gain: the only way to a flat tummy is through the hard work of repeating these exercises").

70   Effective explanations and instructions alike often have a visual   70 element. Drawings can show how the parts of a mechanism fit together or help readers recognize the differences among the elements of a natural process, such as the growth of an insect or the eruption of a volcano. Pictures can help readers identify ingredients or components and show them what a finished product will look like.

To guide readers through the steps or stages of a process, to remind them of changes that will occur, or to highlight the sequence of events, consider using words that point out relationships among the various elements.

Words identifying different stages—*step, event, element, component, phase, state, feature, occurrence*

Words emphasizing relationships in time—*after, next, while, first, second, third, fourth, concurrently, the next week, later, preceding, following*

Words indicating changes—*becomes, varies, transforms, causes, completes, alters, revises, uncovers, synthesizes, cures, builds*

Make sure you include enough details to allow readers to visualize the steps or stages of the process, but not so many that the details become confusing. Present major steps (or stages) in considerable detail, minor ones in less. If you choose to write in the second person (*you*), as in a set of directions ("You should then blend the ingredients"), make sure you use this point of view consistently and do not shift to the first person (*I* or *we*) or the third person (*he, she, it*, or *they*) without good reason. If you choose the first person or third person for your perspective, make sure likewise that your presentation is consistent.

Analyzing *Cause-and-Effect* Relationships

Writing built around cause-effect analysis addresses questions like "Why did that happen?" and "What is likely to happen next?" It can grow from simple curiosity about the *why* of events or from a practical desire to avoid unpleasant or unforeseen consequences. Above all, cause-effect analysis focuses on relationships, the links between one phenomenon and another. When you employ the pattern in expository writing, you need to do more than identify possible causes or consequences. You need to establish a reasonable relationship among them by showing how both logic and the available evidence point to the relationship. After all, two things that often occur together, such as storms and tornadoes, are not *necessarily* related. Since many storms occur without the accompaniment of tornadoes, a cause-effect analysis would focus first on identifying those kinds of storms frequently associated with the appearance of tornadoes, then isolate specific causal features that can be demonstrably linked to funnel clouds and destructive winds.

A search for cause and effect can be rigorously scientific ("Researchers debate possible links between caffeine consumption and heart disease") or it can be personal ("Why do I always end up arguing with my parents over things we all know are unimportant?"). It can take the form of causal analysis, trying to identify all the links in a causal chain: remote causes, necessary conditions, and direct causes to immediate effects and more distant consequences. Or it can identify the many conditions and forces that work together in no particular pattern to shape a person's life, create a particular situation, or help bring about events.

75   Most expository uses of the pattern do not require scientific rigor, 75 however. For social or cultural events, like the growth of a political movement or the rise of a new form of art, we can seldom hope to pinpoint exact causes and effects. Instead, we can identify the roots of contemporary phenomena and develop an awareness of the kinds of changes that may be going on today. This is the kind of explanation provided by the following paragraph, which looks at the early development of a popular kind of music.

> Rap started in the discos, not the midtown glitter palaces like Studio 54 or New York, New York, but at Mel Quinn's on 42nd Street and Club 371 in the Bronx, where a young Harlemite who called himself D.J. Hollywood spun on the weekends. It wasn't unusual for black club jocks to talk to their audiences in the jive style of the old personality deejays. Two of the top black club spinners of the day, Pete (D.J.) Jones and Maboya, did so. Hollywood, just an adolescent when he started, created a more complicated, faster style, with more rhymes than his older mentors and call-and-response passages to encourage reaction from the dancers. At local bars, discos, and many illegal after-hours spots frequented by street people, Hollywood developed a huge word-of-mouth reputation. Tapes of his parties began appearing around the city on the then new and incredibly loud Japanese portable cassette players flooding into America. In Harlem, Kurtis Blow, Eddie Cheeba, and D.J. Lovebug Star-ski; in the Bronx, Junebug Star-ski, Grandmaster Flash, and Melle Mel; in Brooklyn, two kids from the projects called Whodini; and in Queens, Russell and Joey, the two youngest sons from the middle-class Simmons household—all shared a fascination with Hollywood's use of the rhythmic breaks in his club mixes and his verbal dexterity. These kids would all grow up to play a role in the local clubs and, later, a few would appear on the national scene to spread Hollywood's style. Back in the 1970s, while disco reigned in the media, the Black Main Streets of New York were listening to D.J. Hollywood, and learning.

—Nelson George, *The Death of Rhythm and Blues*

Why Use Cause-Effect Analysis?

Some causes and effects are not very complicated; at least their explanation requires only a simple statement. New parking facilities are not built because a college (or town) lacks the money in its budget. But frequently a much more thorough analysis is required. New parking facilities are not built partly because of expense and partly because they simply seem to encourage more traffic and rapidly become jammed. The college (or town) delays the project until it can study *why* parking facilities quickly become overloaded. In writing, cause-effect as an expository pattern helps address these kinds of complicated relationships.

Writers often respond to puzzling or intriguing phenomena with causal explanations. In its simplest form, the strategy consists of a description of a puzzling phenomenon (the persistence of alcoholism in families, for example) followed by an explanation or an examination of possible causes. The simplicity of this pattern gives it considerable power and flexibility. Writers speculating about social patterns and individual behavior often use the strategy or vary it to consider possible consequences. In dealing with effects, the strategy consists of discussion of a new or previously unnoticed phenomenon whose consequences are unfamiliar followed by consideration of its likely effects, or it begins with discussion of desired effects followed by examination of actions or arrangements most likely to produce these consequences.

Causal explanations appear frequently in academic and research writing. Scholars often look for a particularly puzzling element in a subject or for a point over which there has been much disagreement and then build an essay in an attempt to explain the phenomena: "Perhaps the most interesting feature of early jazz is…."; "Over the last decade researchers have argued about the role of aggressive behavior in corporate organizations…."

Choosing a Strategy

To explain fully the causes of a phenomenon, writers must seek not only *immediate* causes (the ones encountered first) but also *ultimate* causes (the basic, underlying factors that help to explain the more apparent ones). Business or professional people, as well as students, often have a pressing need for this type of analysis. How else could they fully understand or report on a failing sales campaign, diminishing

471

church membership, a local increase in traffic accidents, or a decline in crime and the use of drugs? The immediate cause of a disastrous warehouse fire could be faulty electrical wiring, but this might be attributed in turn to the company's unwise economic measures, which might be traced even further to undue pressures on the management to show large profits. The written analysis might logically stop at any point of course, with the actual strategy a writer employs depending on the purpose of the writing and the audience for which it is intended.

80 Similarly, both the immediate and ultimate *effects* of an action or 80 situation may, or may not, need to be fully explored. If a 5 percent pay raise is granted, what will be the immediate effect on the cost of production, leading to what ultimate effects on prices and, in some cases, on the economy of a business, a town, or perhaps the entire region?

Whatever the extent of the reasoning your writing task demands, you need to make certain strategic choices. Will you focus on causes, effects, or both? Will you focus on a single clear chain of causes and effects or provide a more general discussion, highlighting many contributing factors? How will you use the opening of your writing to convince readers of the importance of understanding the causes or effects of a phenomenon or situation and interest them in reading about the topic?

Because causes and effects often form intricate, potentially confusing relationships, you should develop a straightforward plan for your writing—an organization that will help readers understand the order you have discovered within the complexity. This is particularly important when a phenomenon has multiple causes, as in the following example.

Introduction: Example of a diverse audience at a horror movie responding with fear and pleasure to the film

Tentative thesis: People choose to watch horror films for many different reasons, each depending on the individual's taste and psychological makeup.

Cause 1: The "thrill" of being shocked and scared

Support: Some people are psychologically disposed to get pleasure from danger, especially when it is imaginary.

Support: Certain people's brain chemistry may mean that they (like people who engage in extreme sports) get a feeling of well-being after feeling that they have placed themselves in danger.

Cause 2: The twists and turns of the plot
Support: Many people enjoy the kinds of complicated, surprising plots they find in horror movies (similar in some ways to the kinds of plots people enjoy in adventure stories).
Cause 3: The pleasure of "escape"
Support: The dangers faced by characters in the films allow viewers to escape for a short time from their somewhat less serious but more real everyday problems.
Cause 4: Fashion
Support: Horror movies are popular. Going to them with friends and talking about them afterwards is a pleasant social experience.
Summary

Your writing will need to do more than identify causes and effects. It will need to provide readers with evidence that you have correctly identified the relationships. As a result, much writing that employs this pattern relies on detailed research. Printed sources, television documentaries, and interviews can provide you with useful information. You should keep such research focused, however, so you don't stray too far into areas that are interesting but not really related to the causes or consequences you will be discussing.

Developing Cause-Effect Analysis

Discussions of causes and effects can easily become complex and confusing, so consider using the following strategies for alerting readers to the relationships among causes and effects. A concise statement near the beginning of an essay can point out relationships you plan to examine. Statements in the body of an essay can remind readers of the points you are making and the supporting details and reasoning you are providing. Likewise, terms that identify causes and effects or that indicate their relationships can help guide readers' attention:

result	effect	accomplishment	development
outcome	antecedent	source	first
cause	instrument	as a result	second
means	thus	motive	third
consequence	reason	agent	next

When you analyze causes and effects, your readers must always have confidence in the thoroughness and logic of your reasoning. Here are some ways to avoid the most common faults in causal reasoning:

1. Never mistake the fact that something happens with or after another occurrence as evidence of a causal relationship—for example, that a black cat crossing the road caused the flat tire a few minutes later, or that a course in English composition caused a student's nervous breakdown that same semester.

2. Consider all possible relevant factors before attributing causes. Perhaps studying English did result in a nervous breakdown, but the cause may also have been ill health, trouble at home, the stress of working while attending college, or the anguish of a love affair. (The composition course, by providing an "emotional" outlet, may even have helped postpone the breakdown!)

3. Support the analysis by more than mere assertions: offer evidence. It would not often be enough to *tell* why Shakespeare's wise Othello believed the villainous Iago—the dramatist's lines should be used as evidence, possibly supported by the opinions of at least one literary scholar. If you are explaining that capital punishment deters crime, do not expect the reader to take your word for it—give before-and-after statistics or the testimony of reliable authorities.

4. Be careful not to omit any links in the chain of causes or effects unless you are certain that the readers for whom the writing is intended will automatically make the right connections themselves—and this is frequently a dangerous assumption. To unwisely omit one or more of the links might leave the reader with only a vague, or even erroneous, impression of the causal connection, possibly invalidating all that follows and thus making the entire writing ineffective.

5. Be honest and objective. Writers (or thinkers) who bring their old prejudices to the task of casual analysis, or who fail to see the probability of *multiple* causes or effects, are almost certain to distort their analyses or to make them so superficial, so thin, as to be almost worthless.

Using *Definition* to Help Explain

Few barriers to communication are as great as those created by key terms or concepts that have various meanings or shades of meaning. For this reason, expository writing often provides definitions of words and ideas whose precise meaning is important to the writer's purpose. Sometimes **definitions** merely clarify meanings of concrete or noncontroversial terms. This simple process is similar to that often used in dictionaries:

1. providing a synonym, for example
   cinema: a motion picture
   or
2. placing the word in a class and then showing how it differs from others of the same class, for example

Term	Class	Details

   metheglin: an alcoholic liquor made of fermented honey

Often, however, definitions specify the meanings of abstract, unusual, or newly minted terms. Definitions of this sort are particularly useful when the experiences or knowledge of readers does little to help them with the meaning of a term or idea that is nonetheless a key element of an overall explanation.

Sometimes a term or concept (or perhaps a process, a natural phenomenon, a group of people, or a relationship) is itself the subject of an explanation, leading to an *extended definition,* as in the following example.

> This is *orienteering,* a mixture of marathon, hike, and scavenger hunt, a cross-country race in which participants must locate a series of markers set in unfamiliar terrain by means of map and compass. The course, which may range from an acre of city park to twenty square miles of wilderness, is dotted with anywhere from four to fifteen "controls," red-and-white flags whose general locations are marked on the map by small circles. At each control there is a paper punch that produces a distinctive pattern on a card the racer carries. In most events the order in which the card must be punched is fixed; the route taken to reach each control, however, is up to the participant.
>
> —Linton Robinson, "Marathoning with Maps"

Extended definitions may take a paragraph or two or may be the primary pattern for all or most of an essay, depending on the complexity of the subject being defined, the amount of controversy or confusion it has generated, the likely interest of readers in the discussion, and the writer's purpose.

Why Use Definition?

When your subject requires you to write about terms, ideas, or phenomena likely to be unfamiliar to your audience, or when the concepts and words you are using have conflicting or controversial meanings, then you probably need to prepare an extended definition for your readers. For years, discussions of how much people work each week excluded housework and other time spent on activities important to home and family. The definition of *work* included only labor outside the home for a specific wage. Women were rightly angered by this definition, which excluded the hours many of them labored creating homes and maintaining families. If you were to write today about how much work people do in an average week, you would need to provide an extended definition of work including such activities. Few people would argue your definition, but they would expect you to be aware of the different (and conflicting) meanings of the term and to make your choice among them clear. If some readers are likely to disagree with your choice, however, you will need to present reasons for it. You might even need to stipulate (or dictate) the meaning of the term as you use it in the essay so that your audience will not misread your essay by substituting their preferred meaning for your own.

When your writing focuses on a fashion, artistic trend, social phenomenon, political movement, or set of ideas or behaviors whose impact is widespread enough to interest most readers but new enough to require definition, you might consider creating an essay that presents an *informative definition*, one that explores and explains the various aspects of your subject. In contrast, when your readers already have some ideas about your subject, but you think these ideas (or perspectives) need to be changed, you could create a *redefinition* essay. A redefinition begins with the ideas readers hold and tries to substitute new and different ones. For example, people often try to make pets of wild animals because they consider the creatures cute, cuddly, or amusing. You might attempt to redefine the favorable images people hold of animals like koala bears, monkeys, boa constrictors, ocelots, or raccoons to show that these and similar creatures are likely to make troublesome, unpleasant, or even dangerous pets.

Choosing a Strategy
Extended definitions, unlike the simple dictionary type, follow no set pattern. Often when extended definitions are part of an essay, readers are not specifically aware of the process of definition. This lack of specific awareness arises because the definitions are frequently part of the overall subject, are written in the same tone as the rest of the exposition, and are closely tied to the writer's thesis and purpose.

When an extended definition is the primary pattern for an essay, however, the essay itself may follow one of several broad strategies. An informative definition often begins by explaining the reason for the subject's current importance as well as the need to define it. It may then move to a brief, sometimes formal definition; continue with a discussion of the historical background and present instances; and conclude with a review of the subject's features. The following informal plan for an essay includes these strategies in an order appropriate to the subject.

Introduction
> Tentative thesis: If you look carefully at your calendar for the month of December, you are likely to come across the holiday Kwanzaa, which may be unfamiliar to you but which is celebrated each year by an increasing number of your friends, coworkers, and neighbors.
> Current importance: Examples

Definition
> Brief formal definition
> Historical background
> Features: Seven principles, various activities, clothing, participants, meaning of celebration, food, stories, and materials and resources
> Present instances: Current and growing popularity

Conclusion: Summary and sources for further information

A redefinition essay grows from the assumption that readers already have some ideas about the subject but these ideas should be modified or discarded altogether. Redefinitions often begin in the same matter as informative definitions—by creating interest in the topic. Then they generally proceed to mention the ways the subject is normally interpreted, following each with an alternate interpretation, or redefinition. Or they review various aspects of the subject and suggest fresh ways of looking at each.

Developing Definitions

95 A definition helps writers and readers agree on the meaning of a term, 95 concept, or phenomenon by providing answers to some important questions. As you develop a definition, try keeping in mind the questions you will need to address in order to help readers understand your subject. These sample questions can provide a start.

For subjects that can be observed, measured, and known:	For concepts, values, or terms whose meaning depends on the ways people use them:
What are its features?	How do people use it?
What is its history?	What has its meaning been historically, and how has the meaning changed?
What does it do?	
What doesn't it do?	
	How is this set of values or concepts different from others? Similar?

Definitions use many familiar techniques of expository writing, including examples, comparisons, and classifications. There are, however, some techniques peculiar to definition. You can give the *background* of a word, answering the question "What is the history of the term or concept?" (that is, its *etymology*) and providing valuable hints to its meanings. For example, *catholic* originally, in ancient times, meant pertaining to the universal Christian church. Its present meaning—of or concerning the Roman Catholic Church—retains some of the original force because the Roman Catholic Church views itself as the direct descendant of the ancient, undivided Christian church.

You can also enumerate the *characteristics* of the term or subject, sometimes isolating an essential one for special treatment. In defining a social group, such as triathletes, for example, you might list the physical qualities they share (endurance, strength, versatility, and exceptional fitness), their mental qualities (high endurance for pain, desire to exceed normal levels of achievement, and pleasure in physical exertion), and their social preferences (tolerance for solitary training routines, desire to excel, and preference for individual achievement rather than group membership). In so doing, you would be explaining the common elements that define the group and distinguish it from other groups.

You might define by *negation*, sometimes called "exclusion" or "differentiation," by showing what is *not* the meaning of the term, concept, or phenomenon. (This is an important technique for a redefinition essay.) To do this, you answer the question, "What is it *not?*": "*Intelligence* is neither a puzzle-solving activity that enables people to do well on a standardized example like the SAT or ACT, nor the ability to remember columns of facts and figures that may have no real use." If you employ this technique, however, remember that readers will expect you also to provide a positive definition, indicating what the definition *is* as well as what it *is not*.

But perhaps the most dependable techniques for defining are basic expository patterns. You can illustrate the meaning of a term or define a phenomenon by drawing *examples* from your own experience, from newspaper or online reports, from books and magazines, or from interviews and surveys. For instance, you might help explain the range of behaviors included in the term *deviant behavior* by offering examples not only of thieves, drug dealers, and pornographers, but also of people who live alone in the wilderness for spiritual enlightenment or who participate in dangerous sports. You might even include yourself in the category by telling how you climbed the side of a glacier or parachuted from a bridge into a river gorge. Or you might define by *classifying*, sorting kinds of deviant behavior into those that are socially acceptable, even honorable (the search for spiritual enlightenment); those that are harmful only to the individual (dangerous sports); and those that harm other people (thievery and other activities generally considered criminal).

100   *Comparisons* are useful, too, both those that identify *synonyms* 100 (*naive* means innocent, unsophisticated, natural, unaffected, and artless) or that distinguish among concepts with similar, though not identical, meanings, such as *consensus* (general agreement among a group of people on their attitude toward an issue or problem) and *dissensus* (general agreement among a group of people on the ways

their attitudes toward an issue or problem differ). Comparisons respond to the question "What is the subject like or unlike?" So, too, do *similes* and *metaphors,* two techniques that are especially useful in defining concepts and attitudes that are difficult to grasp directly ("an *epiphany* is a moment of sudden clarity and insight, like the moment your eyes become accustomed to the dark and you can suddenly see your surroundings," "a *transition* in writing is a bridge between ideas").

A narrative or an account of a process can also help you define. An explanation of *courage,* for example, might include the story of a 10-year-old saving a friend from drowning in an icy pond. A discussion of *open-heart surgery* might include a description of the process.

Few extended definitions would use all these methods, but the extent to which you use them should depend on three factors: (1) the term or concept itself, since some are more elusive and subject to misunderstanding than others; (2) the function the term serves in your writing, since it is foolish to develop several pages defining a term that serves only a casual or unimportant purpose; and (3) your prospective audience, since the extent of your readers' knowledge and their likely responses to your definition of a disputed or controversial concept or phenomenon should lead you to choose the most convincing or persuasive strategies for the particular audience.

Finally, remember that reference works can be valuable sources for definition. The *Oxford English Dictionary,* for example, traces the meanings of a word during various historical periods; the *Dictionary of Slang and Unconventional English* or the *Encyclopedia of Pop, Rock, and Soul* can provide you with surprising and useful information. A reference librarian or an Internet search engine can provide you with many more sources.

Explaining with the Help of *Description*

You can make your expository writing more vivid, and hence more understandable, with the support of **description,** sometimes even using the pattern as the basic plan for an exposition. In writing, you can use sensory details—sight, sound, touch, taste, and smell—to re-create *places:* a portrait of the steamy closeness of the Brazilian jungle; the gray stone, narrow streets, tall houses, and church spires of an Eastern European city. You can create portraits of *people, qualities, emotions,* or *moods:* a beloved aunt whose cheerfulness was part of a long fight against pain and illness, the physical and spatial on-court "intelligence" of a star basketball player, the despair of a child crying for her puppy just killed by a car, or the contrasting moods of a city where excited theatergoers pass a drunk slumped against a building.

105   Descriptive writing depends on detail, and your first and most   105 important job as a writer employing description is to select the details to be included. There are usually many from which to choose, and it is easy to become so involved in a subject—especially one that is visually or emotionally intriguing—that you lose sight of the expository purpose of your writing. As you draft and revise, therefore, you need to keep in mind the kind of picture you want to paint with words, one that accomplishes *your* purpose for *your* intended audience. Such a word picture need not be entirely visual, for the dimensions of sound, smell, and even touch can create a vivid and effective image in your readers' minds.

When used as a pattern for much or all of an expository essay, description does more than set a mood, add a vivid touch to an explanation, or provide an occasional supporting detail. It becomes the primary strategy for explaining a subject or supporting a thesis, as in the following example.

Makes me think of a frozen like

It's not winter without an icestorm. When Robert Frost gazed at bowed birch trees and tried to think that boys had bent them playing, he knew better: "Icestorms do that." They do *describing* that and a lot more, trimming disease and weakness out of the *the* tree—the old tree's friend, as pneumonia used to be the old *ice* man's. Some of us provide life-support systems for our precious shrubs, boarding them over against the ice, for the icestorm takes the young or unlucky branch or birch as well as the rotten or feeble. One February morning we look out our windows over yards and fields littered with kindling, small twigs and great branches. We look out at a world turned into one diamond, ten thousand carats in the line of sight, twice as many facets. What a dazzle of spinning refracted light, spider webs of cold brilliance attacking our eyeballs! All winter we wear sunglasses to drive, more than we do in summer, and never so much as after an icestorm, with its painful glaze reflecting from maple and birch, granite boulder and stone wall, turning electric wires into bright silver filaments. The snow itself takes on a crust of ice, like the finish of a clay pot, that carries our weight and sends us swooping and sliding. It's worth your life to go for the mail. Until sand and salt redeem the highway, Route 4 is quiet. We cancel the appointment with the dentist, stay home, and marvel at the altered universe, knowing that midday sun will strip ice from tree and roof and restore our ordinary white winter world.

—Donald Hall, *Seasons at Eagle Pond*

Why Use Description?

Descriptions help readers create mental images of a subject or scene. To do this, the writer uses concrete, specific detail ("The floodwater turned the carpet into a slippery mess that smelled like dead fish and covered the electronic insides of the TV with a thin coat of black mud") rather than abstract, general impressions ("The flood soaked everything in the living room"). You can put descriptive detail to work for a variety of purposes, however.

You might choose to focus on a particular place or scene, using description to convey and support your thoughts and conclusions about it. Writing of this sort often appears in brief essays focusing on a limited scene: a beach in winter, a small corner of the Sonoran Desert, or a mall parking lot just before Christmas, for example. On the other hand, a description of a typical family apartment in Cairo might provide important conclusions and support for a study of family structure in Egypt, or descriptions of the Arctic landscape might contribute to an understanding of the habits of polar bears. When used for such expository purposes, descriptive writing goes beyond simply recording details to offering conclusions and explanations of the effects of a setting on those who live in it.

You might also use descriptive writing to create a portrait of a person. To do this, you combine descriptive detail with narration, usually in the form of brief but representative incidents. Your aim is to highlight the characteristics of your subject: details of appearance, speech, action, and feeling. In such a context, descriptive detail serves to support and convey your understanding of an individual's outlook and motivation, a sense of his or her personality, and your insight into the individual's influence on others.

Technical descriptions, common in scientific and professional writing, are another use for descriptive writing. In this form of writing, you provide a precise understanding of the elements of a subject and their relationship, and in so doing you convey necessary information or evidence to support your conclusions. Biologists, for example, might describe features of a frog that are marks of evolution or function; art historians might focus on color, line, shape, and brush stroke as a way of supporting a thesis about an artist or a particular painting.

Choosing a Strategy

Descriptive writing generally follows one of two strategies—*objective* description or *subjective* description—though some overlapping is also common. In objective description you aim at conveying the details of a subject thoroughly and accurately without suggesting your feelings or biases and without trying to evoke an emotional response from readers. Scientific papers, business reports, and academic writing often take this stance. In choosing details, writers of objective descriptions aim at precision and try to avoid emotional overtones. In arranging the details for presentation, writers either pay attention to the need to support a conclusion or to the function of the object or process being presented, as in the following example.

Cathode Ray Tube

The most familiar example is a television picture tube, and the simplest kind is the black and white. The inside of the tube is coated with a *phosphor,* a substance that glows when struck by electrons. At the rear of the tube (the neck) is an electron gun that shoots a beam of electrons toward the front. Electromagnetic coils or electrically charged metal plates direct this stream from side to side and top to bottom, forming a glow-picture of the "message" being received by the cathode ray tube. Color tubes are similar except that the face is coated with thousands of groups of dots. Each group, called a *pixel* (picture element), consists of three dots, one for each of the three primary colors—red, green, and blue.

—Herman Schneider and Leo Schneider, *The Harper Dictionary of Science in Everyday Language*

In subjective description, however, you make your values and feelings clear and often encourage readers to respond emotionally. Often, instead of describing how something *is* objectively, you describe how it *seems* subjectively. To do this, you may make occasional use of direct statement, but you are likely to find it more effective to rely on a choice of vivid, concrete, or emotionally laden detail or on the connotations of words. *Connotations* are the feelings or associations that accompany a word, not its dictionary or literal meaning. Subjective descriptions express your conclusions about a subject or your attitudes toward it. Thus, in arranging details for presentation, you should pay attention to the dominant impression or interpretation you wish to convey as well as to the arrangement of details in the setting (right to left, top to bottom, for example).

In creating a subjective description, pay attention to the dominant impression you create, making sure it conveys and supports your overall purpose or interpretation. In the following passage, for example, the dominant impression clearly conveys the writer's insights into the effects of atmosphere—in this case, fog—on human perceptions, even though she does not directly state this conclusion.

It begins in late afternoon, a wall of gray blocking the entrance to the harbor, moving imperceptibly, closing in. The sun becomes a bright thing in the sky for a moment before a thick grayness takes over. Trails of vapor drift by. Roads taper off into mist. Pine trees, encircled by the fog, take on different shapes. Inside vacation houses, people make tea, read books, play cards with old decks. Outside, the air smells of soaked wharves. Down by the rocks the surf crashes, but it is a muffled sound, heard while asleep. Bay bushes hunch together, woolly and wet. Walking through fields of Queen Anne's lace, lupine, and goldenrod, their colors muted, is like moving through dreamland. A foghorn blows. Other people are out—a figure appears near the raspberry bushes, spectral, with a basket. A dog runs by, and from the leaves drops fall.

—Susan Minot, "Lost in the Light of Gray"

Developing Description

The first and most important job in descriptive writing is to select the details. The questions you ask about a subject can help you identify significant details and suggest ways of interpreting it.

For scenes or objects:

- What does it look like (colors, shapes, height, depth)?
- What does it sound like (loud, soft, rasping, soothing, musical, like a lawn mower)?
- What does it smell like (smoky, acrid, like gasoline, like soap, like a wood fire)?
- What does it feel like (smooth, sticky, like a cat's fur, like a spider's web, like grease)?
- What does it taste like (bitter, salty, like grass, like feathers)?

For emotions or ideas:

- What effect does it have on behavior (anger: red face, abrupt gestures)?
- What is it like (freedom: like taking a deep breath of air after leaving a smoky room)?

For people:

- What does the person look like (hair neatly combed, rumpled blouse, muddy boots)?
- What are some characteristic behaviors (rubs hands on skirt, picks ear)?
- What has the person done or said (cheated on a chemistry test, said cruel things to friends)?
- How do others respond to the person (turn to her for advice, call him a "slob")?

115   Successful subjective descriptions generally focus on a single *dominant impression,* which can act in place of a conclusion or thesis. To create a dominant impression, you select those details that will help create a mood or atmosphere or emphasize a feature or quality. But more than the materials themselves are involved in creating a dominant impression. The words you choose, and both their literal and suggestive meanings (denotations and connotations), convey an impression. So, too, do the arrangements of words in sentences, as in the use of short, hurried sentences to help convey a sense of urgency or excitement.

The actual arrangement of the material is perhaps less troublesome in description than in most other expository patterns. Nonetheless, you need to follow a sequence that is clear to your reader and that helps you achieve your purpose or support your thesis. A clear spatial organization, for example, will help readers understand a visually complex subject. You can move from left to right, top to bottom, or near to far. You can describe a person from head to toe, or vice versa, or begin with the most noticeable feature and work from there. Or you could start with an overall view of a scene and then move to a focal point.

A chronological arrangement enables you to look at a scene from several perspectives: early morning, midday, and night, for example, or in different weather conditions. Such a strategy allows you to make a point by contrasting the scenes, and it provides variety and interest. A thematic organization emphasizes the dominant impression or thesis through focus and repetition. You might emphasize by repeating clusters of key words (grim, grasping, hard, short-tempered) or images (pink ribbons, the scent of violets). You might also arrange segments of the description by increasing order of importance or in another manner that best supports a thesis.

You can also choose a point of view, either first person ("I looked...") or third person ("He sighed....," "It moved...."). You might also choose a perspective, including the location of the observer and any limitation on the observer's ability to see and understand, perhaps observing a familiar family scene from a child's perspective to provide a new understanding of relationships.

Whatever techniques you choose, however, try to avoid excessive description, which creates confusion and boredom, or description without a clear purpose, which offers your readers no goal or reward for their effort.

Using *Narration* as an Expository Technique

120 When is narration a pattern of exposition rather than a story told for 120 its own purposes? The answer: when it serves to explain a subject, present conclusions, or support an interpretation or a thesis. For example, a writer who wishes to explain the role of risk-taking individuals (rather than corporations) in developing new ideas and products might tell the story of an entrepreneur who perfected the frozen French fry in the early 1950s only to discover that there was little demand for his product. The story would emphasize his perseverance in struggling to develop a market for the product—a perseverance that paid off for all concerned a decade later when the rapidly

growing fast-food industry discovered the usefulness of frozen fries for ready-in-a-minute menus.

Whether you use narration as the pattern for an entire essay or for support and explanation within an essay, your readers will expect you to do certain things. They will expect your narrative to help them understand *what happened,* including the *who, where, what,* and *to whom* of events. They will expect the narrative to *re-create* events, showing (through concrete detail or the actual words of participants) rather than merely telling what happened (through summary). Finally, your readers will expect your narrative to help them understand the *significance* of the events. They will look for the point you are making, for what you have to say about the events, or for the way the events supports your thesis.

In a book explaining the extraordinary character and physical courage of early Antarctic explorers, the writer Edwin Mickleburgh offers the following narrative to support his thesis about the explorer Ernest Shackleton's abilities as a leader and about the courage of his crew.

For anyone who has looked up from the sullen South Georgia shore [an island near Antarctica] towards the soaring, razor-edged peaks and the terrible chaos of glaciers topped by swirling clouds and scoured by mighty winds, the knowledge of the crossing made by these three men adds a wider dimension to an already awe inspiring sight. How they did it, God only knows, but they crossed the island in thirty-six hours. They were fortunate that the weather held, although many times great banks of fog rolled in from the open sea, creeping toward them over the snow and threatening to obscure their way. Confronted by precipices of ice and walls of rock they had often to retrace their steps adding many miles to the journey. They walked almost without rest. At one point they sat down in an icy gully, the wind blowing the drift around them, and so tired were they that Worseley and Crean fell asleep immediately. Shackleton, barely able to

Introduces narrative and its relation to writer's main point

Narrative

SCHWEGLER | RHETORICAL MODES

keep himself awake, realized that to fall asleep under such conditions would prove fatal. After five minutes he woke the other two, saying that they had slept for half an hour.

—Edwin Mickleburgh,
Beyond the Frozen Sea: Visions of Antarctica

Why Use Narration?

Perhaps the most familiar form of expository narrative is the personal narrative, based on personal experience or observation, that offers insights into events or conclusions about relationships and the importance of certain kinds of experience. These include memoirs focusing on the author's personal and intellectual development, on an unusual and significant childhood event, or on other experiences. They include autobiographies of media stars, politicians, and other well-known people, especially those that shed light on the fields in which they have worked or on the important events they have witnessed. And they include personal narratives embedded in other kinds of works in order to give the works a sense of authenticity.

Another use of narrative is to present a profile on an unfamiliar or unusual activity or the people involved in it. Typically, such a narrative begins by presenting an interesting person in action (a day in the life of a computer game creator, for example) or by focusing on an activity (workers changing light bulbs on the spire of the Empire State Building; divers searching in deep water for wreckage from an airplane crash). As a way of creating drama and interest, such narratives frequently reveal surprising tensions or contradictions, such as the quiet home life and personal kindness of an offshore boat racer also known for his fearlessness, abrasiveness, spectacular crashes, and narrow escapes from death.

A narrative can also provide a framework for commentary and analysis, with passages of narrative interspersed with discussions of the significance and implications of the events. Or narratives can add convincing detail or emotional force to explanations built around some other expository pattern, such as comparison, cause-and-effect, or definition.

Choosing a Strategy

A narrative is a chronological account of events. You do not always have to present the events in chronological order or give them all equal emphasis. When you are creating an event for expository purposes, begin your planning process with questions like these:

- What events are most important to my purpose for writing?
- What ideas and emotions surrounding the events are worth sharing with my readers?
- What point do I want to make with this narrative?

Your answers to questions like these should help you limit the time frame of your narrative and focus on the most important events of the story. Many writers are gripped by a compulsion to get all the details of a story down—important and unimportant. Radical surgery often helps. Instead of covering a whole week or day, consider focusing on the single most important incident—the four or five minutes when all the forces came together—and summarizing the rest.

Remember that you can arrange the events to suit your purpose(s). In basic form, a narrative sets the scene; introduces characters; presents, in chronological order, episodes that introduce a conflict or prepare for the central event; then, finally, explores in detail the most important incident in which the conflict is resolved or the writer's outlook is made clear. Yet the chronological approach can make it hard to emphasize the most important element. You may instead want to start in the middle of things, perhaps at the climactic episode, and fill in prior events through flashbacks. Or you might stop in the middle of events to provide important background information or comment on the characters and their actions.

And you need to choose whether to provide an explicit thesis statement to organize your narrative and direct commentary on the events, or to let the events speak for themselves, assuming that their relationship to your main point will be sufficiently clear to readers.

Developing a Narrative

130 As you draft and revise a narrative, pay attention to the following 130 concerns that can contribute to the success (or failure) of your efforts.

- **Selection of Details.** You will probably have many more details you might include in a narrative than you need. Keep in mind that too many details can overwhelm readers, making them lose sight about the point the narrative is making or the explanation it is offering. Focused, unified writing makes use only of those details that are most relevant to the writer's purpose and desired effect. Whenever possible, try to include concrete, specific details that make the narrative vivid and believable and that will be likely to hold your reader's interest.

- **Time Order.** You can employ straight chronology, relating events as they happened, or the flashback method, leaving the sequence temporarily in order to go back and relate some now-significant happening of a time prior to the main action. If you use flashback, do so deliberately, not merely because you neglected to mention the episode earlier.

- **Transitions.** Watch out for overly simple and repetitive transitions between events in the narrative: "And then we.... And then she.... And then we ..." As you revise, make a conscious effort to create variety in transitions: "next," "following," "subsequently," "as a consequence," "reacting to," "later," "meanwhile," "at the same time," "concurrently," and the like.

- **Point of View.** Decide whether you want to tell the story from the point of view of a participant, such as yourself or a character, or from the overall perspective of a spectator. The vividness and immediacy possible from a participant's point of view can make the narrative more dramatic, but the spectator's point of view can allow for an easier transition from narrative to commentary and may be especially useful in expository writing. Whichever point of view you choose, keep it consistent throughout the narrative.

- **Dialogue.** Remember that quoting the words of participants can help make narrative more convincing and dialogue, which can reveal conflicting perspectives among the participants, can also be a springboard to your commentary on the meaning of the events.

Appendix III: Links to Sample Essays

Links to Sample Paragraphs and Essays in Various Rhetorical Modes

Sample students papers in various rhetorical modes:

http://www.rscc.cc.tn.us/owl&writingcenter/OWL/Types.html

Narrating an event sample:

http://www.bedfordstmartins.com/hacker/narrating.htm

Personal narrative student sample:

http://www.thewritesource.com/studentmodels/wi-baby.htm

Comparison/contrast sample paragraphs:

http://lrs.ed.uiuc.edu/students/fwalters/compcont.html

Cause and effect sample paragraphs:

http://lrs.ed.uiuc.edu/students/fwalters/cause.html

Descriptive essay sample paragraphs:

http://www.rscc.cc.tn.us/owl&writingcenter/OWL/Describe.html

Process essay student sample:

http://leo.stcloudstate.edu/acadwrite/process.html

Classification essay student sample:

http://www.buowl.boun.edu.tr/students/types%20of%20essays/
Classification%20Essay.htm

Definition essay student sample:

http://www.thewritesource.com/studentmodels/wi-net
_addiction.htm